Understanding Strategic Management

Visit the *Understanding Strategic Management* Companion Website at **www.pearsoned.co.uk/capon** to find valuable **student** learning material including:

- Self Assessment Questions to test your learning.
- Extensive links to valuable resources on the web.
- Interactive online flashcards that allow you to check definitions against the key terms during revision.
- An online glossary to help explain key terms.

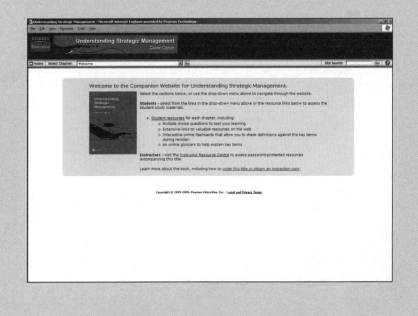

PEARSON
Education

We work with leading authors to develop the strongest educational materials in business, bringing cutting-edge thinking and best learning practice to a global market.

Under a range of well-known imprints, including Financial Times Prentice Hall, we craft high-quality print and electronic publications which help readers to understand and apply their content, whether studying or at work.

To find out more about the complete range of our publishing please visit us on the World Wide Web at: **www.pearsoned.co.uk**

Understanding Strategic Management

Claire Capon
Staffordshire University

FT Prentice Hall
FINANCIAL TIMES

An imprint of **Pearson Education**
Harlow, England • London • New York • Boston • San Francisco • Toronto
Sydney • Tokyo • Singapore • Hong Kong • Seoul • Taipei • New Delhi
Cape Town • Madrid • Mexico City • Amsterdam • Munich • Paris • Milan

Pearson Education Limited
Edinburgh Gate
Harlow
Essex CM10 2JE
England

and Associated Companies throughout the world

Visit us on the World Wide Web at:
www.pearsoned.co.uk

_____

First published 2008

ISBN: 978-0-273-69498-4

British Library Cataloguing-in-Publication Data
A catalogue record for this book is available from the British Library

Library of Congress Cataloging-in-Publication Data

Capon, Claire.
    Understanding strategic management / Claire Capon.
        p. cm.
    Includes bibliographical references and index.
    ISBN 978-0-273-69498-4
  1. Strategic planning.   2. Business planning.   I. Title.
    HD30.28.C3743 2008
    658.4'012--dc22

                                                    2008001027

    10 9 8 7 6 5 4 3 2 1
    12 11 10 09 08

Typeset in Stone Serif 9.5pt by 3
Printed by Ashford Colour Press Ltd., Gosport

The publisher's policy is to use paper manufactured from sustainable forests.

Contents

Contents

Chapter 11 STRATEGIC CONTROL

Chapter 12 MANAGING FAILURE AND TURNAROUND

Supporting resources

Visit the *Understanding Strategic Management* Companion Website at
www.pearsoned.co.uk/capon to find valuable online resources.

Companion Website for students

- Self Assessment Questions to test your learning.
- Extensive links to valuable resources on the web.
- Interactive online flashcards that allow you to check definitions against the key terms during revision.
- An online glossary to help explain key terms.

For instructors

- Instructors manual including suggested teaching plan and notes on the cases in the text.
- Downloadable Power Point sides containing all the exhibits from the book.
- Test bank of question material.
- Additional case studies for each chapter.

Also: The Companion Website provides the following features:

- Search tool to help locate specific items of content.
- E-mail results and profile tools to send results of quizzes to instructors.
- Online help and support to assist with website usage and trouble-shooting.

For more information please contact your local Pearson Education sales representative or visit **www.pearsoned.co.uk/capon**.

List of case studies

Preface

The aim of *Understanding Strategic Management* is to provide students studying strategic management for the first time with a textbook which covers the main areas of strategic management, without being over whelming. Hence the book has been limited to twelve chapters and is suitable for undergraduate, post experience and post graduate students.

Each of the twelve chapters has incorporated within it a wealth of features, which assist lecturers in teaching the subject and students in learning about strategic management. The features include an entry case study, review questions, 'check your understanding', learning outcomes and summary, exit case study and questions, 'widen your horizons', weblinks and further reading.

It is envisaged that students studying strategic management as a level 2 or level 3 module on undergraduate business course (e.g. BA Business Studies and HND Business Studies) or on a postgraduate qualification (masters programmes and CIPD) will find this book useful in gaining an understanding of strategic management.

A website (**www.pearsoned.co.uk/capon**) provides further material for both students and lecturers.

Claire Capon
March 2008

This book is suitable for strategic management modules and the 'Essential strategy' model, shown at the start of each chapter, summarises all that is covered in this book and provides a useful diagrammatic overview of the main strategic management topics.

Chapter 1 of the book introduces the concept of strategy. Chapter 2 goes on to examine the general external environment and the competitive environment, before Chapters 3 and 4 explore resources and financial resources respectively. Chapter 5 examines stakeholders, organisational culture and change in organisations. Chapter 6 looks at management and leadership. The second half of the book focuses on developing strategy and its implementation. Hence the topics covered include competitive strategy and marketing strategy in Chapter 7, which is followed by an examination of growth and expansion strategies in Chapter 8. The idea of developing strategy is continued in Chapter 9 with an overview of the issues relating to international strategy. Issues around implementation are covered in Chapter 10, which is followed by strategic control in Chapter 11. Managing failure and turnaround is considered in Chapter 12.

Chapter 1 What is strategy?

This chapter introduces the reader to some of the well-known definitions of strategy from the mainstream literature. This should allow the reader to gain an understanding of 'What strategy is' and form his or her own views and opinions on the subject.

Chapter 2 Environmental analysis

This chapter seeks to examine the general external environment and the competitive environment. The idea of PEST analysis and the work of Duncan and Ginter are used to consider the general external environment. The regulation of the competitive environment from a UK perspective is examined, before the chapter looks at Porter's 5 forces of competition.

Chapter 3 Managing resources competitively

This chapter examines the assessment of resources in organisations. Initially the straightforward resource audit approach to evaluating resources is examined. This is followed by an overview of core competencies. The value chain, value system and linkages are covered in detail.

Chapter 4 Analysing financial resources

This chapter covers two main areas. The first is the raising of finance, including loans, debentures and flotation. The rest of the chapter looks at ratio analysis and covers both calculating and interpreting ratios.

Chapter 5 Stakeholders, culture and change

This chapter examines stakeholders in an organisation and how they can be managed, given the position they occupy with respect to the organisation. The chapter then goes on to consider what certain stakeholders contribute to the determination of organisational culture, which is examined via the cultural web. Organisational culture is often affected by change in organisations, which is then explored.

Chapter 6 Management and leadership in organisations

This chapter looks at both management and leadership in organisations and definitions of both are examined. Managerial style, management efficiency and effectiveness, along with the role of trust and respect in managing staff are all covered. Styles of leadership, leadership power and role of leadership in organisations are also examined.

Chapter 7 Developing competitive and marketing strategy

This chapter covers a number of approaches to competitive strategy and achieving competitive advantage, including Porter. The underpinning of competitive strategy by marketing strategy is then examined and market segmentation, targeting and positioning are covered.

Chapter 8 Growth for success

The chapter explores how organisations can grow and expand. The material in this chapter covers organic growth and exporting, before looking at external growth via licensing, franchising, strategic alliances and acquisitions.

Chapter 9 Developing international strategy

The aim of this chapter is to give an overview of the issues for companies seeking to expand internationally. Therefore many aspects of international strategy including the international external environment, human resource management and foreign direct investment are explored.

Chapter 10 Structure, culture and groups in organisations

This chapter looks at many of the areas organisations need to consider when planning for the implementation of strategy. They include organisational structure and its link with culture via Handy's work. To conclude, the role of groups in organisations is examined.

Chapter 11 **Strategic control**

This chapter covers strategic control and is structured around the strategic control of the organisation's activities as per the value chain and value system.

Chapter 12 **Managing failure and turnaround**

This chapter explores the recognition that organisations don't always succeed and do on occasions need to plan to avert decline, or even come back from failure in some way.

Teaching with this book – module delivery

To aid the tutor in delivering strategic management modules, there is a clear chapter structure and a number of features appear in each chapter.

Chapter structure

Essential strategy model
Chapter objectives
Entry case study
Introduction
Main text, including margin definitions, 'Review questions' and 'Check your understanding' activities throughout
Conclusion
Learning outcomes and summary
Exit case study with learning outcomes and questions
Discussion topic
'Widen your horizons'
Weblinks
Further reading

Essential strategy model

The essential strategy model is shown at the start of each chapter and shading indicates the areas examined in that particular chapter. This allows readers to see at a glance what is covered in a chapter.

Chapter objectives

Chapter objectives provide a broad overview of the material covered in a chapter and allow both lecturers and students to gain a broad overview of a chapter before proceeding to study the material in more detail.

Entry case study

Each chapter has an entry case study, which provides a practical view and application of the main themes covered in the chapter. The 'Check your understanding' activities dotted throughout each chapter on occasion ask the reader to return to the entry case study and undertake some work in relation to the case study.

Margin definitions

The margin definitions aim to make it easy for the reader to see at a glance the meaning of business words or phrases with which they may not be familiar.

Review questions

The review questions usually appear at the end of major sections in each chapter and allow the reader to evaluate their own learning as they progress through each chapter.

Check your understanding

The 'Check your understanding' features appear throughout the text and allow the reader to apply their learning to real life and practical situations in business. On occasion this is done via referring back to the entry case study.

Learning outcomes and summary

The chapter learning outcomes and summary allow the reader to evaluate whether they have achieved the objectives set out at the start of each chapter and gained a full understanding of the material covered.

Exit case study and questions

The exit case studies and questions provide an opportunity for students to apply the knowledge and skills gained from studying each chapter to a real-life situation. Learning outcomes also allow the exit cases to be used for coursework assessments.

Discussion topic

The discussion topic relates to an article of further reading, which allows students to extend their knowledge of and critical thought around a strategic management topic. Many of the papers used in this feature can be found in *The Strategy Process*, Mintzberg, Lampel, Quinn and Ghosal, Harlow: Prentice Hall, 2003. It is envisaged that this feature is most likely to be used with postgraduate students.

Widen your horizons

This feature provides students with an opportunity to undertake some further research on a strategic management topic and apply some of the theory from the chapter to a real organisation or situation.

Weblinks

The weblinks provided are relevant to the material in the chapter, and should be viewed as an initial guide to web-based sources.

Further reading

The further reading is broken down into relevant topic areas for each chapter and provides information on where alternative views and approaches to the strategy topics covered in the chapter can be found.

About the author

Claire Capon teaches strategy in the Business School at Staffordshire University. She previously taught strategy in the Business School at Sheffield Hallam University and worked at Huddersfield Polytechnic and UMIST as a researcher in the areas of strategic management and the use of design by SMEs.

Claire Capon is also the author of *Understanding Organisational Context*, 2nd edition, FT/Prentice Hall, 2004.

Guided tour

Navigation and setting the scene

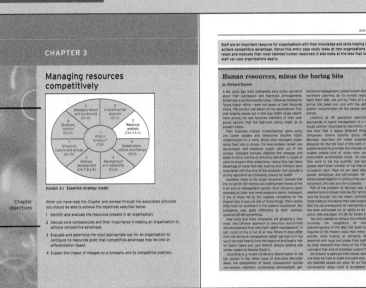

Navigational strategy model reminds you of where you are in the structure of the book and what topics are going to be discussed in that particular chapter.

Chapter objectives enables you to focus on the topics you should be able to understand by the end of the chapter.

Entry case studies give you an insight into how the major themes in each chapter are applied in practice.

Strategy in focus

Exit case studies conclude each chapter to help you consolidate the major themes and encourage you to apply what you have learnt to real life scenarios facing organisations.

Business illustrations focus on one particular organisation so you can learn more about its strategy.

Aiding your understanding

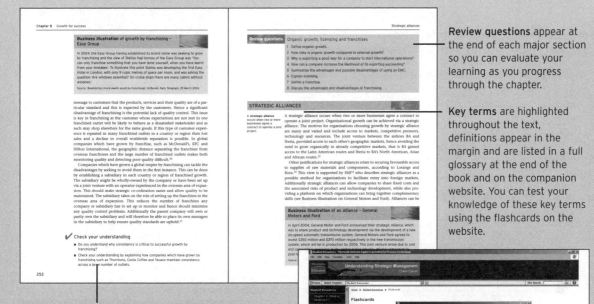

Review questions appear at the end of each major section so you can evaluate your learning as you progress through the chapter.

Key terms are highlighted throughout the text, definitions appear in the margin and are listed in a full glossary at the end of the book and on the companion website. You can test your knowledge of these key terms using the flashcards on the website.

Check your understanding allows you to apply your learning to real life and practical situations in business. Where possible this is done by referring back to the organisation featured in the entry case study.

Summary sections succinctly recaps and reinforces the key points to take away from the chapter. Each summary section is also mapped to the chapter learning outcomes so you can evaluate whether you have achieved these objectives.

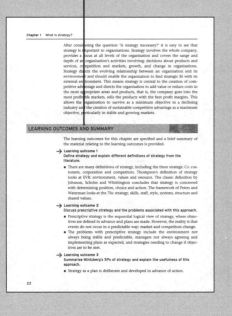

Self assessment questions on the companion website test your understanding of the topics covered in each chapter.

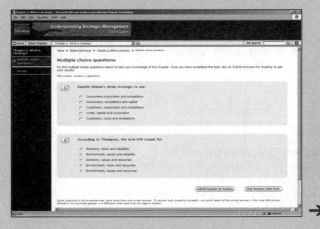

Discussion topics give you thought provoking questions on an article of further reading allowing you to extend your knowledge and think critically about a specific strategic management issue.

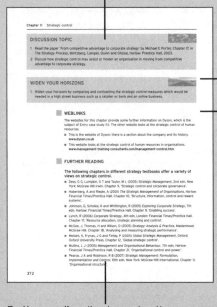

Widen your horizons gives you suggestions for further research so you can apply theory to a real organisation situation.

A list of relevant **weblinks** are included so you can explore more about the areas discussed in the chapter. There are also **weblinks** to the websites of the organisations featured in the entry and exit case studies on the companion website where you can learn more about each company and its strategy.

Further reading directs you to other sources where you can explore alternative views and approaches to the strategy topics covered in the chapter.

Acknowledgements

We are grateful to the Financial Times Limited for permission to reprint the following material:

Exit case study 3.2 Eurostar seeks a speedy transformation, © *Financial Times*, 29 September 2003; Entry case study 4.1 Speedel plans IPO to finance further trials, © *Financial Times*, 28 April 2005; Exit case study 4.2 Creating links with recycled mobile phones is the Eazy way to success, © *Financial Times*, 3 March 2007; Exit case study 5.2 Vratislav Kulhanek of Skoda, © *FT.com*, 11 October 2002; Entry case study 6.1 Industry maps DNA of 21st-century movers and shakers, © *Financial Times*, 10 November 2006; Exit case study 6.2 Engineer with tools to rebuild an airline, © *Financial Times*, 11 February 2007; Entry case study 7.1 Viacom agrees China deal, © *Financial Times*, 24 March 2004; Exit case study 7.2 Nike overtakes Adidas in football field, © *Financial Times*, 19 August 2004; Entry case study 8.1 P&G set to buy Gillette for $57bn, © *Financial Times*, 29 January 2005; Exit case study 8.2a Napster attacks delays in European music licensing, © *Financial Times*, 26 January 2004; Exit case study 8.2b MTV in European video licensing row, © *Financial Times*, 24 March 2004; Entry case study 9.1 Disney to unveil international strategy, © *Financial Times*, 28 September 2004; Exit case study 9.2 Burberry tailors a fresh image in Japan, © *Financial Times*, 15 April 2004; Entry case study 10.1 Sony takes first step towards leaner structure, © *Financial Times*, 27 February 2006; Exit case study 10.2a Unilever to keep dual structure, © *Financial Times*, 20 December 2005; Exit case study 10.2b Royal Dutch/Shell to unify structure and move HQ, © *Financial Times*, 28 October 2006; Entry case study 11.1 Designers win the right to control spare parts, © *Financial Times*, 9 March 2006; Exit case study 11.2 We believe in being in control, © *Financial Times*, 7 March 2006; Entry case study 12.1 Ford pares management as part of turnaround, © *Financial Times*, 12 February 2006;

We are grateful to the following for permission to use copyright material:

Entry case study 1.1 from Google's random genius is no accidental strategy. Can it last?, *The Financial Times Limited*, 1st February 2005, © Robert Austin and Lee Devin; Entry case study 3.1 from Human resources, minus the boring bits, *The Financial Times Limited*, 5 February 2004, © Richard Donkin, author of *Blood, Sweat and Tears, The Evolution of Work*. www.richarddonkin.com.; Exhibit 1.4 EVR diagram, figure 1.7, p.12 and Exhibit 1.5 The levels of strategy, figure 1.1, p.30 from *Strategic Management*, 4th edition, Thomson Learning (Thompson, J.L. 2001); Exhibits 1.6, 5.3, 5.6 from *Exploring Corporate Strategy: Text and Cases*, 7th edition, Johnson, G., Scholes, K. and Whittington, R., Pearson Education Limited. © FT/Prentice Hall, 2005; Exhibit 1.8 The McKinsey 7s Framework from IN SEARCH OF EXCELLENCE: LESSONS FROM AMERICA'S BEST RUN COMPANIES by THOMAS J. PETERS and ROBERT H. WATERMAN, JR. Copyright © 1982 by Thomas J. Peters and Robert H. Waterman, Jr. Reprinted by permission of HarperCollins Publishers; Exhibits 2.17, 3.5, 3.7 and 7.2 Reprinted with the permission of The Free Press, a Division of Simon & Schuster, Inc., from COMPETITIVE ADVANTAGE by Michael E. Porter. Copyright © 1985, 1998 by Michael E. Porter. All rights reserved; Exhibits 5.2, 5.7 and 5.10 from *Understanding Organisational Context*, 2nd edition, Financial Times/Prentice Hall, (Capon, C. 2004); Exhibit 7.9 from *Principles of Marketing*, European Edition, Prentice Hall, London (Kotler, P., Armstrong G., Saunders,

J. and Wong, V. 1996); Exhibits 7.10, 7.11, 7.12 and 7.13 Reprinted from *Long Range Planning*, Vol. 23, No. 5, Press, G., Assessing competitors' business philosophies, pp. 71–75, Copyright (1990), with permission from Elsevier; Exhibits 10.18, 10.19, 10.20 and 10.21 The Power Culture, The Person Culture, The Role Culture and The Fast Culture from *Understanding Organizations*, pp. 188, 195, 190, 193, Charles Handy (Penguin Books 1976, Fourth Edition 1993) Copyright © Charles Handy, 1976, 1981, 1985, 1993, 1999. Reproduced by permission of Penguin Books Ltd.; Exhibit 12.5 The feasibility of recovery, figure 18.1, p.533 adapted from Slatter, S. (1984) Corporate Recovery, Penguin in *Strategic Management*, 4th edition, Thomson Learning (Thompson, J.L. 2001); Exit case study 1.2 Royal Bank rides the dragon in *The Daily Telegraph*, 10 November 2006 (Griffiths, Katherine) © Telegraph Media Group Ltd.; Exit case study 2.2 Cadbury looks to burst Wrigley bubble in *The Daily Telegraph*, 6 February 2007 (Litterick, David) © Telegraph Media Group Ltd.; Exit case study 12.2 New HP boss plans 14,500 job cuts: 100% of workforce will go to create 'nimbler, quicker' firm in *The Guardian*, 20 July 2005 (Teather, David) © Guardian News & Media Ltd.

In some instances we have been unable to trace the owners of copyright material, and we would appreciate any information that would enable us to do so.

CHAPTER 1

What is strategy?

Exhibit 1.1 Essential strategy model

Chapter objectives

The aim of strategy is to provide organisations with direction, whether that is a carefully developed plan or a series of related opportunities which the organisation follows, or a combination of plans and opportunities. This chapter examines different definitions of strategy from the literature and seeks to allow the reader to see the relevance and importance of having a strategic overview, and of developing and implementing coherent strategy. The other chapters in this book provide ideas and guidance for developing and implementing strategy in greater detail.

When you have read this chapter and worked through the associated activities you should be able to achieve the objectives specified below.

1 Define strategy and explain different definitions of strategy from the literature.

2 Discuss prescriptive strategy and the problems associated with this approach.

3 Discuss emergent strategy, its advantages and disadvantages.

4 Summarise Mintzberg's 5Ps of strategy and explain the usefulness of this approach.

5 Summarise Mintzberg and Waters' approach to prescriptive and emergent strategy.

This case study looks at Google's approach to strategy and how it seeks to succeed in the face of competitors such as Microsoft. Google's approach to strategy is evolving or emergent and this is looked at in this chapter. This approach to strategy contrasts with the planned or prescriptive approach to strategy, which is also examined.

Google's random genius is no accidental strategy. Can it last?   FT

by Robert Austin and Lee Devin

Googlemania has been in full swing for more than a year. Unless you devote your life to the subject, you have probably struggled to keep pace with the adventures of Sergey, Larry and their hoard of gifted geeks. After months of wall-to-wall media coverage, you might even be asking yourself: do I really care? Stepping back for a minute from the frenzy, there are two important reasons why you should. The first has to do with Google's business model, the second with how the world's most written about company is run. What does the original, eponymous search engine have in common with Gmail, Google News, Google Earth and the myriad other services to have poured forth from Mountain View, California? They are all piped to your computer via the internet and they are all free, in the sense of being funded by targeted advertising. Thus Google has found a way to turn almost anything you look at on your computer screen into advertising-supported media.

For traditional media companies, including the Financial Times, this is worrisome. Advertisers suddenly have a nifty new way to spend their money. For software companies – notably, but not only, Microsoft – the implications are super-scary: why should consumers pay for software if Google and its imitators can provide the basics (word processing, e-mail, calendars, spreadsheets) for free? Perhaps even more significant than the business model, however, is the way Google is run. The company is reluctant to let management journalists roam freely around the Googleplex, but it seems to be engaged in nothing less than a giant experiment in 'emergence'. Management gurus have for years been telling companies to abandon the traditional top-down, process-driven approach to strategy. Harness the imagination of employees, they exhort. Do not be afraid to experiment. Create an internal market for ideas. Place bets. Build a 'portfolio' of initiatives from which a winning strategy can emerge. Yet old habits die hard. The strategic planning process remains an annual ritual. Chief executives talk about the need to experiment, then mete out punishment when experiments go wrong, or fail to champion unconventional projects when it matters most.

Now compare that with Google, where software engineers can spend up to 20 per cent of their time on projects of their own choosing. This would be unremarkable in a research lab, where 'skunk works' are quietly encouraged. But since when did big companies allow such latitude? Imagine what delights might result if General Motors followed suit. Command-and-control managers will respond that such practices are a recipe for slacking and wasted resources. A more enlightened interpretation is that Google is trying to harness the collective wisdom of employees about how resources should be allocated. Interesting projects attract talent, irrespective of whether they have been sanctioned by top management. While some initiatives at Google seem to be driven from the top, the company remains open to the possibility that internal market forces will come up with better decisions than committees.

To see the portfolio approach in action, dig around the nether regions of google.com. There lurk dozens of services in either beta (ready for final testing by users) or 'labs' (still fairly clunky) mode. Want to help Stanford

→

University researchers fold proteins? Or talk to distant relatives over the internet? Or buy a teapot online? Google has a service to help. Where is this eclectic mix of internet-based services leading? I do not know. Neither, I suspect, does the company's management. Rivals certainly do not, which is what makes Google so devilishly difficult to compete against. The company is bounded only by a couple of open-to-interpretation phrases ('organise and make accessible the world's information', 'don't be evil') and its collective imagination.

If there is strategic intent in the conventional sense (annihilate Microsoft? Run rings around Yahoo?), we do not know about it. In fact, it may not make sense to talk about Google's strategy at all. Its strategy is a collection of some of the finest computer science brains on the planet and an unconventional approach to organisation. There is nothing accidental about this. In Eric Schmidt, Google has a chief executive who has seen the best (Sun Microsystems at the height of its pomp) and worst (dark days at Novell) of technology sector management. He may not talk much in public about management tech-

nique but he thinks long and hard about creativity, innovation and strategy. This is, after all, the man who three years ago wrote the preface to *Artful Making*, an interesting but obscure management book that drew parallels between the work of actors in rehearsal and software engineers.

None of this implies that Google is free from the normal headaches of project management. Froogle, its online shopping search service, has been in beta for so long that it is a standing Silicon Valley joke. Nor does its riotous run imply that the emergent approach will continue to deliver results. What works for a few dozen or even a few hundred programmers may not produce results in an international company of several thousand employees. The business model may have almost limitless potential, but will the organisation scale? This, as of the time of writing, is a $126bn (£71bn) question. Expect more mania to come.

Source: from 'Artful Making: What managers need to know about how artists work', *Financial Times*, 1 February 2005.

INTRODUCTION

What is strategy? There are many and varied definitions of strategy with almost every textbook on the subject offering its own definition and this textbook is no exception. The Exhibit that appears at the start of this chapter and every subsequent chapter shows the strands, which the author believes, go to make up strategy. Common to nearly all strategy is an understanding of the external environment and the resources available to compete in the external environment (see Chapters 2–4). The understanding, management and leadership of stakeholders (internal and external), organisational culture and change are usually key in determining the type of place an organisation is to work in or interact with as an external stakeholder, such as a customer (see Chapters 5 and 6). Developing strategy is often concerned with markets, competition and growth both domestically and internationally (see Chapters 7–9). This may necessitate changes to structure and culture or the existing set-up in the organisation may be sufficient for taking the organisation forwards (see Chapter 10). Organisations, which are concerned with their progress, will seek to control and evaluate their success or identify areas of actual or potential failure (see Chapter 11). Hence the last Chapter in this book looks at managing failure and turnaround (see Chapter 12). Every organisation's strategy will be different and place different emphasis on which strands of strategy are important for it to succeed.

This Chapter examines these strands of strategy via Chapters 2–12. Hence the reader will be able to make up his or her own mind on what constitutes strategy and this will be influenced by what the reader has read on the subject and how strategy unfolds and operates in organisations with which the reader is familiar. Different approaches to strategy can be seen by contrasting the more planned approach taken by HSBC (see Business illustration of strategy – HSBC) and the more evolving approach taken by Google (see Entry case study 1.1).

Business illustration of strategy – HSBC

In November 2005 the chief executive of HSBC, Michael Geoghegan was developing a strategy for HSBC branch banking in the UK. HSBC held only 14 per cent market share for current accounts and mortgages in the UK, compared with market leaders Lloyds TSB holding 20 per cent market share. HSBC want to close this market gap by focussing on attracting students and young professionals. The strategy being followed to achieve this was to modernise the face of HSBC branch banking by opening 60 super branches in the UK. Inspiration for the new branches was to be taken from the new Apple computer store in central London, which includes designer interiors, escalators and interactive TV.

Source: 'HSBC seeks to lure new blood with "super banks"', Kim Hunter Gordon, *The Observer*, 20 November 2005.

In summary the advantages of developing and implementing strategy allow an organisation to make best use of its resources and opportunities in achieving its objectives (see **Exhibit 1.2**).

Exhibit 1.2 Advantages of strategy

- Involves the whole organisation and provides a focus and overview for managers and employees at all levels of the organisation.
- Focuses on the relationship between the organisation and its environment.
- Includes the management and leadership of both internal and external stakeholders.
- Covers the full range of activities the organisation undertakes, including products, services, competition, markets, growth and change.
- Is central to the creation of competitive advantage via added value or reduced costs.
- Allows organisations to see how they may create sustainable competitive advantage as a maximum objective or survive as a minimum objective if in a declining marketplace.

DEFINITIONS OF STRATEGY

This section looks at some definitions of strategy from the mainstream literature. The work of Ohmae, Thompson, Johnson, Scholes and Whittington, Lynch, and Peters and Waterman is presented and the intention is to provide the reader with the opportunity to see some of the common themes of strategy from different definitions of strategy. The common themes from the definitions include environment, resources, culture and vision, customers and markets, competitors, growth, systems and structure.

The **three strategic Cs** are customers, corporation and competitors.

The **external environment** is where the opportunities and threats arise from to confront the organisation.

The three strategic Cs

The **three strategic Cs** – customers, corporation, competitors – are introduced by Ohmae in his book, *The Mind of A Strategist*.[1] Ohmae suggests strategy is about trying to influence, where possible, the **external environment** in which the company operates; differentiating to add unique value to products and services; and thoroughly understanding the marketplace, its segmentation and the customers. The three strategic Cs all interact and try to

Exhibit 1.3 The three strategic Cs

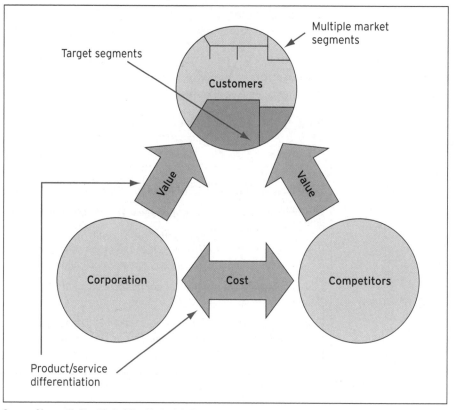

Source: Ohmae, K, *The Mind of the Strategist*, The Penguin Business Library.

influence one another and the Ohmae model shows those interrelationships (see **Exhibit 1.3**).

Corporations or companies seek to beat direct competitors on cost or seek to add more value for the same cost than competitors are able to do. However, the added value has to be perceived as such in the eyes of the paying customer. Google (see Entry case study 1.1) seeks to offer more than competitors such as Yahoo and, at the moment, advertisers and users of Google perceive them to be doing so. This is not so with HSBC who are struggling to compete with market leaders for current accounts in the UK, Lloyds TSB (see Business illustration on HSBC).

The EVR model

An organisation's **resources** include its facilities, staff, know-how and money.

Values are the beliefs of the organisations that in turn determine the expected behaviours from managers and employees.

An alternative definition of strategy is provided by Thompson,[2] presenting the view of strategy as the interaction of the external environment, the **resources** and **values** of the organisation (see **Exhibit 1.4**). Ideally an organisation wants a close match with its environment which is underpinned by its resources and values. The Business illustration of ITV and Friends Reunited provides an example of a likely EVR mismatch with the takeover of Friends Reunited by ITV.

Exhibit 1.4 EVR Diagram

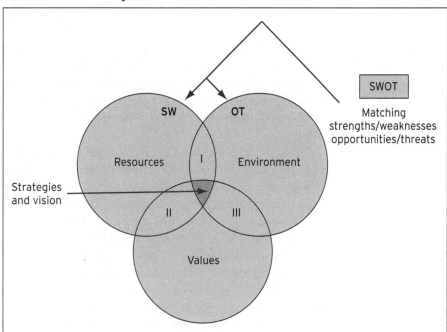

Source: Thompson, J L (2001) *Strategic Management*, 4th edn, London: Thomson Learning.

Business illustration of EVR mismatch – ITV and Friends Reunited

In December 2005 ITV (a TV company) paid £175 million for Friends Reunited, a five-year-old Internet business which puts former school friends in touch with each other. In 2005 Friends Reunited had 15 million registered UK members, with 1 million paying for subscription services and earnings of £8.9million from a turnover of £18.7million. Some ITV shareholders regarded the deal as a strange move; a fifty-year old TV company and a five-year-old web-based business.

The downside of the deal could be seen as ITV not understanding the web-based environment and being unable to deal with a 'pull' medium like the web, which has active and informed consumers. This is seen as contrasting with the television environment, which is a 'push' medium where the viewer is largely seen as passive. Additionally the view could also be taken that ITV were likely to lack the necessary knowledge and skills (part of resources in EVR) to successfully manage Friends Reunited. The mismatch of environment and resources and quite possibly values suggests that this acquisition is unlikely to succeed.

Source: 'When push comes to pull, can the ITV dowager make new friends?', John Naughton, The *Observer*, 11 December 2005.

The external environment is where the opportunities and threats arise from and confront the organisation. Opportunities arise in the form of new customers and new geographic markets, which can be exploited, via exporting through to acquisition (see Chapter 8). Google (see Entry case study 1.1) has created and taken advantage of many opportunities to sell advertising and provide services ranging from helping 'Stanford University researchers fold proteins' through to buying 'a teapot online'. In contrast threats usually arise from competitors having better prices, more customers and greater market share.

Resources which organisations have access to include facilities, staff, know-how and financial resources. These are used to combat threats and build on opportunities in the external environment. The more effective use of resources than that undertaken by competitors is a strength and poor use of resources a weakness (see Chapter 3). The unconventional use of both resources and staff time at Google serve as strengths at the time of writing.

Values are the beliefs of the organisation that, in turn, determine the expected behaviours from managers and employees which are often seen by other stakeholders as the image of the organisation. For example the beliefs or values of The Body Shop centre on its green and fair-trade approach to doing business around the world. This results in many consumers seeing The Body Shop as having a 'green image' and being a morally good place to shop. These values and The Body Shop's success at creating and using its image is clearly very different from those created and used by Virgin Trains. The values of Virgin Trains will be those of good customer service and efficiency, to create an image of a train service which is clean, efficient and runs on time. Many customers hold the view that Virgin Trains appears to find it hard to consistently create its desired image, as on occasions it is unable to provide a clean, efficient, on-time service to customers. The behaviour of managers and employees can influence how well resources are used to achieve the aim of success in the environment. Again this is illustrated at Google (see Entry case study 1.1) where there are few constraints other than 'organise and make accessible the world's information' and 'don't be evil', which produces the highly innovative behaviour required of staff at Google.

Exhibit 1.5 The levels of strategy

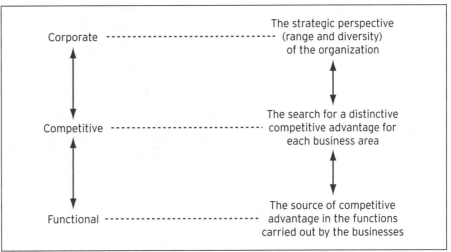

Source: Thompson, J L (2001) *Strategic Management*, 4th edn, London: Thomson Learning.

Thompson and many writers on strategy stress the need for co-ordination to give a coherent and overall strategic direction to the organisation and for this to happen strategy must exist at different levels. Thompson highlights this by defining the **levels of strategy** as corporate, the company-wide overview; competitive, the divisional level; and functional, the operational level (see **Exhibit 1.5**). All these levels should be involved in the development of strategy as all levels view and implement strategy from differing perspectives, and all are important in creating cohesive strategy.

The **levels of strategy** are corporate, competitive, and functional.

Position, choice and action

The Johnson, Scholes and Whittington[3] definition of strategy is well known and suggests that, when actually deciding and planning strategy, a framework is needed. Johnson, Scholes and Whittington define strategy as being concerned with **position**, **choice** and **action** (see Exhibit 1.6). Position is concerned with environmental analysis, strategic capability or resource evaluation, the expectations of stakeholders and impact of culture from both within and

Position is concerned with analysis of the external environmental, resources, stakeholders and culture.

outside the organisation, which are all covered in Thompson and Ohmae's definitions of strategy. This definition of strategy is often viewed as prescriptive.

Exhibit 1.6 Position, choice and action diagram

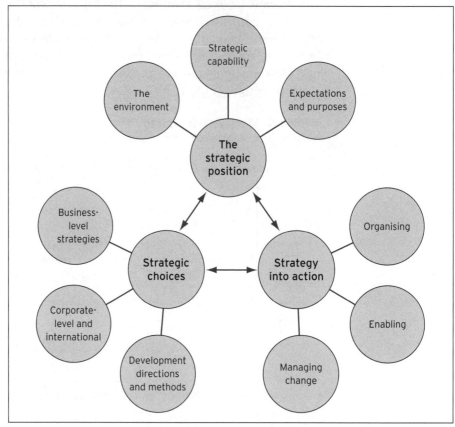

Source: Taken from Johnson, G, Scholes, K and Whittington, R (2005) *Exploring Corporate Strategy*, 7th edn, London: Financial Times/Prentice Hall.

Choice is about strategic options, including competitive strategy, corporate strategy, international strategy, market options and growth strategy.

Choice is about what the organisation wants to do and involves identifying strategic options, which include competitive strategy, corporate strategy, international strategy, market options and growth strategy. Competitive strategy is covered in Chapter 7 and involves the company deciding to be a low-cost or added-value producer in a mass or niche market. Market options are also covered in Chapter 7 and include market penetration, product development, market development or diversification. Growth strategy covers how an organisation chooses to expand and there are various options, including organic growth, acquisitions and strategic alliances. These and other methods of growth are examined in Chapter 8. International strategy is covered in Chapter 9 and examines how companies can develop international strategy and expansion. Johnson, Scholes and Whittington argue a company should select and review all possibilities for strategy, and select those which are feasible and sustainable. This identifies the need to evaluate current and potential strategy to ensure its cohesiveness.

Action is about allocating resources and making the chosen strategic options happen.

Action covers implementation, which involves deciding how resources are going to be used and allocated to make the chosen strategic options happen. This action or implementation involves both managing and controlling the resources used to pursue the chosen strategic options. If necessary actions can also cover alterations to the organisation's structure to allow strategic options to proceed and this can involve the management of significant organisational change (see Chapters 5, 10, 11 and 12).

Elements of strategic decisions

The definition of strategy presented by Lynch[4] identifies the core areas of strategy, as being analysis, development and implementation and this is clearly similar to the position, choice and action presented by Johnson, Scholes and Whittington.[5] However Lynch[6] goes on to develop the idea of strategy by defining five key elements of strategic decisions shown in **Exhibit 1.7**. Many of the strategic decisions made by Google (see Entry case study 1.1) have these characteristics, which are what make it difficult for Microsoft to compete effectively with Google.

Exhibit 1.7 Key elements of strategic decisions

- Sustainability and maintaining change over time resulting in success and profitability.
- Distinctiveness is concerned with being different from competitors and achieving sustainable competitive advantage.
- Creating links that cannot be easily duplicated by competitors.
- Spread the risk, go for a range of different customers in different markets and industries.
- Create clear vision, clear values and strong culture.

Source: Lynch, R (2006) *Corporate Strategy*, 4th edn, London: Financial Times/Prentice Hall.

McKinsey 7-S framework

The **7-S framework** covers strategy, skills, staff, style, systems, structure and shared values.

The McKinsey **7-S framework** was developed by Peters and Waterman[7] as a tool for managing and covering all aspects of strategy in an organisation (see **Exhibit 1.8**). All components of the framework, strategy, skills, staff, style, systems, structure and shared values are equally important and interconnected. Hence altering one component is likely to impact on the others, illustrating the point that effective strategy is not only one element of the framework. Effective strategy is determined, in part, by the relationship between strategy, structure, systems, staff, skills, style and shared values in the framework.

Exhibit 1.8 The 7-S Framework

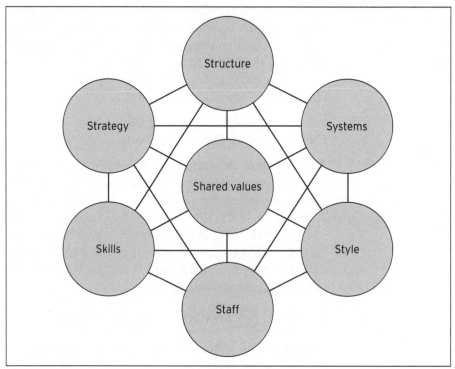

Source: Peters, T J and Waterman R H (1982) *In Search of Excellence*, New York: Harper & Row.

The idea of strategy as position has been well documented (see earlier definition by Johnson, Scholes and Whittington) and is concerned with an organisation understanding its position in its external environment. If an organisation's position in the external environment is clear then development inside the organisation should aim to achieve strategic fit with the external environment. The idea of fit can be developed by managing and changing the components of the 7-S framework. Strategy and structure determine how an organisation's activities are organised and grouped together (see Chapter 10). In Google (see Entry case study 1.1) this is done very loosely as staff are allowed to experiment and spend up to 20 per cent of their time working on projects of their own choosing. Systems allow resources to be allocated and managed appropriately when being delivered, used or distributed as finished goods (see Chapter 3). The staff and skills are key in the providing knowledge and know-how to deliver a company's products and services (see Chapter 3) and also in the case of Google (see Entry case study 1.1). Management style and leadership are key in managing staff and resources, and in providing strategic direction and leadership for the organisation (see Chapter 6). The shared values and culture (see Chapter 5) are to a greater or lesser extent interdependent upon all of the other components of the model; with who leads, who does what, how things are allocated and organised, determining the type of place an organisation is to work or vice versa.

✔ Check your understanding

- Do you understand what strategy is?
- Check your understanding by stating what you think the strategy is for each of the following:

    1 David Beckham (LA Galaxy soccer player)

    2 Oxfam (A charity raising money for the Developing World)

    3 Gordon Brown (Prime Minister of UK)

    4 Ryanair (A low-cost airline)

    5 T.K. Maxx (A cut-price retailer of designer clothes)

Review questions | **Definitions of strategy**

1 Write your own definition of strategy in 100 words.

2 Identify common strands of strategy from the definitions of strategy you have read about.

3 Explain why it is important that strategy is about both the external environment and the inside of organisations.

PRESCRIPTIVE AND EMERGENT STRATEGY

Prescriptive strategy is the sequential, logical view of strategy.

In the literature there are many definitions of strategy and definitions, like the ones looked at earlier in this chapter, can be viewed as prescriptive or emergent. **Prescriptive strategy** is the sequential, logical view of strategy that can be demonstrated, for example, by the earlier definition of Johnson, Scholes and Whittington, which suggests that determining position is followed by strategic choice, which is followed by strategic action. This means an overview of the organisation is taken, objectives are defined in advance and everything is considered in developing strategy (see Business illustration on Lloyds of London). The environment is analysed and the future anticipated, and this clear understanding of the external environment means resource requirements can be predicted. Next, choices are made and strategy is developed, prior to implementation, after which it is all evaluated. However, in reality events do not occur in a neat and logical sequence and some of the difficulties of prescriptive strategy are shown in **Exhibit 1.9**.

Exhibit 1.9 The assumptions and problems of prescriptive strategy

Assumptions of prescriptive strategy	Problems with prescriptive strategy
■ Prescriptive approach assumes the future can be highly predictable and this may be so if the organisation operates in an environment which is very simple, stable and static.[8]	■ Not so if the environment is very turbulent.
■ Chosen strategic options can and will be implemented correctly.	■ Not necessarily the case; managers make mistakes, have their own agenda and may only seek a satisfactory outcome, rather than the best outcome for the company.
■ Clear decisions are made concerning strategic options and all decision-makers agree on everything.	■ Not likely; some decision-makers will strongly support the decisions made, others will strongly disagree and some will remain in the middle. Therefore not all managers will be pulling in the same strategic direction.
■ Strategy once developed is never adjusted or changed.	■ Very unlikely for most organisations, as change in the environment often necessitates a change in strategy

Business illustration of prescriptive strategy – Lloyds of London

In January 2006, the insurance broker Lloyds of London announced it was to appoint a new chief executive. The unusual condition of the appointment was that the new chief executive would be expected to implement the company's three year strategic plan which had already been drawn up, rather than the develop his or her own vision and strategy for Lloyds. There was debate about whether this very prescriptive approach to strategy and leadership would hinder the ability of Lloyds to attract top level candidates to the post.

'To try to recruit a chief executive merely to implement a predetermined strategy for the company can limit the calibre of the person that the company is able to attract' was the view of Samuel Johar of headhunters Buchanan, Harvey & Co. Other views expressed were that the implementation of a predetermined and prescribed strategy would be best achieved by the appointment of an internal candidate with an operational background, rather than an external candidate with strategic or entrepreneurial background.

Source: 'Lloyd's says its next chief will be expected to stick to agreed strategy', Andrea Felstead, *Financial Times*, 25 January 2006.

Emergent strategy develops over time and is an ongoing process, which usually has unclear objectives but which become clearer over time.

In contrast **emergent strategy** is strategy which evolves, and there are different ways of explaining the concept of emergent strategy. Emergent strategy at its most basic is when all three areas position, choice and action are interlinked rather than sequential[9] and the final objective is unclear and only emerges over time. Managers and staff will be consulted for their views and, as managers can only handle so much data and information at once, the final decisions will be made from a selected number of strategic options. It should also be noted that managers could be biased in their interpretation of data and information.

In reality a company may decide to follow a particular strategy, for example producing and selling low-cost products. However this decision will be evaluated and adjustments made as matters proceed, that is, as competitors adjust prices and products the company's strategy will emerge. In contrast adjustments to a prescriptive strategy would not be made as matters proceed, even if the strategy was failing; changes would only be made once the project reached its end and the strategy had been evaluated. Hence emergent strategy is more of an ongoing process and in contrast to prescriptive strategy, emergent strategy often has unclear objectives, which develop and become clearer over time as the strategic situation develops – as per Google's approach. However the advantages of emergent strategy lie in its reflection of reality and flexibility (see **Exhibit 1.10**). Google appears to be driven from the top, but retains real openness to the view that the 'internal market forces will come up with better decisions' that will then be pursued and allowed to shape strategy at Google (see Entry case study 1.1). Hence Google's approach to strategy is emergent and as such is flexible and reflects reality. The evaluation of emergent strategy occurs on an ongoing basis and its flexibility allows adjustments to strategy to be made as required ensuring objectives are met and failure avoided.

Exhibit 1.10 Advantages of emergent strategy

- Reflects reality, corresponds with actual practice in organisations.
- Considers organisational culture.
- Implementation is integrated into emergent strategy.
- Flexibility allowed, emergent strategy adjusts as the organisation's strategic situation and environment change over time.

The downside of the emergent approach to strategy is that it lacks planning and therefore the organisation lacks any sense of strategic direction and strategic control. Equally managers operating in an organisation and environment in which strategy is highly emergent may be subjective in how they interpret information and make decisions (see **Exhibit 1.11**). Hence in many organisations the process of developing and implementing strategy is actually part prescriptive – with some things planned – and part emergent, with the organisation responding to its environment as appropriate.

Exhibit 1.11 Disadvantages of emergent strategy

- Managers can be biased in their interpretation of data when making decisions.
- Managers seek satisfactory solutions rather than maximise objectives of the organisation.
- No planning takes place, meaning a lack of strategic control and direction; the organisation muddles through.

✔ Check your understanding

- Do you understand the prescriptive approach to strategy?
- Check your understanding by explaining if Lloyd's prescriptive approach to strategy will help or hinder the new chief executive in achieving success for Lloyds (see Business illustration of prescriptive strategy – Lloyds, earlier in this chapter).

Review questions | **Prescriptive and emergent strategy**

1 Explain why the prescriptive approach to strategy is useful to organisations.
2 Explain why the emergent approach to strategy is useful to organisations.
3 Discuss how you might warn an organisation against using only the emergent approach to strategy?

MINTZBERG ON STRATEGY – 5PS OF STRATEGY

Mintzberg is a well-known author in the area of strategy and has made a significant contribution, hence the inclusion of a section which looks at some of his work including both prescriptive and emergent strategy. This section looks at some of Mintzberg's definitions of strategy, namely the 5Ps and forms of strategy.

Business illustration of strategy as a plan – GlaxoSmithKline

Jean-Pierre Garnier, head of the pharmaceutical company GlaxoSmithKline, plans the strategy for GlaxoSmithKline by drawing a cross on a piece of paper, with each arm of the cross representing key success factors for GlaxoSmithKline. They are research and development productivity, operational excellence, reinvention of marketing and pricing initiatives. These four areas knit together to give GlaxoSmithKline a coherent strategic direction.

Improved productivity of research and development leads to more drugs undergoing clinical trials and eventually more GlaxoSmithKline products on the market. Operational excellence is the drive for efficiency and reduced duplication of activities, all on a global basis. In 2006 reinvention of marketing involved looking for new ways of selling and using GlaxoSmithKline's salesforce. Pricing initiatives involve managing pricing challenges in the US and Europe and considering a reduction in the price of GlaxoSmithKline drugs in countries which are 'resource poor markets'. This would make drugs to treat HIV and Aids more easily available in countries like South Africa and GlaxoSmithKline would likely benefit as the lower price would generate a greater sales volume.

Source: 'Garnier outlines four-point strategy to improve GSK's health', Andrew Jack, *Financial Times*, 31 December 2005.

Mintzberg[10] suggests that strategy like marketing – which has its four Ps (product, price, place, promotion) – should have five Ps, namely **plan**, **ploy**, **pattern**, **position**, and **perspective**.

Strategy as a plan

Strategy as a plan is deliberate and developed in advance of action.

Plans are made deliberately and developed in advance of the actions to which they are to apply. Plans can be formally stated or they can be allowed to remain formally unstated, in which case they should remain clear in someone's mind. This appears to be the approach taken at Lloyds (see Business illustration on Lloyds) and at GlaxoSmithKline (see Business illustration on GlaxoSmithKline). Both companies have planned predetermined strategies, which then need to be applied and followed.

Strategy as a ploy

Strategy as a ploy is the threat to act in response to a competitor's actions.

A ploy is defined as a plan which threatens to counteract a competitor's actions or planned actions. The strategy is the threat to act in response to a competitor's actions, not the plan to act. The same ploy cannot be used repeatedly, because as a ploy the threat will never be carried out, and so it will cease to be an effective strategy.

Strategy as a pattern

Strategy as a pattern is a stream of actions with consistency.

Strategy as a pattern takes into account planned actions as well as the behaviour, which the strategy produces. Therefore the intended and the actual strategies are both considered. In describing strategy as a pattern, Mintzberg describes a pattern as a 'stream of actions'.

The use of a 'pattern' to describe strategy suggests consistency in the resulting behaviour and this could infer the presence of a plan behind the consistency of the company's behaviour. It must however be remembered that strategies are the result of human actions and to assume a plan behind the pattern may be incorrect. For a pattern or strategy to result from a plan (a plan being a statement of intent), the actions stated must be realised without being influenced or adjusted by either the internal or external environment and it should be clear that this is very unlikely. It is equally unlikely that a truly emergent strategy would produce the required consistency in behaviour without any indication of its intention. Therefore Mintzberg suggests that **realised strategy** has two components, **intended strategy** and emergent strategy (see **Exhibit 1.12**).

Realised strategy is the planned and emergent strategy which actually occurs.

Intended strategy is the planned strategy of an organisation.

Strategy as a position is the company's point in its external environment, which seeks to allow it to compete effectively with other companies.

Strategy as a position

Strategy as a position is how the company is placed in its external environment and it will likely be in competition with companies, which are in similar

Exhibit 1.12 Deliberate and emergent strategies

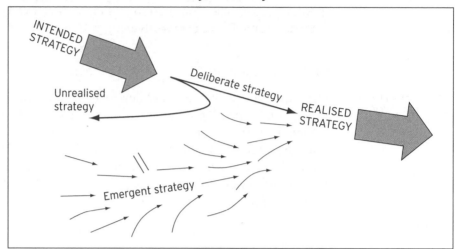

Source: Mintzberg, H (1987) 'SPs for Strategy', *California Management Review*, Fall.

positions in the external environment. The link which Mintzberg suggests between position and environment can be examined in another light, in that a company occupying a niche is a company which occupies a position in which competition is limited or can be avoided, and this is the company's strategy. Hence strategy can exist as position as in the case on Renault which is seeking to position itself such that it is competing in the luxury car market and avoiding some of the very fierce competition in the family car market (see Business illustration on Renault).

Business illustration of strategy as position – Renault

In February 2006 Carlos Ghosn, chief executive of Renault, announced his strategy for Renault. The strategy is based on position. Carlos Ghosn seeks to launch the new Laguna model in the luxury market segment competing with the BMW 3-series, with the aim of Renault doubling its sales of luxury cars. Renault will also move away from heavy reliance on the Megane model and launch 26 new products, including SUVs and 4x4s, which are market segments in which Renault does not currently compete.

Source: 'Ghosn unveils ambitious strategy for Renault', Tom Griggs, *Financial Times*, 9 February 2006.

Strategy as a perspective

Strategy as a perspective is a view or concept which is shared by members of the organisation.

Mintzberg[11] states that perspective is to strategy what 'personality is to the individual'. This leads to the suggestion that strategy is a concept. Concepts and hence strategies are abstract and exist only in people's minds. The key point is that strategy as perspective will be shared by members of an organisation, via their intentions and/or actions.

Relationships between plans, ploys, patterns, position and perspectives

The relationships between the 5Ps of strategy are many and varied. Mintzberg suggests that strategy as a perspective is compatible with **strategy as a plan** and/or as a pattern. An alternative suggestion is that **strategy as a perspective** may give rise to plans and/or patterns. The opposite of this type of behaviour is that strategy emerges, step by step, is recognised as a pattern and then made deliberate; that is, pattern evolves, rather than plan evolving pattern. This is illustrated by Google's approach to strategy which evolves as a result of the company employing 'some of the finest computer brains on the planet' and not as the result of planning (see Entry case study 1.1).

If plans and patterns are dispensable, perspective in that it is like a person's personality or character is extremely difficult to change. With this in mind it is possible to see that perspective is more like pattern (consistency in behaviour) than plan (statement of intent). Therefore if perspective is virtually impossible to change, then plan and position can only be changed in a way which is compatible with existing perspective.

The definitions of strategy, which have been discussed, compete with one another and are used in place of each other. This is perhaps not surprising, as some plans will become patterns; some patterns which develop will have been planned, while others will emerge. Some ploys are less than positions, while some strategies are more than positions, but less than perspectives.

A plan introduces the idea of stating intent and pattern introduces the notion of behaviour and emergent strategies. Additionally pattern and position also introduce the idea of rooting the strategy in the external environment and hence the existence of competition, while perspective states that strategy is a concept and is a collection of plans, ploys, patterns and positions.

Forms of strategy

Strategy is often thought of in terms of a long-term plan, which is drawn up by the organisation's leaders in order to meet the organisation's objectives. This common approach to strategy is reflected in many definitions of strategy, including those looked at earlier in this Chapter and they often suggest that strategy be developed prior to implementation. Mintzberg[12] makes the point that this view is limited and a wider perspective of strategy is often useful to leaders and managers charged with providing strategic direction and strategy for an organisation.

Mintzberg[13] goes on to establish the view of strategy as a stream of decisions containing patterns. The next point is to understand that streams of decisions and the associated behaviour can be identified and patterns recognised, based on the relationship between the intent of leaders and what the organisation actual does. This is illustrated in **Exhibit 1.12**, which shows the two large arrows the one on the left-hand side representing 'intended strategy' and the one on the right-hand side representing 'realised strategy'. This illustrates realised strategy as arising from the planning and intent of leaders and from decisions and patterns which emerge and are realised, without prior planning or intent from the organisation's leaders.

All or some elements of the intended strategy of an organisation, as planned or prescribed by its leadership, may actually happen; these become part of the realised strategy (see **Exhibit 1.12**). Some of the decisions made and intended actions may not actually happen, these become **unrealised strategy** (see **Exhibit 1.12**). If all the decisions made with intent, become realised strategy, there are no unrealised decisions and hence no unrealised strategy. Additionally if there is no emergent strategy, then the organisation's strategy is a pure deliberate strategy; hence, intended strategy is exactly the same as realised strategy.

Unrealised strategy is the planned or intended actions which do not actually happen.

Mintzberg and Waters[14] stress that three conditions must exist for a company to have a 'pure deliberate' strategy. First, detailed and precise plans have to exist. Next, the plans have to be absolutely accepted by everyone in the organisation, and thirdly the intended decisions have to be implemented without any adjustment or changes. This third point means the organisation's external environment has to be very stable or completely predictable or fully controlled by the organisation. It is unlikely all these conditions will be met by an organisation, but some do come close to meeting one or some of the conditions and consequently will have a 'fairly deliberate' or 'highly prescriptive' strategy. The obvious example is a firm of funeral directors: the external environment is fairly predictable, plans exist for the business to operate on a day-to-day basis and, providing the staff or family members don't fall out, agreement on plans and operation of the business exist.

In contrast a 'perfectly emergent' strategy arises when there is a lack of intent, but actions are consistent in what the organisation actively does. Thus the '**perfectly emergent**' strategy is expected to be as unlikely as the 'purely deliberate' strategy. However Mintzberg and Waters do suggest that an organisation may operate with a strategy which is close to being 'perfectly emergent' if the external environment dominates the organisation and its industry in some way. This is the case with Google as the marketplace for electronic information dominates the environment Google operate in (see Entry case study 1.1).

Perfectly emergent strategy arises when there is no intent, but there is consistency in what the organisation does.

Hence Mintzberg and Waters suggest that 'purely deliberate' and 'perfectly emergent' strategies form opposite ends of a continuum, with most organisations falling somewhere between the two in terms of their strategy. This means most organisations will have a realised strategy, which is part deliberate or prescriptive and part emergent; hence some strategy is planned and some is emergent. Organisations may of course be closer to one end of the continuum and their strategy may be either more deliberate or more emergent, and additionally, their position on the spectrum may alter over time. This is discussed further in the Mintzberg paper.[15] In conclusion, deliberate strategy focuses on managing strategic direction and control to get things done. In contrast emergent strategy focuses on strategic learning and crafting strategy,[16] which means leadership is flexible and responsive to the organisation, its staff and its position in the external environment.

✔ Check your understanding

- Do you understand what is meant by deliberate and emergent strategy?
- Check your understanding by applying Mintzberg and Waters' approach to deliberate and emergent strategy to Google and Microsoft. Explain what type of strategy you think each company is following.

Review questions | **Deliberate and emergent strategy**

1 Which of Mintzberg's 5Ps of strategy are prescriptive and which are emergent?
2 Explain the difference between pure deliberate and perfectly emergent strategy.
3 Explain why Mintzberg and Waters' approach to strategy is more useful to organisations than either the prescriptive or emergent approaches on their own.

CONCLUSION

Definitions of strategy such as those examined earlier in this chapter implicitly suggest that strategy is something organisations need. This raises the question 'Is strategy necessary?'. Clearly an organisation with no strategy will make resource savings, as no strategic analysis and development will be undertaken and potential opportunities are not limited as the company's strategy does not have to achieve its strategic objectives. There would be no defined strategic direction. The disadvantages of not having a strategy are summarised in **Exhibit 1.13**.

Exhibit 1.13 The disadvantages of a lack of strategy

- Lack of focus inside and outside organisation, strategic fit will not be achieved.
- Employees will lack depth of knowledge and be unable to spot good opportunities.
- Decision makers plunge into making decisions without awareness of risks or refuse to make decisions without knowledge of the risks
- Efficiency and effectiveness of resources are not measured as strategy is not reviewed and evaluated.
- Cannot anticipate change which will impact on the organisation.
- Risk of managers doing nothing or acting at cross-purposes, i.e. not all pulling in the same direction.

After considering the question 'Is strategy necessary?' it is easy to see that strategy is important to organisations. Strategy involves the whole company, provides a focus at all levels of the organisation and covers the range and depth of an organisation's activities involving: decisions about products and services, competition and markets, growth, and change in organisations. Strategy directs the evolving relationship between an organisation and its environment and should enable the organisation to find strategic fit with its external environment. This means strategy is central to the creation of competitive advantage and directs the organisation to add value or reduce costs in the most appropriate areas and products, that is, the company goes into the most profitable markets, sells the products with the best profit margins. This allows the organisation to survive as a minimum objective in a declining industry and the creation of sustainable competitive advantage as a maximum objective, particularly in stable and growing markets.

LEARNING OUTCOMES AND SUMMARY

The learning outcomes for this chapter are specified and a brief summary of the material relating to the learning outcomes is provided.

→ **Learning outcome 1**
Define strategy and explain different definitions of strategy from the literature.

- There are many definitions of strategy, including the three strategic Cs: customers, corporation and competitors. Thompson's definition of strategy looks at EVR: environment, values and resource. The classic definition by Johnson, Scholes and Whittington concludes that strategy is concerned with determining position, choice and action. The framework of Peters and Waterman looks at the 7Ss: strategy, skills, staff, style, systems, structure and shared values.

→ **Learning outcome 2**
Discuss prescriptive strategy and the problems associated with this approach.

- Prescriptive strategy is the sequential logical view of strategy, where objectives are defined in advance and plans are made. However, the reality is that events do not occur in a predictable way; market and competitors change.
- The problems with prescriptive strategy include the environment not always being stable and predictable, managers not always agreeing and implementing plans as expected, and strategies needing to change if objectives are to be met.

→ **Learning outcome 3**
Summarise Mintzberg's 5Ps of strategy and explain the usefulness of this approach.

- Strategy as a plan is deliberate and developed in advance of action.

- Strategy as a ploy is the threat to act in response to a competitor's actions.
- Strategy as a pattern is a stream of actions with consistency.
- Strategy as position is the company's point in its external environment, which allows effective competition.
- Strategy as perspective is a view or concept which is shared by members of the organisation.
- The 5Ps approach is useful as it allows organisations to view their strategy and development in different ways, which can be useful if the organisation is unable to move forward with the approach currently being used.

→ **Learning outcome 4**
Discuss emergent strategy, its advantages and disadvantages.

- Emergent strategy is an ongoing process, which often has unclear objectives, but which develop and become clearer over time. Emergent strategy reflects reality and corresponds with what actually happens in organisations and their environment. The flexibility of emergent strategy allows implementation to be integrated and modified as events unfold for the organisation.
- The downside of emergent strategy is that no planning takes place and the organisation muddles through, with managers who are biased and happy to seek only satisfactory implementation rather than maximising the objectives of the organisation.

→ **Learning outcome 5**
Summarise Mintzberg and Waters' approach to prescriptive and emergent strategy.

- The elements of the intended strategy of an organisation which actually happen become part of the realised strategy. Intended actions which do not happen become unrealised strategy. A 'perfectly emergent' strategy arises when there is a lack of intent, but actions are consistent in what the organisation actively does.
- Mintzberg and Waters suggest that 'purely deliberate' and 'perfectly emergent' strategy form opposite ends of a continuum, with most organisations falling somewhere between the two in terms of their strategy.
- Mintzberg and Waters stress that three conditions must exist for a company to have a 'pure deliberate' strategy. First, detailed and precise plans have to exist. Next, the plans have to be absolutely accepted by everyone in the organisation and, third, the intended decisions have to have been implemented without any adjustment or changes.

This exit case study looks at a company developing a different strategic direction and can be used to assess the learning outcomes below.

Learning outcomes	Check you have achieved this by	
Understanding and identifying possible strategies.	Applying the EVR and 7-S framework to the Bank of China.	Answering exit case study question 1.
Discuss the advantages and disadvantages of a particular strategy.	Identifying and explaining the pros and cons of strategy for different companies.	Answering exit case study question 2.

Royal Bank rides the dragon

by Katherine Griffiths

Above a branch in central Beijing, Royal Bank of Scotland is embarking on its Chinese adventure. In a room smaller than the average RBS high street outlet, the Scottish bank and its partner, Bank of China, are producing credit cards they hope will appeal to China's rising class of wealthy people. RBS and Bank of China have just two pristine new credit card machines to cater for a country with a population of 1.3 billion. Even that, the banks say, produces more cards than are needed.

But RBS, which also owns NatWest, and Bank of China are gambling on a rapid rise in demand. They will launch one million cards this year. By 2010, the number in issue in China will catch up with the UK. It is almost a year since Sir Fred Goodwin, RBS's chief executive, paid $1.6bn (£900m) for just over 5pc of Bank of China, the country's second biggest bank, and began the partnership he hopes will make RBS a major player there.

Sir Fred, known for his iron grip on detail and willingness to commit 'mercy killings' by taking over weaker rivals, realises the challenge of RBS's latest major strategic gamble, but is guardedly optimistic. 'There are real communication difficulties which means it takes more time to agree things but I'm happy with how things have been going. Could it go quicker? 'Yes'. Could it go slower? 'Yes', said Sir Fred, as he attended a bi-monthly meeting in Beijing of the senior RBS and Bank of China people who are overseeing the joint venture.

Having been castigated by shareholders when rumours of its ambitions in China first emerged, RBS is now looking clever. Its $1.6bn stake is now worth $4.7bn, though the increase is a paper profit and RBS is locked into owning the shares for three years. Sir Fred also has a seat on Bank of China's board. Having started off with credit cards and corporate banking, the

agreement between the two has broadened and deepened.

The partners are beavering away on plans for an exclusive service which will help China's swelling class of wealthy people manage their money. Built on RBS's skills from owning Coutts, bankers to the upper crust, the operation is looking for a swanky office in the heart of Beijing and will span out across China's eastern cities where money is accumulating fast, such as Shanghai and Tianjin.

RBS is helping Bank of China expand its corporate banking operation via services such as lending to companies and selling on their debt in the financial market. RBS will do about $1bn in joint transactions with Bank of China this year and launch a joint general insurance operation.

Despite the frustrations, from the frequency of trips on RBS's private jet to China, as well as the amount of time other senior RBS managers are investing, Sir Fred appears to firmly believe China is worth it. He has said the stake RBS took in Bank of China is a 'ticket to the game'. He is not alone in wanting a ringside seat.

The list of other banks around the world putting a stake in the ground in China include HSBC, Citigroup, Bank of America, UBS, Deutsche Bank and Goldman Sachs. Of its UK competitors, HSBC – which has a long history in Asia – has taken stakes in the giant Bank of Communication and the smaller Bank of Shanghai and is also opening its own branches in China. Standard Chartered – whose biggest market is Hong Kong – has invested in a Chinese start up, Bohai Bank. Other UK high street banks are doing very little, though Barclays has shown interest in Korea. China's attractions are obvious for western banks, which operate in mature markets where GDP growth is sluggish and people already have current accounts and credit cards.

China's GDP has grown at about 10pc a year for the past 15 years and is set to continue at or near that pace. It has between 300,000 and 400,000 inhabitants with more than $1m (£524,000) of disposable assets, making it the second largest concentration of 'high net worth' individuals in Asia after Japan. The middle class is also expanding rapidly. There about 60m Chinese earning $5,000 – the sum RBS believes is viable for offering a credit card – and that is forecast to double to 120m people by 2010.

Yet the risks of doing business in China are massive, and perhaps one of the reasons Sir Fred, one of the most adventurous chief executives in the FTSE 100 and almost certainly the most daring chief of a UK bank, is so attracted to the country. Before they even get started in China, foreign banks face steep regulatory hurdles. The most basic is that a single foreign investor can own a maximum of 20pc of a Chinese bank, and a consortium of outsiders may hold up to 25pc. That is likely to change, but no one knows when. As part of China's entry into the World Trade Organisation in 2001, some restrictions are being lifted, but there is uncertainty over the timetable for deregulation.

Wealth management is set to be opened up to foreigners next month, while the rule preventing all banks in China from doing insurance business may be scrapped next year, but more likely in 2008. The Communist country may even reverse some planned reforms if the backlash about foreigners snapping up Chinese banks 'on the cheap' becomes too great. All of this has big implications for RBS.

Sir Fred acknowledges the agreement upon which RBS's major strategic move into China is based is 'vague' because China's banking laws currently do not allow more definite arrangements. Instead RBS has had to set things up according to a 'principle of equal sharing'. This means that, while the Scottish bank cannot formally own half of the wealth management and credit card joint ventures, it is bearing at least half of the set up costs, and hopes future profits will be divvied up equally. Sir Fred also knows that, at some point, Bank of China may wish to buy it out of the joint ventures. If so, 'we'll find ourselves on the street with hopefully a not insubstantial cheque and a body of RBS people with knowledge of how to run things in China', he says.

There are also economic risks for banks in China. Bert Hofman, a China expert at the World Bank, believes, despite its fast growth, 'there is no overheating in China'. But he has 'concerns' about the inflationary risks caused by the huge amount of money being pumped in building and other projects in China. The amount of money spent by middle class Chinese households is still far lower than the UK, Germany and US.

Conspicuous wealth has also carried risk. When Forbes published a Chinese Rich List in 1999, it became known as the 'death list' as many of them were hit by allegations of tax evasion. Analysts believe all this is changing. Banks are beginning to have to deal with the opposite problem – more young Chinese defaulting on credit cards than in other countries. There is far less data on people's credit histories than is available in the West.

RBS likens its Chinese venture to the deal it struck with Tesco in 1997 to sell banking products through the supermarket chain. After years of heavy investment the business went into the black in 2000, and is now a major generator of profits.

He Liping, professor of finance at Beijing Normal University, believes there is a lot of 'room for improvement' in China's banking sector. But he says much as already been done: 'China's banks have been recapitalised. Formally separated boards of directors have been set up. Banks that traditionally lend to companies or producers are increasingly lending to individuals. The banking market is being opened up to foreigners and the IPOs of a number of banks have led to significantly increased profits'.

The biggest worry over Chinese banks concerns bad debts. In 2004 and 2005, China wiped out $60bn of bad debts from its main banks, but a further $250bn of losses remain in the system, according to UBS.

China's high-speed growth in the past few years has meant its banks' ability to withstand a downturn has not been even remotely tested. All of China's biggest banks remain majority-owned by the government. Inside each is a Communist Party controlled committee whose role is opaque. Yet the country's largest banks have undergone big reforms. Bank of China's commercial decisions are taken by the board of directors.

In preparation for its dual flotations in Hong Kong and then Shanghai, Bank of China shed about 11pc of its staff, cutting it to 230,000 and closed hundreds of branches (now fewer than 12,000). It has introduced performance related pay and its board includes heavyweight external directors such as Patrick de Saint-Aignan, a Morgan Stanley veteran.

Zhu Min, Bank of China's assistant president who masterminded its flotation and previously worked on Wall Street, said 'culturally there is a still a big issue' in reforming the bank. But he adds that much is being done, for example by 'centralising risk management and

→

moving it from being committee-based to focused on the individual'.

RBS says that, if nasty bad debts are lurking in Bank of China, it can exercise warrants agreed at the time it took its stake which protect the value of its stake. In practice, the bank might find it difficult to call on this insurance policy. RBS also believes that in choosing Bank of China it has picked a bank the government would never allow to go down.

Much will depend on the relationship between Sir Fred, an accountant by training, and his opposite number at Bank of China, Li Lihui. Both Mr Li and Sir Fred have much to lose. Perhaps they also have something to gain.

Source: *Daily Telegraph* 10 November 2006.

Exit case study questions

1 Using the EVR model of strategy and the McKinsey 7-S framework determine the strategy of the Bank of China.

2 Explain the advantages and disadvantages of the Bank of China's strategy for both themselves and the Royal Bank of Scotland.

DISCUSSION TOPIC

1 Read the paper 'What is strategy?' by Michael E Porter, Chapter 1, in *The Strategy Process*, Mintzberg, Lampel, Quinn and Ghosal, Harlow: Prentice Hall, 2003.

2 Explain how Porter's definitions of strategy underpin and support or contradict the definitions of strategy summarised in Chapter 1 of this textbook.

WIDEN YOUR HORIZONS

1 Widen your horizons by summarising NASA's strategy for the future in 250 words. Visit the NASA website, www.nasa.gov. From the home page, click on 'Missions Section' and then on 'Future Missions'.

2 Widen your horizons by identifying and discussing the advantages and disadvantages of doing business in Russia. The article 'Corruption casts a shadow on resourceful Russia', by Rebecca Bream and Neil Buckley in the *Financial Times* on 1 December 2006 provides a useful starting point.

WEBLINKS

The websites for this chapter provide some definitions of strategy and some discussion concerning the question 'What is strategy?'

■ This paper reviews various definitions of strategy.
  http://home.att.net/~nickols/strategy_definition.htm

■ Read the paper 'What is strategy?' by Michael E Porter, from the *Harvard Business Review*, November-December 1996.
  http://faculty.washington.edu/castlej/ENTRE475/Articles%20of%20interest/What%20is%20Strategy-Porter.pdf

■ An article which discusses what strategy is and isn't.
  www.camagazine.com/index.cfm/ci_id/9654/la_id/1.htm

FURTHER READING

The following readings provide a variety of views on strategy.

- Dess, G G, Lumpkin, G T, Taylor, M L (2005) *Strategic management*, 2nd edn, New York: McGraw Hill Irwin. Chapter 1, 'Strategic management'.
- Jenkins, M and Ambrosini, V (2002) *Strategic management: A multi-perspective approach*, Basingstoke: Palgrave Macmillan. Chapter 1, 'Strategy as multi-perspectives'.
- Johnson, G, Scholes, K and Whittington, R (2005) *Exploring Corporate Strategy*, 7th edn, Harlow: Financial Times/Prentice Hall. Chapter 1, 'Introducing strategy'.
- Lasserre, P (2003) *Global Strategic Management*, Basingstoke: Palgrave Macmillan. Chapter 2, 'Designing a global strategy'.
- Lynch, R (2006) *Corporate Strategy*, 4th edn, London: Financial Times/Prentice Hall. Chapter 1, 'Corporate strategy'.
- Lynch, R (2006) *Corporate Strategy*, 4th edn, London: Financial Times/Prentice Hall. Chapter 2, 'A review of theory and practice'.
- McGee, J, Thomas, H and Wilson, D (2005) *Strategy: Analysis and Practice*, Maidenhead: McGraw Hill. Chapter 2, 'Strategy and organisation'.
- Mellahi, K, Frynas, J G and Finlay, P (2005) *Global strategic management*, Oxford: Oxford University Press. Chapter 1, 'Introduction to global strategic management'.
- White, C (2004) *Strategic management*, Basingstoke: Palgrave. Chapter 1, 'Introducing strategy and strategy making'.
- White, C (2004) *Strategic management*, Basingstoke: Palgrave. Chapter 2, 'Thinking and acting strategically'.

REFERENCES

1. Ohmae, K (1983) *The Mind of the Strategist*, The Penguin Business Library.
2. Thompson, J L (2001) *Strategic Management*, London: Thomson Learning.
3. Johnson, G, Scholes, K and Whittington, R (2005) *Exploring Corporate Strategy*, 7th edn, London: Financial Times/Prentice Hall.
4. Lynch, R (2006) *Corporate Strategy*, 4th edn, London: Financial Times/Prentice Hall.
5. Johnson, G, Scholes, K and Whittington, op. cit.
6. Lynch, R, op. cit.
7. Peters, T J and Waterman R H (1982), *In Search of Excellence*, New York: Harper & Row.
8. Richardson, B and Richardson, R (1992) *Business Planning*, 2nd edn, London: Pitman.
9. Lynch, R, op. cit.
10. Mintzberg, H (1987) 'Five Ps for strategy', *California Management Review*, Fall; in Mintzberg, H, Lampel, J, Quinn, J B and Ghosal, S, (2003) *The Strategy Process*, Harlow: Prentice Hall.
11. Ibid.
12. Mintzberg, H (1988) 'Opening up the definition of strategy', in Quinn, J B, Mintzberg, H and James, R M, (1988) *The Strategy Process*, New Jersey: Prentice Hall.
13. Ibid.
14. Mintzberg, H and Waters, J (1985) 'Of strategies deliberate and emergent', in De Wit, B and Meyer, R (1994) *Strategy: Process, Content, Context*, St Paul, MN: West Publishing Company.
15. Mintzberg, H (1988) op. cit.
16. Mintzberg, H (1987) 'Crafting strategy', *Harvard Business Review*, July-August; in Mintzberg, H, Lampel, J, Quinn, J B and Ghosal, S (2003) *The Strategy Process*, Harlow: Prentice Hall.

CHAPTER 2

Environmental analysis

Exhibit 2.1 Essential strategy model

Chapter objectives

The aim of environmental analysis is to help a company understand its current position in the external environment. This chapter introduces two key approaches to environmental analysis, namely PEST analysis and analysis of the competitive environment. PEST analysis allows a company to identify and understand the broad general factors impacting upon it, such as legislation and social behaviour of current or potential customers. Analysis of the competitive environment considers the role of regulation and the factors driving competition. The factors driving competition are assessed by use of Porter's five forces of competition model. This type of environmental analysis allows an organisation to develop a broad picture of its environment and hence an understanding of its own position in that picture. This understanding is key if a company is to develop and implement effective strategy.

When you have read this chapter and worked through the associated activities you should be able to achieve the objectives specified below.

1 Analyse the general external environment by use of PEST and the competitive environment by use of Porter's five forces model.

2 Summarise the benefits of undertaking environmental analysis.

3 Discuss the process for analysis of the general external environment and the competitive environment.

4 Understand the reasons for regulation of competition and how it can be implemented.

This entry case study looks at the changes occurring in the external environment in Vietnam, which will benefit both local and international businesses operating in the country. Approaches to analysing the external environment are looked at in this chapter.

Investors rush to join fray to say good morning to FT Vietnam

by Mark Kleinman

There are not many places Lloyd Blankfein flies to on business where Goldman Sachs, the Wall Street bank he heads, is not a heavy-hitter. But as the Goldman corporate jet took off from RAF Brize Norton late last Monday evening, Blankfein – fresh from collecting the prestigious Thomson Financials International Financing Review (IFR) Bank of the Year Award – was heading for uncharted territory.

Along with several high-ranking colleagues, Blankfein was on his way to court policymakers in one of Asia's fast-emerging economic success stories: Vietnam. His timing was impeccable. During Blankfein's trip, when he met central bankers and other government officials, Vietnam celebrated its formal accession to the World Trade Organisation.

Arriving not long after the US Congress granted Vietnam the status of permanent normal trade relations, it is a development that many believe will provide a springboard for this country of 84m people to punch its weight on the global economic stage, not much more than three decades after it was torn apart by war.

'By opening the country up to greater foreign competition, [WTO accession] will yield dynamic benefits over the longer term,' said a recent report by HSBC on Vietnam's growth prospects.

For Blankfein and Goldman Sachs, Vietnam is an opportunity waiting to happen. While rivals such as Citigroup and ABN Amro have secured retail banking licences, a business in which Goldman does not compete, and Merrill Lynch is part of a securities joint venture, the real riches are yet to be unlocked.

The statistics tell their own story. Vietnam boasts the fastest growing major economy in South-East Asia, with growth of 8.4pc in 2005 and an average of 7.2pc over the past decade. Its gross domestic product (GDP) has grown from $31bn to $60bn (£15.8bn to £30.5bn) over the past four years and exports are booming. That growing wealth is filtering through to cities such as Hanoi and Ho Chi Minh, where the expanding middle classes want luxuries unimaginable just a few years ago: a recent report from AT Kearney, the management consultancy, said consumer spending rose 16pc in 2005.

The parallels with Vietnam's near neighbour, China are inescapable. It is easy to see that for consumer goods multinationals such as Britain's SABMiller, the FTSE-100 brewer which last year struck a joint venture with Vinamilk, the state-owned dairy firm, the relaxation of foreign direct investment rules has prised open a highly attractive door. Yesterday, the Hong Kong conglomerate Hutchison Whampoa joined the fray when its telecoms subsidiary announced the launch of HT Mobile, a national mobile phone service for Vietnam.

Investors may not have to wait long before the steady flow of deals becomes a flood. The country's Communist government said last week it aimed to privatise as many as 100 state-owned firms by the end of next year, ranging across industries including oil and gas, textiles and the national flag-carrier, Vietnam Airlines. The process is a

→

far cry from the days when the economy was held in an iron grip and the state resisted any outside influence.

But perhaps foreign investors should not rejoice too much – yet. The Vietnamese government remains committed to a 'socially-oriented market economy', which analysts interpret as a shot across the bows of those hoping for unfettered access to the country's economic riches.

Its growth surge has come from a low base: it has only had an equity market for seven years. At the end of December, companies listed on the Ho Chi Minh stock exchange had a combined value of about $9bn, a similar size to Yell, the British Yellow Pages publisher.

Hanoi's attempt to project an image of a country open for business was undermined last year when ABN Amro, the Dutch bank, found itself embroiled in a bitter dispute with Incombank, a state-owned lender, over the loss of about $5m in foreign-exchange deals executed by ABN. The conflict was settled by ABN forking out about $4.5m

despite insisting it had done nothing wrong, yet the authorities' intentions towards four of its employees arrested during the row remain unclear.

'Corruption and non-transparency of bureaucratic decision-making remain significant obstacles', warned the HSBC report. Many investors think it a risk worth taking. Like Blankfein, the private-equity industry is also saying good morning to Vietnam. A recent research note published by Spencer White, a leading equity strategist at Merrill Lynch in Hong Kong, pointed to funds worth well over $650m being raised to invest in the country.

'We believe that state control will be steadily reduced over the coming years in non-strategic holdings, increasing the free float in the market,' said Don Lam, managing partner of VinaCapital, a Vietnam-focused investor with a fund quoted on AIM.

Source: *Daily Telegraph*, 16 January 2007.

INTRODUCTION

This Chapter introduces the idea of organisations analysing their external environment in order to make sense of the volatile world in which they operate, such that appropriate management and business decisions can be taken. In contemplating the complex and dynamic world in which they operate, organisations have to consider many influences and issues. For example in 2005 the US motor industry was facing a turbulent environment in the form of fierce competition and loss of market share to Asian car producers, with both Ford and General Motors having to make many thousands of staff redundant. Additionally the US companies were facing increasing raw materials costs and healthcare costs for its workers.[1]

PEST analysis is analysis of the external environment by considering political, economic, socio-cultural and technological factors influencing an organisation.

Analysis of the external environment can be done at a broad general level by use of **PEST analysis** and this is often considered along with analysis of competition, which is an important part of any company's external environment. Both are covered in this chapter.

Business illustration of competition – French wine

Traditional French wines have suffered a loss of market share due to the fierce competition by the new world producers in California, New Zealand and Australia. To fight back some French producers such as Vignerons Catalans, a big group of growers based around Perpignan, are producing wines such as the Fruite Catalan wines which come in pink screw top bottles, designed to appeal to the young and female markets.

Source: 'It's pink and garish, but it's the new look of French wines', Felicity Lawrence, *Guardian*, 25 June 2005.

UNDERSTANDING AND ANALYSING THE EXTERNAL ENVIRONMENT

The **external environment** is literally the big wide world in which organisations operate. Whatever the nature of their business, organisations do not and cannot exist in splendid isolation from the other organisations or individuals around them – be they customers, employees or suppliers. It is therefore clear that the external environment of any organisation is a large and complex place.

The term 'environment' in this case refers to much more than the ecological, 'green' issues that the word commonly evokes, although being environmentally friendly and reducing the carbon footprint can be part of an organisation's strategy (see Business illustration on Marks & Spencer). 'Environment' here is more appropriately interpreted as the external context in which organisations find themselves undertaking their activities. Companies operating in Vietnam will be operating in a dynamic and changing external environment (see Entry case study 2.1). Each organisation has a unique external environment which has unique impacts on the organisation, due to the fact that organisations are located in different places and are involved in different business activities, with different products, services, customers and so on. In addition to this unique context, individual organisations all have their own distinctive view of the world surrounding them, leading them to interpret what is happening in the external environment correctly or incorrectly, depending on their ability to understand the external forces affecting them. This begins to suggest how crucial it is for organisations to undertake external environmental analysis and to gain a correct understanding of the external environment's impact.

Business illustration on reducing the carbon footprint - Marks & Spencer

In January 2007 Marks & Spencer announced it was to spend up to £200m on implementing an 'eco-plan' throughout its business and supply chain to become carbon neutral by 2012. This means reducing the emission of greenhouse gases from its outlets and transport fleet, as well as sending no waste to landfill. Becoming carbon neutral means operations do not contribute to climate change.

Achieving a carbon neutral status means using new equipment such as low energy lighting and vehicles, which run on fuels derived from plants, such as electricity or bio-fuels. M&S plans to offset any remaining emissions by investment in projects such as wind-farms or solar energy. Other environmental initiatives for M&S include seeking to use only sustainable sources of wood and fish, and recycling plastic rather than using oil to make polyester.

Source: 'M&S plans £200m green push', Elizabeth Rigby and Fiona Harvey, *Daily Telegraph*, 15 January 2007.

Careful and accurate analysis of the external environment benefits organisations by providing overall greater understanding and an appreciation of the context in which the organisation operates. The key benefits of external environmental analysis are best realised if it is undertaken on a long-term, ongoing basis. The key benefits of analysing the external environment are shown in **Exhibit 2.2**.

Exhibit 2.2 Benefits of external environmental analysis

- Managers in the organisation achieve a greater understanding and appreciation of the external environment leading to improvement in long-term and strategic planning.

- The principal external environmental influences generating change are highlighted.

- Anticipation of threats and opportunities occurs within a time-scale of long enough duration to allow responses to be considered.

Source: based on Duncan, Peter M and Ginter, W Jack (1990) 'Macro-environmental analysis for strategic management', *Long Range Planning*, 23 (6), December.

PERFORMING EXTERNAL ENVIRONMENTAL ANALYSIS

The external environment is an immensely complex and dynamic place and, therefore, performing an analysis of the external environment of an organisation requires access to a wide range of information. Information concerning the external environment may already exist within the organisation or it may have to be sought, collected and collated from other sources.

Sources of information within an organisation will encompass information from the four key functional areas of marketing, production, finance and human resource management. This information will include sales reports; customer/client survey results; reports on staff skills and availability; and budgets and cash-flow statements detailing the amount and availability of cash. In addition, information should be available on the systems in place in the organisation, including information on their capability and capacity, and efficiency and effectiveness. This type of information provided by internal sources, if it is up to date, will provide details of the resources available to deal with current influences in the external environment.

External information sources are compiled by organisations other than the one undertaking analysis of its external environment. The external information sources most widely available and accessible to everyone are the press, television and radio. The annual report and accounts of a company also provide a summary of recent activities and may offer clues to or an indication of future activities. The annual report and accounts of publicly quoted companies are readily available from the companies themselves or via their website, so are easily obtainable by competitor companies. Specific information concerning an industry will be available from industry- or trade-specific publications.

The Internet and electronic databases are other sources of information, which are widely available in organisations. An immense and extensive amount of information is available on the Internet, although one must be aware of whom or which organisation originated the information, as this will affect its reliability and accuracy. Much printed and broadcast material can now be accessed via the Internet and many organisations have their own website. The other method of accessing information electronically is via the use of subscription databases such as Lexis/Nexus, which gives access to the world's press. Other subscription databases which can be found in libraries include MINTEL, FAME and journal databases.

✔ Check your understanding

- Do you understand the importance of information gathering and its reliability in undertaking external environmental analysis?
- Check your understanding by stating where you would search for reliable information on the following types of influences: political; economic; socio-cultural; and technological.

DUNCAN AND GINTER ON PERFORMING EXTERNAL ENVIRONMENTAL ANALYSIS

A process for analysing the external environment is presented in Duncan and Ginter's work[2] and the principles can apply equally to a company operating in a domestic or world-wide environment. Duncan and Ginter pose a number of questions for organisations, the answers to which determine the need for external environmental analysis by the company, see **Exhibit 2.3**.

Exhibit 2.3 Assessing the need for external environmental analysis

If the answer to at least some of the questions is yes, then environmental analysis is required.

Questions

- Have previous long-term plans been significantly altered due to unexpected changes in the external environment?
- Have there been any 'nasty' surprises in the external environment?
- Is the influence of the external environment increasing?
- Is the company becoming concerned about its markets and customers?
- Is the allocation of capital influenced by the external environment?
- Is management unhappy with previous forecasting and planning efforts?

Source: based on Duncan, Peter M and Ginter, W Jack (1990) 'Macro-environmental analysis for strategic management', *Long Range Planning*, 23 (6), December.

Monitoring is identifying current influences on the company.

Scanning is concerned with identifying future influences on the company.

Forecasting is concerned with anticipating how current environmental influences may change in future.

Assessing is concerned with evaluating the impact and potential impact of both current and future external environmental factors on the organisation.

Duncan and Ginter take the mainstream view that external environmental analysis is concerned with the broad nature of the external environment in which organisations operate. The mainstream view is that external environmental analysis includes PEST analysis and the nature of the competitive environment, which is examined via Porter's five forces model. Both PEST and Porter are examined in this chapter, while market analysis and segmentation are covered in Chapter 7. However, Duncan and Ginter go on to identify the activities companies need to undertake to perform this type of analysis, namely **monitoring**, **scanning**, **forecasting** and **assessing**, see **Exhibit 2.4**. Overall environmental analysis is concerned with the PEST, competitive and market factors affecting and influencing the organisation now and in the future, and how these factors will change and impact on the organisation now and in the future.

Exhibit 2.4 Monitoring, scanning, forecasting and assessing the external environment

Monitoring is identifying current influences on the company and ensuring they continue to be tracked. Examples may include interest rates and the increasing impact of technology, which can both be tracked or monitored
Scanning is similar to monitoring, but it is concerned with identifying future rather than current, influences on the company. Future influences on the company once identified via scanning the external environment need to be monitored.
Forecasting is concerned with anticipating how current environmental influences may develop and change in future. For example current trends affecting a company may change and have a more positive impact on the company, their impact may be more detrimental or their impact on the company may remain unchanged.
Assessing is concerned with evaluating the impact and potential impact of both current and future external environmental factors on the organisation. For example the potential impact of changes in interest rates and the impact of technology on the organisation can be assessed. Hence allowing the organisation to anticipate and proactively manage its external environment.
Source: based on Duncan, Peter M, and Ginter, W Jack (1990) 'Macro-environmental analysis for strategic management', *Long Range Planning*, 23 (6), December.

PERFORMING PEST ANALYSIS

Performing a successful PEST analysis is concerned with identifying and understanding PEST factors influencing the organisation and the equally important second stage. The second stage is concerned with evaluating the impact of the identified PEST factors on the organisation, which allows conclusions to be drawn concerning the critical opportunities and threats facing the organisation, see **Exhibit 2.5**. The main PEST factors in each category are discussed; however, the PEST factors shown in **Exhibit 2.6** are not definitive lists.

Exhibit 2.5 Guidelines for PEST analysis

Stage 1 – Identifying and understanding PEST factors

- Identify the factors affecting the organisation.

- Categorise the factors; decide whether individual factors are **P**olitical, **E**conomic, **S**ocio-cultural or **T**echnological.

- Make sure you can explain how and why a particular factor is affecting an organisation. Remember that elements in the external environment do not exist in isolation and can impinge on and influence one another.

Stage 2 – Evaluating the impact of PEST factors on the organisation

- Select and judge which categories are most important to the company, for example, economic influences.

- Select key individual factors from the important categories.

- Consider the important categories and factors you have identified. Do any of these pose threats or opportunities to which the company must react immediately or in the longer term, when anticipating and planning the future?

- How should the organisation react to and deal with the opportunities and threats? Do short-term opportunities take priority over long-term threats or vice versa?

Exhibit 2.6 Generic PEST factors

Political	Economic
- National government - National bodies - Alliances and agreements	- Central bank - Stock market - Trading blocs and bodies
Socio-cultural	**Technological**
- Demographics - Cross cultural issues	- Information technology - Communications technology

✔ Check your understanding

- Do you understand the process for performing PEST analysis?
- Check your understanding by explaining the arrangements a business should put in place to undertake successful PEST analysis.

Review questions | **External environmental analysis**

1 Explain why organisations undertake external environmental analysis.

2 Summarise where organisations get information from to assist in undertaking environmental analysis.

THE POLITICAL ENVIRONMENT

The **political environment** comprises bodies which have a political viewpoint regarding how business operates

The **political environment** comprises many organisations. The key elements of the political environment facing businesses include local and national government, trade unions, employers' bodies, political **alliances and agreements**, which all represent a political viewpoint (see **Exhibit 2.7**). There are many areas of overlap between the political and **economic environments** as national and global economies are largely organised and run by governments, and this is the reason the European Union appears in both the political and economic sections of this chapter. This chapter examines the impact that external environmental elements have on organisations (see Entry case study 2.1), but inevitably it will become clear that organisations also affect the external environment around them. This is perhaps especially so for employers' organisations, as will be seen later.

Exhibit 2.7 Generic PEST grid showing political factors

Political	Economic

■ National government
  - Devolution in Scotland and Wales
 	
■ National bodies
  - Employers bodies
  - Employees bodies
 	
■ Alliances and agreements
  - The European Union
  - The UK and the USA
  - The UK and China	

Socio-cultural	**Technological**

National government

The ways in which the national government manages the economic environment are dealt with under the relevant section below. As a result of the UK's membership of the **European Union**, the distinction of a national political environment is becoming blurred. Acts that appear on the surface to have been the British Parliament making laws governing British businesses turn out to have originated in Brussels and required all member countries to implement them. Two examples of European decisions enacted by the national British government are the fitting of seatbelts to coaches, vans and lorries, adding costs to transport companies; and the abolition of duty-free goods within the European Union, meaning that tax-free shopping has come to an end except for inter-continental flights.

Examples of the purely national political environment affecting organisational activity are therefore increasingly hard to find, but largely focus on the legislation passed regarding permissible commercial activity, production and service functions, and human resource strategies. An example is the introduction of legislation in England banning smoking in enclosed public spaces, which has meant the hospitality industry in England now has to operate smoke-free premises since the legislation voted for in February 2006 came into force on 1 July 2007.

Although its effects could be said to be largely economic, the national government's political decision making affects most citizens directly through its annual budget. Government has to raise money to provide for its services. It does this via taxation revenue which it uses to pay for publicly funded services such as education, the National Health Service, public transport subsidies, and social and welfare services such as the state pension for those too old to be economically active. Some of the money raised by taxation is distributed via local government, and some is distributed and spent directly by national government.

Decisions with an economic effect on business, then, may be classified as political when taken by government. From this it can be seen that the link between the national political and economic environments is clear. Politicians are elected by the people and run the economy. In doing so, they decide the economic policy that affects both individuals and organisations operating at the national level of the environment.

Devolution in Scotland and Wales

The Labour Government elected on 1 May 1997 had promised in its election manifesto to hold referendums on devolution in both Scotland and Wales. This was duly implemented. In Wales the referendum was held on 18 September 1997 and 50.1 per cent of the electorate turned out to vote, with 50.3 per cent voting for a Welsh Assembly and 49.7 per cent voting against. In Scotland the referendum on 11 September had a turnout of 60.4 per cent, with 74.3 per cent of those who voted supporting the creation of a Scottish Parliament and 63.5 per cent voting to give the Scottish Parliament limited tax-varying powers.

The Scottish Parliament appointed a First Minister, Donald Dewar, who in turn appointed members to and headed the Scottish Executive. The First Minister and Scottish Executive are drawn from the party or group commanding the majority in the Scottish Parliament. The Scottish Parliament is able to pass laws in a number of areas for Scotland, including: health, education, local government, housing, economic development, trade, transport, criminal and civil law, courts, prisons, police and fire services, animals, the environment, agriculture, food standards, forestry, fisheries, sport and the arts. The Scottish Parliament also has powers to repeal legislation passed at Westminster as far as Scotland is affected.

Business illustration of devolution and legislation – no smoking

The advent of devolution in the United Kingdom has meant different legislation in different countries governing a variety of issues. One example is the 'no smoking' legislation. Scotland passed no smoking legislation in November 2004 and the ban on smoking in enclosed public spaces came into force in Spring 2006. In 2005 the Welsh Assembly was expecting a ban on smoking in enclosed public spaces to be in place in three years' time. While in February 2006 Westminster voted for a ban on smoking in enclosed public spaces in England that came into effect in July 2007.

Sources: 'Welsh blanket smoking ban planned', *BBC News*, http://news.bbc.co.uk/1/hi/wales/4654369.stm, 5 July 2005.

'Scotland smoking ban to go ahead', *BBC News*, http://news.bbc.co.uk/1/hi/scotland/3996587.stm 10 November 2004.

The Welsh Assembly contains 60 directly elected seats and 40 additional seats. In contrast to the Scottish Parliament, the Welsh Assembly does not have powers governing the establishment of legislation and the repeal of Westminster legislation. The areas of responsibility devolved to the Welsh Assembly include economic development, agriculture and food, industry and training, education, local government, health and personal social services, housing, environment, planning, transport and roads, arts and culture, the built heritage, and sport and recreation. The Secretary of State for Wales has the power to make secondary legislation in these areas. For example, the Secretary of State for Wales is able to decide the school curriculum in Wales.[3]

National bodies

National bodies represent businesses and employees, presenting views on employment and trade issues to one another, and to the government and opposition parties. Both employer and employee organisations try to shape and influence events in the external environment for the benefit of their members. Employer and employee national bodies are often closely aligned themselves with the government or a particular political party. Employers' organisations traditionally support the Conservative Party, while the Labour Party is linked financially and in terms of membership to the trade unions. For the Labour Party to achieve victory at the 1997 general election, it was thus crucial for it to have gained support from both sides of the negotiation table.

Employers' bodies

Examples of national employers' bodies include employers' organisations such as the Institute of Directors (IOD) and the Confederation of British Industry (CBI). The IOD was formed in 1903 and its members are individual company directors from large FTSE 100 companies through to smaller entrepreneurial start up businesses. The IOD provides members with information, advice, training, conferences and publications. In addition the IOD seeks to be an influential organisation in representing the concerns of its members to government and does this via lobbying and the media.

The CBI was founded in 1965, bringing together several industry bodies. Members of the CBI are companies, including both multinationals and small and medium sized enterprises (SMEs) as well as trade associations and employers' organisations. The CBI seeks to provide UK industry with a forum for developing and influencing policy in a host of areas which impact on business organisations, such as the economy, legislation and technology. Additionally the CBI seeks to encourage efficiency and competitiveness in UK industry and in doing so develop the contribution of UK industry to the economy.

These organisations provide a forum for employers or owners of businesses to put forward their views and be represented on issues affecting businesses, such as the national minimum wage, the euro and work–life balance. Both the IOD and CBI frequently use the printed and broadcast media to do this.

Business illustration The Institute of Directors

The Institute of Directors will often comment on political and economic decisions impacting on businesses. Examples include interest rates and in February 2006 the IOD agreed with the Bank of England that the decision not to change interest rates and that keeping the base rate at 4.5 per cent was the right thing to do. However, in the same press release the IOD did indicate that they thought a cut in interest rates in the summer should be possible.

Source: 'Time not right for rate cut', Institute of Directors, Press Release, 9 February 2006.

Employees' bodies

In contrast, trade unions are national bodies representing employees. Examples of trade unions are NATFHE, representing teachers in further and higher education; UDSAW, representing shop workers; and UNISON, representing public-sector employees. Trade unions represent their members in negotiations with employers on issues concerning pay and conditions, whether in the private or public sector. They are linked to the Labour Party, although reforms made to party membership after Labour's 1992 election defeat attempted to reduce the unions' impact and promote the concept of 'one member, one vote'. Most trade unions are affiliated to the Trades Union Congress (TUC), which is the largest voluntary organisation and the largest pressure group in UK. The TUC operates to represent its member unions collectively at a national level.

Alliances and agreements

Alliances and agreements occur between two or more countries for mutual benefit.

Alliances and agreements occur between two or more countries for mutual benefit. The countries involved concur to support each other in global politics or in bilateral or multilateral economic activity. In extreme cases, consent may be given to the merger of countries into a single entity, or one country may consent to divide into separate countries to fulfil ideals of cultural identity, national integrity or economic benefit.

The European Union

In 1957 the European Economic Community was established by the Treaty of Rome. There were six founding countries with a further nine countries joining the European Union (EU) by 1995 (see **Exhibit 2.8**). The recent expansion of the EU has included ten new members in 2004 and a further two member states in 2007 (see **Exhibit 2.8**).[4]

Exhibit 2.8 European Union member countries

Year of entry	European Union member countries		
1957	■ Belgium ■ Italy	■ France ■ Luxembourg	■ Germany ■ Netherlands
1972	■ UK	■ Denmark	■ Ireland
1981	■ Greece		
1986	■ Spain	■ Portugal	
1995	■ Austria	■ Finland	■ Sweden
2004	■ Cyprus ■ Czech Republic ■ Latvia ■ Poland	■ Estonia ■ Lithuania ■ Slovakia	■ Hungary ■ Malta ■ Slovenia
2007	■ Romania	■ Bulgaria	

Source: http://europa.eu.int

The euro became legal currency for trade and financial markets on 1 January 1999 in all participating EU countries, and coins and notes were introduced on 1 January 2002. (See also the section on the European Union later in this chapter.)

The 1997 Treaty of Amsterdam covered new rights for EU subjects concerning issues such as freedom of movement and employment. The Agenda 2000 blueprint presented to the European Parliament in July 1997 allowed the EU to expand eastwards and for former Communist countries of Eastern Europe (see **Exhibit 2.8**) to become members. Enlargement of the EU is viewed as an opportunity to unite Europe, and extend and consolidate political stability and economic prosperity. The criteria laid down by the European Council in Copenhagen in 1993 require potential member states to demonstrate democracy, human rights, a functioning market economy, and a commitment to the EU's aims covering political, economic and monetary union. The political and economic conditions of applicant countries have to be judged to be satisfactory by the EU before it allows their admittance. Negotiations to admit new members are complex and examine how the significant differences in economic and social development between member and potential member states can be tackled.[5]

In 2004 ten new countries were admitted to the EU (see Exhibit 2.8) and, with the exception of Cyprus and Malta, they were all former Eastern bloc countries which experienced major change after the dissolution of the USSR. The major changes were to their political and economic systems, with elections taking place in many countries, and greater opportunities for international trade and commerce becoming available. Some of the opportunities for trade and commerce allow Western companies to invest and manufacture in countries, for example Volkswagen taking over Skoda and Peugeot investing in manufacturing facilities in Slovakia

In geographic terms Poland, Hungary and the Baltic states of Latvia, Lithuania and Estonia remained unchanged; in contrast Czechoslovakia and Yugoslavia have altered significantly. Czechoslovakia, for reasons of national and economic identity, split into two countries – the Czech Republic and Slovakia. The 1990s' civil war split Yugoslavia into several independent countries: Croatia, Bosnia and Herzegovina, the Former Yugoslav Republic of Macedonia and Slovenia, with Montenegro and Serbia remaining as a rump Yugoslavian Federation – with only Slovenia becoming an EU member in 2004. The second wave of expansion occurred in 2007 when Romania and Bulgaria joined the EU. The next stage of expansion is likely to be when Turkey and Croatia join and negotiations started in 2005 (see **Exhibit 2.9**).

Exhibit 2.9 European Union membership sought

Candidate countries	
■ Turkey	■ Croatia

Source: http://europa.eu.int

The UK and the USA

A good example of an alliance in which two countries concur to support each other is the close and special relationship between the UK and the USA. Although there are few formal bilateral treaties, a special relationship exists as a result of the two countries' historical and linguistic ties. In the 1980s the close friendship and mutual support of Conservative Prime Minister Margaret Thatcher and US Republican President Ronald Reagan personified the relationship between the UK and the USA. Both headed conservative governments in their respective countries and combined radical free-market agendas with strong global politics. This caused some difficulty for President Reagan during the UK–Argentine Falklands War in 1982, as his special relationship with the UK required support of Britain's efforts, while US links with the rest of the American continent precluded actual aggression against Argentina. On a separate occasion in 1986, Margaret Thatcher approved the use of US airbases in the UK to launch bomb attacks against Libya.

The relationship and support continues, embodied in Labour Prime Minister Tony Blair and US Republican President George W Bush. In 2003 there was close agreement between the UK and the USA to liberate Iraq, while France and Germany were in less agreement over the decision to enter Iraq without a UN mandate. There had been greater global consensus over the 1991 Gulf War, where international forces – UK and US among them – liberated Kuwait from Iraqi invasion.

The UK and China

China is extremely important on the global political stage because of its sheer size: geographically, politically and economically. The Chinese market is an important part of Britain's overseas trade. The return of Hong Kong is an example of an agreement at the global level of the external environment, which was designed to promote business stability and minimise political and economic risk for British business in China. On 1 July 1997, the British Colony of Hong Kong was handed back to China after 99 years of British rule under the terms of a lease forced from the Chinese at the height of Britain's imperial activity. This was unlike the fate of any of the UK's other colonial possessions, which all left the Empire to become independent countries in the Commonwealth. Hong Kong, however, had not been independent before the colony was established, but had always been part of China, so was returned at the end of the lease.

The negotiations governing the return of Hong Kong to China were started in the early 1980s by Margaret Thatcher and Deng Xiaoping, China's then paramount leader. In the late 1970s Deng Xiaoping engineered economic reforms in China and allowed the slow development of a more market-based economy, while retaining strict political control over personal liberty. He died on 19 February 1997 prior to the deadline for Hong Kong's return to China, which duly went ahead. China described itself as 'one country – two systems', referring to the promise to continue unchanged for a minimum of 50 years Hong Kong's capitalist free-market economy under Chinese communist rule. This free-market economy has long been the gateway to the Chinese market for foreign businesses and for Chinese exports to the world. Over half the value of China's foreign trade has been directed via Hong Kong, so it is greatly in China's interest to maintain the status quo.

Review questions   ## The political environment

1   Explain the impact of national government on an organisation.
2   Identify and briefly discuss the opportunities an expansion of the EU offers business.
3   Why are political alliances between countries important?

THE ECONOMIC ENVIRONMENT

The **economic environment** comprises bodies, which make economic decisions that affect businesses and may also be shaped by political decisions.

The **economic environment** faced by organisations is shaped and influenced by the political environment as well as by the economic bodies that are constituents of the external environment (see **Exhibit 2.10** and Entry case study 2.1). The previous section examined the political elements of the external environment. In this section the roles of economic bodies such as banks, stock markets, **trading blocs** and the World Trade Organisation are considered.

Exhibit 2.10 Generic PEST grid showing economic factors

Political	Economic

	■ Central bank
	  - Bank of England
	  - European Bank
	■ Stock markets
	■ The WTO

Socio-cultural	Technological

Political decisions, which have an economic impact, obviously have an influence on businesses and the trade they undertake. Political decisions which have an economic impact include taxation and other economic decisions outlined in the annual budget presented by the Chancellor of the Exchequer each year. Details of the latest budget can be found at the Treasury website (see weblinks section at the end of this chapter).

Value added tax (VAT) is a sales tax and is payable on many goods and services in the UK.

The most common forms of taxation are income tax, corporation tax, **value added tax (VAT)** and duty on imports/exports. VAT is payable on many goods and services, currently standing at 17.5 per cent for most goods in the UK. The Conservative government of the 1990s increased the rate of VAT across the board from 8 to 17.5 per cent and also increased the number of categories of items on which VAT is charged.

The rate of taxation affects businesses as higher income tax lessens the amount of disposable income that people have to spend on goods and services, and VAT makes goods and services more expensive to the consumer than the price set by the manufacturer or service provider. Therefore it is crucial to the standard of living of the individual citizen, to the profitability of private-sector organisations and to the standard of public services that a balance is achieved between taxation and public spending. Businesses are affected by corporation tax as the higher the rate, the greater the amount of tax due on any profits made and hence the lower the amount of money available to fund dividends and expansion activities, such as product development.

Although much of the above is concerned with affecting the economic environment of the country, the decision making behind the management of the economy is essentially political, as it can be political parties' economic strategies that voters find key at the ballot box. Additionally, budgets from opposing political parties often show different approaches towards solving the same problems. Hence political decisions and the economic environment influence the value of cash and investments held by businesses and individuals, which in turn determine the amount of cash available in the economy (see Entry case study 2.1).

The central bank

Bank of England

The **Bank of England** has two core purposes, monetary and financial stability.

In the UK the central bank is the **Bank of England** and it has two core purposes, monetary and financial stability. In May 1997 the new Labour Chancellor of the Exchequer, Gordon Brown, gave independence in the setting of the base rate of interest to the Bank of England and its Governor. Under the previous system, the Chancellor of the Exchequer and the Governor of the Bank of England would meet regularly and jointly agree changes to the base rate of interest.

The new system separates out the economic and political decision-making processes concerning interest rates for the first time in the UK's history. The Bank of England's Monetary Policy Committee judges and sets the base interest rate to meet the target inflation rate required by the government. The base rate set by the Bank of England is then implemented via the financial markets and banks, which in turn set interest rates for their borrowing and lending based on the Bank of England base rate.

The base rate directly influences businesses and individuals as repayment of overdrafts, loans or mortgages will increase with higher interest rates, hence reducing the amount of activity in the economy. For example, when interest rates are high businesses spend less on new equipment, advertising and product development; and individuals spend less on the goods and services produced by businesses. The effects of the government handing over decision making on base interest rates to the central bank is that the influence of short-term political need on economic management is removed. Interest rates, a key economic management tool, should be decided from a purely economic perspective.

> **Business illustration** of political involvement in the economy – interest rates
>
> Nigel Lawson, Chancellor of the Exchequer in 1987, manipulated interest rates for political advantage before the 1987 election. This created the so-called 'Lawson Boom' that led directly to the recession of the early 1990s in the United Kingdom. The Bank of England, in contrast, would only take rational, objective decisions about long-term economic strategy. This is in line with other European countries' practice, and further prepares the UK for the possibility of entry to the euro at some date in the future.

The European Bank

The European Central Bank (ECB) is based in Frankfurt in Germany and is the central bank for the euro. The Governing Council is the main decision-making body and includes six executive members and the governors all the national central banks (NCBs) from each of the countries that have adopted the euro – twelve in total (see later section on the EU in this chapter). The ECB seeks to maintain the euro's purchasing power and stability in the **euro-zone** and its tasks are shown in **Exhibit 2.11**.

The **euro-zone** is the geographic area made up of the countries which have adopted the euro as their currency.

Exhibit 2.11 Tasks of the European Central Bank

- Define and implement monetary policy, including interest rates for the euro-zone.
- Conduct foreign exchange operations.
- Hold and manage foreign reserves.
- Promote the smooth running of payment systems.
- Authorise the issuing of euro banknotes.
- Collect and collate statistical information.
- Ensure smooth running and supervision of credit institutions and financial systems.
- Maintain working relations with relevant institutions both within the EU and internationally.

Source: www.ecb.int

European Bank for Reconstruction and Development

The European Bank for Reconstruction and Development (EBRD) was established in 1991 and its role is to support and help develop the private sector in democracies in Eastern European and former Soviet bloc countries (see **Exhibit 2.12**). The aim is to create market economies and democracies in such countries.

Exhibit 2.12 The work of the EBRD

- Structural and sectoral reforms.
- Competition privatisation and entrepreneurship.
- Stronger financial institutions and legal systems.
- Infrastructure development to support the private sector.
- Adoption of strong corporate governance, including environmental sensitivity.
- Promotion of co-financing and foreign direct investment (FDI).
- Mobilisation of domestic capital.
- Provision of technical assistance.

Source: www.ebrd.com

The EBRD usually invests in private businesses, often with commercial partners, but some investment does occur in assisting publicly owned companies to either privatise or re-structure and improve public services. This work helps countries to manage the transition economy and move closer to having a full market economy, assisting in the establishment of a sound banking system.

The stock market

The stock market is where shares of publicly quoted companies are traded. The stock market in the United Kingdom is in London, which is a centre of international as well as financial opportunity. Company names and share prices are published in daily newspapers and online. The shares of a company will trade on the stock market at a market price and the price will go up or down depending on the performance of the company and how the City views it. For example, a company that announces good profits is likely to see a rise in its share price and vice versa. However, good performance can be measured by factors other than profit (see Business illustration on Rolls-Royce).

> **Business illustration** of share prices –
> **Rolls Royce**
>
> At the start of February 2006 shares in Rolls-Royce peaked at 450 pence due in no small measure to its development work on military vertical take off and landing technology and profits from the civil aviation market which rose from £194 million to £454 million, meaning pre-tax profits for the company rose nearly 50 per cent to £584 million.
>
> Source: 'Blue Skies for Rolls as profits soar 50 per cent', Roland Gribben, *Daily Telegraph*, 10 February 2006.

The value of shares will also be altered by overall movements in the stock market. If the economy is doing well, and unemployment and inflation are low, then trading conditions will be viewed as generally favourable. In this type of situation the stock market will be buoyant and overall share prices will rise. However, if share prices rise too much or the economy performs less well, then share prices generally may fall.

The World Trade Organisation

The **World Trade Organisation** (WTO) is located in Geneva, Switzerland and officially came into existence on 1 January 1995, replacing its predecessor, the General Agreement on Tariffs and Trade (GATT). The WTO, whose role is summarised in **Exhibit 2.13**, has 132 member countries and 34 observer governments, of which 33 have applied for membership.[6]

Exhibit 2.13 Role of the World Trade Organisation

- Administer WTO trade agreements.
- Provide a forum for trade negotiations.
- Handle trade disputes.
- Monitor national trade policies.
- Provide technical assistance and training for developing countries.
- Co-operate with other international organisations.

Source: www.wto.org

The biggest change in the WTO in recent years has been the conclusion of China's long-term efforts and negotiations to become a WTO member, successfully joining from 11 December 2001. China's drive to become a member of the WTO has been long and slow, since it first applied to join GATT in 1987. Consequently in 1997 the thawing of previously frosty political relations between China and the USA provided an opportunity for progress on China's entry to the WTO and negotiations took place in Geneva. Final agreement on the terms of China's entry to the WTO was reached on 15 November 1999. In 2007 Vietnam, a neighbour of China, also gained membership of the WTO and the status of permanent normal trade relations with the USA (see Entry case study 2.1).

Review questions | **The economic environment**

1 Explain the link between political decisions and the economic environment.
2 Why is it important that the setting of interest rates is an economic decision rather than a political decision?
3 Summarise the role of a central bank.
4 Explain the benefits of WTO membership.

✔ Check your understanding

- Do you understand the benefits to Vietnam of joining the WTO?
- Check your understanding by referring to the Entry case study 2.1, 'Investors rush to join chorus saying good morning Vietnam', and explain the benefits to individuals, Vietnamese businesses and international companies of Vietnam's membership of the WTO.

THE SOCIO-CULTURAL ENVIRONMENT

The **socio-cultural environment** includes changes in ages and structures of populations and cross-cultural issues.

The **socio-cultural environment** includes the age and structure of a population, and the way people in a population behave in their own and in different societies (see **Exhibit 2.14**). Hence, this section looks at demographics and cross-cultural issues and how they impact on organisations.

Exhibit 2.14 Generic PEST grid showing socio-cultural factors

Political	Economic
Socio-cultural	**Technological**
■ Demographics - United Kingdom - Europe - Asia and Africa ■ Cross-cultural issues - Language - Behaviour - Culture shock	

Demographic changes

Demographic changes are changes in the age and structure of a population.

Demographic changes in different populations, including the United Kingdom, Europe, Asia and Africa are considered below.

United Kingdom

In the UK population there are three fundamental demographic changes occurring. First, the number of people aged 45–60 in the population is increasing and these are those born in the post-war baby boom years of 1950–64. If people in this group have held good jobs and experienced the consumer boom of the 1980s, then they are likely to continue to be generous consumers. These people have become the 50-plus population of today. Secondly, there is a shrinking youth population, defined as those aged 15–24 years. The youth population is viewed, in general, as not being affluent as many young people are unemployed, in training or in tertiary education, none of which provide a large disposable income. This reducing youth population should mean the media's obsession with youth markets declines. However, youth programming has grown significantly on television and advertisers continue to be willing to pay for access to young people in their late teens and early twenties. These young consumers are perceived as being easier to persuade to switch between brands than older people, who are viewed as having established purchasing habits. The wisdom of this approach by advertising agencies has to be questioned as in the UK only 5 per cent of advertising spending is aimed at the third of the UK's population over 50 (20 million people), who have access to over 45 per cent of disposable income.[7]

Finally, there is an increasing older population, those aged 50, in the United Kingdom. In 1961 there were 16 million people aged over 50 in the UK, by 2021 there will be 22.5 million people – an increase of 40 per cent against an overall population increase of 15 per cent.[8] In 1995 people aged over 50 formed one-third of the UK's population; the number of people aged 75 will have doubled by 2045.[9] While the 2001 census showed, for the first time since the first census in 1801, that there are now more people aged over 60 than under 16 in the UK population, with 1 million of those older people aged over 85 years – five times more than in 1951.[10] A significant number of these older people, 3–4 million, are white-collar workers of social class ABC1. This type of person will tend to have a good retirement income from an occupational pension scheme, savings, and own his or her home, with the mortgage paid off. Retired people in this situation are inclined to spend their relatively large disposable incomes on themselves, and consumers aged 50 plus are the largest buyers of winter sun holidays and cruises.[11]

However, there is also a large group of less affluent older people, aged 60 plus, for whom the main source of income in old age is the state pension. These people, like the rest of the population, are likely to live longer and require medical treatment and a state pension during their longer life. The effect on the working population is an increase in their tax contributions. It is estimated that in the UK National Insurance contributions will have to rise from 12.5 per cent of the wage bill in 1990 to 18 per cent by 2030. The increase in taxes paid by the employed and industry will prompt governments to alter the welfare system fundamentally, to encourage more people to save for a pension of their own. Tony Blair's Labour Government targeted those currently in work but not contributing to an occupational pension scheme. This type of encouragement is crucial, as provision of retirement income needs to be boosted for the majority. This need is evidenced by the fact that in 2001, 5.2 million pensioner couples and 4.1 million single pensioners had no income from an occupational pension scheme.[12]

This increasing difference in income between different groups of older people is a reflection of what is happening more broadly in society, leading to an increasing income gap between rich and poor people. This is likely to continue as the proportion of pensioners in the UK's population is forecast to increase from 20 per cent in 2000 to 34 per cent in 2050.[13] and significant numbers of people, especially women, continue to fail to undertake financial planning for retirement.[14] This is also supported by the fact that public spending on pensions is not going to be a substitute for occupational pensions. In the UK public spending on pensions was 5 per cent of gross domestic product (GDP) in 2002 and this is set to fall to 4.8 per cent by 2052. This contrasts starkly with other European countries where public spending on pensions can be as high as 17 per cent.[15]

Europe

The European Union's economic growth rate will potentially shrink to 1.25 per cent a year, due to its ageing and therefore less productive population. This is half the US growth rate of 2.5 per cent per year. One view on tackling the issue of the decline of Europe's economy is to raise the retirement age by five years, significantly increase pension funding and also increase productivity, while reducing unemployment.[16] The alternative view to tackling this problem is for Europe to re-examine its current approach to immigration.

It is estimated that without significant policy changes in the EU, Europe's share of world output may decrease from its current 18 per cent to 10 per cent by 2050.[17] This trend is mirrored in Japan, whose share of world output could fall from 8 per cent to 4 per cent. This is in stark contrast to the USA where it is estimated that its share of world output could rise from 23 per cent to 26 per cent over the same period.[18] This is attributed to the higher levels of immigration in the US, which brings both more workers and increasing fertility rates as immigrants tend to be young and of childbearing age.[19] This argument that Europe's demographic problem may be helped by immigration is also echoed by the British Venture Capitalist Association (BVCA) which sees at least part of the solution to Europe's demographic problems lying in an enlightened approach to economic migration. The BVCA also points to the 'influx of South American economic migrants' into the US, who will contribute to the expected buoyancy in the US economy.[20]

Asia

Changes in populations at a global level impact on companies and the opportunity for doing business in different countries and regions around the world. For example significant reductions in fertility rates in Asia during the 1980s resulted in a sizeable reduction in levels of absolute poverty, which is defined as the percentage of a population surviving on less than a dollar a day.[21] The impact of lower fertility rates and the resultant slower population growth is that there is faster economic expansion along with a reduction in poverty.[22] Faster and improved economic expansion is logically due to smaller families having fewer expenses and being able to earn more, which in turn improves the opportunities people have to spend and save.[23] However, it is estimated that around 50 per cent of improvement in economic growth in developing countries arises from a one-off 'demographic window' which occurs when large numbers of working adults support fewer children and older people.[24]

Africa

The demographics and populations of some countries and hence their economic development is affected by HIV and Aids. HIV and Aids is forecast to make the populations of the 53 most affected countries 480 million fewer than expected by 2050. The total population of these countries is over 4 billion and the percentage reduction will be 8 per cent by 2050.[25] The impact of HIV and Aids is greatest in Africa, with the population of the 38 most affected countries being 16 million lower in 2000 than was expected. This figure is expected to reach 320 million by 2050, which is 19 per cent or an almost one fifth reduction in the population.[26] In most of these countries high fertility rates will likely result in growing populations, however Botswana, Lesotho, South Africa and Swaziland are forecast to have lower populations in 2050 than today.[27] This is supported by the projected life expectancy in these countries: in Botswana life expectancy in 2003 was 40 years, against the predicted 68 years without the impact of HIV and Aids; in South Africa, life expectancy was 48 years against the expected 67 years. In 2050, life expectancy in these countries is forecast to be only 56 years.[28]

In conclusion, overall during the next fifty years the world's population is expected to age faster than ever before, see **Exhibit 2.15** which shows median ages (the age that divides a population into two halves). During the same period of time the world's population will grow at an annual rate of 1.2 per cent, giving a net increase of 77 million people every year, with 50 per cent of the increase arising from just six countries: India, 21 per cent; China, 12 per cent; Pakistan, 5 per cent; and Bangladesh, Nigeria and the USA, 4 per cent each.[29]

Exhibit 2.15 Median ages

	2000 – median age	2050 – median age
Least developed countries	18.1 years	27.1. years
Developing countries	24.1 years	35.7 years
Developed countries	37.3 years	42.5 years
Overall	26.4 years	36.8 years

Source: 'People, plagues and prosperity', M Wolf, *Financial Times*, 26 February 2003.

Cross-cultural issues

Organisations have to consider political and economic circumstances in other countries when contemplating international business operations. Culture also plays an important part in determining how international business is undertaken in different countries and regions of the world. The cross-cultural issues which commonly have to be understood and dealt with when doing business and working abroad are language, behaviour and culture shock.

Language

The most obvious illustration of culture is language. Investing in accurate language assistance when operating in another cultural context is a vital but largely underestimated consideration for organisations assessing the potential costs of international operations. The cost of getting it wrong is often much greater, but this is often ignored in short-term decision making. It is only necessary to consider how many misunderstandings occur between native speakers of English who originate from the UK, the USA and Australia to begin to appreciate the difficulties of translating and interpreting other languages. For example the British lecturer will invigilate an exam, while an American will proctor the exam. Similarly, British tourists on holiday in Australia will want to buy flip-flops to wear on the beach and may be confused when the shop assistant offers a pair of thongs instead.

> **Business illustration** of language and branding – car models
>
> Proton, Malaysia's national car manufacturer, decided not to introduce its basic model to the UK under its Malaysian name as 'Saga' is the brand name of products targeted at senior citizens, to whom Proton did not wish to limit sales.
>
> The General Motors' 1980s mini hatchback Vauxhall Nova was branded Opel Corsa in mainland Europe as 'Nova', which was meant to have connotations of new, actually translates as 'does not go' in many European languages.
>
> The Rolls-Royce Silver Mist had to be renamed for the German-speaking market because *mist* in German is a colloquial word for excrement.

However, translation or the choice of words meaning other things in different languages is not the only skill required overseas. Interpreting – which is not simply translating the words, but rather saying the right thing in the target language – is a crucial skill. At a business meeting between British and Chinese businesspeople, when the British host says 'We hope you have enjoyed your stay in the UK', a direct translation will sound arrogant and rude. Therefore a skilled interpreter would replace this phrase with the customary, 'We are sorry we did not look after you properly', thereby fulfilling the courtesy requirements of both sides.

Behaviour

Other types of cross-cultural issues would relate to the consumption of alcohol in Muslim states and of beef in India, where the cow is sacred to Hindus (McDonald's had to substitute a Hindu-friendly version of the burger). How much physical contact or personal space people are customarily allowed is also problematic, as some cultures remain physically very distant from each other, while in others regular touching is commonplace. Again, whether or not physical contact is permissible between the sexes or between people of the same sex is an issue. For example, in many Middle and Far Eastern cultures, any touching between the sexes is unacceptable, while man-to-man hand-holding and bodily contact are quite normal. This understandably becomes a minefield of danger to the foreign executive. In Japan, blowing one's nose in public is taboo, while in China the public expectoration of such waste is unsurprising.

Therefore, the behaviour of foreign executives, the design of products and services, and the labelling, packaging and advertising of goods and services must all be subject to intense scrutiny.

Culture shock

The greater the distance between home and host culture, the more likely it is that the host culture will provide elements of everyday life that shock the individual travelling there. From language to food, from individual behaviour to collective customs, culture shock is a real and debilitating influence on the individual businessperson abroad. As it is based in experience, it is difficult to know how culture shock can be dealt with until it has been experienced, since there is still a huge difference between knowing something is going to be experienced and actually experiencing it. Nevertheless, organisations can invest in pre-departure orientation programmes, training people for overseas postings through contact with people native to the host country, visits and access to expatriates who have already lived in that culture. It is essential to consider not only the expatriate executive, but also the relocation and comfort of family members as well (see Chapter 9).

Review questions | **The socio-cultural environment**

1 Summarise the impact of ageing populations on businesses
2 Briefly discuss why immigration is a good thing for business.
3 How does poor health, such as that caused by HIV and Aids, impact on a country's economy?
4 Explain the impact of language and behaviour on a company undertaking international business.

THE TECHNOLOGICAL ENVIRONMENT

Technology has an influence on all aspects of business from the very general to the very specific. To provide a flavour of the impact of technology this section identifies and discusses the general impact of technology and illustrates its specific impact on the banking industry (see Business illustration on the banking industry).

The advent of technology has made it easier for people to communicate with each other, whether they operate in the political, economic, social or general business arena. Communications technology takes the form of mobile phones, fax machines, video conferencing, the Internet and the World Wide Web, and its key benefit is that staff are contactable all the time while at work, and should be able to contact customers and clients without having to return to an office.

Video conferencing is becoming increasingly popular among businesses. Large companies such as British Petroleum (BP) have been using video conferencing since 1983 and have in-house studios in global locations. The greatest benefits of video conferencing are conferred when people in two or more places in different parts of the world use it. SmithKline Beecham has over thirty video conferencing studios worldwide and is able to carry out video conference meetings (see **Exhibit 2.16**). It is likely that the increased threat of international terrorism and the potential spread of illnesses such as the SARS virus and avian flu will result in an increased use of video conferencing by organisations seeking to reduce the risks to which their workforce may be exposed.

Exhibit 2.16 Benefits of video conferencing

- Less time spent travelling to and from meetings, therefore reducing the cost and stress of travelling.

- More people can attend meetings and be called into the meeting at relatively short notice if their knowledge and expertise are required.

- Eye contact and body language are seen, a clear advantage over phone conferencing.

- Enhancement of team working and communication among teams whose work is spread out across the globe.

The Internet is an array of interconnected networks to which millions of computers around the world are attached. There are a large number of Internet sites that hold information, for example company sites such as the *Financial Times* site. The World Wide Web (WWW) allows the linking of Internet sites and research and retrieval tools – hence WWW and the Internet are often seen as one and the same. Search engines such as Google enable searches to be carried out very easily and it is an equally simple task to repeat and refine any searches that have previously been carried out.[30]

Companies can take up a presence on the Internet by setting up a website. This will give a company worldwide exposure on the Internet 24 hours a day, 365 days a year. Companies are able to use their Internet presence to advertise their products and services, and to collect addresses and details from potential customers who visit the site, with a view to e-mailing or posting further information to them. The Internet is equally accessible by both large and small companies, although large companies may have more money to spend on designing a site.

A company that has set up an Internet site also has to consider how it is going to persuade people to visit the site. Many companies advertise in the more traditional media, such as the television and press, and include their Internet address in the advertisement. An additional method is to be included on search engines so that when users type in a keyword such as 'books' or 'beer' the relevant Internet sites are listed. Companies are also able to advertise on search engines by paying to have their logo appear, although costs are high.[31]

Business illustration of industry specific technology – banking industry

The banking and financial services is a good example of an industry where service delivery has been continually altered and modernised since the late 1970s. In banking the most obvious application of technology has occurred in the development of the automatic teller machine (ATM).

The other main technological development has been in the use of central computer-based systems to hold customer details and account records. These applications of computer technology allow any customer with a passbook or debit card to withdraw money from their bank or building society account anywhere in the country and even overseas.

This greater reliance on technology to perform at least some routine tasks has been part of the reason that both banks and building societies have been able to use and train their staff to sell a much wider range of financial services.

The development of new ways of delivering banking and financial services has continued to develop and today internet banking is common.

Review questions

The technological environment

1 Identify and discuss types of technology which may impact on an organisation.
2 Explain the benefits to an organisation of adopting and using technology.

✔ Check your understanding

- Do you understand the impact of PEST factors on a high street retailer, such as Boots or River Island?
- Check your understanding by explaining how relevant PEST factors can impact on the business of a retailer.

THE COMPETITIVE ENVIRONMENT AND ITS REGULATION

Earlier sections of this chapter have examined the broad general external environment in which organisations operate. The rest of this chapter deals with the competitive environment, which is a key part of the external environment faced by organisations, and its regulation.

The regulation of competition in the UK

The UK economy is a mixed economy, which means that there is some influence and regulation of the competitive behaviour of firms. Some of the regulation of competition is by bodies that may intervene if there is a likelihood of anti-competitive behaviour occurring. These bodies are the **Office of Fair Trading**, the **Competition Commission** and the **Restrictive Practices Court**.

Office of Fair Trading

The **Office of Fair Trading (OFT)** is an independent professional organisation, which seeks to promote and protect consumer interests.

The Office of Fair Trading (OFT) was established in 1973 and is a government funded body which seeks to promote and protect consumer interests, and ensure companies compete in a fair and competitive manner. The OFT is headed by the Director General of Fair Trading and is accountable to Parliament.

The OFT's activities fall into three areas: enforcement of competition and consumer protection rules; investigation into how markets are working; and communication to explain the benefits of fair competition. The OFT aims to seek out and deter anti-competitive behaviour including cartels. Additionally the OFT will refer mergers and acquisitions that could significantly lessen competition to the Competition Commission. The OFT may investigate markets for specific products or services to ensure that they are working fairly for consumers. Investigations by the OFT can lead to enforcement of the competition rules and legislation or to recommendations to government. Finally the OFT seeks to ensure that all interested stakeholders, such as businesses and consumers, understand how the competition rules and laws apply to them.

Business illustration of the OFT – No referral to the Competition Commission

In February 2006 the OFT announced the outcome of its investigation into the proposed takeover of Alliance UniChem by Boots. The OFT was satisfied that Boots had offered to divest outlets in around 100 local areas where there would be reduced competition as a result of the takeover. Therefore the bid was not referred to the Competition Commission.

Source: Press release from OFT, 7 February 2006.

Three key pieces of competition legislation are the Fair Trading Act 1973, the Competition Act 1998 and the Enterprise Act 2002. The Fair Trading Act 1973 was introduced to deal with complex and scale monopolies. A scale monopoly exists if one firm has a minimum of 25 per cent market share and a complex monopoly exists if two or more firms together account for more than 25 per cent market share and engage in similar behaviour. The Fair Trading Act 1973 is the piece of legislation by which the Director General of Fair Trading, the Utility Regulators and the Secretary of State can refer possible monopoly situations to the Competition Commission for investigation. If the Competition Commission find that a monopoly situation exists and operates against the public interest, remedies may be imposed. These can take the form of behavioural remedies, which is the stopping of particular practices, or structural remedies, which may include closing or divesting specified parts of the business.

Business illustration of the OFT - Referral to the Competition Commission

The proposed acquisition by Waterstones of rival booksellers Ottakars was referred to the Competition Commission in December 2005. The two main reasons for this referral were that, first, substantial competition would be eliminated from the market particularly where an Ottakers and Waterstones were sited close to each other. The second main reason is the legislation which states that a merger should be referred to the Competition Commission if the turnover in the UK of the resulting company would exceed £70 million or if market share would exceed 25 per cent.

Source: Press release from OFT, 6 December 2005.

The Competition Act 1998 makes anti-competitive agreements, cartels and abuses of a dominant position unlawful from the start and gives the Director General of Fair Trading new powers to stop anti-competitive behaviour from the outset. Competitors and customers who are victims of anti-competitive behaviour are able to seek damages, and perpetrators are liable to financial penalties of up to 10 per cent of UK turnover for up to three years.

The Enterprise Act 2002 came into force in summer 2003 and established the OFT as a corporate body with the Director General of Fair Trading at its head. The main reforms of the Enterprise Act were in the areas of competition measures, consumer protection measures, and insolvency reforms. The main changes to competition measures were an increase in criminal sanctions, with up to five years in prison for those convicted of dishonestly operating hardcore cartels, and greater opportunity for victims of cartels to gain redress – including allowing consumer bodies to make claims on behalf of individual consumers.

Consumer protection measures were increased by the extension of Stop Now Orders to protect consumers from traders who fail to meet their obligations, for example covering failure to carry out building work to a satisfactory standard. This is complemented by the OFT approving codes of practice which should allow consumers to more easily identify trustworthy traders, for example an honest car repair business. Additionally consumer bodies will be able to make 'super-complaints' about features of a market which they feel harm consumers.

Insolvency reforms include reforming corporate insolvency law such that the process is simplified and streamlined, and the provision of an updated bankruptcy regime to encourage entrprenuership, with limited restrictions of up to 12 months for those who failed through no fault of their own. In contrast, restrictions on bankrupts who abuse their creditors and the public will range from 2 to 15 years.

Competition Commission

The **Competition Commission** carries out monopoly and merger inquires and hears appeals against decisions of the OFT and Regulators.

The Competition Commission (CC) was established by the Competition Act 1998 and replaced the Monopolies and Mergers Commission (MMC) on 1 April 1999. The Competition Commission has two distinct areas of activity; the first is taking over the role of the MMC in carrying out inquiries referred to it by the other UK competition authorities, including the OFT and other industry regulators such as OFGEM. The reporting panel at the Competition Commission undertakes this work. The second area of activity for the Competition Commission is the Appeals Tribunals, which hear appeals against decisions of the Director General of Fair Trading and the Regulators concerning infringements of the competition legislation and abuse of a dominant market position. The appeals panel at the Competition Commission undertakes this work. Finally the specialist panels for utilities (electricity and gas), telecommunications, water and newspapers assist in some of the regulatory inquiries.

Restrictive Practices Court

The **Restrictive Practices Court** controls practices that are presumed to be against the public interest, including the price and supply of goods.

The Restrictive Practices Court was established in 1956 and controls practices that are presumed to be against the public interest. Restrictive practices can relate to the price of goods, conditions of supply, qualities or descriptions, processes, or areas and persons supplied. A case in which the Restrictive Practices Court has recently ruled is that of over-the-counter medicines. In 1999 the Office of Fair Trading launched an investigation into the price-fixing agreement for over-the-counter medicines such as aspirin, vitamins, and cough and cold remedies. In the 1970s this agreement guaranteed small pharmacies a reasonable profit and living by virtue of an assured profit margin on over-the-counter medicines. However, by the mid-1990s 40 per cent of the market for over-the-counter medicines was held by large supermarket chains. The Office of Fair Trading investigation began when one such supermarket chain, Asda, challenged the protected position of these medicines. In March 1999 the Restrictive Practices Court announced that it would allow the Office of Fair Trading to launch a full-scale hearing into the 30-year-old price-fixing agreement. In January 2003 the OFT recommended removing restrictions on entry to the community pharmacy market, which includes the abolition of the 1970 price-fixing agreement for over-the-counter medicines. This move saves consumers around £30 million a year.

Regulatory bodies for privatised utilities and industries

Regulatory bodies for privatised utilities and industries encourage competition and see that customers are not unfairly exploited.

The privatised utilities in the UK are monitored by regulatory bodies. Regulators exist for communications, energy, water and rail transport. Their responsibility is to encourage competition and see that customers are not unfairly exploited where there may only be one supplier of a service, such as the supply of water to domestic premises.

Office of Communications

OFCOM regulates the communications sector, covering television, radio and telecommunications.

The Office of Communications (**OFCOM**) was established by the Office of Communications Act 2002 and is the regulator for the communications sector. OFCOM became operational in 2003 and brought together five existing regulatory bodies: the Independent Television Commission (ITC), the Broadcasting Standards Commission (BSC), the Office of Telecommunications (OFTEL), the Radio Authority (RAu), and the Radiocommunications Agency (RA).

The role of OFCOM

- Furthering the interests of consumers in relevant markets.
- Securing the optimal use of the radio spectrum.
- Ensuring the availability of a wide range of television and radio services in the UK.
- Protecting the public from offensive or potentially harmful effects of broadcast media.
- Safeguarding people from being unfairly treated in television and radio programmes.

Source: www.ofcom.org.uk

Office of Gas and Electricity Markets

OFGEM seeks to promote effective competition in the energy market for present and future customers.

The Office of Gas and Electricity Markets (**OFGEM**) replaces the Office of Gas Supply (OFGAS) and the Office of Electricity Regulation (OFFER). OFGEM's powers are provided under the Gas Act 1986, the Electricity Act 1989 and the Utilities Act 2000, and its main objective is to promote effective competition in the energy market for present and future customers.

The role of OFGEM

- To enforce licence obligations, competition and consumer law to protect customers, for example, from rogue doorstep salesmen.
- To regulate the monopoly networks of fuel supply, by regulating the wholesale market and prices.
- To ensure that competitive supply arrangements mean competitive prices for customers as well as direct regulation of the prices customers pay for their fuel.
- To improve the quality of service to customers by encouraging effective long-term investment in the gas and electricity networks in the UK.

Source: www.ofgem.gov.uk

Office of Water Supply

OFWAT regulates water supply and pricing to domestic and industrial customers.

The Office of Water Supply (**OFWAT**) is a government department led by the Director General of Water Services which regulates water supply and pricing to domestic and industrial customers. OFWAT checks that prices for different types of customers – metered or unmetered, large or small, urban or rural – are fair. Generally the prices charged by water companies should reflect the cost of supplying clean water and getting rid of dirty and draining water from homes and premises.[32]

The role of OFWAT

- To limit the amount companies can charge customers.
- Ensuring companies can carry out their responsibilities under the Water Industry Act 1991.
- To protect the standard of service customers receive.
- Encouraging companies to be more efficient.
- Working to encourage competition where appropriate.
- To work closely with the Environment Agency, which implements water quality standards in inland waters, estuarial and coastal waters, and with the Drinking Water Inspectorate, which regulates standards for drinking water.

Source: www.ofwat.gov.uk

Review question | ### Regulation of competition

1 Explain why it is necessary to regulate private companies in the energy, communications and water industries.

THE NATURE OF COMPETITION – THE FIVE FORCES

Porter[33] presents a model for examining competition in an industry or sector, (see **Exhibit 2.17**). He argues that five basic forces drive competition in an industry: **competitive rivalry**; **threat of new entrants**; **threat of substitute products or services**; **bargaining power of buyers**; and **bargaining power of suppliers**. These five forces need to be examined and understood if the nature of competition in an industry or sector is to be fully appreciated (see **Exhibits 2.17** and **2.18**).

Exhibit 2.17 The five forces that determine industry profitability

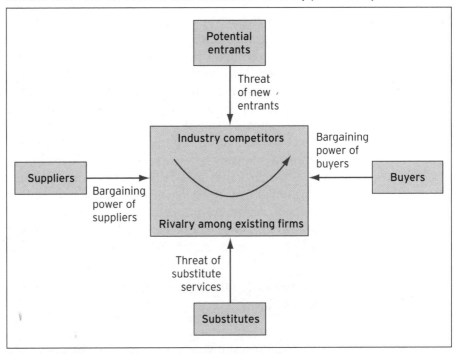

Exhibit 2.18 Guidelines for assessing competition

Competitive rivalry	■ Identify present and potential competitors in the industry or sector. ■ Assess the intensity of competition between the different organisations. Is this likely to change?
Threat of new entrants	■ Does a threat of new entry into the industry exist? From which organisations does it arise? ■ Identify the industry in which potential entrants currently operate. ■ Evaluate the likelihood of new entrants coming into the industry.
Threat of substitute products and services	■ Identify alternative products and services. ■ In what industry are present and potential substitute products located? ■ Assess the likely impact of substitute products and services on the organisation and industry being analysed.
Bargaining power of buyers	■ Name the buyers of the organisation's products and services. ■ Identify and evaluate any sources of power the buyers have with regard to the organisation being analysed.
Bargaining power of suppliers	■ Name the suppliers of the organisation's key resources and inputs. ■ Identify and evaluate any sources of power the suppliers have with regard to the organisation being analysed.

Competitive rivalry

Competitive rivalry is the nature of competition between companies in the same industry.

The first of the five forces examines the nature of competitive rivalry within a particular sector or industry. There are a number of factors affecting how fierce competitive rivalry is in an industry or sector and consequently how difficult the market is for organisations operating there. The key questions to examine concern who the present and potential competitors are, and how intensive the competition is between them. In some industries there are numerous competitor companies, all of a similar size and capacity, all holding comparable market shares and all seeking to dominate the industry. There may be no dominant company or companies within the sector and little to distinguish between the brands and products that are available to the customer. The market itself may be established or mature, with little prospect of major innovation or design surprises. In such an industry or sector, the intensity of competitive rivalry will be very high, as mature companies have to battle to retain market share, sustain **differentiation** and maintain their customer base.

Business illustration of competitive rivalry – UK supermarkets

The supermarket industry in the UK is a good illustration of extremely fierce competitive rivalry. Tesco is dominant in terms of market share, but other players all have high profiles and similar market presence. For many customers there is little real difference between the big supermarket chains, with Tesco, Sainsbury's, Asda and Morrisons all offering very similar ranges of products and services. Supermarkets compete ruthlessly and do so by offering an ever wider range of differing services, including those complementary to their core business. Supermarkets have opened banks to provide financial services, in addition to a range of ancillary services that are now standard, including dry cleaning, cafés, photo processing, clothes stores, recycling collection points and pharmacies.

Threat of new entrants

Threat of new entrants arises from companies likely to enter an industry to compete with existing operators.

The second of Porter's five forces is the threat of new entrants to an industry or sector. It is necessary to identify which companies are likely to be able to enter the market in order to compete with existing operators, and to recognise the other markets in which these potential new entrants currently operate. The threat of new entrants will be greatest if an industry is attractive enough to entice them. The attractiveness of an industry depends on there being a sufficient customer base to support the new entrant's business along with existing organisations. High potential profits and low set-up costs make an industry attractive; low financial risk combined with high potential returns is always an attractive combination.

> **Business illustration** of new entrants - Fine fragrances
>
> The entrance of Superdrug, in the 1990s, into the business of retailing upmarket perfume and aftershave was undertaken as there was an opportunity to make good profits. The standard profit margin made by an authorised retailer on a bottle of upmarket perfume or aftershave was 40 per cent. Hence Superdrug was able to cut its profit margin to, say, 20 per cent and still make an attractive profit. This, combined with the relatively low set-up costs to exploit the opportunity, the cost of the perfume and securing supplies, meant it was too good an opportunity for Superdrug to miss. This move by new entrant Superdrug changed the face of fine fragrance retailing in the UK and price competition is now commonplace, with retailers offering cut price fragrances. Boots now routinely offer fragrances for sale with a third off, and promote this in the run up to Christmas and Valentine's day.

Threat of substitute products

Threat of substitute products arises from a product or service providing the same function as the good it seeks to replaces.

When considering the nature of competition, the alternative products or services available to be purchased require consideration. A substitute product or service provides the same function as the good for which it is a replacement. Straightforward examples of substitute products include tea as a substitute for coffee, or cans and cartons as substitute forms of packaging that have largely replaced glass bottles as containers for milk and soft drinks. Other examples include carpet and laminate flooring. In the UK, carpet manufacturers have suffered a downturn in business due to the popularity of laminate and wooden floors, which are in some cases cheaper than carpet.

Substitute products or services will be a threat if customers perceive that the alternatives perform a similar or equally good function. The threat from substitutes will be greater if the alternatives provide better value for money. This can be achieved by the substitute being equally good and cheaper, or by it being equal on price, but offering a better product or more added value. For many customers the convenience of Amazon makes it an acceptable substitute for shopping on the high street for books, CDs and DVDs, for example.

Bargaining power of buyers

The **bargaining power of buyers** depends on the opportunities to shop around for the same or substitute goods.

Organisations have varying degrees of dependence on their customers and suppliers and Porter's five forces of competition model refers to this as the 'bargaining power of buyers and suppliers'. There are two types of buyer: the industrial or commercial buyer: who purchases goods on a large scale, on behalf of the organisation for whom he or she works, and the individual consumer.

The bargaining power of a commercial buyer depends on a number of factors. If, for example, the threat of substitutes is strong, then a number of choices exist and the buyer will shop around to find the best deal and most suitable choice. The bargaining power of the buyer is also strengthened if alternative sources for the supply of a product exist. In this situation the buyer will have the upper hand when negotiating supply and price. In the UK the supermarket sector is a good example of a group of organisations that have high bargaining power as buyers. In purchasing food to sell to the general public the supermarkets purchase in bulk, and there are many substitutes and alternative sources of supply for them to capitalise on. Hence they can drive a hard bargain in terms of price and product.

Business illustration of buyers – Fruit and vegetables

In buying fruit and vegetables, supermarkets require suppliers of products like apples or tomatoes to grow a particular variety, and supply fruit of uniform appearance and of a predetermined size. This allows for attractive in-store displays to tempt customers to buy the produce, which is aided by the uniform appearance of the fruit and vegetables, and which also limits the amount of handling and rummaging though the goods by customers. If the size of a particular fruit or vegetable is important to the supermarket, then that will be specified in the contract with the grower, along with the variety and delivery date. For round fruit and vegetables, size is specified as the circumference in millimetres. For example, in February 2006 Marks & Spencer sold pre-packaged South African plums, labelled as being of the Flavor King variety, size 55/60mm. It should be noted that powerful buyers like supermarkets often work closely with their suppliers in developing new products and the systems for producing them.

The individual consumer is usually much less powerful as a buyer compared with a large organisation. The bargaining power of an individual buyer is influenced by factors similar to those for commercial buyers. The strong threat of substitutes and the number of choices available will allow the individual consumer to shop around for the best deal. The city centre office worker who goes out to buy his or her takeaway lunch everyday has a number of choices. They can buy a sandwich, drink and packet of crisps from a city centre store like Marks & Spencer or Boots; a bakery from a local chain; or a sandwich shop like Deli France. Other substitutes are available for the individual consumer to consider, such as a burger, fries and drink from a fast-food outlet like McDonald's or Burger King. Individual consumers are free to exercise choice but have no real power as individuals to negotiate over the price they pay for their lunch.

Bargaining power of suppliers

The **bargaining power of suppliers** depends on the alternative sources of supply available to the buyer.

The other side of the transactional relationship is the power exerted by suppliers. There are a number of different cases when the bargaining power of suppliers is high. In industries or sectors where there are few possible suppliers, then they will be able to exert a good deal of influence on the organisations to which they supply raw materials, components or finished goods for retail. In the supply of highly specialist technology, of highly prized or rare materials where the quantity is low and price is high, the supplier is more powerful as it controls something that is greatly sought after. Thus oil-producing nations have the ability to bring the world to its knees since the most modern industrialised nations are entirely dependent on the supply of crude or refined oil. In some cases, suppliers may not be entirely satisfactory and alternatives may be available, but the cost of switching from one supplier to another is too high in the short term to be affordable – even if, in the long term, the savings would be greater. Hence, where there are few suppliers who cannot be easily substituted, supplier power is high.

Business illustration – Supply to perfume houses

The suppliers of fragrances to French perfume houses such as Yves Saint-Laurent and Chanel are family-based firms located in the Grasse area of France. These firms are not paid for the research and product development work they undertake. They only receive payment if they win a contract with a fragrance house, which is issued once the fragrance house is satisfied with the fragrance that has been developed for them. The developers of the fragrances will be competing against other similar firms and they stand a one in ten chance of being successful and winning a contract with a perfume house like Chanel. Hence the bargaining power of the fragrance developers as suppliers to the fragrance houses is very low indeed.

✔ Check your understanding

- Do you understand the forces driving competition in an industry?
- Check your understanding by explaining the competitive forces driving competition in the food retailing industry for your home country.

Review questions | **The nature of competition**

1 Summarise the factors, that create fierce competitive rivalry.
2 Explain what makes an industry attractive to new entrants.
3 Name three possible substitutes for a skiing holiday.
4 Explain the difference between what makes a buyer powerful and those factors which make a supplier powerful.

CONCLUSION

The key elements of the external environment include the general external environment and the competitive environment. The general external environment is analysed by PEST analysis and this approach allows organisations to unravel the confusion of the external environment. Making sense of the external environment enables organisations to identify key factors impacting upon it, for example economic factors such as interest rates or trading blocs such as the EU.

The competitive environment is analysed using Porter's five forces model, which allows the factors driving competition to be evaluated. If three or more of Porter's five forces are strong, then competition facing the company and in the industry will be fierce. The identification of the five forces shaping competition allows companies to see where to focus their efforts in managing competition, for example targeting suppliers or substitutes.

A clear understanding of the general external environment and competitive environment allows the company to understand the changes going on around it. This in turn means the company can develop and adjust strategy and plans to take best advantage of identified opportunities and perform to the best of its ability.

LEARNING OUTCOMES AND SUMMARY

The learning outcomes for the chapter are specified and a brief summary of the material relating to the learning outcomes is provided.

→ Learning outcome 1
Analyse the general external environment by use of PEST and the competitive environment by use of Porter's five forces model.

- Organisations analyse their external environment in an effort to understand what it is that impacts upon them. In general terms factors impacting on organisations arise from the PEST factors (political, economic, socio-cultural and technological) and competition.

- Political influences on organisations include government, legislation, trade unions, and agreements between countries. Economic influences include the impact of banks and trading blocs, such as the EU and NAFTA. Socio-cultural influences cover age, structure and behaviour of populations. The impact of technology is wide reaching and includes computer hardware, computer software, communications technology and electronic media.

- Porter's five forces of competition drive competition in an industry and the five forces model is used to analyse competition. Competitive rivalry is fierce if there are numerous competitors in an industry; markets are mature, with little differentiation and innovation. The threat of new entrants will be high if an industry is attractive, that is there are enough customers, profit margins are high, and set-up costs are low.

- Substitute products are a threat if they perform the same function as the product or service they replace. A substitute which provides more or is better value for money is a greater threat.

- Buyers generally are powerful if they have the opportunity to shop around for the best deal and they purchase a significant amount of a product. Suppliers are powerful if there are few suppliers of a good or service, as the buyer is denied the opportunity to shop around for a good deal.

→ **Learning outcome 2**
Summarise the benefits of undertaking environmental analysis.

- Undertaking external environmental analysis allows managers to better understand the external environment, and hence have an improved idea of how to respond to threats and opportunities in the external environment.

→ **Learning outcome 3**
Discuss the process for analysis of the general external environment and the competitive environment.

- PEST analysis is best performed by first identifying and understanding PEST factors, before evaluating the impact of those PEST factors upon the organisation.

- Information for analysing an external environment exists both inside and outside the organisation, and takes the form of sales reports, budgets, press articles and media sources.

- According to Duncan and Ginter external environmental analysis can be undertaken by monitoring, scanning, forecasting and assessing PEST, competitive and market forces upon the organisation.

→ **Learning outcome 4**
Understand the reasons for regulation of competition and how it can be implemented.

- Competition in the UK is regulated by the Office of Fair Trading (OFT), the Competition Commission (CC), the Restrictive Practice Court (RPC) and a host of regulators for privatised utilities, industries and service sectors.

This exit case study looks at Cadbury's launch of Trident chewing gum on the UK market and can be used to assess the learning outcomes below.

Learning outcomes	Check you have achieved this by	
Explain which factors make an industry or marketplace attractive to new entrants.	Summarising the reasons behind a company's decision to enter a new marketplace.	Answering case study question 1.
Demonstrate the nature of competition faced by organisations.	Applying Porter's five forces of competition to an industry or marketplace.	Answering case study question 2.

Cadbury looks to burst Wrigley bubble

by David Litterick

Cadbury Schweppes will next week launch an all-out assault on the British chewing gum market. The company is attempting to take on Wrigley and burst the bubble of the company that currently has the UK market sewn up. Wrigley pockets 98.5 per cent of the £240m Britons spend on chewing gum every year.

On Monday, Cadbury will roll out one of its single biggest product launches in the UK. With a £10m advertising and marketing budget behind it, few people within the company can remember anything quite so high-profile. Many more millions of pounds have been spent just getting to the launch, making it also one of Cadbury's biggest gambles.

Cadbury hopes that the hundreds of people who have spent the past year in Parsippany, New Jersey, working out how best to crack the UK market have got it right. The company has spent more than $40m (£20m) building what it has dubbed its 'Gum Centre of Excellence'. With the global market reckoned to be worth $15bn a year, and growing by 8 per cent a year, there is much at stake. Cadbury's share of the global market is 26 per cent, up from 4 per cent in 2001 due to its take-over of Adams. Wrigley is market leader with 36 per cent.

Cadbury has traditionally been a small player in chewing gum, but its acquisition of Adams in 2003 pro-pelled it into second place and sparked plans to launch a new front in the chewing gum war in Britain's newsagents. The UK lags the rest of the world in gum. The average chewer consumes around 130 sticks a year, compared with 180 in the US. For the past two years, even that amount has been shrinking. After months of market research and testing among its target audience, Cadbury chose to launch its Trident brand in the UK and is now getting the product to shops ahead of the marketing blitz.

In New Jersey, it's clear how much work has already been put in. Even a traditional stick of mint-flavoured gum starts off with more than 30 varieties of mint. Each one of those is made up of 1,000 different compounds that give different varieties a particular essence. At Cadbury's new site, scientists process the oils gathered from different plants, boosting the presence of some compounds and reducing others to create what they hope will be a winning flavour.

Panellists with specially trained pallets assess and compare the flavours for sweetness and intensity. The panellists work part time, fewer than 15 hours a week, but so crucial is their job that 10 per cent of those that apply are rejected for failing to have a sensitive enough palate. Those that make the cut receive 12 months of training before they are considered experienced enough to judge a flavour.

An on-site lab prepares hundreds of pieces of gum for testing, tweaking flavours and textures in a process that can last months. Each piece of chewing gum is made up of four key components – the gum base, texture modifiers, flavourings and sweeteners – and Cadbury spends years trying to ensure that the balance will create a successful product. Jesse Kiefer is a Cadbury vice-president in charge of new technology development for chewing gum, although most people here call him the 'gumologist'. He rarely uses the word 'gum' however, describing it as a 'piece of technology' that functions as a 'flavour delivery system'.

Part of his job is to deal with the question posed by Lonnie Donegan more than 45 years ago – 'Does your chewing gum lose its flavour on the bedpost overnight?'. He has developed secret chemical compounds designed to surround the flavour molecules. When the flavour is then attached to the gum, and the gum is chewed, the compounds are supposed to regulate the rate at which the flavours are released, in much the same way as slow release drugs are designed.

The panellists are often required to chew the gum for hours to check the technology has worked, although the company does use chewing machines to simulate gum masticated for hours on end.

Finally, each individual piece of gum is sprayed 45 times with an outer coating in a process than can take eight hours.

Sadly for street cleaners, Mr Keifer has yet to crack the problem of developing a chewing gum that does not stick to the pavement. 'It's the Holy Grail, but we're not there yet,' he said.

Source: *Daily Telegraph*, 6 February 2007.

Exit case study questions

1 Explain why Cadbury have chosen to enter chewing gum market in the United Kingdom.

2 Analyse the competitive environment of the chewing gum market in the United Kingdom by use of Porter's five forces of competition.

DISCUSSION TOPIC

1 Read the paper 'Competitive strategy in emerging industries' by Michael E Porter, Chapter 13, in *The Strategy Process*, Mintzberg, Lampel, Quinn and Ghosal, Harlow: Prentice Hall, 2003.

2 Discuss the relevance of 'Common structural characteristics', 'Early mobility barriers', 'Strategic choices' and 'Timing entry' for high street retailers moving to Internet retailing in addition to retaining their high street operations.

WIDEN YOUR HORIZONS

1 Widen your horizons by analysing the competitive environment for the Online Next Directory. Christmas 2006 was very successful for Next's online business and research of the business press in January 2007 will help with analysing the competitive environment.

2 Widen your horizons by discussing how the opening of high street stores in the UK (instead of out-of-town stores) will impact on the IKEA's external environment. The announcement by IKEA to open high street stores in the UK was made in January 2006.

▨ WEBLINKS

The websites for this chapter are for some of the key bodies impacting on organisations.

■ The following website is for the House of Commons.
www.parliament.uk/commons/index.cfm

■ The following website is for the Scottish Parliament in Edinburgh
www.scottishparliament.uk

■ The following website is for the Welsh Assembly in Cardiff
www.wales.gov.uk

■ The following website is for the Bank of England
www.bankofengland.co.uk/

- The following website is for the London Stock Exchange.
  www.londonstockexchange.com/Default.asp

- The following website is for the Trade Union Congress (TUC), which is an umbrella for trade unions in the UK.
  www.tuc.org.uk

- The following website is for the European Union.
  www.europa.eu

- The website for the European Free Trade Area is shown below.
  www.efta.int

- The website of the European Bank of Reconstruction and Development is shown below.
  www.ebrd.org

- The following website is for the Council of Baltic Sea States.
  www.cbss.st

- The website for NATO is shown below.
  www.nato.int

- The website of the World Trade Organisation is shown below.
  www.wto.org

- The website of the World Bank Group is shown below.
  www.worldbank.org

- The following website is for the International Monetary Fund.
  www.imf.org

- The website of the Organisation for Economic Co-operation and Development is shown below.
  www.oecd.org

- These are the weblinks for two important bodies in the regulation of the UK economy.
  Office of Fair Trading (OFT)
  www.oft.gov.uk
  HM Treasury
  www.hm-treasury.gov.uk

- The website of the Competition Commission provides the web addresses for other regulatory bodies in the UK and overseas regulatory bodies in Europe, North America and Australia. To find the list of regulatory bodies for overseas countries visit the Competition Commission website and type in 'overseas links' into the search facility on the website
  www.competition-commission.org.uk.

  The first resulting match is 'Competition Commission – Links and Contacts' – click on this to see overseas regulators.

- These are the websites for the regulatory authorities for some of the privatised sectors.
  Office of Communications (OFCOM)
  www.ofcom.org.uk
  Office of Gas and Electricity Markets (OFGEM)
  www.ofgem.gov.uk
  Office of Water Services (OFWAT)
  www.ofwat.gov.uk

FURTHER READING

The following readings provide a variety of views on analysing the external environment.

- Capon, C (2004) *Understanding Organisational Context,* 2nd edn, Harlow: Financial Times/Prentice Hall. Chapter 8, 'The external environment'.
- Capon, C (2004) *Understanding Organisational Context,* 2nd edn, Harlow: Financial Times/Prentice Hall. Chapter 9, 'The composition of the external environment'.
- Capon, C (2004) *Understanding Organisational Context,* 2nd edn, Harlow: Financial Times/Prentice Hall. Chapter 10, 'The competitive environment'.
- Dess, G G, Lumpkin, G T and Taylor, M L (2005) *Strategic Management*, 2nd edn, New York: McGraw Hill Irwin. Chapter 2 'Analysing the external environment of the firm'.
- Johnson, G, Scholes, K and Whittington, R (2005) *Exploring Corporate Strategy*, 7th edn, Harlow: Financial Times/Prentice Hall. Chapter 2, 'The environment'.
- Lasserre, P (2003) *Global Strategic Management*, Basingstoke: Palgrave Macmillan. Chapter 1, 'Globalisation of markets and competition'.
- Lynch, R (2006) *Corporate Strategy*, 4th edn, London: Financial Times/Prentice Hall. Chapter 3, 'Analysing the environment – basics.
- Lynch, R (2006) *Corporate Strategy*, 4th edn, London: Financial Times/Prentice Hall. Chapter 4, 'Analysing markets, competition and co-operation'.
- Mellahi, K, Frynas, J G and Finlay, P (2005) *Global Strategic Management*, Oxford: Oxford University Press. Chapter 2, 'Global business environment: the external macro environment'.
- Mellahi, K, Frynas, J G and Finlay, P (2005) *Global Strategic Management*, Oxford: Oxford University Press. Chapter 3, 'Global business environment: the industry environment'
- White, C (2004) *Strategic Management*, Basingstoke: Palgrave. Chapter 5, 'Reading the competitive environment'.

REFERENCES

1 Teather, D (2005) 'Asian competitors and falling sales drive down Ford profits', The *Guardian*, 21 April.
2 Duncan, Peter M and Ginter, W Jack (1990) 'Macro-environmental analysis for strategic management', *Long Range Planning*, 23 (6), December.
3 www.wales.gov.uk
4 http://europa.eu.int
5 Barber, L (1997) 'No turning back from brave new Europe', *Financial Times*, 17 July.
6 www.wto.org.
7 Brown, K (2002) 'A lost generation leaves Britain older and calmer', *Financial Times*, 5 October.
8 Nicholson-Lord, D (1995) ' "Greys" take over from the young as big spenders', *Independent*, 27 January.
9 Braid, M (1995) 'Tomorrow belongs to them', *Independent*, 1 October.
10 Brown, op. cit.
11 Nicholson-Lord, op. cit.
12 Braid, op. cit.
13 Brown, op. cit.

14 Blitz, R (2003) 'Ageing population trend heightens pension fears', *Financial Times*, 30 January.

15 Timmins, N (2002) 'Public spending on pensions set to fall despite ageing population', *Financial Times*, 28 November.

16 Parker, G (2002) 'Brussels warns of ageing population crisis', *Financial Times*, 11 December.

17 Ibid.

18 Ibid.

19 Ibid.

20 Gimbel, F (2003) 'BVCA to call for immigration increase', *Financial Times*, 23 March.

21 Williams, F (2002) 'UN finds link between fertility rate and wealth', *Financial Times*, 3 December.

22 Ibid.

23 Ibid.

24 Ibid.

25 Wolf, M (2003) 'People, plagues and prosperity', *Financial Times*, 26 February.

26 Ibid.

27 Ibid.

28 Ibid.

29 Ibid.

30 Shankar, B and Sharda, R (1997) 'Obtaining business intelligence on the Internet', *Long Range Planning*, 30 (1), February.

31 Bird, J (1996) 'Untangling the web', *Management Today*, March.

32 www.ofgem.gov.uk.

33 Porter, M E (1985) *Competitive Advantage*, New York: Free Press.

CHAPTER 3

Managing resources competitively

Exhibit 3.1 Essential strategy model

Chapter objectives

When you have read this Chapter and worked through the associated activities you should be able to achieve the objectives specified below.

1 Identify and evaluate the resources present in an organisation.

2 Discuss core competencies and their importance in helping an organisation to achieve competitive advantage.

3 Evaluate and determine the most appropriate way for an organisation to configure its resources given that competitive advantage may be cost or differentiation based.

4 Explain the impact of linkages on a company and its competitive position.

Staff are an important resource for organisations with their knowledge and skills helping organisations achieve competitive advantage. Hence this entry case study looks at how organisations can harness, retain and motivate their most talented human resources; it also looks at the idea that losing talented staff can cost organisations dearly.

Human resources, minus the boring bits

FT

by Richard Donkin

A few years ago most companies were highly secretive about their succession and fast-track arrangements. Sometimes even the anointed ones – those earmarked for future higher office – were not aware of their favoured status. The secrecy was based on two assumptions: first, that singling people out in this way might cause resentment among the less favoured members of their peer group; second, that the fast-track status might go to people's heads.

Then 'business process re-engineering' came along and career ladders and hierarchies became highly unfashionable for a while. White-collar managers began losing their jobs in droves, the one-company career was discouraged, and employee loyalty went out of the window. Graduate trainees digested the message and began to think nothing of switching jobs after a couple of years to broaden their experience. Ideally they had taken advantage of some first-rate training and intensive work experience with the kind of big employer that enjoyed a strong reputation as a breeding ground for talent.

Suddenly many of the larger employers realised that the 'no job for life' mantra was costing them money at the front end of management careers. Such concerns rarely extended to older and more expensive senior managers. If any of those fell by the wayside, competing for the biggest jobs, it was just one of those things. There seems little room for sentiment in the modern corporation. But companies look quite differently at their carefully groomed 20-30-somethings.

Now more and more companies are adopting a relatively new US-style approach to executive recruitment and development that calls itself 'talent management'. In fact, much of this is not at all new. Where it does differ from the old-style management ladder perhaps is in the way it borrows heavily from the legacy of McKinsey's 'war for talent' ideas and Jack Welch's zealous grading and review system at General Electric.

According to a recent Conference Board report in the US, quoted in the latest issue of *Executive Recruiter News*, the components of talent management include recruitment, retention, professional development, performance management, measurement and feedback, and workforce planning. So it's human resources management then? Well, yes and no. Think of it as HR with the boring bits taken out, and with the addition of some greater concentration on top people and potential top people.

Listening to HR specialists describing their own approaches to talent management at a recent London-based seminar organised by Korn/Ferry International, it was clear that it means different things to different companies. Valerie Scoular, group HR director at Barclays, described the 'talent proposition' that was designed for the top level of the bank in 2001. The old system tended to promote the interests of a very recognisable urbane kind of white male and did not set measurable performance levels. 'So everyone thought they were in the top quartile,' she said. Before this, people didn't know whether or not they were part of the succession plan. 'Now we are open about it. It brings people recognition and self-esteem. We bring our talented people together in communities and they share the enjoyment, the pain and the successes.'

Part of the problem for Barclays was defining what a talented person should look like. For left-brained bankers, says Ms Scoular, this has meant confronting their emotional sides by discussing their past experiences. It seems that the old prerequisite for maintaining a stiff upper lip has been exchanged for an ability to let the bottom lip quiver now and again. It's OK for bosses to cry.

You only needed to witness the emotional scenes surrounding the resignation of Greg Dyke as director-general of the BBC last week to grasp what is required of the modern boss. How many other bosses, I wonder, were looking on enviously at the way he departed with hugs and kisses from staff waving 'Don't go Greg' banners? How many of the FTSE's finest could command that kind of employee support?

Ms Scoular is adamant that bosses have to change. 'At one time we tried to make everyone grey. But exceptionally talented people are spiky. So we have a continuing conversation about what is acceptable spikiness and

→

what isn't,' she says. The other difference is that 'upper quartile' managers now know exactly where they sit. They also know that their continued status depends on continued superior performance. When your talent is under-management, you must understand that your halo can slip.

Tony Bloxham, part of the senior executive team at AstraZeneca, the international pharmaceuticals company, played an instrumental HR role in integrating the staffs of the old Astra and Zeneca companies when they merged in 1999. At the time, he said, the company identified 'the absolute key people who could make or break the merger' depending on whether they stayed or left. These 650 people, he said were 'touched' by an allocated senior manager whose job it was to take them to one side and tell them: 'Whatever you're feeling during this period of instability, don't worry because you will have a significant job in the new organisation.' Having never been touched myself, I was gratified to hear Chris Bones, group organisation effectiveness and development director for Cadbury Schweppes, the international beverage and confectionery company, take a less elitist view of talent. 'I think everybody is talented so we don't use the term. We want to harness the power of the 55,000 people we employ and create opportunities for all of these people to show how talented they are.'

All of this, you would think, sounds like bad news for head-hunters such as Korn/Ferry. But I didn't see any of their people quaking in their boots. Perhaps this is because clearly identified talent pools will make their fishing expeditions that much easier. In the long run I suspect that some of these approaches will need to be carefully managed in case they backfire. The more you cosset people, the greater the temptation they face to become ever more demanding. It seems, anyway, that many young people coming in to companies these days have their focus pinned not so much on the boss's job but on the next big holiday. 'A lot of them have the attitude that they want to work for six months and they will work intensively for long hours then 'live' for six months,' says Mr Bones. He calls it 'binge' working.

Companies are responding to this blasé attitude to work by trying to create ever more attractive support systems for the people they want to nurture. We have come some way from the lifelong careers of managers who worked their way up, learning every aspect of the business and giving their all before, so often, slipping into early retirement or finding themselves redundant. There was talent there too, and a great deal of it has been wasted.

Source: *Financial Times*, 5 February 2005.

INTRODUCTION

This chapter seeks to look at how an organisation can identify and evaluate its resources, before considering how its resources can be configured or organised to achieve cost or differentiation base competitive advantage by looking at the **value chain**.

One characteristic that all organisations share, irrespective of sector or activity, is the fact that they use resources to deliver products and services to customers and service users. Public sector organisations, for example hospitals, use skilled staff, beds, operating theatres, pharmaceuticals and public money to treat patients. In contrast private sector manufacturing organisations such as Ferrari use a wide variety of components, many manufactured by subcontractors, to build cars. The components will include lights, engine parts, wheels, and luxury leather for the seats, and many of them will be bespoke for Ferrari, to produce a luxury sports car which sells in a niche market. Additionally in the private sector, service organisations such as banks use resources to provide banking services and financial products for customers. The banks are a good example of organisations which have over the last twenty years reconfigured their resources away from carrying out routine banking tasks face-to-face across a counter to developing new financial service products, savings accounts, insurance, mortgages, personal loans. Technology is now used to carry out much of the routine work, first with the ATM and more recently Internet banking. In the future the banking industry will have to use and continue to develop technology to prevent wide-scale electronic theft and fraud. This was initially seen in the introduction of 'chip and pin' systems.

EVALUATING RESOURCES

A **resource audit** examines how resources could be used to improve efficiency and effectiveness and hence profitability.

Organisations identify and evaluate resource strengths and weaknesses to allow clear understanding of what it is possible to achieve in terms of products, markets and growth given the constraints of resource availability which exist in all organisations. The **resource audit** should indicate how resources might be redeployed to improve efficiency and effectiveness, and hence profitability.

Exhibit 3.2 Evaluating resources

- Which resources does the organisation have access to?

- How balanced are the resources?

- How much resource slack is there within the organisation and in which areas does it exist?

- How effective and efficient is resource utilisation?

- How flexible are resources?

- How do the resources contribute to the organisation's strategic fit?

Identifying and evaluating resources requires more than producing a simple list of the resources an organisation utilises. There are four categories of resources – financial, human, tangible and intangible – and a full audit should highlight those resources which provide the organisation with areas of strength (to be exploited and built upon) and areas of weakness (to be minimised). This evaluation process can be undertaken by using the questions in **Exhibit 3.2**, Evaluating resources. This process allows the organisation to identify how it can minimise costs or increase efficiency, and add value for the customer by being more effective in its resource utilisation.

Evaluating human resources

Identifying and evaluating human resources should include an assessment of the number and type of staff in the organisation, their current skills and development potential. This will give an overview of current human resources and in particular their adaptability, which could be key if the organisation is to

Core permanent employees have highly skilled jobs, with relatively good job security and career prospects with the organisation.

The **first peripheral group** are those employees with full-time jobs, often with vocational skills.

The **second peripheral** group will provide workforce flexibility and includes part-time employees, job-sharing employees and subsidised trainees.

External staff can be brought in quickly to meet increased demand and include consultants, subcontractors and temporary agency staff.

undergo change. The type of employees in an organisation can be categorised by use of the flexible firm model, which divides employees into three categories: core, peripheral and external. The **core permanent employees** have highly skilled jobs, with relatively good job security and career prospects, and the expectation is that these employees will be flexible in terms of their role in the organisation and working location. The **first peripheral group** is those employees with full-time jobs, not careers, which often require more vocational-type skills than core employees have. Employees in this group include supervisors, secretaries, assemblers and administrators. The **second peripheral group** will provide a significant component of the workforce flexibility and includes employees on short-term contracts, part-time employees, job-sharing employees and subsidised trainees. The skill level of the second peripheral group will vary depending on the job and contract. For example, a consultant IT expert will have extensive skills and may hold a full-time post for a period with the organisation, carrying out and completing a project before moving on to the next project with another employer. In contrast part-time employees and job-share employees will work on a permanent basis for the organisation, but only for a fraction of the hours of a full-time employee. An example of a subsidised trainee is provided by the Modern Apprenticeships Scheme, where the government covers around 25 per cent of the cost to the organisation of employing and training the apprentice. The final category of staff in the flexible firm model is **external staff**. They can be brought in quickly to meet increased demand and include self-employed consultants, subcontractors and temporary agency staff. The latter may include secretarial staff and administrators. A common view is that subcontracted activities are those that are non-core and can be done more cheaply and satisfactorily by contracted staff, such as cleaning, catering, provision of IT support, and running the payroll. However, it is common in some areas of the public sector where staff shortages exist to subcontract core activities; examples include the use of agency nurses by hospitals and care homes and the use of supply teachers in schools to cover for absent colleagues.

The advent of the flexible workforce owes much to the popularity of downsizing in organisations and the general shift in the economy from manufacturing to service provision. A manufacturer may employ extra staff to meet peak demand or stock goods produced in a quiet time to meet demand in peak times. However, a service provider is unable to stock products to meet peaks in demand and therefore meets that demand by employing extra part-time or temporary staff. This is less expensive than employing a larger number of permanent full-time staff, as during troughs in demand the extra full-time permanent staff would be inactive. Therefore downsizing occurs when organisations reduce the number of core employees, recruiting more part-time or subcontracted employees instead of full-time staff, or when they delayer, removing layers of employees so that the organisation becomes structurally flatter.

Classic examples of flexibility in the labour market include retailers taking on extra staff over Christmas and fruit producers employing seasonal labour during the summer to pick and package the fruit. The catering and hotel industry uses part-time and temporary staff to ensure they can cope during the busy periods, for example summer holidays or Friday and Saturday evenings. Flexible practices may also occur with skilled jobs, for example a GP's practice may employ a doctor on a part-time basis to cover a defined number of surgeries every week.

However, for other organisations such as pharmaceutical companies (e.g. Merck), software companies (e.g. Microsoft) and hospitals (e.g. Moorfields Eye Hospital), the success of the organisation in developing new drugs, software and surgical techniques is dependent on the knowledge and skills of the staff. The ideas of knowledge and intellectual capital are well summarised by Tom Stewart, a *Fortune* writer, who defined 'intellectual capital as knowledge, information, intellectual property, experience, that can be put to use to create wealth.'[1] Equally Entry case study 3.1 refers to the recruitment and development of staff likely to posses knowledge and intellectual capital as 'talent management'. The concept of knowledge comes in two different forms: explicit knowledge and tacit knowledge. Explicit knowledge is easily documented, for example architects' drawings, business plans, patents, processes and techniques. In contrast tacit knowledge is in the minds of employees and is based on their experiences and backgrounds, and is only accessible with the co-operation and consent of the individual.

Overall the capabilities, knowledge, skills and experience of the individual employee or manager are defined as **human capital** and include job relevant knowledge, skills and experience, along with the ability to learn and add to that reservoir of knowledge, skills and experience. The network of relationships that individuals have throughout the organisation and beyond – including, for example, suppliers, customers and alliance partners – is known as social capital. These relationships are critical in sharing and acquiring both knowledge and resources. The challenge for organisations is to attract, develop and retain appropriate human capital.

Human capital is the capabilities, knowledge, skills and experience of the individual employees.

Managing human resources

Having identified the type of workforce the organisation needs and the degree of flexibility required the organisation and its management should ensure that the staff are managed effectively such that they are able to make the necessary contribution to the organisation's strategic **fit** with its environment. The strategic contribution of human resources will be best realised if the senior management team is cohesive and includes a human resources director who is active at the strategic level and, in addition, makes an effective contribution to key human resource areas. The key human resource areas include **succession planning**, human resource planning, management development, performance management and **reward management**.

Succession planning is ensuring the organisation's management provision for the future.

Succession planning is about ensuring the organisation's management provision in the future. In 1999 when the company AstraZeneca was formed by merger, key staff in the future of the organisation were 'touched' by a senior manager whose job it was to offer reassurance that the individual would have a significant role in the future of the company (see Entry case study 3.1). This means identifying gaps which are likely to occur in the management team, and considering how to fill them. The question to ask is: where are the future managers now? The organisation may seek to recruit new employees with management potential, or identify current employees with management potential, and provide extensive development and training to allow these staff to take on management roles in the future. The advantage of this is the organisation has influence over the development of such employees. The disadvantages are that the identified staff may not fulfil their potential or they may fulfil their potential and leave to work for another company – maybe the closest competitor. The other option is to recruit managers as and when the organisation needs them. This can be expensive and the person with the right skills, abilities and attributes may be difficult to find. However, a newly appointed manager will be likely to bring new and different views concerning the job and how it is done, and this can be refreshing for an organisation which is struggling to move forwards. This is perhaps why Barclays Bank has taken the view expressed by Valerie Scoular in the Entry case study 3.1: 'But exceptionally talented people are spiky. So we have a continuing conversation about what is acceptable spikiness and what isn't.'

Clearly succession planning can involve management development. Additionally employee development is something which needs attention if the organisation is to successfully develop its workforce in an appropriate way to ensure the right qualifications, skills and abilities are present in the business, now and in the future. This, in turn, links with human resource planning which is concerned with anticipating the organisation's staff needs over the short and long term. The question to consider is how will the staffing needs change and will the required mix of core, peripheral and external employees remain similar or radically change. Additionally, the likelihood of staff remaining with the organisation or leaving it should be taken into account.

Assessing the performance of staff and the rewards offered are also critical. Performance management is dealt with by determining and implementing the best type of performance evaluation system. Performance targets and key results areas should also be considered and can include appraisal, piece work, meeting targets (sales) and overall performance. Reward management is concerned with deciding on the reward system most likely to be effective in the future and identifying the type of rewards that ought to be linked to the attainment of long-term business goals, which relates back to organisational mission and objectives. Rewards can include more pay, bonus schemes, profit sharing, share ownership and incentives, company car and private health insurance.

Reward management is concerned with implementing an effective reward system linked to the attainment of goals.

Evaluating and managing human resources

1 Why are core employees important to an organisation?
2 Explain the difference between the first and second peripheral groups of employees.
3 Explain the difference between explicit and tacit knowledge in organisations.
4 Define the term human capital.
5 Summarise the advantages and disadvantages of home grown managers in an organisations.

Evaluating tangible resources

Tangible resources are physical assets, such as buildings, offices, factories, warehouses, IT systems, machinery and motor vehicles.

Tangible or physical resources include buildings, offices, factories, warehouses, IT systems, machinery and motor vehicles. An evaluation of **tangible resources** should stretch beyond a mere listing of the number of machines or the production capacity of the company. Questions about the nature of these resources, such as their age, condition, capability and location, will help to determine their productive life and their usefulness in helping the company gaining competitive advantage. In evaluating tangible resources their current rate of usage, changes in this and their continued usage will help managers make decisions regarding the scrapping of tangible resources and their replacement or non-replacement.

Managing tangible resources

The **flexibility of resources** is the effectiveness with which resources can be redeployed to take account of developing strategy and a changing environment.

The **balance of resources** refers to resource excess, efficiency and inefficiency.

Managing tangible resources involves considering a number of issues: the **flexibility of resources**; their balance; and their fit. The flexibility of resources refers to the effectiveness with which resources can be redeployed to take account of both developing strategy and a changing environment. Fixed assets, including plant, equipment and premises, tend to be more useful if a company is pursuing existing and related customers and markets. A strategy of unrelated diversification will be more risky and require different resources and assets.

The **balance of resources** refers to resource excess, efficiency and inefficiency. In successful periods there can be a tendency for organisations to develop resources excesses or slack. Tangible resources such as stock, premises, equipment are plentiful, and they are maintained at higher levels and in greater numbers than might be the case if the organisation was operating at maximum efficiency. Efficiency helps reduce costs and hence its achievement can make a major contribution to competitive advantage. Therefore it is suggested that organisations scrutinise their costs with a view to identifying and eliminating excess costs, thereby improving efficiency and profitability. However a balance does need to be struck and an excessive drive to get 'more for less' can produce a reality of asking 'too much from too little'; the effect may be a reduction in the quality of goods and service, and in turn a loss of customers.

Fit is used as an expression of how cohesive the parts of an organisation, its resources and environment are in relation to one another.

The concept of **fit** should also be considered: how do the tangible resources an organisation has support and fit with other aspects of the organisation, for example human resources, cash, systems and structure? The resources and their configuration should, in turn, all support an effective and competitive strategy for markets and growth. In considering the concept of fit an organisation may reach the conclusion that the organisation is experiencing misfit between its resources and environment. Strategists investigating fit should look for symptoms of misfit. Symptoms of misfit, and potential or actual failure (see Chapter 12), include a decline in financial performance and falling market share.

The intangible resources

Intangible resources are goodwill, image and reputation, and arise from brand names, good contracts, company image and innovative capability.

Intangible resources have traditionally been defined as goodwill, image and reputation, and arise from brand names, good contracts, company image or many other sources, such as the value attached to the innovative capability (such as patented processes). In some businesses, particularly services such as solicitors, retail shops and the catering industry, goodwill could represent a major asset of the company and will result from strong brand names and company image. There should be no doubt that these intangible resources have a value since when businesses are sold part of their value is 'goodwill'.

Review questions   Evaluating and managing tangible and intangible resources

1   Define the terms tangible resources and intangible resources.
2   In evaluating resources, which questions should be asked to determine the usefulness of resources?
3   Why is it advisable that organisations scrutinise their costs?
4   Explain what happens if an organisation is too efficient.
5   Why is the concept of fit important in managing resources?

The financial resources

Financial resources are important for all organisations and these are looked at in detail in Chapter 4. Financial resources include capital from different sources, such as loans and shares, and a key issue is the effective use of the capital. Additionally the amount of cash available in a business is key; too little and cash flow will be poor, with insolvency and liquidation the extreme possibility. Equally, excessive cash in a business could make it an attractive target for a takeover.

CORE COMPETENCIES

Customers are stakeholders in an organisation and fulfilling **key success factors** involves the organisation in meeting the needs and expectations of its customers and other stakeholders (see Chapter 5). For example, key success factors may include good service, reliable delivery or providing good value for money. Fulfilling key success factors requires the organisation to have developed the required competencies. So, for example, an electrical retailer like Currys supplying and delivering domestic electrical goods such as television sets, DVDs, washing machines, fridge-freezers and dishwashers, has as one of its key success factors reliable delivery. Reliable delivery depends on having competencies in managing stock (no customer will wait 10 weeks for a Sony 28" integrated Freeview widescreen television) and logistics, as customers want to know which day and time the goods will be delivered. This has driven companies doing such work to develop systems that are able to give customers a four-hour delivery slot to which they can adhere. In seeking to satisfy stakeholders, especially customers, while at the same time aiming to outperform competitors, organisations should seek to:

- fulfil the key success factors for the industry or market;
- develop competencies that provide competitive advantage (see following discussion);
- utilise competencies to meet the requirements of specific customers in a profitable manner.

Thompson and Richardson[2] describe survival and success for organisations as arising from two types of organisational competence. First, supplying products and services which compete successfully to meet customer needs and wants. Successful competitive strategy, which can be cost based or added-value based, will allow the organisation to achieve competitive advantage over its rivals. This allows maximum income to be generated, which in turn allows the organisation to meet the expectations of other stakeholders: for example, payment of dividend to shareholders or annual pay increase to employees. The other type of organisational competencies are those relating to efficiency of the processes used to deliver a service or manufacture a product. For example, in a call centre efficiency could be measured by the number of calls dealt with in one hour, or in a factory manufacturing calibrated laboratory glassware, the smaller the number of faulty pieces of glassware the greater the efficiency of the manufacturing process. In general terms the greater the efficiency of processes, the better the control of costs and the more likely the chance of achieving superior profits. Thompson and Richardson deliberately refer to organisational success as outcomes that are the end result of the organisation achieving the tangible competencies rather than the competencies themselves. They also, however, acknowledge that tangible and measurable outcomes have been widely discussed in the strategy and marketing literature.

Thompson and Richardson[3] developed eight generic competencies categories and any successful organisation will need to employ the combination of competencies which is appropriate for itself, and the mix of competencies will be likely to cover all eight categories (see **Exhibit 3.3**). Maintaining survival and success will require the organisation to continuously evaluate its capability in achieving competencies and the suitability of the combination of competencies pursued to achieve successful outcomes. Therefore the organisation will need to continually develop and improve its competencies if competitive advantage is to be maintained.

Exhibit 3.3 Thompson's and Richardson's competence categories

- Strategic awareness and control abilities

- Stakeholder satisfaction abilities

- Competitive strategy

- Strategy implementation

- Quality and customer care

- Functional competencies

- Failure and crisis avoidance

- Ethics and social responsibility

Source: based on Thompson, J L and Richardson, B (1996) 'Strategic and competitive success: towards a model of the comprehensively competent organisation', *Management Decision*, 34, 2, pp 5-19.

The views of Prahalad and Hamel[4] are similar to those of Thompson and Richardson and start with the well-established idea that the competitiveness of an organisation arises from the price and/or performance of its product and services. Additionally long-term competitive success depends on the organisation being able to deliver competitive products and services at lower cost and faster than its competitors. This is achieved via an organisation's **core competencies**, which are concerned with both the development of technical skills and the organisation of the work, be it manufacturing or service delivery. The core competencies are developed from the integration of skills, abilities and people from across the organisation, and successful companies are likely to have five or six fundamental competencies. A long list of capabilities does not equal five or six core competencies and to help recognise a core competence Prahalad and Hamel[5] identify three criteria (see **Exhibit 3.4**).

In the long term core competencies need to be nurtured, applied and shared; otherwise they will fade, and skills and knowledge will become dated and may be lost as people leave the organisation. Therefore core competencies are developed from within the organisation and are not something which can be gained from outsourcing; hence, the skills and abilities to develop and maintain the core competencies should come from within the organisation. This helps to ensure that core competencies, and hence sustainable competi-

Core competencies are the skills and abilities developed within an organisation with which competitive advantage can be created and maintained.

Exhibit 3.4 Prahalad and Hamel's criteria for identifying core competencies

- Does the core competence provide the company with access to a range of world wide markets?

- Does the core competence make a major contribution to the perceived customer benefits of the end product?

- Is the core competence difficult for competitors to copy?

Source: based on Prahalad, C K and Hamel G (1990) 'The core competence of the corporation', *Harvard Business Review*, May/June.

tive advantage, are difficult for competitors to reproduce. Prahalad and Hamel[6] identify two clear lessons with regard to core competencies. First, the cost of an organisation losing a core competence can only be partly calculated in advance. Second, due to the development of core competencies taking a long period of time via a process of continuous improvement, lack of a core competence will make it difficult to enter a new or developing market as a major player.

Prahalad and Hamel hold the view that it is vital to distinguish between core competencies, core products and end products due to global competition having different goals and being played by different rules in each area. A company which is successful in developing in all areas – core competencies, core products and end products – will be creating or defending a long-term leadership position. Success in the core competencies area will see the organisation aiming to develop and design world class products and services. Prolonged leadership requires core competencies to be supported by core products and services, selling to a wide variety of customers. This allows feedback, turnover and profit to be generated, which in turn allows the continuing development of the core competencies that are key for the organisation to sustain competitive advantage which is difficult to copy. Finally, the dominant position of a company's end products in the marketplace will allow the shaping of customer and end-user needs and wants. Organisations need to know how successful they are in each of the three areas of core competencies, core products and end products.

Review questions

Core competencies

1 Explain the terms 'core competence' and 'key success factors'.

2 Where do core competencies arise from?

3 Summarise the two types of core competence an organisation needs to meet for survival and success.

4 Why is maintaining core competencies important?

5 How can core competencies be maintained?

THE VALUE CHAIN

The **value chain** is a framework for examining how an organisation configures its resources for competitive advantage.

The **value chain**[7] is a framework for thinking about resources and systems which currently provide competitive advantage and which could provide competitive advantage for an organisation. Gaining, maintaining or improving competitive advantage requires a firm's resources and systems to be arranged to reduce the costs overall or add most value for least cost. Whether an organisation seeks to configure its value chain to reduce the costs overall or add most value for least cost, depends on the type of competitive strategy it is seeking to pursue – cost based or differentiation based. An organisation should be aiming to be the most profitable company in its industry, and its competitive strategy and hence its value chain should help clarify how the required margins can be achieved (see Business illustration on BA). An organisation seeking to be a successful cost leader in an industry, such as the supermarket chain Asda in the UK (owned by the US company Walmart), seeks to cut costs in all areas. Asda does this by reducing the cost of goods it sells and the resources it uses via bulk purchasing and negotiating power. Additionally Asda promotes itself as 'low priced' with the 'Asda Price' slogan in the UK. In contrast a food retailer such as an upmarket delicatessen will sell many specialised items, deal with many small suppliers, and purchase small quantities, with the associated costs being passed on to the customer in the form of higher prices. In contrast to a large supermarket chain the opening hours for a delicatessen are very unlikely to be 24 hours and the staff to customer ratio will be higher.

Business illustration on cutting the value chain margin – BA

In April 2006 British Airways cut its short haul fares in Europe to compete with low-cost airlines such as Easyjet and Ryanair. The aim of BA is to protect their market share on holiday routes where the competition from low-cost carriers is fiercest. Passengers able to book well in advance benefit most from reduced fares on a first come first served basis. In contrast travellers who book at short notice have faced higher prices. All BA fares are inclusive of items such as food and drink, in contrast to the low-cost airlines. This suggests BA is cutting the margin of their value chain to maintain passenger numbers. However BA's approach to competing with low carriers is in contrast to the service offered by SAS, another major European airline. SAS offers a choice of a cheap no-frills seat or a full service journey at a higher price.

Source: 'BA cuts fare to challenge no-frills rivals and the train', D Millward, *Daily Telegraph*, 21 April 2006.

Primary activities are concerned with the manufacture of a product or creation of a service and their delivery to customers.

The value chain includes **primary activities** and support activities (see Exhibit 3.5). Primary activities are directly concerned with the manufacture of a product or creation of a service and the delivery of both to customers. In contrast support activities help improve the efficiency and/or effectiveness of the primary activities.

Exhibit 3.5 The value chain

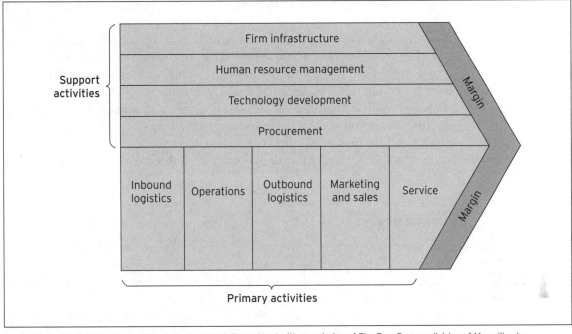

Source: Porter, M E (1985) *Competitive Advantage*, Free Press. Used with permission of The Free Press, a division of Macmillan Inc. Copyright 1985 Michael E Porter.

PRIMARY ACTIVITIES

Inbound logistics

Inbound logistics are concerned with managing incoming materials and components.

Inbound logistics are about ensuring incoming materials and components are delivered on time and undamaged, are easily accessible and link to production requirements, and feed into any JIT (just in time) stock control systems the organisation operates. Expressed in these terms most people would think of inbound logistics as applying to a manufacturing organisation. However, they also apply to service organisations which purchase goods and consumables to use in delivering services to customers. For example in the case of an airline, if good service is to be delivered the planes need to be correctly configured when delivered by the manufacturer, for example Boeing. In the case of Ryanair as many seats as possible, all of economy class standard, will be needed. In contrast Singapore Airlines requires its new Airbus A340-500 planes which are flying between Singapore and Los Angeles to be fitted with 'executive economy' seats (more leg room than economy seats) and 'business class' seats. Equally consumables such as food and fuel need to be delivered at the right time, in the right quantities and stored correctly. Inbound logistics for a service organisation may include how customers are dealt with when they arrive to experience the service offered and will include how they are asked to queue on arrival. A post office which has one big queue for all service windows, with the customer at the front of the queue going to the next available window, is different from the fast food restaurant which has separate queues at every till with customers trying to choose the shortest or fastest moving queue. Organisations like supermarkets ask customers to queue on their way out of the shop; this is part of **outbound logistics**. In the case of an airline how passengers are boarded is part of the inbound logistics. Easyjet with its first come, first served approach to selecting a seat is in contrast to an airline like British Airways which if boarding via a front entrance to an aircraft, on a short haul flight, will often board passengers seated in the rear rows first. On longer haul flights airlines may choose to board first and business class passengers separately, while in economy infirm passengers and those with small children may board first.

Operations

Operations are concerned with delivering products or services of a quality appropriate for the competitive strategy being pursued.

The **operations** section of the value chain is concerned with creating products or services of an appropriate quality for the type of competitive strategy being pursued. For the airline this can be about ensuring planes leave and arrive on time, which is supported by airlines usually having a policy of not allowing late passengers to check in. Many of the low-cost airlines also seek to achieve accurate arrival and departure times by using smaller and less busy airports, however they do have to balance this with their very short turnaround times. A turnaround time of 25 minutes instead of 45 minutes on short haul flights within Europe can mean an airline gets eight flights a day from a plane, instead of six flights – which is an increase in business of one-third. All airlines seek to maximise efficiency by ensuring as many seats as possible on any one flight are occupied; in the industry this is referred to as having a high load factor. Airlines will also double book seats to help ensure high load factors. The double-booked customer will have paid and will be flown on a flight where there are empty seats, thereby increasing the airline's load factor. The pricing strategies, advertising and promotion pursued by the airline will all aim to fill flights as soon as possible, often meaning flights booked close to the day of departure are more expensive than those pre-booked some weeks beforehand. Operations for an airline also covers the correct scheduling of crew; for example the long haul flight which has to make an unscheduled stop due to bad weather may be unable to continue on its way immediately as regulations concerning the amount of time crew have been flying and their rest breaks will need to take priority. Equally the aircraft will need to have undergone the appropriate maintenance and fuelling.

Outbound logistics

Outbound logistics is about rapid and accurate delivery of the product or service to the customer.

Outbound logistics are about rapid and accurate delivery of the product or service to the customer. For manufacturing organisations this is concerned with managing the distribution system to ensure the right goods are in the right place, at the right time for customers. In a company manufacturing gear boxes for Toyota, outbound logistics are concerned with delivering the right gear boxes in the right quantity at the right time to the Toyota factory to connect with the just-in-time (JIT) systems Toyota operate. For service organisations it can be concerned with getting the customers to the right location on time or being accessible to customers in the right place at the right time. For example, the Virgin train from Manchester to London which is terminated at Watford and all passengers are told to disembark is not delivering London-bound passengers to the right location at the right time. Hence this section of the value chain removes value for the customer on this particular occasion. For retail organisations outbound logistics may be concerned with location, opening hours, and as mentioned earlier, queuing systems. The supermarkets, which now open 24 hours a day, are seeking to improve their outbound logistics.

Marketing and sales

Marketing and sales is about the promotion and advertising of goods and services to customers.

Marketing and sales is about the promotion and advertising being closely tied into well-defined market segments and having a well-trained and knowledgeable salesforce. This applies equally to products and services, and is about informing and attracting customers.

Decisions have to be made concerning the advertising media to be used: press, magazines, television, radio or Internet. Alongside the advertising decisions, the promotional activity for a product has to be decided. A combination of advertising and promotional activities is required to create and support a successful product. The combination of activities needs to create an awareness and interest in the product and acceptance of it by the marketplace. The promotional activities that can be used are varied. In supermarkets with loyalty cards, the offer of extra bonus points on certain products or goods entices customers to switch loyalty from one brand to another or to buy products not normally on their shopping list. Magazines are frequently used to offer free samples of cosmetics, CDs or even books to their readership, in the hope of capturing new and potentially loyal customers. The launch of new products can be heralded by the delivery to target households of free samples, discount vouchers or promotional literature. The sponsorship of television programmes is a relatively new activity in the UK, following the deregulation of broadcast advertising, and is an effective promotional method. Thus Cadbury, 'the nation's favourite' chocolate manufacturer, sponsors *Coronation Street*, a popular soap operas on television in the United Kingdom, and uses the sponsorship opportunity at the start and end of each programme to promote Cadbury products, for example Creme eggs at Easter.

The importance of an organisation's advertising and promotion activities is clear if a product is a leading brand and the organisation seeks to maintain that position. The importance of good advertising and promotion is heightened if a competing brand advertises heavily and is easily substituted. Also the advertising and promotion surrounding a product will remind consumers

89

making frequent repeat purchases to purchase the same brand of product as before, which is crucial if customer loyalty to a brand is low. A product's added value or low cost, which will be important to particular groups of customers, can be emphasised by the use of advertising and promotion.

Service

Service in the value chain is concerned with additional services which support the goods and services sold to customers.

In a manufacturing or retail organisation service is concerned with additional **services** which support the goods sold to customers. These take the form of installation, maintenance, repair or service contracts and can be for many types of good, including industrial machinery and equipment, IT systems, cars, photocopiers, and domestic appliances such as washing machines and televisions. The value the service offers the customer will depend on the cost of the service to the customer and the speed with which any maintenance, repair or service can be performed. It should be noted that, depending on the situation, service may be included in the original cost of the good or as is often the case there maybe an additional charge for maintenance, repair or a service contract. In a service industry clearly the overall objective is about delivering good service to customers. However the service section of the value chain is concerned with additional services which the organisation may choose to offer customers. For the airline it is about additional services such as assistance for disabled passengers and special airline meals. In 2003 Ryanair was charging some passengers in need of a wheelchair an additional £18, but argued that as Ryanair flights were very cheap, charging for this type of additional service was acceptable. In February 2004 the courts awarded one such passenger, Bob Ross, £1,336. Airlines which serve meals on their flights usually cater for special dietary requirements with meals which are, for example, kosher, vegetarian, vegan, gluten free, low fat, and suitable for children, nut allergy suffers and those following the Atkins Diet. An airline which requires a customer needing a special meal to order it when the ticket is booked adds less value to its value chain than a more flexible airline which will accept orders for special meals up to 24 hours before the flight departs.

Review questions **The value chain and its primary activities**

1 Discuss the purpose of a value chain.
2 Explain the inbound and outbound logistics of a service organisation.
3 Define 'operations' in the value chain.
4 Explain the 'service' activities in the value chain of a service organisation.

SUPPORT ACTIVITIES

Procurement

Procurement is the process for acquiring and purchasing goods and materials of appropriate quality for all areas of the business. For example, procurement can be involved in both the acquiring of machines and equipment for use in an organisation's operations and in negotiating a promotion or sponsorship deal for the organisation.

For airlines procurement also covers the purchase of new aircraft. During 2001 and 2002 easyJet was involved in year-long negotiations with competing aircraft manufacturers Boeing and Airbus to procure new aircraft. During this process the broadly similar Boeing 737 and Airbus A319 aircraft, and their operating performance, were both examined in minute detail. This allowed easyJet to reach the conclusion that if the price was right, the airline could successfully make the switch to Airbus and in so doing achieve a 10 per cent reduction in operating costs. Hence in October 2002 easyJet announced that Airbus was to be appointed as its preferred aircraft supplier. The deal was large: 120 Airbus A319 planes for delivery from September 2003 over five years, with price protection on a further 120 Airbus A319 planes until 2012. Details of the deal easyJet have done with Airbus have not been made public, but easyJet appears to have negotiated a sizeable reduction on the list price of £4 billion ($6.2 billion) for the Airbus planes. In addition it seems that Airbus were willing to support the cost of integrating the Airbus planes into the easyJet fleet. easyJet aim for its Airbus and Boeing planes eventually to be interchangeable on all easyJet routes. Up to October 2002 easyJet had always flown Boeing 737s and held the view that flying one type of aircraft gave it efficiency and low costs in terms of operating the planes, staff training and maintenance.[8&9]

Equally procurement at easyJet will cover the negotiations with LWT (London Weekend Television) for the 'fly on the wall' programme *Airline*, which has seen the making of seven series of the *Airline* programme since 1998.[10] The TV programme provides easyJet with wide television coverage which is different in type and amount of coverage to that which would be gained from advertising on television.

Technology development

This area of the value chain considers technology in the broadest possible sense: that is, all activities in the value chain have a technology or 'know-how'. The

technology development may be concerned with research and development for new products or new resources, such as improved raw materials or components, or it may be the use of IT to improve delivery of a product or service to the customer. Equally a company can use technology to assist in the management of resources and staff (see Business illustration on B&Q). Additionally pharmaceutical companies such as Wellcome and GlaxoSmithKline Beecham will invest heavily in research and development in the hope of discovering new drugs which can be used to treated or cure common diseases and chronic conditions, such as diabetes and Alzheimer's disease. This type of use of technology will potentially add value to the products offered to doctors and patients and will be part of a competitive strategy of differentiation. Equally many service organisations such as retail chains, airlines and banks have used technology to manage stock more efficiently and allow easier customer access to the services, be it banking online or booking a flight or holiday online. In the case of banks and airlines, the use of technology has reduced staffing costs and increased convenience for many customers by providing 24-hour access to an organisation's services. This is often part of a cost-based competitive strategy.

Business illustration of streamlining HR in the value chain - B&Q

In 1999 B&Q started conducting first interviews for vacancies at its shops over the telephone by an automated system. Successful candidates are shortlisted, with information on ethnicity, gender and age removed, before selection for final interview which is conducted by a B&Q store manager. B&Q identifies several advantages to this system, the process of dealing with 200,000 applications for 15,000 jobs is streamlined and bias is completely removed from the initial stages of the recruitment process. Additionally staff turnover has fallen from 35 per cent to 29 per cent since the introduction of the automated selection process in 1999.

Source: 'The right personalities in store', S Overell, *Financial Times* 5 December 2002.

Human resource management

HRM is concerned with recruiting, managing, training, developing and rewarding staff to help the organisation achieve competitive advantage.

The area of **HRM** is important in the value chain as it applies to all of the primary activities and also applies equally to manufacturing and service organisations. A manufacturing organisation will look for team leaders who can organise staff and are good at producing quality products, while a service organisation may look for team leaders who can supervise other staff, be customer focused, and handle difficult customers politely and well. HRM is concerned with recruiting, managing, training, developing and rewarding staff in order to help the organisation achieve competitive advantage. The way in which these HRM activities are performed will also help determine the type of structure the organisation adopts. Staff who are recruited to work on their own initiative and in teams will mean a flexible and decentralised structure, such as the divisional or matrix structure, will prevail. In contrast, if most of the staff are recruited to very specific roles in the organisation then a more rigid structure, such as the functional structure, will be more likely. The recruitment of staff is underpinned by their management, training, development and reward – which can all impact on motivation and staff turnover.

Infrastructure

Infrastructure includes structure, culture and systems, which are likely to reflect what it is important for the organisation to control and manage.

The **infrastructure** of an organisation includes the structure, culture and systems. An organisation operating in a turbulent environment will require a flexible structure (for example, divisional or matrix) if it is to develop a value chain which is nimble enough to continually provide a strategic match between the organisation and its environment. Equally an organisation in a static and stable environment will be able to develop successfully with a more rigid structure (simple or functional). The type of culture an organisation adopts can be viewed as linked to the structure, with flexible organisations having a culture which tends towards Handy's task culture and the less flexible organisation being likely to have a power or role culture. Finally in terms of systems these will be likely to reflect what it is important for the organisation to control and manage for the achievement of competitive advantage (see Chapter 5). Examples of such systems include: financial systems for budgeting and costing, stock control systems, queuing systems for both customers and their phone calls, quality systems, and information management systems.

Review questions | **The value chain and its support activities**

1 Explain the difference between 'inbound logistics' and 'procurement'.

2 Summarise activities which technology development encompasses.

3 Why is HRM an important part of the value chain for an organisation pursuing a low-cost competitive strategy?

4 Contrast the infrastructures adopted by companies operating in stable and in turbulent environments.

✔ Check your understanding

- Do you understand the difference between primary and support activities in the value chain?

- Check your understanding by matching the following action by a company to the correct value chain activity.

  1 Renault carry out a market research survey for a new car.

  2 MFI deliver a new sofa to a customer's house.

  3 McDonalds negotiate a better deal with a new supplier of bread products.

  4 A small erector of garden sheds and garages starts to inspect all parts and components when they arrive from the supplier.

  5 GAP specify the working conditions in a factory in Vietnam.

  6 Nike use a computer-based design system for its sports shoes.

  7 Toyota manufactures cars.

  8 A mail order company switches from using the Royal Mail to using a courier company.

  9 Marks & Spencer restructure and cut 500 head office jobs.

LINKAGES IN THE VALUE CHAIN AND VALUE SYSTEM

Linkages represent the interrelationships and interdependencies between value chain activities and are sources of competitive advantage.

The interrelationships and interdependencies between value chain activities are sources of competitive advantage and are represented by **linkages**. The use of IT to deliver training by B&Q is an example of such a linkage between the value chain activities of IT and HRM. B&Q uses DVD-Roms and Docent (a US-based e-learning specialist) to deliver a computer-based learning programme for its 28,000 staff. The aim is to add value for the customer by having staff on the shop floor who are able to assist customers and by keeping costs low[11]. This type of linkage between different parts of an organisation's value chain is termed an **internal dependency** by Emery and Trist[12] and can be a way for the organisation to add value and/or reduce costs for the customer (see **Exhibit 3.6**).

Internal dependencies are the linkages between different parts of an organisation's value chain.

Exhibit 3.6 Environmental linkages

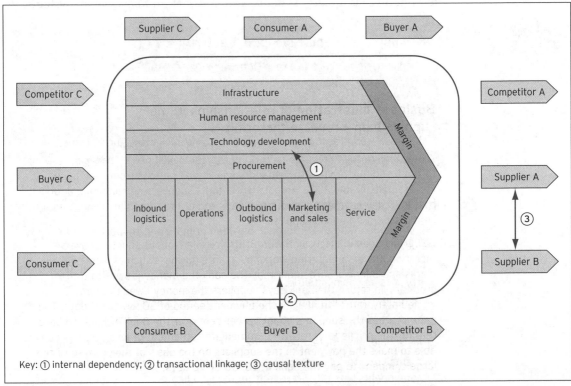

Key: ① internal dependency; ② transactional linkage; ③ causal texture

Source: based on Emery, F E and Trist, E L (1965) 'The causal texture of organisational environments', *Human Relations*, 18, pp 21-32.

The **value system** is a set of inter-organisational links between the value chains of an organisation and its suppliers, distributors and customers.

The **value system** (see **Exhibit 3.7**) is a set of inter-organisational links between the value chains of an organisation and its suppliers, distributors and customers. The decisions for any organisation in developing **transactional linkages** in its value system concern the initial decision to outsource a particular activity, for example the distribution or to purchase from a particular

Transactional linkages are between an organisation and another organisation, such as a supplier, distributor or customer.

supplier. Secondly there is the informed choice of company with which to link up; and finally to decide what form that relationship should take, for example a contract to buy or sell from each other, a joint venture or an acquisition.

Exhibit 3.7 The value system

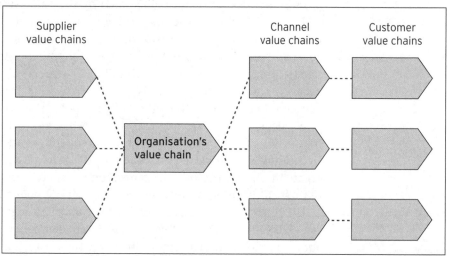

Source: Porter, M E (1985) *Competitive Advantage*, Free Press. Used with permission of The Free Press, a division of Macmillan Inc. Copyright 1985 Michael E Porter.

Business illustration of relationships in the supply chain – reverse factoring

A mechanism called reverse factoring has been developed by banks in response to the trend for retailers to demand longer credit periods from their suppliers. For example in July 2006 Arcadia wrote to its suppliers demanding a doubling of the 30 day payment period to 60 days and at the same time requested a 1 per cent discount on goods supplied.

HSBC has been in discussion with British retailers about adopting reverse factoring. Reverse factoring works by a large business such as New Look or Marks and Spencer agreeing to pay the bank the money it owes to trade creditors. In return the bank pays suppliers the money owed to them immediately, rather than after the payment period of 30, 60 or 90 days. The bank charges the suppliers about 1.5 per cent over the Bank of England base rate for the privilege of receiving immediate settlement of invoices. The bank is able to make the payment to the suppliers on the basis of the promise of the large company to pay the bank in 30, 60 or 90 days.

Clearly reverse factoring means suppliers were paid early, but it does not address the problem that suppliers still ended up paying for early settlement of the invoices they have issued for the supply of goods. The Forum of Private Business, a trade group is lobbying the European Commission to introduce a standard 30-day payment period throughout Europe via the late payment directive. However, large companies could still extend payment terms but would have to pay their suppliers for the privilege.

Source: 'Suppliers offered a fast track to their cash', R Tyler, *Daily Telegraph* 15 August 2006.

It is unusual for an organisation to undertake all activities from design through to delivery to the final customer itself; it is more usual for other organisations such as suppliers, distributors and even the final customers themselves to be involved. The relationships between an organisation and its suppliers, distributors and customers can be illustrated by the value system (see Exhibit 3.7), with value for the end user in part being created by these other players in the value system. Emery and Trist term this type of linkage between one organisation and another organisation, such as a supplier, distributor or customer, a transactional linkage (see Exhibit 3.6). There is normally a relationship between the two organisations which involves a transaction taking place between them, such as the selling of parts or finished goods and such transactional dependencies are managed by negotiation with the other parties. The transactions can be simple or complex, frequent or rare, consistent or one-off. Depending on the kind of transaction, the level of dependence between the organisation and the other organisation in its environment may change (see Business illustration on reverse factoring, on the previous page).

Causal textures are interdependencies outside the organisation in the external environment.

The third type of linkage which Emery and Trist identify is **causal textures** (see Exhibit 3.6). Causal textures are interdependencies outside the organisation in the external environment, which can have an effect on the organisation. The causal texture in which an organisation operates is called that because there is a cause-and-effect relationship between what elements of the external environment do and how this affects third-party organisations (see Business illustration on Clan Douglas). The simplest example of causal

---

Business illustration of causal texture – Clan Douglas

Clan Douglas is a manufacturer of luxury cashmere sweaters based in the Borders area of Scotland, whose biggest market is the USA. In March 1999 the US government began a 'banana row' with the EU, with Britain being the most affected European country. The row centred around Britain's favouring of bananas produced by small farmers on Caribbean islands that are former British colonies, as opposed to bananas produced by US companies on plantations in South America. The USA viewed this as unfair trade and therefore imposed a 100 per cent import tax on certain luxury goods imported by US companies from Britain and Europe. These goods included cashmere sweaters, which sell for $350, and fountain pens made by Mont Blanc and Watermans, which retail at $300. The doubling of the price of these goods to over $600 would effectively kill the US retail market and hence put affected manufacturers out of business. Hence a company like Clan Douglas in the Borders would be severely affected by such outside linkages or causal texture. Such companies have absolutely no influence over the banana war, nor could they have been reasonably expected to have anticipated the disagreement.

Sources: *BBC Breakfast News*, 2 March 1999, and 'NY trade in luxuries becomes a victim', A Edgecliffe-Johnson, *Financial Times* 6/7 December 1999.

texture would be two suppliers agreeing to fix prices (this is illegal) to the detriment of retail buyers. This causes the cost of supplies to go up for buyers, who in turn increase prices charged to members of the public, which results in lower sales and reduced profits. This type of linkage or causal texture is difficult for organisations to uncover and manage effectively, so responses to such linkages may be slow and apprehensive and hence contribute to an organisation's doubt and uncertainty in managing the external environment.

✔ Check your understanding

- Do you understand the three types of linkages which can impact on an organisation?
- Check your understanding by giving one example of your own for each type of linkage.

Review questions | **Linkages**

1 Discuss the concept of the value system.
2 Explain the difference between an internal dependency and a transactional linkage.
3 What type of linkage is there between a small business and its venture capitalist?
4 Why are causal textures a threat to companies?

CONCLUSION

There are a variety of different issues to consider when seeking to manage resources such that competitive advantage is achieved. A straightforward resource audit will provide an overview of the resources which the organisation has access to and their 'condition'. This, along with a understanding of the organisation's strategy (see Chapter 1), should provide an indication of whether or not a gap exists between the resources an organisation has and those it needs to successfully implement its strategy.

An understanding of core competencies adds to strategy as it enables an organisation to understand what it should be seeking to do well if it is to achieve and maintain competitive advantage. The application of the value chain to an organisation's activities provides a picture of where resources are effectively used and core competencies pursued to achieve successful outcomes.

LEARNING OUTCOMES AND SUMMARY

The learning outcomes for this chapter are specified and a brief summary of the material relating to the learning outcomes is provided.

→ **Learning outcome 1**
Identify and evaluate the resources present in an organisation.

- Organisations have a variety of different types of employees: core employees who hold highly skilled jobs; first peripheral employees who hold vocational jobs; second peripheral employees who hold part-time and short-term contracts; external staff who are subcontractors and temporary staff.

- Managing human resources requires attention to the key areas of succession planning, human resources, management development, performance management, and reward management.

- Tangible resources include buildings, factories and IT systems, and managing these resources requires the consideration of a number of issues namely flexibility, balance and fit. Flexibility refers to the effectiveness with which resources can be redeployed given a developing environment and strategy. The balance of resources is concerned with resource excess, efficiency and inefficiency. The resources and strategy should fit each other, that is the resources and their configuration should support effective competitive and market strategy.

- Intangible resources include goodwill, image, reputation and human capital and organisations need to develop and maintain the intangible resources which are key to their competitive advantage.

→ **Learning outcome 2**
Discuss core competencies and their importance in helping an organisation to achieve competitive advantage.

- Development of core competencies allows an organisation to achieve its key success factors. Organisations should seek to develop competencies that provide competitive advantage and utilise those competencies to meet customer requirements.

→ **Learning outcome 3**
Evaluate and determine the most appropriate way for an organisation to configure its resources given that competitive advantage may be cost or differentiation based.

- The value chain is a framework for thinking about resources and systems, which currently provide competitive advantage and which could provide competitive advantage for an organisation. Gaining, maintaining or improving competitive advantage requires a firm's resources and systems to be arranged to reduce the costs overall or add most value for least cost.

- The primary activities in the value chain are directly concerned with the manufacture of a product or creation of a service. The primary activities are inbound logistics, operations, outbound logistics, sales and marketing, and service.

- The support activities help improve the efficiency and effectiveness of the primary activities. The support activities are procurement, technology development, human resource management, and infrastructure.

→ **Learning outcome 4**
Explain the impact of linkages on a company and its competitive position.

■ A linkage between different parts of an organisation's value chain is an internal dependency. A linkage between an organisation and an external stakeholder such as a supplier or customer is a transactional linkage. Causal texture is a linkage between two third parties, which does have an effect on an organisation. Linkages can improve an organisation's competitive advantage or may have a negative impact, as is often the case with causal texture.

This exit case study looks at Eurostar and the transformation it is seeking to make by using its resources to improve its operations and can be used to assess the learning outcomes below.

Learning outcomes	Check you have achieved this by	
1. Evaluate the operations of a company by using appropriate theory and models.	Using the value chain to assess an organisation's operations.	Answering exit case study question 1.
2. Recommend changes needed to transform an organisation.	Describing the changes a company could make to improve its position.	Answering exit case study question 2.

Eurostar seeks a speedy transformation

FT

by Robert Wright

Passengers leaving London by Eurostar this week will start with a familiar experience. The 18-coach trains will leave London on congested commuter lines, as they have done since mainland Britain's only international train service started nine years ago. The maximum speeds will be barely half those of which the train is capable. Yet then, after 36km, the train will speed up.

For the first time in the UK, the train will travel much of the last 74km stretch to the Channel tunnel at 300kph, the train's maximum velocity on high-speed lines in continental Europe. The improved performance follows the completion of the first stage of the new, high-speed Channel tunnel rail link, which opened to passengers yesterday. Opening of the line should make Eurostar's services more reliable and cut an average of 20 minutes off journey times between London and Eurostar's continental European destinations.

However, the link is only part of a comprehensive effort to restructure operations and relaunch the Eurostar service. Traffic, which has been declining since 2000, has never come close to pre-opening forecasts for the service, which mainly runs to Paris and Brussels via the Channel tunnel, as well as serving some tourist destinations. Alongside the reduced journey times, the relaunch effort will feature improved conditions for passengers, such as reduced check-in times and better mobile phone reception. Eventually, Eurostar also hopes to introduce services to a wider range of continental European destinations.

For Eurostar managers, however, it is almost as important to simplify decision-making. Until now, even minor problems have been hard to solve because Eurostar's French, British and Belgian operating companies all had to agree any change. 'The business has not been able to work as effectively as it should in a more dynamic transport sector,' says Paul Charles, director of communications for Eurostar Group. 'The world has changed and Eurostar in the last few years has been slightly hamstrung by the very structure that was set up to make it a success.'

Many of the problems stem from the complex arrangements set up when Eurostar was first planned. The French and Belgian operating companies are owned by the state-owned national railways - SNCF in France and SNCB in Belgium. The British operating company is

→

owned by London & Continental Railways, the private company that has built the Channel tunnel rail link. It is run under contract by Inter-Capital and Inter-Regional Railways, whose largest shareholder is National Express, the bus and rail operator. Each of the three operators has traditionally had a high degree of autonomy. Decision-making, meanwhile, has been made harder by complex revenue and cost-sharing arrangements. According to Rob Holden, chief executive of London & Continental Railways, the agreements gave SNCF incentives to aim for high yield per passenger but not necessarily high volumes. The British company was better rewarded if it achieved high volume – but not necessarily high yield. 'Frankly, the railways have not worked together as efficiently as they might have done in order to provide the best possible Eurostar service from a business and commercial perspective,' Mr Holden says. 'There's an unbelievable tension created between the French and British, which has necessarily meant that compromises have had to be made on both sides in bringing the business together.'

The proposed solution is Project Jupiter, which would put all Eurostar operations under one company with centralised management and decision-making. Although negotiations on the exact terms are continuing, it is intended to be owned 55 per cent by SNCF, 40 per cent by LCR and 5 per cent by SNCB. The management arrangement with ICCR for the UK operation would end. It is hoped the new company will come into existence early next year. Even before Project Jupiter comes fully into operation, Eurostar is already seeking to behave more like one operation. Under Richard Brown, chief executive since August last year, managers of Eurostar UK have been running aspects of operations at Eurostar Group, an umbrella company set up in 1999. The most pressing issue they face is declining traffic. Passenger numbers – which under pre-opening predictions would have been 17m this year – peaked at 7.66m in 2000, when revenue was £429m. The service carried only 7.1m passengers last year and earned revenues of only £412m. Figures for the first half of this year showed a continued decline.

The company has never issued profit and loss figures but the operation is thought to be heavily loss making with its current numbers of passengers. Nick Mercer, commercial director for both the UK and group operations, says the group is working on a three-year plan to improve market share. Although Eurostar currently has about 64 per cent of the London–Paris air and rail market and 46 per cent of London–Brussels, the service still has plenty more room to grow if it is to emulate the success of Thalys, a French-Belgian-Dutch high-speed operator, which has almost eliminated airline competition between Paris and Brussels.

One of Eurostar's main goals is to have the company in a better financial position by 2007, when the second stage of the Channel tunnel rail link – from Ebbsfleet in Kent to London St Pancras – is due to open. The link will reduce journey times by another 15 minutes. Journeys will then be fast enough for Eurostar to consider new routes, including London-Amsterdam. It is also examining ways it could serve big European airports, since Eurostar trains from Amsterdam's Schiphol or Paris's Charles de Gaulle airports should then be able to take passengers to central London more quickly than a connecting air flight. 'We know where we want to be in 2007,' Mr Mercer says. 'You will see in the course of those three years a series of planned actions that will both improve the passenger experience significantly and improve our market share.'

One of the first changes could be to Eurostar's inflexible price structure. Although Eurostar has successfully promoted £59 returns to Paris and Brussels over the summer, the cheap tickets have no flexibility and open, standard-class returns still cost £298, which is expensive compared with low-cost airlines. Meanwhile, Mr Mercer also plans improvements suggested by market research. Mobile phone reception will be improved along the high-speed line and there will be on-board internet access and in-seat catering for passengers who request it in standard class. At present, only first-class passengers have this. Check-in times are also set to be cut as the service moves away from modelling itself on airline practice. 'Two messages come to us clearly [from market research],' Mr Mercer says. 'One is "Just make this really simple for us". The other is "Do this with a bit of style".'

Given Eurostar's history of unforeseen problems, however, many observers will be sceptical about the rail group's chances of pulling off such a transformation. As well as suffering disappointing passenger numbers, Eurostar had its inaugural train break down at London Waterloo in 1994, endured a two-day service suspension last year after a storm blew sea salt on to tracks and overhead wires near Calais, and has been hit by French and Belgian public-sector strikes. Nevertheless, Eurostar's management insists that, with its new, shorter journey times, it can not only overcome its past problems but also start to do what was originally planned for the Channel tunnel.

The 1986 Franco-British treaty agreeing on the project expresses hope that the tunnel and train services through it will so transform cross-Channel travel that Britain's relationship with continental Europe becomes closer. 'This is a business that recognises its failures in the past,' says Paul Charles, the communications director. 'It's under no illusion whatsoever about the amount of work it has to do. But, if all goes well during the following year, it has a rosy future.'

Source: *Financial Times*, 29 September 2003.

Exit case study questions

1 Indicate and explain which areas of Eurostar's value chain add value and which remove value for the customer.

2 Identify and discuss the three main areas of Eurostar's value chain, which need attention if the 'speedy transformation' is to be achieved.

DISCUSSION TOPIC

1 Read the paper 'From competitive advantage to corporate strategy' by Michael Porter published in the *Harvard Business Review*, May–June, 1987.

2 Consider the following quote from the paper and critically evaluate the use of the value chain in helping the diversified business develop a corporate strategy.

'Corporate strategy concerns two different questions: what business the corporation should be in and how the corporate office should manage the array of business units.'

WIDEN YOUR HORIZONS

1 Widen your horizons by selecting ten different job adverts from a variety of sources and decide if the jobs you have identified are core, first peripheral, second peripheral or external.

2 Widen your horizons by visiting the website for the Ritz Hotel in Paris, www.ritzparis.com, and drawing up a value chain for the Ritz Hotel.

WEBLINKS

The websites for this chapter provide some further information on the exit case study Eurostar and an illustration of how organisations may use core competencies to define their staff and the training that they provide.

■ The official website for Eurostar.
www.eurostar.com

■ The CIPD website outlines the ten core competencies that underpin its professional standards.
www.cipd.co.uk/mandq/standards/corecomp.htm

FURTHER READING

Resources

- Bennis, W and O'Toole, J (2000) 'Don't hire the wrong CEO,' *Harvard Business Review*, May/June.
- Cook, S (2004) 'So that's your aptitude', *Management* Today, April, pp 50-3.
- Hall, R (2000) 'The management of external resources', *Journal of General Management*, 26 (1), Autumn.
- Hansen, M T (1999) 'What's your strategy for managing knowledge', *Harvard Business Review*, March/April.
- Miller, R (2001) 'Managing intranet content', *Knowledge Management Review*, May/June.
- Myerson, J (2003) 'Workspace heaven', *Management Today*, June, pp 53-61.
- Reeves, R (2004) 'Symptom of insecurity', *Management Today*, July, pp 29.
- Rivette, K G and Kline, D (2000) 'Discovering new value in intellectual property', *Harvard Business Review*, January/February.
- Wenger, E C and Snyder, W M (2000) 'Communities of practice', *Harvard Business Review*, January/February.

Core competencies

- Hamel, G and Prahalad, C K (1989) 'Strategic intent', *Harvard Business Review*, May–June, in Mintzberg, H, Lampel, J, Quinn, J B and Ghoshal, S (2003) *The Strategy Process*, Harlow: Pearson Education.
- Prahalad, C K and Ramaswamy, V (2000) 'Co-opting customer competence', *Harvard Business Review*, January/February.

Value chain and system

- Fill, C and Visser, E (2000) 'The outsourcing dilemma: a competitive approach to the make or buy decision,' *Management Decision*, 38 (1), pp 43-50.
- Garrett, A (2003) 'Assessing a rookie supplier', *Management Today*, July, pp 76.
- Rooney, B (2002) 'How to negotiate', *Management Today*, June.
- Sawhnwy, M and Parikh, D (2001) 'Where value lives in a networked world', *Harvard Business Review*, January.

REFERENCES

1   Stewart, T A (1997), *Intellectual Capital: The New Wealth of Organizations*, New York: Doubleday, in Dess, G, Lumpkin, G T and Taylor, M L (2004) *Strategic Management*, New York: McGraw Hill.
2   Thompson, J L and Richardson, B (1996) 'Strategic and competitive success: towards a model of the comprehensively competent organisation', *Management Decision*, 34 (2), pp 5-19.
3   Ibid.
4   Prahalad, C K and Hamel, G (1990) 'The core competence of the corporation', *Harvard Business Review*, May/June.
5   Ibid.
6   Ibid.

7   Porter, M E (1985), *Competitive Advantage: Creating and Sustaining Superior Performance*, New York: The Free Press.

8   www.easyjet.com

9   www.bbc.co.uk

10 www.easyjet.com

11 Pritchard, S (2003) 'B&Q: DIY programme suits DIY staff', *Financial Times*, 2 April.

12 Emery, F E and Trist, EL (1965) 'The causal texture of organisational environments', *Human Relations*, 18, pp 21-32.

CHAPTER 4

Analysing financial resources

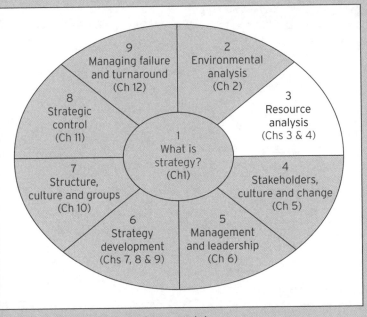

Exhibit 4.1 Essential strategy model

Chapter objectives

When you have read this chapter and worked through the associated activities you should be able to achieve the objectives specified below.

1 Determine the main source of finance for a company.

2 Explain the processes for listing on the London Stock Exchange.

3 Explain how loans and debentures work.

4 Define and explain the performance ratios which can be used in evaluating a company's success.

5 Define and explain the financial status ratios which can be used in evaluating a company's success.

6 Define and explain the stock market ratios which can be used in evaluating a company's success.

Companies need to be able to raise funds to expand their operations and this entry case study looks at why Speedel has chosen to undertake an initial public offering (IPO) to raise funds for its development.

Speedel plans IPO to finance further trials

by Simonian Haig

Speedel, the Swiss drugs group backed by Novartis' venture capital fund, yesterday added its name to the list of European biotech groups planning an initial public offering. The company said it hoped to complete its IPO by the end of next month. More details are expected in the next two to three weeks, but the company has already appointed UBS and Merrill Lynch as lead managers.

Speedel differs from some recent biotech launches in having an unusually strong potential pipeline, along with a possible blockbuster drug. Some analysts believe Aliskiren, a hypertension treatment currently under phase three clinical trials, could open the door to a new form of treatment for this common ailment. The compound, of significant interest to Novartis, is seen as a potential successor to the Swiss pharmaceutical group's blockbuster Diovan treatment for high blood pressure. Diovan is expected to lose patent protection around 2012, giving Aliskiren, which could come on the market as early as 2007, sufficient time to develop momentum as a successor.

However, Speedel's main motive for seeking additional funds now is to finance costly further trials for another new product, aimed at treating diabetic kidney disease. 'Our timing is predetermined by the fact that we have reached a size that requires access to the public markets,' said Dr Alice Huxley, chief executive. Dr Huxley, who formerly worked for Novartis, founded Speedel and has, with venture capitalists and private investors, ensured its funding over the past six years.

Speedel declined to comment on the amount it planned to raise, or possible pricing. However, the company said it was looking for 'several hundred million' Swiss francs to finance its plans for the next three to four years. After that period, growth could be bank-rolled by royalties from Novartis for Aliskiren. Analysts said the IPO was likely to be significantly bigger than the SFr97m–SFr118m ($81.3m–$99m) currently being sought by Arpida, another Swiss biotech group going public.

Source: *Financial Times*, 28 April 2005.

INTRODUCTION

Financial resources or money is important for all organisations, whether public, private or charitable, as it is money which allows organisations to obtain the resources required to meet their aims and objectives. The level of funding an organisation has and how well it manages that money will determine its level of success or failure in meeting its aims and objectives.

The financial aims of many companies will include efficient use of money, making profit and a good return for shareholders. This chapter looks at sources of finance for organisations, their advantages and disadvantages, and the evaluation of a company's financial position. An efficient financing strategy requires a company to be aware of different sources of finance and their pros and cons, hence enabling the required funds to be raised at the best or lowest possible cost. There are two broad categories of funding: internal finance and external finance. Basic evaluation of a company's financial position can be undertaken by ratio analysis.

SOURCES OF FINANCE

Internal finance

Internal finance is cash generated by a company which is not needed to meet operating costs, interest payments, tax liabilities, dividend payments or the replacement of fixed assets, and is known as retained earnings. The more efficient management of working capital can also improve retained earnings, that is improved management of short-term assets and liabilities to reduce costs. Improvements in the management of debtors, stock and cash in the business lead to reductions in overdraft and interest charges and increased cash reserves.

Companies may prefer internal finance in the form of retained earnings, as the decision on the level of dividend to pay out to shareholders, and hence the amount of retained earnings, is an internal decision. This type of internal decision does not require the backing or approval of a third party such as the bank or venture capitalist. The use of internal finance means the current owners do not face a reduction in their level of control of the business, as would occur if a venture capitalist or share issue were used to raise funds. Additionally retained earnings are a source of ready cash and there are no restrictions on how the cash may used in the business or associated costs. This is in contrast to both a new loan from a bank, which will be for a specified purpose and attract interest costs, and a share issue, which will incur associated costs. The use of reserves to fund expenditure also means that the level of scrutiny to which the organisation's management is subjected is less exacting than if funds were raised from external sources.

The level of retained earnings available will be determined by a company's cash flow and it will be possible for many companies to finance some capital investment from retained earnings. However, most companies need to consider external sources of finance for major projects or expansion. If cash flow from existing operations is high, a larger proportion of the finance for investment projects can be met internally. In contrast if the cash flows from current operations are low, a company will be more dependent on external financing. Therefore, the decisions concerning the relative proportions of internal and external finance to be used for a capital investment project will depend upon: the size of the project; the level of finance required; existing cash flows; and the balance between internal and external finance required by financial stakeholders.

External finance

Generally there is a wide range of external sources of finance available to businesses. External finance can be split into different types, namely equity (share) and debt finance, as well being classified as short term (less than one year), medium term (1 to 5 years), or long term (more than five years). Accessibility to the different types of finance depends on an individual organisation's situation. For example, a company which is not listed on the stock market cannot raise funds via a share issue and a company which has a high gearing (that is, it already has a high level of borrowing) will find it difficult to raise further funds via loans. Equally a company which consistently returns earnings to shareholders via dividends will have a lower level of retained earnings and will be more likely to seek external finance.

Share finance

Equity finance is money raised via the sale of ordinary shares in a company to investors.

Share finance, often known as **equity finance**, is money raised via the sale of ordinary shares in a company to individual or corporate investors. Companies raise money when shares are initially listed on the stock market and also when **rights issues** are undertaken. A rights issue is the raising of further finance by issuing more shares, which are offered for sale to existing shareholders.

Ordinary shares carry ownership rights entitling the holder of the shares to attend the Annual General Meetings and any Extraordinary General Meetings of the company. Shareholders are entitled to one vote per share owned on important decisions including: the appointment of directors of the company; the appointment, payment and removal of auditors; the use of shares as payment or part payment for an acquisition; and alterations to share capital. The ordinary shareholder also has the right to receive a copy of the company's annual report and accounts and a dividend if the company issues one. Dividends are a distribution of profits to the owners/shareholders of the company and can be raised or lowered as the company sees fit. Dividend payments are usually expressed in the form of so many pence per share owned. For example, if a company announces a dividend of 17.5p per share, a shareholder owning 200 shares would receive a payment of £35.

Most companies seek stability or a slight upward trend in their dividend payments with the aim of keeping shareholders satisfied. For example, when in March 2004, the American company PepsiCo announced a dividend of 92 cents per share, a shareholder owning 200 shares would receive a payment of $184.[1] However if performance is poor a company may reduce its dividend. Delta, the company which manufactures the chemicals used in Duracell batteries, experienced decreases in turnover and profits in 2002 and 2003. Therefore Delta decided to reduced its dividend for the year end January 2004 from 8 pence the previous year to just 3 pence. Therefore a shareholder with 200 shares in Delta would receive just £6.[2]

Shareholders are either individual members of the public investing relatively small sums of money (thousands of pounds) in shares or corporate investors with large amounts of money to invest (millions of pounds) for the company or their clients. For investors shares are a form of investment that is more risky than keeping money on deposit earning interest, but a better long-term return is likely. The increased risk for the ordinary shareholder arises from the possibility that the whole investment could be lost. If a company is

In the event of bankruptcy **secured creditors** have their claims settled first, e.g. debenture holders.

In the event of bankruptcy **unsecured creditors** such as suppliers have their claims settled second.

In the event of bankruptcy **preference shareholders** have their claims settled third and ordinary shareholders last.

liquidated or goes bankrupt there is a strict legal order of precedence governing the distribution of any remaining cash or cash raised from selling off assets. The first creditors to have their claims settled in full are the **secured creditors**, such as debenture holders and banks. Next the claims to be settled in full are those of **unsecured creditors** such as suppliers. The next call on any remaining cash is by **preference shareholders** and finally, should any cash remain, the **ordinary shareholders** are entitled to receive payment. In early 2005 the chain of department stores Allders went into liquidation and the secured creditors – including Barclays Bank, the property company Minerva and the investors group Epsilon – received 90 pence in the pound, while employees also received most of the pay and paid holidays owed to them.[3] The receivers for Allders had clearly managed to sell many of the company's assets, including eight Allders shops which were sold to Debenhams for £34 million.[4]

However, not surprisingly, it is often the case that when a company has gone into liquidation there is nothing remaining to pay the ordinary shareholders. Usually, if there is any cash left, it is distributed on the basis of pence per share, so each shareholder receives some payment proportional to the number of shares owned in the liquidated business. In contrast, it is possible for ordinary shareholders to make significant gains from liquidation due to their entitlement to all that remains once the claims of creditors and preference shareholders have been fully met.

The Rover car company based near Birmingham in the UK went into receivership in April 2005 and the receivers were unable to recover remaining cash or assets to pay the company's debts as many of the valuable assets had already been sold. The land on which the Rover car plant stood was owned by St Modwen Properties, the MG Rover spares company was owned by the US company Caterpillar, the rights to the engine series K, KV and L were owned by Shanghai Automotive, and the Rover badge was under licence to BMW. Hence the £200 to £300 million Rover owed to suppliers and trade creditors could not be paid and the following week's wage bill of £6.5 million for its 5,500 staff could not be met without a government loan, hence receivership was inevitable.[5&6]

The risk the ordinary shareholder takes is in part derived from their position at the bottom of the list of creditors to be paid in the event of ultimate failure of the company. Therefore ordinary shareholders carry a higher risk than any other providers of long-term finance, such as banks or preference shareholders, and hence expect to receive a higher return on their investment. It should be expected that dividend payments will be higher than interest payments or preference dividends, meaning that the cost of ordinary share capital is greater than the cost of debt or preference shares.

Rights issues

A **rights issue** is a company raising capital by issuing new shares to existing shareholders.

A company wishing to raise capital by issuing new shares is legally required by law to offer them first to existing shareholders; this is called a rights issue. It should be noted that a rights issue is not appropriate if the amount of finance to be raised is large as the funds available to individual shareholders are likely to be limited. In a rights issue ordinary shareholders are offered new shares in proportion to those they already own. For example, if a shareholder owns 500 shares in a company and the rights issue is a one for five offer, then the shareholder will be entitled to purchase one new share for every five already owned, tht is 100 new shares in total. In March 2004 the Danish brewer Carlsberg announced a rights issue of 15.2 million new shares in a one for four issue. Therefore a shareholder already owning 500 shares in Carlsberg would be entitled to buy another 125 shares for DKr 255 each.[7]

Rights issue shares are normally offered at price around 15 to 20 per cent below the stock market valuation, to make the investment appear attractive to the existing shareholders. The price of shares already being traded on the stock market prior to the rights issue will increase to reflect the value of the right to receive any new shares at a discount; this increased price is called the cum-rights price. After a number of weeks and just before the rights issue, the list of shareholders will close and buying a company's shares on the open stock market will no longer confer the opportunity to buy discounted shares via the rights issue. Hence the price quoted on the stock market will fall; this is called the ex-rights price.

If shareholders take up the rights issue by purchasing the shares, then the shareholder breakdown remains the same. If the existing shareholders do not buy the new shares and the rights issue is a failure, then the shares will eventually be sold on the open market by the underwriters and the shareholder profile of the company will be likely to change, offering the opportunity for a hostile takeover bid. A failed rights issue may point to the possibility that the company is not doing well. Therefore investors should examine closely a company's reasons for undertaking a rights issue. A company using the money raised by a rights issue to expand the business, with the aim of seeing profits, share price and dividends rise in the future, will clearly be a better investment than a company using the money to pay off old debts and avoid business failure.

Although rights issue shares are usually offered at a price equal to or below the stock market price to make the investment appear attractive to the shareholders, the pricing of a rights issue should be carefully considered. The insurance group Royal & Sun Alliance was seeking to bolster its reserves by about £800 million after asbestos claims in the United States. Royal & Sun Alliance's shares were trading at 154 pence when in September 2003 it announced a one for one rights issue, priced at 70 pence per share.

If the existing shareholders do not buy the new shares and the rights issue is a failure, then the shares are offered on the open market by the underwriters. The cost of underwriting a rights issue is usually from 1 to 2.5 per cent depending on the discount offered and the level of risk or likelihood that the rights issue will fail. In the example referred to above, Royal & Sun Alliance, which was not in a strong position, paid its underwriters (Merrill Lynch,

Goldman Sachs and Czenove) a huge 3.5 per cent. In October 2003 Royal & Sun Alliance declared the rights issue a success with a 92 per cent take-up rate and the company's share price had climbed back to 96 pence.[8&9]

Sources of finance

1 Describe the benefits of internal finance.

2 Summarise the rights of an ordinary shareholder.

3 Specify the order in which creditors are paid if a company goes bankrupt.

4 How does a rights issue differ from a share issue?

5 Briefly discuss the failure of a rights issue.

SHARES AND THE LONDON STOCK EXCHANGE

The London Stock Exchang (LSE) is where the ordinary shares of many large UK companies are brought and sold. Companies pay an annual fee to have their share price listed or quoted on the stock exchange. The LSE and its business are regulated by the Financial Services Authority (FSA), under the Financial Services and Markets Act 2000. In carrying out this regulatory role it is referred to as the UK Listings Authority (UKLA), and has responsibility for maintaining the lists of quoted companies/shares; admitting shares/companies to the lists; the regulation of **sponsors**, normally merchant banks; enforcing the legislation; suspending and cancelling listings when necessary. Therefore a company seeking to issue shares and have them listed on the London Stock Exchange (LSE) will need to appoint a sponsor and a **broker**, often both the same company. The sponsor, normally a merchant bank, will assemble the prospectus which will outline the company, its business and the shares being offered for sale; manage the listings process; and liase with the stock exchange. The role of the broker is to advise on an appropriate issue price for the new shares and to market the shares to potential investors.

A **sponsor** will assemble the prospectus outlining the company and the shares being offered for sale, and liaise with the stock exchange.

A **broker** will advise on the issue price for the new shares and market the shares to potential investors.

Not surprisingly the cost of obtaining a listing on the London Stock Exchange is substantial. The cost includes the sponsor's fee, the broker's fee, legal fees, accountants' fee – all likely to be a minimum of £100,000 each – while the admission fee to the London Stock Exchange will be between £5,000 and £250,000. There will also be ongoing fees to maintain the listing and an increase in the level of financial disclosure is required, for example the annual report and accounts will need to be made more widely available as there is a whole new group of stakeholders to keep informed and satisfied.

Listing on the London Stock Market

There are a number of new issue methods for a company to obtain a stock market listing. The two main methods of issuing ordinary shares in the UK are

A **placing** is when the broker approaches potential institutional investors to enable shares to be issued at a fixed price to the investors.

The **offer for sale** sees shares offered direct to the public with the help of the sponsor and the broker.

An **offer for sale by tender** is where the public is invited to bid for the available shares at a price above the minimum set by the issuing company.

An **initial public offering** is the offering and marketing of shares to investors for the first time.

The **intermediaries' offer** is stock exchange members applying for shares in an offer and selling or passing the shares to their clients.

An **introduction** is when a listing is granted to existing shares in a company, as it already has a wide ownership base.

a **placing** and an **offer for sale**. A placing is a low-cost method of issuing shares, as the broker approaches potential institutional investors before the share issue and the shares are issued at a fixed price to a number of institutional investors. The issuing company's sponsor underwrites the issue. The offer for sale, which is often made at a fixed price, is normally used by companies coming to the stock market for the first time and which therefore have a large number of shares to issue. The offer for sale method sees shares offered to the public with the help of the sponsor and the broker. The broker will help the company set an issue price for its shares which will be high enough to raise the required finance without issuing more shares than necessary, but at the same time being low enough to attract investors. The issue is normally underwritten by institutional investors, hence guaranteeing the issuing company its required finance, as the unsold shares are brought by the underwriters at an agreed price.

The obvious alternative to an offer for sale at fixed price is an **offer for sale by tender**. The public is invited to bid or tender for the available shares at a price above the minimum set by the issuing company. The price at which all the shares on offer will be sold is the striking price. The available shares are allocated on a pro rata basis to those investors who bid at or above the striking price, with all investors paying the striking price. Offer for sale by tender issues were common in the 1980s.

Other share issue methods include an **initial public offering** (IPO); an **intermediaries' offer**; and an **introduction**. An initial public offering is the offering and marketing of shares to investors for the first time. In April 2005 Lazard, the American investment bank, announced it was to end its 157-year partnership and seek a listing on the New York stock market by selling 30 million shares priced at between $25 and $27 each, which represented around a third of the company's shares. The remaining two-thirds of shares would remain with 'working members', including former partners in the business. The company launched what it called a 'roadshow' to attract investors and explain the business's potential as an investment opportunity.[10]

The intermediaries' offer sees stock exchange member firms act as intermediaries by applying for shares in an offer and subsequently selling or passing the shares to their clients. This method is quicker and cheaper than an offer for sale at fixed price as the broker, sponsor and accountants will not be needed, but the company's shares will be owned by a wide variety of investors.

An introduction is where a stock exchange listing is granted to the existing ordinary shares of a company with an already wide ownership base. An introduction does not involve selling any new shares; hence no new finance is raised. However an introduction can allow a company to obtain access to capital markets and increase the marketability of its shares.

In summary, there are a number of various ways to obtain a stock market listing and a company seeking a listing needs to select the method which best suits its requirements and budget.

London Stock Exchange regulations

The listings rules for the London Stock Exchange, commonly known as the purple book, and the Public Offer of Securities Regulations 1995 govern the issuing and listing of new shares. The regulations require that any company seeking a listing is required to publish a prospectus detailing information on company activities and performance, including a forecast of expected future performance and accounts for at least the previous three years. The prospectus should provide any potential investor with enough information to make an evaluation of the company and its likely success as an investment. The company must also have a minimum market capitalisation of £700,000 and a minimum of 25 per cent of the company's shares in public ownership when trading in the shares commences.

Underwriting

Underwriting is the form of insurance companies adopt against a share or rights issue failing. Companies seek to avoid having a share or rights issue fail as: it will fail to raise the finance it is seeking; unsold shares will be left with the underwriter; and it will make raising future finance by share or rights issue more expensive and difficult. Additionally during the time between the announcement of a new share or rights issue and its completion there is always the possibility of adverse share price movements, which may make the issue unattractive to investors and therefore a failure. The main underwriter for an issue is normally the merchant bank organising the share or rights issue, who will appoint a number of sub-underwriters, thereby further spreading the risk of the issue. In return for the underwriting fee, should the share or rights issue fail, the role of the underwriters is to take up the shares not initially sold on the market. Therefore via underwriting the company is certain of raising the required finance. However, a share or rights issue would still be regarded as unsuccessful if most of the shares were taken up by underwriters rather than by the market.

Advantages and disadvantages of listing on the stock market

There are a number of benefits that may be obtained by a company becoming listed on a stock market and any one of them may encourage the directors of a company to seek a listing. In broad terms the benefits of listing on the stock market are that finance is raised and it is easier to raise finance in the future, as rights issues can be considered and a listed company is more likely to attract institutional investors. Overall this makes it easier to raise money for growth and expansion of the business. Additionally it is usually easier for quoted companies to raise capital finance via long-term debt, as lenders tend to perceive quoted companies as more secure and therefore of lower risk, hence reducing the cost of debt for the quoted company.

In contrast unquoted companies can find it more difficult to raise finance and this can restrict the opportunities for growth. The finance 'gap' for unquoted companies is to an extent filled by venture capitalists. Venture capitalists normally provide capital funding in return for a stake in the company in which they are investing. After a number of years it is expected that the unquoted company will have achieved growth, partly by use of the funds provided by the venture capitalist. Hence it is at this point in the unquoted company's development it may choose to list on the stock market to raise further funds and/or provide the venture capitalists with an opportunity to realise their investment and hopefully take their profit.

However obtaining a stock market listing will not be the best option for all companies wishing to raise finance. The disadvantages of obtaining a stock market listing include the cost of listing; increased financial disclosure and scrutiny; and greater stakeholder expectations. The substantial cost of obtaining a listing is discussed earlier in this chapter.

There will be greater financial disclosure to comply with stock exchange regulations, which also incurs another cost. The greater financial disclosure results in greater public scrutiny of the company and its performance by, among others, the media, shareholders and customers. Equally any company which obtains a listing will find itself having to satisfy a powerful group of stakeholders, namely institutional shareholders. The expectations of institutional shareholders will be likely to include a focus on short-term profitability and dividend income. Failure to meet these expectations results in dissatisfied shareholders; their support for a hostile takeover bid would then be more likely.

LOANS, DEBENTURES AND LOAN STOCK

Loan finance

Long-term loans can be provided by banks, with the borrowing organisation gaining capital in return for repayment of the capital with interest over a number of years, for example five or ten. Loans are for a definite period and repayable with interest. The amount of interest payable depends on the interest rate charged, which is driven by the base rate of interest set by the Bank of England. The level of risk taken by the bank in lending money to the borrower will be influenced by the security offered against the loan and what the money is to be used for. All these will, in turn, also influence the interest rate charged on the loan. It is common for long-term loans to be secured against company assets. Securing the loan reduces the risk for the bank and thus the interest rate for a secured loan will be lower than for an unsecured loan.

The interest payments on loans come out of profit and cannot be reduced by the borrowing business if profits and trading conditions are unfavourable. This contrasts with **dividend payments**, which a company can alter depending on profits and trading conditions. A further characteristic of loans is that they do not carry ownership rights, which is in contrast to **ordinary shares** that do. If a company is unable to meet the loan and interest payments, then the bank or lender may decide to foreclose on the loan and appoint a **receiver** to take day-to-day control of the company. The receiver has to decide if the business is able to continue trading under its guidance and generate enough cash to pay the bank and other **creditors**, or whether the business should be closed, the assets sold off and the cash generated used to pay the bank and other creditors.

Debentures and loan stock

Debentures and loan stock are written acknowledgements of indebtedness.

Debentures and loan stock are written acknowledgements of indebtedness; a debenture is a bond that is secured against corporate assets, while loan stock refers to an unsecured bond. The debenture will be secured against the corporate assets by a fixed or floating charge. A fixed charge will be on specified assets and the assets, which are usually fixed assets, cannot be disposed of while the debt is outstanding. In contrast a floating charge will be on current assets and hence disposal of some assets is allowed. However, should the company default, for example on interest payments, the floating charge reverts to a fixed charge on specified assets, which prevents their disposal until the required payments are made.

Loan stock and debentures are both long-term bonds and debt securities and have a par value, which is usually £100 in the UK. The market price of the bonds is determined by how they trade in the bond markets. The interest rate or coupon, payable on debentures and loan stock is based on the par value. For example, a fixed interest 10 per debenture or loan stock will pay the holder £10 per year in interest (10% of the par value of £100). Like dividends, debenture or loan stock interest may be paid twice a year, with part of the interest paid half way through the financial year and the remainder at the year-end. The interest payable on debenture and loan stock is tax deductible; hence the overall cost to a company of servicing debt is lower than the interest rate. On a fixed interest 10 per cent debenture with corporation tax at 30 per cent, the cost of interest to the company is actually 7 per cent per year.

Review questions   ## Shares and the London Stock Exchange

1. Describe the roles of broker and sponsor for a company seeking a stock market listing.
2. Briefly compare and contrast a placing and an offer for sale.
3. Summarise the role of the underwriters in a share or rights issue.
4. Identify the advantages and disadvantages of listing on the stock exchange.
5. Explain how debentures operate.

EVALUATING FINANCIAL PERFORMANCE

An evaluation of a company's financial performance should indicate the level of profit created, the efficiency with which resources are used and managed, and for publicly quoted companies an indication of stock market success. This type of evaluation is most commonly undertaken by ratio analysis. The majority of the information required to undertake ratio analysis would appear in a company's balance sheet and profit & loss account. Other pieces of information, such as the company's share price, will need to be found from other sources such as the business press.

Ratios for any given financial year on their own are meaningless and therefore need to be looked at in conjunction with other information. Comparison with a previous year's ratios can indicate improvement or decline in performance. Comparison with a competitor can be a useful indicator of how far behind or ahead of a competitor a company is. However, the ratios for both companies need to be calculated in the same way, using financial statements which have been drawn up using similar accounting policies and procedures. Therefore ratio analysis can be used to identify areas which the company needs to scrutinise further and to pinpoint the areas in which the company holds competitive advantage or could develop further advantage. Finally, the outcome of a ratio analysis should be four or five key points for the company to address and keep under close review in the following 12 months.

The ratios presented in this chapter are a selection of some of the most common ratios and provide a framework within which to evaluate many aspects of a company's financial performance. The ratios are categorised into three main groups: **performance ratios**; **financial status ratios**; **stock market ratios** (see **Exhibit 4.2**). The worked examples in this Chapter refer to the financial statements for Global Books found in **Exhibit 4.3**.

Performance ratios evaluate profitability and efficiency.

Financial status ratios evaluate liquidity and solvency.

Stock market ratios evaluate the success on the stock market of ordinary shares.

Exhibit 4.2 Financial ratios

Performance ratios	Financial status ratios	Stock market ratios
■ Gross profit margin ■ Net profit margin ■ Return on capital employed ■ Return on shareholders' funds ■ Debtors collection period ■ Creditors collection period ■ Stock turnover ■ Fixed assets turnover	■ Current ratio ■ Acid test ratio ■ Gearing ■ Interest cover	■ Earnings per share ■ Price earnings ratio ■ Dividend yield

Exhibit 4.3 Accounts for Global Books 2005–06

Global Books plc Trading and profit and loss account for the year ended 31 March		
	2005	**2006**
Sales	5000	7000
less Cost of sales	3000	4500
Gross profit	2000	2500
less Expenses (including debenture interest and depreciation)	1500	1200
Net profit before tax	500	1300
less Corporation Tax	100	280
Net profit after Tax	400	1020
less Dividend (paid and proposed)	60	100
	340	920
Balance b/f	860 (2004)	1200 (2005)
	1200	2120

Global Books plc Balance sheet as at 31 March			
		2005	**2006**
Fixed assets			
Cost		1500	3250
less Depreciation		340	1020
WDV	(A)	1160	2230
Current assets			
Stock		600	500
Debtors		500	940
Bank		460	160
	(B)	1560	1600
less **Current liabilities**			
Trade creditors		270	405
Proposed dividend		50	70
	(C)	320	475
Net worth	(A) + (B) – (C)	2400	3355
Ordinary share capital (in £1 shares)		600	1000
Share premium account		–	280
Retained earning (P&L account balance)		1200	1775
	(D)	1800	3055
Long term debt			
12% debenture	(E)	600	300
Capital employed	(D) + (E)	2400	3355
Extra Information		**2005**	**2006**
Interest		£92(000)	£50(000)
Share price		£1.50	£1.75

PERFORMANCE RATIOS

Profitability ratios

The profitability ratios examine the return which is being gained by the business. The profitability ratios looked at in this chapter are **gross profit margin**, **net profit margin, return on capital employed** and return on shareholders' funds. The figures used refer to Global Books (see **Exhibit 4.3**).

Exhibit 4.4

$$\text{Gross profit margin (\%)} = \frac{\text{Gross profit}}{\text{Sales}} \times 100$$

Exhibit 4.5 Gross profit margin (%)

2005	2006
$\dfrac{£2000}{£5000} \times 100 = 40\%$	$\dfrac{£2500}{£7000} \times 100 = 35.7\%$

The **gross profit margin** indicates the profit made in relation to the sales the business has made.

The gross profit margin indicates the profit made in relation to the sales the business has made during a particular time period. It can be worked out using a basic formula (see **Exhibit 4.4**) and provides a useful comparator (see **Exhibit 4.5**). A small percentage increase or decrease in the gross profit margin will have a significant impact upon the profits if dealing with thousands of pounds worth of business. A fall in gross profit margin could be due to a reduction in the selling price of goods; an increase in the cost of materials; stock loss due to pilferage; poor storage; or obsolescence. In the case of Global Books this could mean the price of books being reduced as titles are sold as 'remainders', an increase in paper prices, staff stealing books, books being damaged due a flood in a warehouse or books becoming out of date as new editions are published. Equally tackling problems such as poor storage and pilferage or finding a more competitive printer could lead to an increase in the gross profit margin.

Exhibit 4.6

$$\text{Net profit margin (\%)} = \frac{\text{Net profit}}{\text{Sales}} \times 100$$

Exhibit 4.7 Net profit margin (%)

2005	2006
$\dfrac{£500}{£5000} \times 100 = 10\%$	$\dfrac{£1300}{£7000} \times 100 = 18.6\%$
i.e. £10 for every £100 of sales	i.e. £18.60 for every £100 of sales

The **net profit margin** indicates the profit made after the deduction of expenses.

The other commonly calculated profitability margin is the net profit margin (see **Exhibit 4.6**), which is affected by the level of overheads, expenses and depreciation. An increase in the net profit margin is due to a reduction in overheads, expenses and depreciation. Overhead expenditure may be reduced by moving to premises with lower rent and/or business rates; changes in depreciation policy; a reduction in bad debts and/or their provision; paying less interest on debentures; and/or a reduction in staff or overtime worked. Hence if Global Books were to move from an expensive warehouse in the south east of England to one based in the north of England it is likely that the cost of premises would be reduced. Equally if expenses such as overtime payments and distribution costs increase there will be a reduction in the net profit margin.

Exhibit 4.8 Return on capital employed (%)

$$\text{ROCE} = \frac{\text{Net profit before tax and interest}}{\text{Shareholders' funds + long term loans}} \times 100$$

Exhibit 4.9 Return on capital employed (%)

2005	2006
$\dfrac{£500 + £92}{£2400} \times 100 = 24.7\%$	$\dfrac{£1300 + £50}{£3355} \times 100 = 40.2\%$

The **return on capital employed** (ROCE) ratio, gives an overall indication of productivity of the capital invested.

Financial management is concerned with the productivity of all the capital employed. The return on capital employed (ROCE) ratio provides the overall indication of productivity of the capital invested (see **Exhibit 4.8**) and can be used as a comparator (see **Exhibit 4.9**). The ROCE ratio is sometimes referred to as return on investment (ROI). Definitions of profit and capital do vary and the definitions used in this Chapter are some of the most common. ROCE is calculated using net profit before tax and interest and shareholders funds plus long-term loans, which allows an overall look at the productivity and profitability of the company. Net profit before tax and interest is the net profit figure with the interest figure added back, while shareholders' funds are the ordinary share capital, reserves and retained profits. Long-term loans are often provided by banks or debenture holders. Changes in ROCE are due to fluctuations in net profit, gross profit, expenses, and share capital, reserves and long-term debt.

Exhibit 4.10

$$\text{Return on shareholders' funds (\%)} = \frac{\text{Net profit after tax}}{\text{Shareholders' funds}} \times 100$$

NB. shareholders' funds = share capital plus reserves

Exhibit 4.11 Return on shareholders' funds (%)

2005	2006
$\frac{400}{1800} \times 100 = 22.2\%$	$\frac{1020}{3055} \times 100 = 33.4\%$

Return on shareholders' funds is a measure of the return on the investment which shareholders have made after the company has paid its expenses.

The return on shareholders' funds ratio is a measure of the return on the investment that ordinary shareholders have made in the company (see **Exhibit 4.10**). The ratio looks at what is left for the ordinary shareholders after Global Books has paid its business expenses, hence it is a ratio which reflects the interest of the ordinary shareholders. The increase in the return on shareholders funds (see **Exhibit 4.11**) is due to a reduction in expenses, such as the move to a cheaper warehouse in the north of England, which in turn has seen net profit increase.

✔ Check your understanding

■ Do you understand what changes may have occurred to a company's finances if the following changes occur to its financial ratios?

■ Check your understanding by explaining possible changes to a company's profit and loss account, balance sheet or stock market performance if the following changes occur to its financial ratios.

1 Gross profit margin increases.

2 Net profit margin reduces.

3 Return on capital employed increases.

4 Return on shareholders' funds decreases.

Review questions | **Profitability ratios**

■ In 2007 Global Books made a gross profit of £2,750,000 on sales of £7500000 and incurred expenses of £1,200,000. The tax liability was £300,000, dividend payments were £100 000 and interest payments totalled £62,000. The long-term debt for 2007 was £300,000. Share capital remained unchanged at £1,000,000 and retained earnings were £2,000,000.

■ Use the information given above to calculate the ratios listed below for Global Books in 2007.

1 Gross profit margin.

2 Net profit margin.

3 Return on capital employed.

4 Return on shareholders' funds.

Efficiency ratios

The efficiency ratios are of interest to management because they provide a measure of how productively the company is managing its assets and working capital. The common efficiency ratios, which are looked at in this chapter, cover debtors, creditors, stock and fixed assets. The figures used refer to Global Books (see **Exhibit 4.3**).

Exhibit 4.12

$$\text{Debtors collection period (days)} = \frac{\text{Debtors}}{\text{Sales}} \times 365$$

Exhibit 4.13   Debtors collection period (days)

2005	2006
$\frac{500}{5000} \times 365 = 36.5$ days	$\frac{940}{7000} \times 365 = 49$ days

The **debtors ratios** shows how long it takes the company to collect money it is owed.

The **debtors ratio** shows how long it takes the company to collect its debts or money owed to the company (see **Exhibit 4.12**). Therefore it is of particular importance to the company's financial managers. From the example shown in **Exhibit 4.13** it can be seen that Global Books have allowed their credit control to weaken, with money owing from debtors, i.e. booksellers, who can be online and/or high street retailers, coming in much more slowly in 2006 compared to 2005. If the industry average were 40 days, then the company's credit control function would appear to be struggling.

Exhibit 4.14

$$\text{Creditors collection period (days)} = \frac{\text{Creditors}}{\text{Sales}} \times 365$$

Exhibit 4.15   Creditors collection period (days)

2005	2006
$\frac{270}{5000} \times 365 = 19.7$ days	$\frac{405}{7000} \times 365 = 21.1$ days

The **creditors ratio** measures how long it takes the business to pay its suppliers.

Suppliers from whom goods and services have been purchased on credit are creditors and represent a source of short-term finance. In the case of Global Books the suppliers are the printers and typesetters. Financial managers will be interested in the **creditors ratio** to see if the company is paying off its debts too slowly or too quickly (see **Exhibit 4.14**). If the industry average is 45 days, it would appear from **Exhibit 4.15** that Global Books is paying off its debts too quickly, particularly in 2006, when it was settling debts in 21 days and its debtors were taking 49 days to pay Global Books (see Exhibit 4.13). However, a low creditor collection period may indicate that prompt payment secures generous cash discounts from suppliers, which could be very worthwhile over a long period of time.

Exhibit 4.16

$$\text{Stock turnover (times)} = \frac{\text{Cost of sales}}{\text{Stock}}$$

Exhibit 4.5 Gross profit margin (%)

2005	2006
$\frac{3000}{600} = 5$ times	$\frac{4500}{500} = 9$ times

Stock turnover shows how fast or slowly stock is moving through the business.

Stock turnover shows the number of times which the stock is sold in a given period or how fast or slowly stock is moving through the business (see **Exhibit 4.16** for the formula). Hence, as stock represents capital tied up, it is preferable to have a rapid rate of stock turnover to ensure that it is tied up for a minimum amount of time. The higher the rate of turnover, the shorter the period of time for which stock is held. Hence, Global Books, who have improved their stock turnover ratio, are tying capital up for a shorter period of time (see **Exhibit 4.17**). It is also likely there will be a reduction in wastage caused by books going out of date and being superseded by new editions. A rapid rate of turnover equals fast moving stock and less capital tied up. A business such as Global Books will experience variation in demand and will need to incorporate peaks and troughs in demand into the stock control system. Global Books will experience a peak in demand for academic books in August for the start of the academic year in September; similarly the demand for fiction and lifestyle books will peak in Autumn in time for Christmas sales whereas demand for books at Easter time will be lower.

Exhibit 4.18

$$\text{Fixed assets turnover (times)} = \frac{\text{Sales}}{\text{Fixed assets}}$$

Exhibit 4.19 Fixed assets turnover (times)

2005	2006
$\frac{5000}{1160} = 4.3$ times	$\frac{7000}{2230} = 3.14$ times

This **fixed asset turnover ratio** provides a measure of asset utilisation, measuring how many times the fixed assets are covered by sales revenue.

This **fixed asset turnover ratio** provides a measure of asset utilisation and measures how many times the fixed assets are covered by sales revenue (see **Exhibit 4.18**). The higher the ratio or the more times fixed assets are covered by sales revenue, the greater the recovery of investment in the fixed assets. The figures in **Exhibit 4.19** show that Global Books became less efficient in 2006, generating a lower sales figure per £1 invested in fixed assets. This may be due to a number of reasons; if new fixed assets were not in place until late in 2006, their full benefit will not be felt until 2007. Equally the company may have been caught out by a downturn in the economy.

✔ Check your understanding

- Do you understand what changes may have occurred to a company's finances if the following changes occur to its financial ratios?
- Check your understanding by explaining possible changes to a company's profit and loss account, balance sheet or stock market performance if the following changes occur to its financial ratios.
  1 Debtors ratio falls.
  2 Creditors ratio rises.
  3 Stock turnover ratio increases.
  4 Fixed asset turnover ratio decreases.

Review questions | **Efficiency ratios**

- In 2007 turnover or actual sales for Global Books increased to £7,550,000 with the cost of sales at £4,750,000. Global Books held stock on average worth £450,000, while debtors were £750,000 and creditors £550,000. Fixed assets have a WDV (written down value) of £2,850,000.
- Use the information given above to calculate the ratios listed below for Global Books in 2007.
  1 Debtors collection period.
  2 Creditors collection period.
  3 Stock turnover.
  4 Fixed asset turnover.

FINANCIAL STATUS RATIOS

Liquidity ratios

Liquidity ratios measure the extent to which a company's assets can be turned into cash and provide a measure of the company's ability to pay its debts. Companies can be quite profitable but still have liquidity problems. The liquidity ratios provide an indication of whether or not the company has liquidity problems or excess liquidity. The liquidity ratios included in this Chapter are the **current ratio** and the **acid test ratio**. The figures used refer to Global Books (see **Exhibit 4.3**).

Exhibit 4.20

$$\text{Current ratio} = \frac{\text{Current assets}}{\text{Current liabilities}}$$

Exhibit 4.21 Current ratio

2005	2006
$\dfrac{£1560}{£320} = 4.88$	$\dfrac{£1600}{£475} = 3.37$
i.e. for every £1 owing to current liabilities there is cover of £4.88	i.e. for every £1 owing to current liabilities there is cover of £3.37

The **current ratio** indicates how easy it is for the company to cover its short-term debts immediately.

The current ratio is normally in excess of one, if this not the case the company may face difficulties in finding sufficient cash to cover its short-term debt immediately (see **Exhibit 4.20**). However many companies survive quite successfully with a current ratio of less than one as it is likely that short-term liabilities do not need to be settled immediately, but over the next 12 months. It can be difficult to comment on the current ratio without a useful benchmark, so assuming the industry average is around 2:1 it would appear that in 2005 Global Books had excess liquidity, which has been reduced in 2006, but liquidity still remains high (see **Exhibit 4.21**). It is likely that the reduction in liquidity, which has occurred between 2005 and 2006, is due to the redemption of debentures and the investment in new fixed assets. This is supported by a high bank balance in 2005 of £460,000,000, with the corresponding figure in 2006 being £160,000,000.

Exhibit 4.22

$$\text{Acid test ratio} = \frac{\text{Current assets less stock}}{\text{Current liabilities}}$$

Exhibit 4.23 Acid test ratio

2005	2006
$\dfrac{£1560 - £600}{£320} = 3$	$\dfrac{£1600 - £500}{£475} = 2.32$
i.e. for every £1 owing to current liabilities there is cover of £3.00	i.e. for every £1 owing to current liabilities there is cover of £2.32

The **acid test ratio**, like the current ratio, measures the company's ability to cover its short-term debts, but stock as an asset is not counted.

The acid test ratio, like the current ratio, measures the company's ability to cover its current liabilities (see **Exhibit 4.22**). However, the view is taken that stock may take some time to convert into cash, therefore the stock figure is subtracted from the current assets figure. As a rule of thumb, this ratio should be around 1.00; however, many industries survive successfully with a ratio of less than one. If the industry average for the acid test ratio is around 1, then the ratios of 3.00 and 2.32, signify excess liquidity (see **Exhibit 4.23**). Global Books should seek to ensure the excess liquid cash is used efficiently by the business.

✔ Check your understanding

- Do you understand what changes may have occurred to a company's finances if the following changes occur to its financial ratios?
- Check your understanding by explaining possible changes to a company's profit and loss account, balance sheet or stock market performance if the following changes occur to its financial ratios.

  1 Current ratio falls.

  2 Acid test ratio increases.

Review questions | Liquidity ratios

- In 2007 Global Books had current assets totalling £1,650,000, of which £450,000 was attributable to stock. Current liabilities were £640,000.
- Use the information given above to calculate the current ratio and acid test ratio for Global Books in 2007.

Solvency ratios

The solvency ratios look at how capable a company is of paying its long-term debts and interest payments. Hence the two ratios looked in this chapter are the **gearing** and **interest cover**. The figures used refer to Global Books (see **Exhibit 4.3**).

Exhibit 4.24

$$\text{Gearing (\%)} = \frac{\text{Long-term debt}}{\text{Shareholders funds}} \times 100$$

Exhibit 4.25 Gearing (%)

2005	2006
$\frac{600}{1800} \times 100 = 33.3\%$	$\frac{300}{3055} \times 100 = 9.8\%$

Gearing measures the proportion of capital which comes from long term debt.

The gearing ratio is concerned with the proportion of capital which comes from long-term financing, including preference shares, long-term loans, and debentures (see **Exhibit 4.24**). A highly geared company will have raised a high proportion of its capital from sources other than ordinary shares. In contrast a company which has raised a low proportion of its capital from preference shares, long-term loans and debentures has low gearing. In tougher economic conditions more highly geared companies will be more likely to struggle as their obligations to make interest payments, loan and debenture repayments will be greater. External providers of capital, for example banks and venture capitalists, will be interested to know a company's gearing ratio before lending further funds.

The gearing calculations in **Exhibit 4.25** show that the gearing for Global Books has gone down significantly during 2006 due to some of the debentures being redeemed and new ordinary share capital and share premiums being issued. What is high or low gearing depends upon the industry in which the company operates, for example below the industry average could be classed as low, above could be classed as high.

Exhibit 4.26

$$\text{Interest cover (times)} = \frac{\text{Net profit before interest and tax (NPBIT)}}{\text{Loan and debenture interest}}$$

Exhibit 4.27 Interest cover (times)

2005		2006	
Net profit before tax	500	Net profit before tax	1300
Add back debenture interest	72	Add back debenture interest	36
NPBIT	527	NPBIT	133
$\dfrac{572}{(92 + 72)} = 3.5$ times		$\dfrac{1336}{(50 + 36)} = 15.5$ times	

Interest cover is an income-based measure of gearing and shows how well a company can cover its interest payments.

Interest cover is an income-based measure of gearing and it shows how well the company can cover its interest payments (see **Exhibit 4.26**). It can be seen that the reduction in gearing (see **Exhibit 4.25**) and the increase in profits has lead to a dramatic improvement in the interest cover for Global Books (see **Exhibit 4.27**). The low gearing of 9.8% in 2006 and increased investment in fixed assets, which represents additional security, means Global Books is in a very strong position to raise further debt capital – that is long-term loans and debentures – should more finance be required.

✔ Check your understanding

- Do you understand what changes may have occurred to a company's finances if the following changes occur to its financial ratios?
- Check your understanding by explaining possible changes to a company's profit and loss account, balance sheet or stock market performance if the following changes occur to its financial ratios.

  1 Gearing falls.

  2 Interest cover rises.

Review questions   Solvency ratios

- In 2007 Global Books made a net profit before tax of £1,550,000 and paid £35,000 in interest. Long-term debt was £300 000 and ordinary share capital remained at £1,000,000.
- Use the information given above to calculate the following ratios for Global Books in 2007.

  1 Gearing.

  2 Interest cover.

STOCK MARKET RATIOS

This group of ratios looks at the financial performance of the company relating to the ordinary shares. The financial managers, existing ordinary shareholders, would-be investors, analysts and competitors will be interested in these ratios. The figures used again refer to Global Books (see **Exhibit 4.3**).

Exhibit 4.28

$$\text{Earnings per share (£)} = \frac{\text{Net profit after tax}}{\text{Number of ordinary shares issued}}$$

Exhibit 4.29 Earnings per share (£)

2005	2006
$\frac{£400}{600} = £0.67$	$\frac{£1020}{1000} = £1.02$

Earnings per share ratio is a measure of the earning power of each share and is closely linked to the share's market value.

The **earnings per share ratio** (EPS), is a measure of the earning power of each share and is closely linked to the share's market value (see **Exhibit 4.28**). Thus, it shows the amount generated per share for the period (see **Exhibit 4.29**) and usually a portion of these earnings will be paid out as dividends and the rest of the balance ploughed back into the business or kept as retained profits.

Exhibit 4.30

$$\text{Price earnings ratio} = \frac{\text{Market price per ordinary share}}{\text{Earnings per ordinary share}}$$

Exhibit 4.31 Price earnings ratio (times)

2005	2006
$\dfrac{£1.50}{£0.67} = 2.24$ times	$\dfrac{£1.75}{£1.02} = 1.72$ times

The **price earnings ratio** measures the relationship between a company's ability to generate profits and market price of its ordinary shares.

The **price earnings ratio** (P/E) measures the relationship between a company's ability to generate profits and the market price of its ordinary shares (see **Exhibit 4.30**). The higher P/E in 2005 (see **Exhibit 4.31**) indicates higher market expectations for Global Books in 2005. A higher P/E ratio means a high price in relation to earnings and this may reflect market expectations of great things to come, which appears not to have been realised in the case of Global Books.

Exhibit 4.32

$$\text{Dividend yield (\%)} = \frac{\text{Dividend per share}}{\text{Market price per ordinary share}} \times 100$$

Exhibit 4.33 Dividend yield (%)

2005	2006
(Dividend per share = £50/600 shares = £0.08)	(Dividend per share = £70/1000 shares = £0.07)
$\dfrac{£0.08}{£1.50} \times 100 = 5.34\%$	$\dfrac{£0.07}{£1.75} \times 100 = 4\%$
i.e. generating £5.56 for every £100 invested at the share price concerned	i.e. generating £4.00 for every £100 invested at the share price concerned

The **dividend yield ratio** relates the dividend to the market price of an ordinary share, giving a potential investor an indication of expected return.

The **dividend yield ratio** simply relates the dividend to the market price of an ordinary share (see **Exhibit 4.32**). However, it does give some idea to a potential investor of the expected return on investment in terms of cash paid out, at the present share price. See **Exhibit 4.33** for an example using Global Books. This ratio only takes account of dividend earnings and does not take account of any capital gain from increases in the share price.

Exhibit 4.34

$$\text{Dividend cover (times)} = \frac{\text{Earnings per share}}{\text{Dividend per share}}$$

Exhibit 4.35 Dividend cover (times)

2005	2006
$\frac{£0.67}{£0.08} = 8.4$ times	$\frac{£1.02}{£0.07} = 14.6$ times
i.e. for every £1 required for dividend payment £8.40 has been generated	i.e. for every £1 required for dividend payment £14.60 has been generated

The **dividend cover ratio** shows the number of times that current earnings cover ordinary dividend payments.

The **dividend cover ratio** shows the number of times that the current earnings cover the ordinary dividend which has been paid or is proposed (see **Exhibit 4.34**). The dividend cover ratio provides an indication of the likelihood that Global Books will be able to maintain its dividend payments while also being able to plough profits back into the business and/or boost retained profits (see **Exhibit 4.35**).

In conclusion the five key points for Global Books to consider for the next 12 months are listed below.

1 Ensure expenses don't creep back up.
2 Check money is not being paid out faster than it is being collected in, unless there is a good reason, like significant discounts from suppliers. Keep the debtors and creditors ratios under review.
3 The stock turnover ratio has increased from 2005 to 2006; ensure that any continued increase in this ratio does not result in the company running out of stock.
4 Keep the fixed asset turnover ratio under close review; ensure the benefit of investment in new fixed assets, including the new warehouse, does occur.
5 Deal with the excess liquidity in the business; make the excess cash work for the business.

✔ Check your understanding

- Do you understand what changes may have occurred to a company's finances if the following changes occur to its financial ratios?
- Check your understanding by explaining possible changes to a company's profit and loss account, balance sheet or stock market performance if the following changes occur to its financial ratios.

 1 Earnings per share increases.

 2 Price/earnings ratio falls.

 3 Dividend yield decreases.

 4 Dividend cover increases.

Stock market ratios

- In 2007 Global Books made a net profit after tax of £1,250,000. Ordinary shares remained at 1,000,000 shares, trading at £2.35 each and dividend amounted to £75,000.
- Use the information given above to calculate the following ratios for Global Books in 2007.
    1 Earnings per share.
    2 Price/earnings ratio.
    3 Dividend yield.
    4 Dividend cover.

CONCLUSION

This chapter has sought to examine aspects of finance which companies need to consider and undertake if they are to successfully pursue their chosen strategy. In the first half of the chapter sources of finance are defined and examined. There is no one ideal way of raising finance; it does quite simply depend on a company's size, situation and standing. For example, a company which has never issued shares before would be unable to undertake a rights issue, a small company would not have the resources to list on the stock market, and a company which is already highly geared would find it difficult to raise further finance via borrowing.

The second half of the chapter looks at undertaking ratio analysis to evaluate a company's success in financial terms. Ratio analysis should always conclude which financial actions need to be undertaken to maintain or improve the company's financial success. There are three categories of financial ratios, namely performance ratios, financial status ratios, and stock market ratios. The performance ratios look at profitability and efficiency, financial status ratios cover liquidity and solvency, and stock market ratios examine the performance of a company's ordinary shares.

LEARNING OUTCOMES AND SUMMARY

→ **Learning outcome 1**
Determine the main source of finance for a company.

- Financial resources are important for all organisations as money allows organisations to achieve their aims and objectives. For commercial organisations financial aims include efficient use of cash, making profit, and a good return for shareholders.
- Internal finance is cash generated by the company which is not needed to meet operating costs, expenses, tax, and dividend payments. Companies

may prefer internal finance as approval of external parties, such as lenders or venture capitalists, is not needed when making decisions to spend the money.

■ External finance can be split into equity (share) finance and debt finance. Equity finance is raised via the sale of ordinary shares, which carry owner-ship rights and entitle the owner to a dividend payment if one is made.

■ A rights issue occurs when an existing company seeks to raise share capital by offering new shares to existing shareholders. There is a legal requirement to first offer any new shares to existing shareholders. If shareholders take up the rights issue by purchasing the shares, then the shareholder breakdown remains the same and a hostile takeover bid is unlikely.

→ Learning outcome 2
Explain the processes for listing on the London Stock Exchange.

■ The London Stock Exchange (LSE) is where the ordinary shares of many large UK companies are brought and sold. A company seeking a listing will need to appoint a sponsor to assemble a prospectus and manage the listing process. A broker will also need to be appointed to advise on the issue price and market the shares to potential investors. The overall cost of obtaining a listing on the LSE is substantial and is unlikely to be less than £400,000 in total.

■ The main methods of obtaining a stock market listing are a 'placing' and an 'offer for sale'. A placing uses a broker for approaching institutional investors before the share issue, who will agree to accept the issued shares at a fixed price. The 'offer for sale' is the offering of shares at a fixed price to the public, which includes institutional and individual investors, with the help of the sponsor and broker.

→ Learning outcome 3
Explain how loans and debentures work.

■ Debenture or loan stocks are written acknowledgements of indebtedness, with a debenture being secured against corporate assets, while loan stock is an unse-cured bond. Both debentures and loan stock have a par value, usually £100 in the UK, and interest is paid as a percentage of the par value, for example an interest rate of 10 per cent means payment of £10 or 10 per cent of the par value of £100. This interest is tax deductible for the company making the payment.

→ Learning outcome 4
Define and explain the performance ratios which can be used in evaluating a company's success.

■ The performance ratios look at profitability and efficiency. Profitability ratios examine the return which is being gained by the business, and include the profitability ratios, gross profit margin, net profit margin, return on capital employed and return on shareholders funds.

■ The return on capital employed (ROCE) ratio provides an overall indication of productivity of capital invested and is sometimes called the return on investment (ROI). ROCE is calculated as 'net profit before tax and interest as a percentage of shareholders funds plus long-term loans'.

■ The efficiency ratios are of interest to management because they provide a measure of how productively the company is managing its assets and working capital. The common efficiency ratios are those covering debtors, creditors, stock and fixed assets.

→ **Learning outcome 5**
Define and explain the financial status ratios which can be used in evaluating a company's success.

■ The financial status ratios look at liquidity and solvency. Liquidity ratios measure the extent to which a company's assets can be turned into cash and provide a measure of the company's ability to pay its debts. The common liquidity ratios are the current ratio and the acid test ratio.

■ The solvency ratios look at how capable a company is at paying its long-term debts and interest payments, and two ratios which do this are gearing and interest cover. The gearing ratio is the percentage of capital which comes from long-term financing, and interest cover is an income-based measure of gearing and it shows how well the company can cover its interest payments.

→ **Learning outcome 6**
Define and explain the stock market ratios which can be used in evaluating a company's success.

■ The stock market ratios look at the performance of the company's shares, their price, earnings and dividends. The earnings per share ratio (EPS) is a measure of the earning power of each share and is closely linked to the share's market value.

■ The dividend yield ratio relates the dividend to the market price of an ordinary share and does give some idea to a potential investor of the expected return on investment in terms of cash paid out, at the present share price. The dividend cover ratio provides an indication of the likelihood that the business will be able to maintain its dividend payments while also being able to plough profits back into the business.

This exit case study looks at Eazyfone and its development, including its sources of finance and can be used to assess the learning outcomes below.

Learning outcomes	Check you have achieved this by	
Discuss a company's turnover.	Examining and commenting on trends in turnover.	Answering exit case study question 1.
Identify current and possible sources of finance.	Discussing current sources of finance and suitable sources of finance for the future.	Answering exit case study questions 2 and 3.
Understand how costs and expenses can deplete profits.	Explaining which costs need to be reviewed and how they might run out of control.	Answering exit case study question 4.
Summarise a potential strategy for an organisation.	Briefly develop a longer-term plan or strategy for a company.	Answering exit case study question 5.

Creating links with recycled mobile phones is the Eazy way to success

FT

by Jonathan Moules

Pete Petrondas is a great believer in finding new uses for things. The 30-year-old entrepreneur has even recycled his company, Eazyfone. His original business plan, selling mobile phones to corporate customers, suffered a near-fatal blow just a year after he started trading in 2001 when his main supplier pulled out of its contract without warning.

Mr Petrondas was forced to dismiss all 10 of his employees but worked furiously to keep the business afloat. 'I had to come up with a new idea,' he recalls. 'Just wrapping up the business was not an option.' The opportunity, Mr Petrondas realised, lay in the handsets customers were sending him whenever they got an upgrade from their mobile network provider. He knew that people in Africa and eastern Europe were willing to pay good money for these handsets. So instead of marketing new contracts to UK customers, he started collecting and refurbishing disused handsets at his Macclesfield headquarters, selling them on to retailers in Dubai, eastern Europe and South Africa. 'There are 90m used or redundant phones lying around in drawers in the UK and only 1 per cent are recycled,' Mr Petrondas says. 'With 18m new handsets being sold each year, I realised that there was a business opportunity staring me in the face.'

People who send their old handsets to Eazyfone for refurbishing either receive cash, a credit at Argos stores or can elect to have the money donated to charity. Eazyfone, which makes a margin on each handset it sells, has paid out more than £1m in cash to date through its Envirofone.com consumer brand and donated more than £1m to children's nurseries, schools, colleges and youth clubs through fones4schools.co.uk and foneaid.com, its charitable businesses.

Turnover rose from £339,000 in the 12 months to March 2005 to £2.4m a year-and-a-half later. Mr Petrondas expects the company to break through the £5m mark by the end of this financial year and to make its first pre-tax profit 12 months later on a turnover of £12.5m. Eazyfone is backed by £4m of private equity money from London-based Frontiers Capital, raised in two funding rounds by Mr Petrondas. 'We had very ambitious growth plans and I believed the best way to achieve this was by raising finance from the right investors.'

Headcount has risen to 75 people, including a team of 15 mainly Polish and Slovakian workers who return the used phones sent to Eazyfone to good working order. Poland and Slovakia have a ready supply of mobile phone technicians, who have worked for the network operators in their home country, according to Mr Petrondas. He adds that they are attracted to the UK by the better wages, although these are much lower than the rates he would have to pay home-grown talent. Many also prefer the fast-moving start-up environment of a company such as Eazyfone to the established mobile phone companies, Mr Petrondas adds. The Slovakian man who now heads the refurbishment operation, for example, was one of Eazyfone's first hires and rose through the ranks to his current position.

'Right now we have kept this operation at head office because it means we are more able to control it,' Mr Petrondas says. However, he admits that there may come a time when it will be better to outsource this activity to a lower cost country than the UK.

Brand recognition is key to Eazyfone's success, so marketing is among the company's biggest outlays at present. 'It is up there with labour costs,' Mr Petrondas admits. The company just spent a significant amount on a television advertising campaign, although Mr Petrondas stresses that the return on investment was 'more than 100 per cent'. A less expensive method of getting the Eazyfone brands in the public eye has been to allow third parties, such as *Metro*, the free daily newspaper, to piggyback on the envirofone.com website for their own phone recycling service. Mr Petrondas has also sought family help.

He hired his father, who had run his own homeopathic medicine business for 25 years, as sales and distribution head for Eazyfone in 2003. They each now hold about half the equity of the business. 'My father is very much an entrepreneur,' Mr Petrondas says. 'He was the iron hand that the business needed and I couldn't have got here without him.'

Eazyfone is also marketing its back-end systems, used for collection and redistribution of phones, as a way for other companies to comply with new rules governing the recycling of waste electrical and electronic equipment (WEEE). From July, all UK producers of electrical and electronic equipment must have the capacity to provide an audit trail of all their output. Eazyfone's systems can enable them to do this and Mr Petrondas has already signed contracts to do this for more than 20 companies, including LG Mobile, the handset manufacturer.

It will not be easy to win further contracts since Eazyfone is competing against several more established competitors in the market, such as Valpak, which has been involved in recycling electronic goods for many years. Eazyfone may also have trouble signing up other mobile phone manufacturers since most already have contracts with third parties for the safe disposal of their handsets. Mr Petrondas is determined to be positive about his chances. 'I think competition is always healthy so it is always great to see so many names in the market.'

Source: *Financial Times*, 3 March 2007.

Exit case study questions

1 Comment on the growth in turnover at Eazyfone.

2 'Eazyfone is backed by £4m of private equity.' Explain if private equity finance is currently more appropriate for Eazyfone than a stock market floatation.

3 When, if ever, do you think Eazyfone should float on the stock market?

4 Which costs will Eazyfone need to keep under review if it is to avoid damaging the potential for good profit? Explain what may cause the costs to run out of control.

5 In your own opinion, determine Easyfone's strategy for the next 3 years.

DISCUSSION TOPIC

1 Read the paper 'The innovative organisation' by Henry Mintzberg, Chapter 16, in *The Strategy Process*, Mintzberg, Lampel, Quinn and Ghosal, Harlow: Prentice Hall, 2003.

2 Compare and contrast the different sources of finance which could be used by the innovative organisation, the operating adhocracy and the administrative adhocracy.

WIDEN YOUR HORIZONS

1 Widen your horizons by visiting the website of the Alternative Investment Market (AIM) www.londonstockexchange.com/en-gb/products/companyservices/ourmarkets/aim_new/ and also accessing and reading the article 'Aim raises £365m in four-week float spree' by Sophie Brodie in the Daily Telegraph on 4 April 2005. Explain the difference between AIM and the main London stock market.

2 Widen your horizons by visiting the website of the British Venture Capitalist Association, www.bvca.co.uk. Explain the role of venture capitalists in business and give examples to illustrate your explanation.

3 Widen your horizons by identifying and explaining how the following organisations receive their funding: Sheffield City Council; Harvard University; Oxfam; Diabetes UK.

4 Widen your horizons by finding an annual report and accounts for a well-known company of your choice and undertaking a ratio analysis of the company. Decide if you would make a long-term investment in the company.

WEBLINKS

- Both these pages look at ratio analysis. The first page is from the Credit Research Foundation, an American organisation.
  www.crfonline.org/orc/cro/cro-16.html

- The second page provides a comprehensive look at ratio analysis and understanding financial statements. Click on 'Understanding Financial Statements', then on 'Ratio Analysis.'
  www.creditguru.com

- This site provides information of growing and developing a business. Click on 'Grow your business', then on 'Financing growth', to see different sections on financing a business, including floating on the stock market.
  www.businesslink.gov.uk

- The Department for Business, Enterprise and Regulatory Reform (BERR) has replaced the DTI. Visit the BERR website and click on 'Business Link' for help on small businesses
  www.berr.gov.uk

- Further information about financial help available for small and medium sized businesses can be found at the websites below, for the Prince's Trust, British Venture Capitalist Association and Business Link respectively.
  www.princes-trust.org.uk/
  www.bvca.co.uk/
  www.businesslink.org

FURTHER READING

A good introduction to corporate finance can be found in the following book.

- Watson, D and Head, A (2007) *Corporate Finance – The Principles and Practice*, 4th edn, London: Financial Times/Prentice Hall.

The following books all contain chapters on ratio analysis.

- Brett, M (2003) *How to Read the Financial Pages*, 6th edn, London: Random House Business Books.

- Chadwick, L (2001) *Essential Finance and Accounts*, Harlow: Financial Times/Prentice Hall.
- Dyson, J R (2003) *Accounting for Non-Accounting Students*, 6th edn, Harlow: Financial Times/Prentice Hall.
- Wood, F and Sangster, A (2005) *Business Accounting: Volume 2*, 10th edn, London: Financial Times/Prentice Hall.

REFERENCES

1   Liu, B (2004) 'PepsiCo lifts dividend 44%', *Financial Times*, 31 March.
2   Firn, D (2004) 'Delta cuts dividend and rules out break-up', *Financial Times*, 17 March.
3   Rankine, K (2005) 'The Allders creditors will get 90p in £', *Daily Telegraph*, 6 April
4   Rankine, K (2005) 'Debenhams seeks refinancing advice', *Daily Telegraph*, 8 April.
5   Hope, C and Jones, G (2005) 'Rover to call in receivers', *Daily Telegraph*, 8 April.
6   Hope, C (2005) 'Administrators warns of £80m bill for Rover sale', *Daily Telegraph*, 12 April.
7   MacCarthy, C (2004) 'Carlsberg unviels DKr3.3bn rights issue', *Financial Times*, 23 March.
8   Orr, R (2003) 'RSA say rights issue a success', *Financial Times*, 15 October.
9   Dickson, M (2003) 'A tense haul for Royal and Sun's rights issue, heavy trading activity in insurer's shares', *Financial Times*, 3 October.
10 Litterick, D (2005) 'Lazard to sell 30m shares in float', *Daily Telegraph*, 12 April.

CHAPTER 5

Stakeholders, culture and change

Exhibit 5.1 Essential strategy model

When you have read this chapter and worked through the associated activities
you should be able to achieve the objectives specified below.

1 Identify and evaluate an organisation's stakeholders.

2 Discuss the interest, power, legitimacy and urgency of stakeholders.

3 Define organisational culture and explain how an organisation's culture is
   determined.

4 Summarise key actions for helping a company alter its culture.

5 Identify driving and restraining forces for organisational change.

6 Understand and discuss the change process model.

The entry case study examines turmoil at British Airways and the stakeholders involved. It can also be used to think about likely changes at BA and their possible outcomes.

Discord at British Airways

by Claire Capon

In 1996 British Airways (BA), was enjoying peak performance with good profitability and shareholder returns. However BA's management saw the need to cut costs if the company was to remain competitive and successful in the long term. However by 2004 BA had not paid a dividend for three years and although the company was profitable in 2004, it was one of the poorer performers in the FTSE 100. The company was suffering from falling revenues – due in no small part to 9/11 – growing labour costs, as staff demanded ever-higher pay rises, and increasing fuel prices. Oil prices hit $50 a barrel in September 2004; two years previously the price of oil had been closer to $25 a barrel.

BA found itself in this situation, despite, between 2001 and 2004, restructuring to remove 20 per cent from the company's cost base, which resulted in 13,000 jobs losses, of which 25 per cent were management posts. Hence, far from being content with this level of cost reduction, Rod Eddington, chief executive of BA, identified a need for a further reduction of £300 million in staff costs between 2004 and 2006.

The trade unions, including the T&G and GMB unions, who represent baggage handlers, check-in staff and ground staff reached a deal with the airline in August 2004. The deal was for a back-dated 8.5 per cent pay rise over three years and £1,000 bonus which would be payable as a lump sum by September 2006. The lump sum payments were in return for a new sick leave agreement, which sought to reduce the amount of sick leave taken by employees from an average of 17 days each to 10 days within a year. The bonus payments were to be made to employees who had fewer than 16 days sick leave in a two-year period. In excess of 10,000 BA staff were covered by this new pay deal, which was described by BA as being tough on persistent non-attenders while remaining sympathetic to the 'genuinely sick'. The aim was to save BA about £30 million. Around the same time it was indicated by BA and in the media that if improvements in efficiency, including changes to work practices did not occur there may be further redundancies. Industry analysts also stated that BA had a disproportionately large workforce for the number of flights operating compared with some competitors.

So, imagine the surprise when around 3,000 passengers at Heathrow faced delays, disruption and cancellations to their flights at the end of August 2004, due to staff shortages! The ensuing two days of chaos very quickly caused city investors to raise concerns that BA's cost cutting had been excessive. Overall more than 70 of BA's Heathrow European flights were cancelled, affecting in total more than 8,000 passengers. The disruption, caused by a lack of check-in staff, was variously blamed on a high number of staff resignations, delays in security vetting and a policy of not replacing staff.

The chaos in August 2004 was the second wave of disruption to hit BA in a little over a year. In July 2003 there was an unofficial strike at BA over the introduction of swipe cards for clocking in and out of work; this produced a weekend of about 500 cancelled flights, 100,000 affected passengers, bad publicity and damage to bookings, costing the company an estimated £40 million. After the unofficial strike in 2003 BA launched its Industrial Relations Change strategy, bringing together managers and trade union officials on a more regular basis.

One view is that as a former state-owned airline, workers at BA have remained relatively militant and the state employee attitudes remain embedded and the complete move to a commercial culture has proved difficult. This is perhaps indicated by BA pilots flying far fewer than the 900 hours a year maximum imposed by the Civil Aviation Authority (CAA) and check-in staff enjoying generous breaks while on duty. In contrast to the days of state controlled airlines in Europe – a system was dismantled in the late 1980s and 1990s – there are now plenty of alternatives to large national flag carriers and these include the competitive airlines such as easyJet, Ryanair and Virgin Atlantic.

In these turbulent times other issues continue to face BA, including the threat of terrorism. In early 2004, BA, Air France and Continental Airlines all had to ground flights as it was feared terrorist organisations were targeting particular flights. BA flights between London Heathrow and Washington, BA flights to Miami, Air France flights between Paris and Washington, and a Continental Airlines flight from Glasgow to Los Angeles via Newark,

New Jersey were all cancelled on security advice. BA continues to be concerned about security and is likely to accept sky marshalls on flights, providing their deployment is such that in-flight security improves. The use of sky marshalls will likely occur once the government has agreed a protocol for their deployment and the pilots' union has agreed to its members flying with armed guards on board.

INTRODUCTION

Stakeholders are any individual or a collection of individuals with an interest in an organisation.

This chapter examines **stakeholders** in organisations, organisational culture, and organisational change. Stakeholders are covered first and include internal and external stakeholders, such as employees and customers respectively. The **stakeholder's power**, **interest**, **legitimacy** and **urgency** are also looked at. Organisational culture occupies the middle section of this chapter and examines the determinants of organisational culture. This is followed by cultural change and the chapter is concluded with an overview of change in organisations.

STAKEHOLDERS AND THE ORGANISATION

Stakeholders include any individual or collection of individuals with an interest in an organisation. Some stakeholders will be internal to an organisation and others will be external. Internal stakeholders include employees, managers, directors, trade unions and shareholders. External stakeholders include suppliers, customers, competitors, financiers, government and the general public. Various categories of stakeholder will affect or be affected by the organisation in diverse ways, hence stakeholders have different interests or stakes in the organisation. This is shown in **Exhibit 5.2**.

Stakeholders are also able to influence an organisation to act in their best interests. However, the interests of different stakeholder groups will vary and may even conflict with each other. For example, employees may seek high wages and above-inflation pay rises, while in contrast customers would prefer lower prices and lower costs, which are not possible if labour costs are high. The interests of stakeholders in an organisation and the way in which power is exercised by stakeholders are shown in **Exhibit 5.2**.

An organisation's stakeholders will be important for an assortment of different reasons and to varying degrees, therefore different stakeholders will respond to the organisation and its behaviour in different ways. Stakeholders whose interests and expectations are met will tend to remain with the organisation. Unsatisfied stakeholders will leave or remain and use their sources of power in an attempt to persuade the organisation to meet their expectations or interests.

Stakeholders who experience a high level of satisfaction with an organisation will tend to demonstrate loyalty and choose to retain their position as

Exhibit 5.2 Stakeholders' power and interest

Internal stakeholders	Stakeholder interests are:	Stakeholder power arises from:
Employees Managers Directors	■ security of employment ■ wage levels ■ fringe benefits ■ responsibility ■ promotion prospects ■ working conditions	■ job grade or title ■ position in organisational hierarchy ■ personal reputation ■ departmental reputation
Trade unions	■ number of union members in the organisation ■ same as its members ■ (list as above)	■ number of union members ■ nature of bargaining (local or national)
Shareholders	■ profit levels ■ size of dividend payments ■ capital growth in share price	■ number of shares held
External stakeholders		
Suppliers	■ size and value of contracts ■ speed of invoice payment	■ location and availability of other suppliers
Customers	■ quality of goods and services available ■ prices and payment terms	■ location of other suppliers ■ quality of goods and services offered by other suppliers ■ prices and payment terms offered by other suppliers
Competition	■ quality of goods and services available ■ prices and payment terms	■ behaviour of other competitors
Financiers	■ how promptly repayment of large and short-term loans occurs	■ offering better deal (improved quality or better prices and payment terms)
Government	■ payment of corporation tax ■ implementation of legislation (e.g. competition and employment legislation)	■ enforcing the legislation via the legal system if necessary

Source: Capon, C (2004) *Understanding Organisational Context,* 2nd edn, Harlow: Financial Times/Prentice Hall.

stakeholders. For example, employees who feel that their well-paid jobs are secure and offer future prospects are likely to remain with that employer. In contrast, stakeholders who are disappointed with the organisation and its behaviour are more likely to relinquish their stake. The likelihood of an unhappy stakeholder withdrawing their stake in an organisation is increased if better opportunities and potentially greater satisfaction appear to be available by acquiring a similar stake in a different organisation. For example, shareholders in a company who feel that they are not gaining a good enough return on their investment may decide to sell their shares and invest the money in a company that will give a better level of return.

Alternatively, stakeholders who are unhappy with the organisation may decide to retain their stake and attempt to change things. For example, unsatisfied shareholders may decide to try to influence changes to the organisation's leadership and strategies, with the aim of benefiting in the long run. To achieve this they will have to be able to exert the necessary amount of influence on planning and decision making within the organisation. This requires a suitable combination of authority, determination and ability. It is usually large institutional investors who stand the best chance of being successful with this type of approach, as they have greater power than smaller investors.

✔ Check your understanding

- Do you understand the different ways in which stakeholders in an organisation could behave?
- Check your understanding by reading the entry case study 5.1 and explaining how the following stakeholders might behave:

  1 a BA passenger whose flight was cancelled at the end of August 2004;

  2 a BA pilot flying 450 hours per year;

  3 Rod Eddington, the chief executive of BA in 2004.

ANALYSING STAKEHOLDERS

The analysis of stakeholders involves identifying who they are and considering their power and interest with regard to the organisation. Once identified, the relative power and interest of the stakeholders can be mapped on to a power and interest matrix, see **Exhibit 5.3**. Additionally this analysis can be extended to consider the reaction, behaviour and position of stakeholders if a particular strategy or plan were to be implemented by the organisation. An alternative approach would consider the attributes each stakeholder possesses. A stakeholder can possess any one or any combination of the attributes of power, legitimacy and urgency. Organisations will give low priority to stakeholders possessing only one attribute as such stakeholders will have low **salience**. Possession by a stakeholder of more than one attribute in the view of the organisation means the stakeholder has increased salience or is given greater priority by the organisation. This is looked at later in this chapter.

Exhibit 5.3 Power and interest matrix

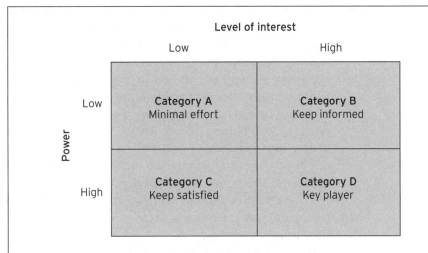

Source: Johnson, G and Scholes, K (1999) *Exploring Corporate Strategy*, 5th edn, Prentice Hall Europe. Reprinted with permission.

Stakeholders with high power and high interest (category D)

Key players are stakeholders with high power and high interest in the organisations.

Stakeholders with high power and high interest are **key players** in organisations and are often involved in managing the organisation and its future. Key players such as category D stakeholders include senior staff: directors and chief executives of organisations. Hence key players will often have responsibility for major decision making in the organisation. Successful decision making is likely to result in good pay and bonuses. Equally, poor decision making can result in loss of employment and the need to account publicly for poor decisions.

This second option occurred in the case of Shell. Philip Watts and Walter van der Vijver, Shell's two most senior executives had been disagreeing about the over-estimation of Shell's oil reserves which had been ongoing since 1993. In January 2004 this was corrected and reserves were reduced by 3.9 billion barrels or 20 per cent.[1] A major outcome of the debacle was the resignation of Watts, van der Vijver and the chief finance officer Judy Boynton. Neither Watts nor van der Vijver had a termination payment clause in their contracts.[2] The shareholders and financial authorities sought investigations into the events at Shell over the period 1993–2004 and hence the key players in Shell. Philip Watts, Walter van der Vijver and Judy Boynton, with decision-making responsibility, did not survive the decisions they made concerning Shell's reserves as other stakeholders very much perceived the decisions as being poor and not accounted for.

Stakeholders with high power and low interest (category C)

Stakeholders with high power and low interest are those who must be kept satisfied. Good examples of stakeholders who must be kept satisfied are the institutional shareholders. In the case of Shell **category C stakeholders** included the Financial Services Authority in the UK, the Securities and Exchange Commission in the US, the US Justice Department and the institutional shareholders.[3] Category C stakeholders such as investors and regulatory authorities will remain compliant and not exert power, while they continue to receive acceptable returns on their investment and are pleased with the organisation's management and activities. However, the ability of category C stakeholders to reposition themselves on the power and interest matrix into category D and become stakeholders with a continuing high degree of power and an increase in their level of interest should not be underestimated. This occurs when category C stakeholders are not kept satisfied and feel that their interests are not being best served. Hence stakeholders with high power and low interest will increase their level of interest to make sure that their interests are met.

> **Category C stakeholders** have high power and low interest and should be kept satisfied.

In the case of Shell and the over-estimation of oil reserves, many category C stakeholders did start to voice their concern and exert their power, requesting an investigation into the ten years' over-estimating of reserves. The shifts in position of unsatisfied category C stakeholders may impede an organisation's plans and prevent the expectations of key players or category D stakeholders being met. At Shell, Watts and van der Vijver (both category D) were no longer able to continue keeping other stakeholders in the dark over the levels of reserves the company held, the publication of Shells audited accounts was delayed and £1.5 billion was wiped of Shell's market value.[4] Shell failed to ensure that the expectations of category C stakeholders were met or that those expectations were adjusted given the reserves issue facing Shell. Shell would have done well to ensure its category C stakeholders were continually kept satisfied. Dissatisfied category C stakeholders are likely to feel marginalised at the expense of the interests of key players, category D stakeholders. Hence a good working relationship and open channels of communication should be developed between category C stakeholders, the organisation, and key players or category D stakeholders.

Stakeholders with low power and high interest (category B)

The stakeholders in category B are those with low power and high interest, and include individual employees and small shareholders. However, due to their low power **category B stakeholders** are unable to exert significant power to influence the organisation and its actions. In contrast, their high level of interest in the organisation means category B stakeholders can voice their concerns if that interest is not being considered in a suitable manner. This was the situation with the small shareholders in Shell, with some acting collectively

> **Category B stakeholders** have low power and high interest and should be kept informed.

via the Dutch Shareholders Group and calling for an explanation of Shell's behaviour over the reserves.[5]

Hence category B stakeholders may act as a collective under the auspices of a trade union or, as in the case of Shell, as a shareholders' group and exert their collective power. Alternatively category B stakeholders may voice their concerns loudly via lobbying or petitions and be able to influence one of the powerful groups of stakeholders in either category C or D, affecting their behaviour. Therefore organisations need to keep category B stakeholders informed of the organisation's activities and decisions, and in doing so convince them that their interests are being taken into account and considered seriously. Shell failed to do this.

Stakeholders with low power and low interest (category A)

Category A stakeholders have low power and low interest, but should not be ignored.

Stakeholders with low power and low interest are those in whom the organisation need only invest minimal effort. However **category A stakeholders** should not be ignored as they may acquire a stake in the organisation by becoming, for example, a customer, supplier, competitor or shareholder, which will mean an increased level of interest and/or power.

Review questions | **Stakeholders and analysing stakeholders**

1   List three things which give employees an interest in an organisation.
2   List three things which give customers power in relation to an organisation they buy from.
3   How will satisfied stakeholders behave?
4   Describe the options for dissatisfied stakeholders.
5   Why are category D stakeholders important to an organisation?
6   Why must category C stakeholders be kept satisfied?
7   Category B stakeholders have low power; how could this change?
8   Why would it be unwise to ignore category A stakeholders?

✔ Check your understanding

- Do you understand the nature of stakeholders' power and interest and how this may change?
- Check your understanding by reading Entry case study 5.1 and undertaking the following tasks.

  1 Identify stakeholders in BA and their sources of power and interest.

  2 Place the stakeholders you have identified on a power/interest (P/I) matrix.

  3 Explain why and how the position of the stakeholders on the matrix could change.

AN ALTERNATIVE APPROACH TO STAKEHOLDERS

Stakeholder identification and salience

Salience is the extent to which managers in an organisation give priority to stakeholder claims.

Stakeholder attributes are power, legitimacy and urgency.

Mitchell, Agle and Wood[6] identify and define stakeholders by the attributes and level of salience they possess. Salience can be defined as the extent to which managers in an organisation give priority to stakeholder claims. Mitchell, Agle and Wood propose that stakeholder salience will be directly related to the number of **stakeholder attributes** (power, legitimacy and urgency) perceived by managers to be held by individual stakeholders.

Stakeholders perceived to hold only one attribute are **latent stakeholders**, those with two attributes are **expectant stakeholders** and those stakeholders with all three attributes are the **definitive stakeholders**. See **Exhibit 5.4** for stakeholder types and their attributes.

Exhibit 5.4 Stakeholder identification

Type	Salience	Attribute(s)	Name
■ Latent	■ Low	■ Power	■ Dormant
■ Latent	■ Low	■ Legitimacy	■ Discretionary
■ Latent	■ Low	■ Urgency	■ Demanding
■ Expectant	■ Medium	■ Power and legitimacy	■ Dominant
■ Expectant	■ Medium	■ Power and urgency	■ Dangerous
■ Expectant	■ Medium	■ Legitimacy and urgency	■ Dependent
■ Definitive	■ High	■ Power, legitimacy and urgency	■ Definitive

Source: based on Mitchell, R K, Agle, B R and Wood, D J (1997) 'Towards a theory of stakeholder identification and salience defining the principle of who and what really counts', *Academy of Management Review*, 22(4), pp 853-86.

A **stakeholder's power** is often based on their position in the organisation and their access to resources.

The attributes are power, legitimacy and urgency. Power is easy to recognise but can be difficult to define.[7] In organisations the power of managers can be based on their position in the organisation and their access to resources. Position and resources allow the powerful stakeholder or manager to bring about the outcomes they desire, even when other people or staff involved may not share that desire and would not otherwise have pursued the desired aim or objective of the manager or powerful stakeholder.

Legitimacy is used to describe stakeholder behaviour, which is right and proper.

Legitimacy is used to describe stakeholder behaviour, which is right, proper and conforms to expected and acceptable standards, in the view of the organisation. Mitchell, Agle and Wood suggest the combination of the attributes of legitimacy and power produces a stakeholder with authority.

Urgency is the requirement for immediate attention and defines the relationship between the organisation and the stakeholder as dynamic.

Urgency is the requirement for immediate or pressing attention and defines the relationship between the organisation and the stakeholder as dynamic. Urgency is the degree to which a stakeholder calls for immediate attention. A stakeholder holds the urgency attribute when their relationship with the organisation is of a time-sensitive nature, that is urgent or critical. A patient with a head injury in the accident and emergency department of a hospital possesses the attribute of urgency. The hospital and doctors will give high priority to the head injury patient. A supplier requiring prompt payment for goods supplied to maintain cash flow and to continue supplying goods may be perceived as possessing the attribute of urgency, particularly if the supplier is either the only or one of very few suppliers of the goods in question.

Check your understanding

- Do you understand there are different types of stakeholder in organisations and that they have different attributes?
- Check your understanding by identifying the type of stakeholder described in each case below and name the attributes they hold (remember this should be done from the point of view of the organisation).
  1. A member of the public having their car, duty free cigarettes and alcohol confiscated by customs official on their return to the UK from France.
  2. A family doctor who is sacked by his/her employer (Health Care Trust) after being struck off by the General Medical Council (GMC) for gross professional misconduct.
  3. A female employee of a city investment bank who earned £750,000 per annum, before bonuses, who is sacked for going on maternity leave for the second time in three years.
  4. The armed robber who holds up a sub-post office with a sawn-off shotgun.
  5. The drunken pilot carrying out pre-flight checks for a long haul flight.
  6. The customer who returns the recently purchased brand new family car (the engine keeps cutting out) to the dealership.
  7. The employee on an overseas assignment who is trapped abroad due to a military coup in the country they where working in.
  8. An uninsured driver who drives into the back of a car which carries fully comprehensive insurance.
  9. Newly-appointed managing director charged with turning around a company from success to failure.
  10. The large high street name purchasing 50 per cent of a supplier's output.

Latent stakeholders

Latent stakeholders possess one attribute and have low salience.

Dormant stakeholders have power, but it is unused as the stakeholder has no legitimate relationship with the organisation.

Mitchell, Agle and Wood[8] define latent stakeholders as those possessing only one attribute. **Dormant stakeholders** possess the attribute of power, but it remains unused and the stakeholder has no legitimate relationship with the organisation. Before making a takeover bid for Marks & Spencer in summer 2004, the UK retailer Philip Green was a dormant stakeholder in Marks & Spencer. Philip Green held the financial power, but had not chosen to legitimately exercise that power. Dormant stakeholders have the power to impose their will on another organisation, but their lack of legitimacy or urgency in their claims means the power remains unused and there is minimal interaction with the organisation. However dormant stakeholders can acquire a second attribute and hence managers in the organisation should remain aware of such stakeholders – and their ability to be dynamic in acquiring a second attribute and becoming more salient. The difficulty lies in predicting which stakeholders will acquire a second attribute.

Discretionary stakeholders possess the attribute of legitimacy, but have no power or urgency in any claim they have on the organisation. Hence there is no pressure on managers in the organisation to engage with the discretionary stakeholder. An active relationship between stakeholder and company is at the manager's discretion. Charitable organisations may receive donations of money, time and other resources from individual and corporate donors. For example, some food retailers will donate food that is almost at its sell-by date to charities helping to feed homeless people and street sleepers. Some organisations give staff an allowance of paid work time in which to do charitable work or community projects. If the company withdraws its donation of food or time, the charitable organisation has no power to claim or retain such donations; it can merely make the best case for donations continuing, it has no right to expect them.

The **demanding stakeholder** possesses the attribute of urgency and is, for organisations, the demanding or annoying stakeholder who has no power or legitimacy and is unable or unwilling to acquire a second attribute. Some insurance companies may see the demanding stakeholder as the traveller who has a serious accident abroad while under the influence of alcohol on holiday, and hospital tests show this. Any insurance claim for medical treatment and assistance is therefore invalidated. For the traveller their claim is urgent; payment for medical treatment and an air ambulance are needed immediately. At this point in time the stakeholders, from the view of insurance company, possess no legitimacy – they were drunk at the time of the accident and have no power to make the insurance company change their mind. Stakeholders possessing only one attribute are called latent stakeholders and have low salience.[9] It is unlikely that managers will give such stakeholders any attention or acknowledgement.

Expectant stakeholders

Expectant stakeholders possess two attributes and have a medium level of salience, which gives them an active stance, in contrast to the passive stance of latent stakeholders possessing only one attribute.

Dominant stakeholders are those with both power and legitimacy, which gives them authority. These stakeholders are dominant as they have a legitimate claim on the organisation and the ability or power to act on any claim they may have with regard to the organisation. Dominant stakeholders can include directors, non-executive directors, shareholders, major creditors, large customers and key suppliers. Stakeholders with power and legitimacy will matter to the company and its managers and this is why the organisation

Discretionary stakeholders possess the attribute of legitimacy, but have no power or urgency in any claim they have on the organisation.

The demanding stakeholder possesses the attribute of urgency and, without a second attribute, is for organisations the annoying stakeholder.

Expectant stakeholders possess two attributes and have a medium level of salience.

Dominant stakeholders are those with both power and legitimacy, which gives them authority.

acknowledges these stakeholders by briefing them. The briefing may occur via: board meetings; management and team briefings; annual reports and accounts; annual general meetings; written policy on the use of suppliers – for example ethical, local, environmentally friendly. Dominant stakeholders expect and receive much attention from the organisation, but are by no means the only stakeholders the organisation has to manage.

Dangerous stakeholders have urgency and power, but do not have a legitimate claim and are often coercive and violent, hence the term 'dangerous stakeholder'. Coercive and violent stakeholders are perceived by the organisation to have an illegitimate status. Examples of coercive and violent stakeholder behaviour include employee sabotage of computer systems by introducing a virus, and terrorism in its extreme form. The world's airlines view al-Qaeda terrorist groups as dangerous stakeholders. The actions of dangerous stakeholders are outside the bounds of legitimacy, although they often damage the relationship between the company and its customers. This happened when in early 2004 BA was forced to cancel several flights to and from the US due to a terrorist threat,[10] leaving customers stranded for a number of days. Dangerous stakeholders should not be afforded any legitimacy; however, they do need to be identified to enable the company or organisation to take action to mitigate against their activities and reduce any likely danger to the organisation, its customers and other legitimate stakeholders. This will often include reviewing and updating security in the organisation as appropriate. Dangerous stakeholders should be identified by the organisation, but never acknowledged as this could give legitimacy and support to their cause.

Dependent stakeholders possess legitimacy and urgency, but lack power. These stakeholders depend upon others for the power to exercise their legitimate and urgent claim on the organisation. The relationship between the stakeholder and the organisation will be one-way, it will not be reciprocal. People leaving care institutions, for example mentally ill people leaving hospital, may require Social Services or a charity such as MIND to act for them – to help meet legitimate and urgent claims for support, benefits and housing. Prisoners leaving prison can require the probation services to help in their resettlement into the community. Young people leaving care on becoming 18 years of age often rely on the Social Services and charities, such as the Princes Trust in the UK, to help them exercise power which will allow them to access housing, training, education and employment.

Definitive stakeholders

Definitive stakeholders have all three attributes – power, legitimacy and urgency – and these are perceived by managers to be present. This gives the stakeholders high salience. Stakeholders with a claim on the organisation which is powerful, legitimate and urgent, need that claim attended to immediately and hence managers give high priority to their claim. Definitive stakeholders are often dominant stakeholders (power and legitimacy) who

Dangerous stakeholders have urgency and power, but do not have a legitimate claim and are often coercive and violent.

Dependent stakeholders possess legitimacy and urgency, but lack power and require others to act for them.

Definitive stakeholders have all three attributes, power, legitimacy and urgency, which gives them high salience.

have developed an urgent claim on the organisation. So a major creditor or supplier who has not been paid and is threatening court action would be a definitive stakeholder. Directors defending a company against a hostile takeover bid are definitive stakeholders: their claim is legitimate, they have power – and given that their reputation and future position with the company is under threat – their claim will have urgency. Hostile bids happen over a period of time and are dynamic in nature; if they are also successful, directors of the company taken over are often the first to leave under the new regime.

Review questions	An alternative approach to stakeholders

1   Define salience.

2   What is a stakeholder attribute?

3   Which stakeholders have low salience?

4   Which stakeholders have medium salience?

5   Which stakeholders have high salience?

6   Which attributes do dangerous stakeholders have?

7   Which stakeholders are key players?

8   Why will managers tend to ignore demanding stakeholders?

9   Who controls the relationship between a discretionary stakeholder and a company?

10   What is the nature of the relationship between the dependent stakeholder and the organisation?

ORGANISATIONAL CULTURE

Strong culture organisations are highly cohesive and have a system of informal rules, indicating to staff exactly what is expected of them.

Weak culture organisations lack cohesiveness and staff will waste time working out what to do and how to do it.

Organisational culture defines the type of place an organisation is for people, be they any type of stakeholder: employee, customer, bank, director. If an organisation is to function effectively it must develop a coherent culture. This is supported by Deal and Kennedy[11] who identify two types of culture: strong and weak. The **strong culture** is highly cohesive and coherent, and has a system of informal rules which indicates to people exactly what is expected of them, so that employees will know how to react and what to do in given situations. In contrast, people operating in a **weak culture**, one lacking in cohesiveness and coherence, will waste time working out what to do and how to do it.

Once an organisation with a weak culture successfully changes the necessary elements of its **cultural web**, for example its **control systems** and routine behaviour, then acceptable behaviour will become the norm and the organisation's culture will start to change, as will the paradigm on the culture web. The changes to the necessary elements of the cultural web, such as cost control and effective work practices, will change the paradigm as the organisation becomes profitable when previously loss making. (See **Exhibit 5.5** for examples of organisational paradigms from two diverse companies.)

Exhibit 5.5 Organisational paradigms for eBay and Royal Doulton

eBay	Royal Doulton
■ Profitable	■ Quintessentially British
■ Growing worldwide	■ Declining market
■ Available to everyone	■ Unprofitable
■ Efficient (don't have to store stock like Amazon)	■ In debt
■ No direct competition	■ Switching manufacture to Far East
■ Difficult to regulate (e.g. people trying to sell Nazi memorabilia and pieces of the Columbia space shuttle)	■ Unfashionable products

Sources: based on Patrick, A (2004) 'Net shoppers drive eBay to £100m', *Daily Telegraph*, 22 October, and Thorniley, T (2004) 'Royal Doulton close to rescue by Wedgwood', *Daily Telegraph*, 22 October.

The exit case study for this chapter shows how changing some of the determinants of organisational culture in Skoda resulted in a stronger organisational culture. The changes in culture arose from the company's takeover by Volkswagen. Volkswagen had to work hard to change some of the determinants of culture in Skoda and perceptions surrounding the company's products, including jokes such as: 'How do you double the value of a Skoda?'; response: 'Put petrol in it.'

THE CULTURAL WEB

The **cultural web** identifies and draws together a number of possible determinants of organisational culture.

The Johnson and Scholes cultural web[12] identifies and draws together a number of possible determinants of organisational culture; the physical indications of organisational culture and the taken-for-granted assumptions or **paradigm** of an organisation. In other words, organisational culture is determined by the entities which exist in an organisation and are shown in the cultural web, see **Exhibit 5.6**.

Routines and rituals

Routines are the scheduled and deliberate practices carried out as a matter of course in the day-to-day life of an organisation.

Routines (see **Exhibit 5.6**) are the scheduled and deliberate practices carried out as a matter of course and form the habits of day-to-day life in an organisation. In normal circumstances routines ensure the smooth running and operation of the organisation. In organisations with a strong culture, routine behaviour is very clearly spelt out and allows employees, particularly new employees, to know and understand 'the way we do things around here'. A good example of an organisation where routine is important is a fast-food restaurant such as Burger King and/or a chain restaurant such as Pizza Hut. Here the actions employees have to take in preparing the food and taking orders are very clearly and explicitly laid down, for example frying the French fries for exactly seven minutes or always asking the customer if they would like side orders of garlic bread or salad with their pizza.

Exhibit 5.6 The cultural web

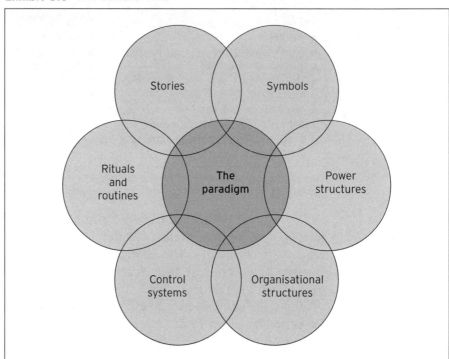

Source: Johnson, G and Scholes, K (1999) *Exploring Corporate Strategy*, 5th edn, Prentice Hall Europe.

Rituals in organisational life can be formal or informal and are used to reinforce the routines.

Rituals in organisational life are used to reinforce the routines and 'the way things are done around here'. Rituals can be formal events that employees are subjected to such as induction courses, training courses or periodic assessments to ensure an employee's performance is up to scratch and conforming to the routine way of doing things. Rituals may also be more informal in nature, for example the office Christmas party, drinks in the pub on Friday at the end of the working week, or gossiping around the office coffee machine. However, they still promote the common routine of the 'way we do things around here'.

Stories

Stories represent the organisation's history and typically highlight significant events and characters in its past.

In any organisation, **stories** will be told by employees to each other, to new recruits who join them and to others outside the organisation. The stories represent the organisation's history and typically highlight significant events and characters in its past. They characteristically focus on the achievements and failures of the organisation and the individuals involved, be they **heroes** or villains. Stories summarise the meaningful and key aspects of an organisation's past and tell people what counts as acceptable conduct today. Doubtless, in the future, stories will circulate at Shell about the demise of Phillip Watts and Walter van der Viljer (see earlier section on stakeholders), indicating that information concerning oil reserves is crucial to Shell and has to be open and honest at all times.

Symbols

The **symbols** present in an organisation can be many and varied and often symbolise someone's position in the organisation or how much that individual is valued by the organisation. Symbols can include titles, office size, company car and salary scales, with all indicating the power and value that an individual possesses with respect to an organisation. In long-established organisations like the Civil Service, many symbols will exist and indicate the power and importance of employees. In such organisations there will be a rigid structure, comprising different jobs at different grades with different salaries, with office accommodation directly dependent on job, grade and salary. Individuals with better offices and higher salaries, and who are further up the hierarchy, will have greater power and may be perceived to be of greater value to the organisation. In contrast, a newer organisation, such as an architects' practice which has all staff on performance-related pay and all working in an open-plan office, displays a different culture by virtue of the symbols that do or don't exist. The message in such an organisation is that all employees are equally valued and succeed on merit.

Power structures

Power structures evolve in organisations over time and consist of individuals with power, who all share a common set of beliefs and values that underpin the way they work together. Membership of the power structure is often determined by seniority and/or length of service in an organisation. Alternatively, power may be based on expertise, with a common source of power being technical expertise that is in short supply and highly valued in the organisation. This may occur particularly in firms where innovation is a key success factor (see Chapter 3). This type of power base will be strengthened if there are many valued experts who group together to promote or resist particular issues in the workplace.

Organisational structure

The structure that an organisation adopts will determine where the power exists within it (see Chapter 10). The location of power in an organisation will define the power relationships and designate the fundamental linkages between the seats of power and control. In centralised **organisational structures**, for example the simple and functional structures, the power will rest with the person or team at the top of the organisation – be that an owner-manager, a small board of directors, or a senior management team. In a decentralised structure, such as the divisional, holding or matrix structure, power will be devolved throughout the organisation. In particular operational and competitive levels decisions will likely be made by managers at the sharp end of the organisation who have day-to-day contact with the customers and marketplace. In the Dixons Group there are three divisions: Electricals, Computing and New Businesses. It is clear that this is a decentralised structure with responsibility devolved as appropriate, allowing Dixons, Currys, PC World to operate in the UK; Elkjop to operate in Norway; PC City in Spain, France, Italy and Sweden; and Electroworld in Hungary and the Czech Republic.

Control systems

Control systems are the mechanisms for control, measurement and reward within the organisation and monitor what is important to it.

The term control systems denotes systems for control, measurement and reward within the organisation. The systems that an organisation puts in place and monitors indicate what is important to it. Control systems include financial control and accounting systems, such as cash flow and budgeting, which are systems for regulating expenditure. Measurement systems examine the output of organisations and their efficiency and effectiveness. The output of an organisation can be the amount of product manufactured or the throughput of customers. Efficiency and effectiveness relate to the aspects of time and resources used to produce the final output/throughput. In some organisations the control of expenditure will be more important than the measurement of output, in others both will be equally important. In fast food restaurants the control of food stores and of cooked food is important and is, in many ways, a measure of efficiency as there is balance between the amount of food cooked and the amount disposed of once it is past its best.

CHANGING ORGANISATIONAL CULTURE

The cultural web is used for identifying the determinants of organisational culture and reaching a conclusion concerning the paradigm (the taken for granted assumptions and beliefs about the organisation). Equally if the determinants of organisational culture change, the cultural web and the paradigm for the organisation change. In organisations where routine behaviour includes poor attendance at work, changes to the routine behaviour can be achieved via the use of control and reward systems. The aim of this is to attempt to change the culture of the company. In seeking to change organisational culture managers will be seeking to change the paradigm (poor attendance and inefficiency) to a new paradigm which includes efficiency and a hard working workforce, which reflects a very different organisational culture. All or any aspect of the cultural web can be changed in an effort to alter organisational culture. The successful alteration of the determinants of culture in the web will result in a transformation of organisational culture and a modified paradigm.

Changes to an organisation's culture will involve changing aspects of its cultural web, hence change may include alterations to any aspect. For example, a change from a functional to a divisional structure, which may also change where the power sits in the organisation: from being centralised with the directors in the functional structure, to being decentralised throughout the divisional organisation, giving middle managers considerable responsibility for the division which they run. Changes to routine behaviour, such as tackling lateness and absenteeism, may only be accomplished by changes to control systems. For example BA (see Entry case study 5.1) had problems with staff clocking on, working half a shift before going home early and getting a friend to do their clocking off. The introduction of swipe cards at BA was an effort to reduce absenteeism and ensure staff members were actually present at work.

An alternative view of changing organisational culture is presented by Deal and Kennedy[13] outlining seven elements required for successful cultural change to be achieved, as discussed below.

Position a hero in charge of the process

Heroes are high achievers in the organisation and personify the organisation's cultural values and hence provide an explicit role model for employees.

Deal and Kennedy define a hero as a high achiever in the organisation and someone who personifies the organisation's cultural values and hence provides an explicit role model for employees. Heroes show every employee 'here's what you have to do to succeed around here'.[14] A hero put in charge of the change process will have to believe strongly in, and be committed, to the proposed changes and be able to inspire belief in and commitment to the change among the affected workforce.

Recognise a real threat from outside

Major cultural change in organisations requires sound reasoning before the change process can be initiated, as well as the appointment of a hero. An organisation's external environment may alter to such an extent that the culture of the organisation and the external environment no longer match one another. The more significant the threat posed to the organisation by the mismatch between its external environment and culture, the more likely it is that the culture can be successfully changed.

Make transition rituals the pivotal elements of change

The involvement of the people to be affected by change in the change process is a common recommendation of both academics and practitioners. Deal and Kennedy suggest a 'transitional ritual' or stage. This is where old ways of doing and organising things cease and new working relationships are established. This is a period of change in which people are encouraged to adopt new work patterns without rushing, while at the same time resisting the temptation to return to the old ways of working. Eventually the new working patterns and relationships become established as the norm.

Provide transition training in new values and behaviour patterns

New working practices and relationships need help to become established. Hence a programme of change will have to be available to all the employees affected. A culture change programme should focus on new values, new behaviour and new language, if new working practices and new relationships are to become permanent and last in the long term.

Bring in outside shamans

An organisation experiencing cultural change needs to drive the change from inside, hence the need for good management and clear direction. However, an outside '**shaman**' or consultant can be useful in helping the people affected by the change to span the gap between the two different organisational cultures. This can be done by defusing the friction and strife and helping those affected by the change to see that the way forward that is suggested by the change in culture can work successfully.

Shamans, in organisational terms, are outside consultants brought in to cure the organisation's problems.

Build tangible symbols of the new direction

People in an organisation affected by cultural change need to see and feel the effects of the change if they are to consider moving forward with the organisation and its cultural change. A good example of this would be a well-managed alteration to the structure of the organisation, as this would send a clear and tangible message concerning the direction in which the organisation was now heading.

Insist on the importance of security in transition

Proposed change in an organisation will always create uncertainty and this needs to be minimised. The greatest uncertainty that people will feel is that surrounding the security of their own jobs, and this needs to be made clear and dealt with swiftly. Those people who are staying with the organisation need to be clearly informed that this is the case. Equally, those who are to be bought off or made redundant also need to be told. Dealing with the issue of job security in an unambiguous way is an crucial part of effective change.

Change is sometimes required in an organisation. Its result can be good or bad. The certainty of change is that it is usually risky, expensive and time consuming. However, if the managers involved are sensitive to the organisational culture, then the change process can be managed successfully.

Organisational culture

1 Briefly compare and contrast strong and weak culture organisations.
2 Define the 'cultural web'.
3 Explain the term 'paradigm'.
4 How are rituals used by organisations?
5 Why are 'stories' important in organisations?
6 What message does the lack of symbols in an organisation convey?
7 Identify the fundamental difference between a centralised and decentralised structure in an organisation.
8 A changing organisation is really altering which aspect of its cultural web?
9 Why are heroes important in organisations?
10 Identify the pros and cons of using an outside consultant in managing change.

MANAGING A CHANGING ENVIRONMENT

Drivers of organisational change

The demand for change in organisations is caused by shifts in the external and internal environments in which they operate. External environmental factors were discussed in Chapter 2. The PEST issues – political, economic, socio-cultural and technological – are all drivers or sources of change that all organisations face. Additionally the behaviour and demands of external stakeholders, including competitors, customers, financiers and shareholders may drive change for an organisation. The influence an organisation has over these **external drivers of change** is often limited, as they usually arise from another organisation or developments over which the company has no or limited influence. The concern voiced by governments and consumer groups over the 'unhealthy' food sold by fast food chains, such as McDonalds and KFC, has been a driver of change for the fast food industry and has prompted fast food companies to offer alternative 'healthy' options including salads and fruit.[15] Drivers of change resulting from the actions of competitor companies or organisations usually require the business to respond. For example, the introduction of a price-cutting strategy by a competitor is clearly an event that requires an immediate reaction if a company is to retain market share. The introduction of a new technology or technologically advanced product by a competitor will require a considered response that may take time to develop.

External drivers of change usually arise from another organisation over which the company has no or limited influence.

Internal sources or drivers of change include employees, trade unions and organisational departments. Demands from employees and trade unions for more pay and/or different wage and salary structures may mean that the rewards system operated by the organisation changes, although this is unlikely to happen in isolation. The likely outcome would be that a deal is struck over working hours or productivity in return for improved wages and conditions of employment. In most organisations undergoing change, at least part of the workforce will be dedicated and faithful to the existing work practices. The news that these practices will have to change will mean that staff feel concerned about their jobs and future with the organisation. Their reluctance to accept and adopt suggested changes forms the restraining forces that contribute to the unbalancing of the status quo. The restraining forces will seek to persuade the organisation to discontinue or alter the recommended changes and so counteract the driving forces of change.

Lewin[16] suggests that change is the outcome of the impact of driving forces on restraining forces, more commonly known as **force field analysis**; see **Exhibit 5.7**. This can be thought of as the status quo that is under pressure to change. The resulting change is a direct outcome of either the driving forces or the restraining forces being more powerful. It is normal for the driving forces of change to have economic attributes. Organisations should seek to strengthen driving forces and weaken or overcome restraining forces.

Force field analysis is used to describe the impact of driving forces upon restraining forces for change in an organisation.

Exhibit 5.7 Lewin's force field analysis

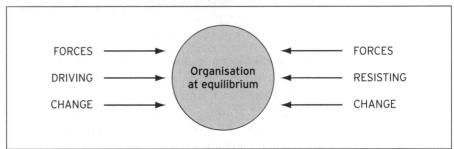

Source: Capon, C (2004) *Understanding Organisational Context*, 2nd edn, Harlow: Financial Times/Prentice Hall.

Managers in organisations experiencing change obviously need to be aware of both driving and restraining forces, see **Exhibit 5.8**. The managers involved should seek to communicate strong justification of the changes by offering a clear and unclouded explanation of the reasons for the changes and any advances in employee empowerment that will result. However, in planning such significant change a careful balance needs to be struck between providing too much information, which may raise fears and queries that cannot yet be dealt with, and providing inadequate information, which leaves people feeling that they have been told nothing and are being kept in the dark. Hence change requires very strong and effective leadership from the managers involved, particularly if structural and cultural changes are to occur. The leadership in any new working teams or groups will have to be particularly strong and focused if the implemented change is to be successful. A strong and effective change manager will disperse resistance to change by highlighting early achievements resulting from the change, which will also help maintain the momentum of the change programme and prevent it suffering from setbacks and periods of slow progress. Recognition that not everyone will support the change and that the feelings of those who are likely to be hurt by it require sensitive handling will help the change process to be managed successfully.

For the management of an organisation which is reacting to, or planning change there will be forces both driving and restraining the change. The forces driving change can be categorised into external and internal forces in relation to the organisation, with the restraining forces being both individual and organisational, see **Exhibit 5.8**. The forces resisting change can prevent new plans and change being developed and prevent their implementation once devised.[17]

Exhibit 5.8 Driving and restraining forces for organisational change

Driving forces	Restraining forces
External forces ■ Political forces e.g. legislation and government policy ■ Economic forces e.g. the condition of the economy; booming or recession ■ Socio-cultural forces e.g. demographics and behaviour in society ■ Technological forces e.g. the development of technology ■ Suppliers' delivery and payment terms and conditions ■ Customers' needs and wants ■ Competitiors' strategy	**Individual resistance** ■ Lack of understanding ■ Fear of the unknown ■ Dislike of uncertainty ■ Ambiguity surrounding change ■ Potential loss of power and control ■ Fear of downgraded job ■ Possible reduction in rewards
Internal forces ■ Directors' desire for growth and improved performance ■ Managers' agendas and aspirations ■ Shareholder expectations ■ Trade union bargaining and negotiation power	**Organisational resistance** ■ Long-established and strong culture ■ Entrenched power (formal and informal) and control systems ■ Weaknesses regarding resources and capabilities

Drivers of change and reducing employee turnover

An organisation, such as a call centre, which is experiencing high levels of employee turnover could map out driving and restraining forces for change to provide an identification of the exact areas which need tackling to reduce employee turnover to acceptable levels (see **Exhibit 5.9**). Guidelines for force field analysis[18] outline the necessary steps for carrying out a force field analysis. The driving and restraining forces identified can be rated as low, medium or high and scored accordingly: 1 for low, 3 for medium, 5 for high. This allows the totals for driving and restraining forces to be calculated and the category of forces requiring most attention to be identified. For some situations involving change it may be the employee resistance category which requires most attention, or it could be the turbulent and fast-moving external environment. Additionally lines of different lengths can be used to identify the relative strength of each individual force on a diagram, before prioritising each force as very urgent, urgent, or not urgent. Thought should then be given to how the very urgent and urgent driving forces are to be strengthened and the restraining forces weakened. The actions which will help achieve change should be identified along with the resources available. This should enable a plan to be drawn up which should include actions, targets, deadlines and responsibilities.

Exhibit 5.9 Driving and restraining forces for reducing employee turnover

Forces driving a reduction in employee turnover	Forces restraining a reduction in employee turnover
External forces ■ Economic forces; economy is moving into recession ■ Competitiors' strategy; a competitor has recently moved their call centre to India	**Individual resistance** ■ Employees dissatisfied with current jobs ■ Lack of stability and job security ■ Poor rates of pay compared to other local employers ■ Limited promotion prospects ■ Flexi-time system does not allow for early finishing
Internal forces ■ Directors' desire for growth and improved financial performance ■ Directors seeking a more motivated and responsive management team and workforce ■ Managers' agendas and aspirations for a career path	**Organisational resistance** ■ Poor recruitment and selection ■ Poor or non-existent induction programmes ■ Poor line management ■ Development and training budget not been increased for 3 years

External forces and reducing employee turnover

Economic forces impact on the availability of labour (see **Exhibit 5.9**). An economy which is moving into recession will tend to have higher unemployment than a buoyant economy. In a recession people will seek to keep their current job as alternative employment will be increasingly difficult to find. Additionally, in a recessionary economy, the withdrawal of a competitor from the local marketplace due to closure or relocation will swell the number of people looking for work in that industry and area. In contrast a buoyant economy where unemployment is low will allow people to move between jobs more easily. There is little any organisation can do to directly weaken or strengthen these macro forces driving change.

Internal forces and reducing employee turnover

The directors, managers and shareholders are often the internal forces which drive change and, as powerful stakeholders in the organisation, will usually be seeking improvements to financial returns and performance (see **Exhibit 5.9**).

For example, managers driving change need to communicate clearly with the existing workforce and if employee turnover is currently 60% per annum and needs to be reduced to 40% per annum within the next year, this sets the organisation and its managers a clear target. Clearly in addition, a more motivated and responsive management team will be needed, if indeed the reduction in employee turnover and the required improvements in performance are to occur. The view is that this will be likely to be tough in an economy moving into recession, but it will put the company in a strong position when the economy eventually recovers – and this should also be communicated. Additionally any improvements which can be made to pay, promotion, training and flexi-time should be highlighted, but promises which cannot be kept or resourced should not be made or mentioned at all.

Individual resistance and reducing employee turnover

If staff in an organisation are dissatisfied, they are more likely to leave; this is what dissatisfied stakeholders in organisations often do. Factors or forces which add to the dissatisfaction levels include poor pay, poor supervision and poor prospects (see **Exhibit 5.9**); people often want better for themselves and their families. Further, lack of flexible hours means employees who are left to work hours which do not suit their domestic situation and lifestyle will inevitably look for another job. In a recessionary economy opportunities may be limited, particularly if there are plenty of people in the labour market with the same skills seeking work. However, this should not mean such problems can be ignored as staff will move at the first opportunity or as soon as things pick up – and the best staff will be the first to leave. Organisations and managers need to listen to employees via consultative bodies, works councils, appraisals, attitude surveys and grievance procedures. This will help employees to voice dissatisfaction and provide them with the opportunity to try to contribute to changing things rather leaving. Staff will be more likely to resist the temptation to look for another job and leave if they are provided with job security, stability, good rates of pay, promotion and training prospects, and flexibility in working hours. Providing job security and taking all possible steps to create a diverse organisation will also help reduce employee turnover.

Organisational resistance and reducing employee turnover

An organisation will add to employee dissatisfaction if their recruitment process is poor. Recruiting the wrong type of employee or the wrongly qualified employees is expensive (see **Exhibit 5.9**). The over-qualified employee will become bored and leave, while the under-qualified employee will be out of their depth and will leave, cause an accident or make a serious mistake. Equally, poor induction to the organisation and the job will leave the new employee unsettled and unsure of themselves in the job, and hence more likely to leave. Similarly, lack of training for existing employees will add to dissatisfaction, as the lack of opportunity for development often also signals lack of promotion prospects in the organisation.

An organisation can start to reduce high employee turnover at the recruitment stage. This involves being realistic with potential employees about the job they are being recruited to, and providing information and access to the potential workplace and colleagues. Once recruited, line managers have a role to play in helping the organisation retain staff and the seriousness of this can be made clear by providing line managers with training in the areas of supervision, absence management and disciplinary procedures. Appraisal of a manager's performance should include their ability to retain staff and manage difficult situations. This may be linked to the organisation's reward system. Organisations may choose to grow their own managers and this can result in internal driving forces for change being strong. This occurs since the resolve of managers will be to establish an individual career and shape a successful future for the organisation at the same time.

Overcoming organisational resistance to change will be difficult to achieve in a recession as expenditure on growth, training, development and promotion will be difficult to justify. Hence the efficient and effective use of the resources available is extremely important. The training which the organisation can afford should be targeted at those who need it most. In the case of an organisation tackling high employee turnover, the recruitment, selection and induction of new staff may be where training is most needed. If the organisation is committed to retaining and developing its own employees – like McDonalds and Enterprise Rent-A-Car – but budgets are tight, the possibility of offering short-term secondments to broaden an employee's experience in the business is an option that could be considered.

In managing a changing environment an organisation can choose to implement changes covering many different aspects of organisational life. These changes can include alterations to organisational size, structure and culture, as well as changes to operational activities and the roles that people undertake in an organisation. Major organisational changes in size and structure will affect hierarchical and reporting relationships, along with communication and decision-making systems. An organisation that decreases the number of middle managers it employs will also be reducing its size and that of its hierarchy. Hence the structure of the organisation will be flatter and more communication will need to occur between those at the top and those further down. At the same time, decision making will have to be either decentralised to those further down the organisation or centralised with those at the top.

A change in organisational culture, which is difficult to achieve, is likely to involve changes in personalities and the position these people occupy in the organisation. Leadership styles and the way in which people are motivated will also change. For employees of an organisation undergoing change, the changes will be felt in the tasks and activities they perform on a daily basis as part of their jobs. This may include minor or major changes in the content of the job and the way the job is undertaken.

Finally, change is either reactive or proactive. Reactive change is where the organisation reacts to an event that has already occurred. In contrast, proactive change is where an organisation plans and prepares for expected and anticipated events, and may even involve working on how to deal with unexpected events.

STRATEGY AND SUCCESSFUL CHANGE

Successful change in organisations requires strategy to have a clarity and coherence that allows it to be clearly understood at all levels in the organisation. The understanding of the strategy at all levels of the organisation means that staff should be clear about the overall strategic vision and their contribution to it (see Chapter 1). This is necessary as different parts of the organisation will be involved to varying degrees in different aspects of change and staff need to understand how the varying aspects of the change relate to each other in providing the coherent strategic vision. There may be many aspects to major change in a large organisation, including restructuring, relocation of outlets, offices and depots, job redesign, new quality systems, redefined service levels and re-equipment (new equipment and technology). The projects implemented, the management style, the interdependencies (see Chapter 2) and resource requirements will form the basis of planning the change. A detailed plan would include an indication of the area or division(s) covered by the plan, what is to be done and by whom, and who is responsible for monitoring progress and final achievement of the plan.

Strong culture organisations, discussed earlier in this chapter, are likely to experience high levels of resistance to change. There will be few natural change leaders in such an organisation and a forceful and extreme approach will be required to break a dominant culture. This type of approach will need to start dismantling resistance to change at the top of the organisation and strong leadership is desirable, as restructuring and redesign of management teams is likely to be required. This approach should allow the organisation to be opened to change and assist management in taking a top-down approach to change. In contrast organisations with a non-dominant culture will naturally be more open to change and it will not be necessary to tackle the resistors to change initially, this can be left until later in the process with minimal risk.[19] In the organisation naturally open to change, a bottom-up approach to change and its achievement in meeting organisational goals should be possible.

Unfreezing

Unfreezing is the acceptance that old behaviour must come to be regarded as unsuitable and must stop.

The Lewin model was developed to identify and examine the three stages of the change process. The first stage is **unfreezing** current attitudes and behaviour (see **Exhibit 5.10**). This unfreezing stage takes the view that if attitudes

Exhibit 5.10 The change process model

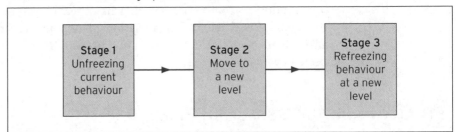

Source: Capon, C (2004) *Understanding Organisational Context*, 2nd edn, Harlow: Financial Times/Prentice Hall.

and behaviour are to change, then old behaviour must come to be regarded as unsuitable and must stop. Hence the necessity for change to be understood by the stakeholders affected for the change to succeed. Senior management need to signal that current behaviours are not allowing organisational goals to be met, and hence the long-term survival of the organisation and its competitive position are in jeopardy. The benefits of the proposed change and how it will help meet organisational goals need to be clearly indicated to the affected stakeholders, hence the importance of an effective communication strategy. Part of the communication at the unfreezing stage concerns senior management highlighting the drivers of change for the organisation. Drivers of change include external factors such as competition and legislation, and internal drivers such as shareholder expectations and the organisation's drive for survival or expansion (see earlier in this chapter). The need for change, where possible, should be supported by data and information, such as sales figures, profit forecasts, market share figures and competitor performance.

In addition to identifying and discussing change, the barriers to change need to be removed; this is part of the unfreezing process. This can often require planned intervention, which can be built into the change process and may involve changing structure, informal networks, control systems, routines, symbols, power structures and stakeholder expectations. The planned interventions also need a timescale and some barriers will be easier to remove and change than others. Senior managers behaving in a manner which supports the message of change they are trying to put across is critical, and of symbolic importance in helping ensure successful development and implementation of the changes. In addition to clear communication and appropriate symbolic activity, further training, education and management development can help to ensure the change process succeeds.

✔ Check your understanding

- Do you understand what is meant by drivers of change?
- Check your understanding by identifying drivers of change for BA (see Entry Case Study 5.1).

Moving to a new level

The second stage of Lewin's change process model is **moving to a new level** (see Exhibit 5.10). A search for answers to the difficulties faced by the organisation has to occur. This involves reviewing alternative solutions, the examination of changing values, culture and structure, along with strategy development and implementation. The organisation will be in a state of flux due to the changes, and different people will have different roles and expectations of organisational change.

Stakeholders with high interest and low power – category B (see **Exhibit 5.3**) – are likely to include employees and some customers. The need is to keep such stakeholders informed of the changes and the potential benefits resulting from them. Communication for minor change can be one way – via circulars, newsletters, memos and email. Information concerning major organisational change is best imparted via two-way communication as this allows stakeholders to ask questions and request information concerning the changes and how they will be affected. This can be done via meetings, team briefings and video conferencing.

Stakeholders with low interest and high power – category C (see **Exhibit 5.3**) – will have virtually no interest in minor changes. However, they need to be kept satisfied and convinced of the benefits of major change, otherwise they may choose to exert their high power and increase their level of interest.

The key stakeholders – category D (see **Exhibit 5.3**) – have high power and high interest and how they are managed will depend on their context. Category D stakeholders are important to organisations and are often staff with seniority or particularly hard to come by skills and knowledge which is highly valued by the organisation. Their interests need to be met if they are not to leave the organisation or exercise their high power and try to change things, that is behave as a dissatisfied stakeholder. The alternative view is that category D stakeholders, which includes senior managers, are often behind major change and as such it is their role to work with employees to analyse the organisation and its environment, and identify the drivers for and against change. This approach should lead to a shared vision of the future for the organisation. The building of teams, departments or groups to enact the changes required should also include identifying and developing team and group leadership, to increase the likelihood that the cohesion and competence needed to move the change forward are harnessed.

Solutions and answers to the difficulties faced by the organisation need to be developed and the essential changes planned. Once this has been achieved the implementation of the planned changes can be arranged. Then the chosen solutions can start to be implemented, which may necessitate running new and current systems and methods of working in parallel. This allows the newly implemented solutions to be assessed as working satisfactorily, before the old method or system of working is withdrawn. There should then be a final review and tweaking of systems and methods of working to ensure that the required level of work and satisfaction is being achieved by the people involved. Maintaining the changes and avoiding the need for repeated major change can be helped by ensuring good communication, and appropriate training and staff development.

Refreezing

Refreezing is the positive reinforcement and support for the implemented changes.

The third stage of Lewin's change process model is **refreezing** attitudes and behaviour (see **Exhibit 5.10**) at the new level. This takes place once acceptable solutions have been found. The refreezing stage involves positive reinforcement and support for the implemented changes. This can be done by highlighting improvements in difficult areas that have occurred as a result of the changes, for example an upturn in sales or improvement in quality, which could include testimony from a satisfied customer reproduced in a company newsletter. Identifying change projects which have a good chance of success and tackling them first will be likely to bring early 'wins'. Early 'wins' help demonstrate that the change is achievable and is going to occur. People from other parts of the organisation not directly affected by the changes also need to be informed of what has been achieved.

Review questions | **Managing a changing environment and successful change**

1 Where do external drivers of change for organisations arise from?
2 Where do internal drivers of change for organisations arise from?
3 Define change.
4 How do organisations ensure the required change occurs?
5 Identify two of each, internal and external driving forces for change.
6 Identify two of each, internal and external restraining forces for change.
7 Explain if it is easy or difficult to effect culture change in a strong culture organisation.
8 Why is 'unfreezing' an important step in the change process?
9 Summarise what occurs in organisations which are 'moving to a new level'.
10 At what point in the change process does 'refreezing' occur?

CONCLUSION

This chapter examines stakeholders in organisations, their power, interest, legitimacy and urgency. The approaches to examining stakeholders can be used to direct strategic thinking around the relative importance of stakeholders to an organisation, as this determines the amount of effort to be invested in them.

The chapter also examines organisational culture and its determinants, which are presented in the cultural web. Using the cultural web to direct thinking about the culture in an organisation allows managers to understand why the organisation is the type of place it is. This can be useful if a change in culture is needed as an analysis using the cultural web may give indicators as to what needs to change, for example the routine behaviour, the structure or the control systems. Changes in organisational culture are usually undertaken in order to change or improve the organisational culture.

This chapter concludes by examining approaches to change in organisations, including cultural change. It provides some general approaches to understanding and examining the change process and how it may occur in organisations.

LEARNING OUTCOMES AND SUMMARY

→ **Learning outcome 1**
Identify and evaluate an organisation's stakeholders.

- Stakeholders are any individual or collection of individuals with an interest in an organisation. Some stakeholders will be internal to an organisation, such as employees; others will be external, for example customers.
- Different stakeholders will have varying levels of power and interest in an organisation – for example employees will have an interest in wage and salary rates – and their power is dependent on their position in the organisation.

→ **Learning outcome 2**
Discuss the interest, power, legitimacy and urgency of stakeholders.

- Stakeholders can be mapped on a power and interest matrix. Category A stakeholders have low power and low interest, and the organisation need invest only minimal effort. Category B stakeholders have high interest and low power and need to be kept informed; while category C stakeholders, with high power and low interest, should be kept satisfied. Key players are the category D stakeholders with high interest and high power.
- Stakeholders can be viewed as being latent, expectant or definitive. Latent stakeholders have low salience and possess only one attribute: power, legitimacy or urgency.
- Dormant stakeholders have the attribute of power, discretionary stakeholders possess legitimacy and demanding stakeholders have urgency.
- Expectant stakeholders are of medium salience and possess two of the three attributes of power, legitimacy and urgency. Dominant stakeholders have power and legitimacy, dangerous stakeholders hold power and urgency, and dependant stakeholders have the attributes of legitimacy and urgency.
- Definitive stakeholders have high salience and hold all three attributes: power, legitimacy and urgency.

→ **Learning outcome 3**
Define organisational culture and explain how an organisation's culture is determined.

- Organisational culture defines the type of place an organisation has become. The determinants of organisational culture are presented in the cultural web, which includes routines and rituals; stories; symbols; power structures; organisational structure; and control systems. All these determinants will have an impact on the type of place an organisation is to work in.

→ **Learning outcome 4**
Summarise key actions for helping a company alter its culture.

- Deal and Kennedy identify seven elements required for successful cultural change. These centre on initially recognising threats from the external environment, and putting a hero in charge of changing the culture and behaviour.
- Job security in the transition process should be emphasised and any necessary redundancies should be dealt with prior to embarking on the culture change.
- The process of changing culture should focus on providing training in new values and expected behaviour, which should be underpinned by transition rituals that mark the change and its success. Achieving this may require the use of outside consultants.

→ **Learning outcome 5**
Identify driving and restraining forces for organisational change.

- The drivers of organisational change can arise from the external environment faced by a company, that is the PEST factors, competitors, markets and customers. Equally causes of change can arise from inside an organisation, namely managers, shareholders and trade unions.
- Restraining forces may be individual in nature, for example an employee's lack of understanding of the proposed changes and associated ambiguity. Equally restraining forces may be organisational in nature and result from long-established culture or weaknesses in required capabilities.

→ **Learning outcome 6**
Understand and discuss the change process model.

- Lewin also developed the change process model, which identifies three stages of the change process. First is the unfreezing stage, in which current behaviour has to become viewed as unsuitable. The second stage is moving to a new level, which involves finding and establishing new behaviours. The third stage is refreezing, when new behaviours become established and the accepted norm.

This exit case study looks at Volkswagen's takeover of Skoda and focuses on the changes at Skoda. It can be used to assess the learning outcomes below. The changes at Skoda can be analysed by using the cultural web model.

Learning outcomes	Check you have achieved this by	
1 Apply the cultural web to an organisation.	Using the cultural web to define an organisation's culture and identify internal drivers for change.	Answering Exit case study questions 1 and 2.
2 Identify the changes to an organisation's cultural web.	Describing the changes to an organisation's cultural web.	Answering Exit case study question 3.

Vratislav Kulhanek of Skoda

FT

by Ross Tieman

'You can't just rely on the British sense of humour'. How do you rescue a consumer business that fell so far behind in technology and quality that its products became the butt of comedians' jokes? Vratislav Kulhanek, the executive chairman of Skoda Auto, the Czech carmaker, allows himself a slow smile at the question. Since he took charge five years ago, the issue of Skoda's blighted reputation has been a constant drag on his efforts to drive the company forward.

Even today, 11 years after Volkswagen Group of Germany bought control of the business from the Czech government, many potential customers in Western Europe still say they wouldn't consider buying a Skoda. But attitudes are changing, as the company's sales and profitability show. Last year, Skoda Auto made and sold 460,000 cars, and 80 per cent of them were bought by customers outside the Czech Republic. Gradually, the company is regaining a reputation for quality and reliability that it last enjoyed in its 1930s' hey-day. But it has been a long haul. 'The important thing about reputation,' says Mr Kulhanek, 'is that you have to work hard to achieve it, and it takes a long time'.

During the communist era, East Europeans were ready buyers of Skoda cars because the market was sheltered from Western competition. Relaxation of import restrictions after the Czech Republic's 'velvet revolution' led to a flood of second-hand Western imports that brought home to the company, and its customers, just how poor its products were by comparison. Skoda Auto, the world's third-oldest car-maker, would almost certainly have disappeared, had not Volkswagen, attracted by wage rates a fraction of those in Germany, taken control and pledged to maintain the marque.

The initial challenge, says Mr Kulhanek, a Czech who joined Skoda from German automotive parts maker Robert Bosch, was to produce a new model of a quality and reliability that would bear comparison with Western rivals. To bring that about, 500 Volkswagen managers were transferred from Germany, to work alongside their Skoda counterparts in every branch of the business. For the Czechs, says Mr Kulhanek, it was a case of 'learning by doing'.

The result was the Felicia, a middle-sized hatchback that was unexciting but reliable and cheap, and enabled the company to satisfy many of its traditional customers while it developed cars that could win new customers and build its market share. Skoda launched its second-generation recovery range with the Octavia mid-sized saloon in 1998. It didn't look like a Skoda. It looked like a car from a Western European or Japanese manufacturer. Sales in Germany, the company's biggest foreign market, ran to target. But in, the UK, its next-largest export market where the company has been selling cars since 1953, they were pitiful. The Octavia wasn't cheap and cheerful enough for traditional British customers, and Skoda's lingering bad reputation deterred the rest. The company learned a hard lesson, but put it to good effect.

Two years ago, when it launched its small Fabia hatchback, Skoda took a deep breath, then unleashed a UK advertising campaign with the slogan: 'The Fabia car is so good you won't believe it's a Skoda.' The effect was remarkable. Sales of the Fabia exceeded the full-year

→

target within months and Skoda UK found itself with a 1,500-car waiting list. Between 1999 and 2001, Skoda's UK sales rocketed from 3,000 cars a year to 28,000. They were up another 20 per cent in the first half of this year, to 21,522, a 1.6 per cent market share. Because Skoda began selling cars in Britain back in 1953, the product's bad reputation had been built up over decades and needed to be tackled head on. But Mr Kulhanek says the appeal to the particular British sense of humour could not be repeated in other export markets, where the challenge was different.

In other countries, where Skodas appeared much later, he says, 'we could count on the view that a Skoda is only a Volkswagen produced in the Czech Republic'. That is a mixed blessing. In these markets, Skoda cars benefit from the halo of Volkswagen's reputation for quality but sell essentially on price. The brand is not necessarily strong enough to win customers in its own right.

The challenge now is to fix with consumers a distinct brand identity for the cars they are building. The first step in this direction was taken this year, when Skoda launched an executive saloon, the Superb, named after one of its finest pre-war models. Skoda's hallmarks, says Mr Kulhanek, are emerging as those the company held dear half a century ago: a kind of conservative new design, underpinned by robustness and reliability. 'There was never a period where we were focused on the latest trends,' says Mr Kulhanek. The target customers, he says, are those who will 'buy a comfortable sofa for their house or flat, rather than the latest designer trend'. This evolution of Skoda's long-drawn recovery, in which focus widens from producing a credible model range to developing a sustainable brand and corporate identity, is now seen as a key step for the company. It is also an important

issue for its parent Volkswagen group, which has to avoid Skoda or its Spanish subsidary, Seat, from cannibalising its own sales.

The attempt to develop distinct brands is evident at the current Paris motor show, where Volkswagen and up-market Audi displays are well separated from Skoda and from Seat, which is meanwhile trying to develop a sporty, Mediterranean style. Skoda, by contrast, turned up with its veteran 1938 Superb, dancers in 1930s costumes, and child-seats buckled in the back of its practical family run-abouts. 'We carry out regular surveys with regard to the brand image,' says Mr Kulhanek. 'Awareness of the brand now equals that of Fiat, and the image is progressing. With every year we are getting closer to our competitors.

'But the handicap of Skoda being an Eastern European brand is very difficult to overcome. For years the communist regime said things were worse in Western Europe and we didn't believe it. People in the West were told things in the East were worse – and they did believe it. I just don't know how many decades it will take for that perception to die away.'

Source: FT. com website, 11 October 2002.

Exit case study questions

1 Using the case study and your own general knowledge apply the cultural web to Skoda prior to its takeover by Volkswagen.

2 Identify drivers for change at Skoda using the case study and your answer to question 1.

3 Discuss the changes to Skoda's cultural web brought about by Volkswagen.

DISCUSSION TOPIC

1 Read the paper 'Transforming Organisations' by Henry Mintzberg, Bruce Ahlstrand and Joseph Lampel, Chapter 6, in *The Strategy Process*, Mintzberg, Lampel, Quinn and Ghosal, Harlow: Prentice Hall, 2003.

2 Consider the following quote from the paper and critically evaluate the relevance of different approaches to change with reference to examples with which you are familiar.

'So should the change process be top down or bottom up?... which approach you use depends on your organisation's goals, needs and capabilities.'

WIDEN YOUR HORIZONS

1 Widen your horizons by undertaking the necessary research and performing a stakeholder analysis, which allows you to compare and contrast stakeholders in the following organisations:

- The International Committee of the Red Cross (ICRC).
- UN (Humanitarian Affairs).
- Médicins Sans Frontières (MSF).

2 Widen your horizons by determining, comparing and contrasting the cultural webs of Arsenal FC (www.arsenal.com) and Fulham Town FC (www.fulhamfc.co.uk).

3 Widen your horizons by considering Asda's advice for creating a winning retail culture, which is: 'respect your people; listen to them; act on what your hear; communicate, communicate, communicate.' Compare and contrast the advice offered by Adsa with that suggested by Deal and Kennedy, see the Deal and Kennedy material in this chapter and the Asda article by D White, 'People power drives Asda's push for top', in the *Daily Telegraph* on 20 November 2003.

4 Widen your horizons by undertaking the necessary research and discussing the stages of the change process which have occurred in an organisation of your choice. Comment on the usefulness of theory in helping you understand the successes and failures of the change which has occurred.

WEBLINKS

The websites for this chapter are for some of the three key areas it covers: stakeholders, culture and change.

- The website below looks at the National Grid and its stakeholders. Visit the website and click on 'Our Stakeholders'.
  www.nationalgrid.com/uk/socialandenvironment
- The website below is for the UK Shareholders Association; shareholders are important stakeholders in organisations.
  www.uksa.org.uk
- This business search engine can provide good articles and information about a range of business and organisational topics, including corporate culture.
  www.business.com
- This site contains articles and information about managing change.
  www.change-management.com
- This is the website of British Airways; the company looked at in Entry case study 5.1. Visit the website and click on 'Company Information' at the bottom of the homepage.
  www.britishairways.com

FURTHER READING

Stakeholders

- Butcher, D (2003) 'Whose company is it anyway?', *Management Today*, July, pp 62-5.
- MacMillan, K and Dowing, S (1999) 'Governance and performance', *Journal of General Management*, 24 (3), Spring.

■ Mills, R W and Weinstein, B (2000) 'Beyond shareholder value – reconciling the shareholders and stakeholder perspectives', *Journal of General Management*, 26 (3), Spring.

■ Mitchell, R K, Agle, B R and Wood, D J (1997) 'Towards a theory of stakeholder identification and salience defining the principle of who and what really counts', *Academy of Management Review*, 22 (4), pp 853–86.

Culture

■ Black, S J and Gregersen, H B (1999) 'The right way to manage expats', *Harvard Business Review*, March/April.

■ Brown, A (1998) *Organisational Culture,* 2nd edn, London: Financial Times/Prentice Hall.

■ Butcher, D (2003) 'How to ditch the disservice culture', *Management Today*, September, pp 62–5.

■ Foster, M J and Minkes, A L (1999) 'East and west: business culture as divergence', *Journal of General Management*, 25 (1), Autumn.

■ Lessem, R (2001) 'Managing in four worlds, culture, strategy and transformation', *Long Range Planning*, February.

■ Martins, E C and Terblance, F (2003) 'Building organisational culture that stimulates creativity and innovation', *European Journal of Innovation Management*, 6 (1), pp 64–74.

■ Ogbonna, E and Harris, L C (1998) 'Organisational culture: its not what you think . . .', *Journal of General Management*, 23 (3), Spring.

■ Shelton, C D, Hall, R F Darling, J R (2003) 'When cultures collide: the challenge of global integration', *European Business Review*, 15 (5), pp 312–23.

Change

■ Balogun, J and Hope Hailey, V with Johnson, G and Scholes, K (2003) *Exploring Strategic Change*, 2nd edn, Harlow: Prentice Hall Europe.

■ Beer, M and Nohria, N (2000) 'Cracking the code of change', *Harvard Business Review*, May/June.

■ Burnes, B (2004) *Managing Change*, 4th edn, Harlow: Financial Times/Prentice Hall.

■ McCracken, D M (2000) 'Winning the talent war for women: sometimes it takes a revolution', *Harvard Business Review*, November/December.

■ Pascale, R and Millemann, M (1997) 'Changing the way we change', *Harvard Business Review*, November/December.

■ Senior, B (2002) *Organisational Change,* 2nd edn, London: Financial Times/Prentice Hall.

■ Strebel, P (1996) 'Why do employees resist change', *Harvard Business Review*, May/June.

■ Welaufer, S (1999) 'Driving change, Interview with Ford's Jacques Nasser', *Harvard Business Review*, March/April.

REFERENCES

1 Waples, J and Kemeny, L (2004) 'Ultimatum for Shell chief after oil reserves bombshell', *The Sunday Times*, 11 January.
2 Hope, C (2004) 'The revolution that shook Shell's politburo', *Daily Telegraph*, 6 March.

3 Durman, P and Kemeny, L (2004) 'Another brutal week for Shell as report makes Watts the fall guy', *The Sunday Times*, 25 April.

4 Kemeny, L (2004) 'Shell finance chief's role in doubt', *The Sunday Times*, 18 April.

5 Hope, op. cit.

6 Mitchell, R K, Agle, B R and Wood, D J (1997) 'Towards a theory of stakeholder identification and salience defining the principle of who and what really counts' *Academy of Management Review*, 22 (4), pp 853–86.

7 Ibid.

8 Ibid.

9 Ibid.

10 BBC News (2004) 'Al-Qaeda threat grounds flights', http://news.bbc.co.uk, 31 January.

11 Deal, T and Kennedy, A (1988) *Corporate Cultures*, London: Penguin Business.

12 Johnson, G and Scholes, K (2002) *Exploring Corporate Strategy*, 6th edn, Chapter 5, Harlow: Financial Times/Prentice Hall.

13 Deal and Kennedy, op. cit.

14 Deal and Kennedy, op. cit.

15 Osborne, A (2004) 'Yes sir, would you like an apple with that?', *Daily Telegraph*, 9 March.

16 Lewin, K (1951) *Field theory in social science*, Harper and Row, quoted in Thompson, J L (1997) *Strategic Management*, London: International Thomson Business Press.

17 Ginsberg, A and Abrahamson, E (1991) 'Champions of change and strategic shifts: the role of internal and external change advocates', *Journal of Management Studies*, 28 (2), pp 173–90, cited in Senior, B (2002) *Organisational Change*, 2nd edn, London: Financial Times/Prentice Hall.

18 Huczynski, A and Buchanan, D (2001) *Organisational Behaviour Student Workbook*, 4th edn, Hemel Hempstead, Financial Times/Prentice Hall, cited in Senior, B (2002) *Organisational Change*, 2nd edn, London: Financial Times/Prentice Hall.

19 Senior, B (2002) *Organisational Change*, 2nd edn, London: Financial Times/Prentice Hall.

CHAPTER 6

Management and leadership in organisations

Exhibit 6.1 Essential strategy model

Chapter objectives

The key purpose of this chapter is to examine the roles of management and leadership in organisations. The starting point is to define management and examine the views of some key writers on the subject such as Peter Drucker and Douglas McGregor. Management is about dealing with people and other resources in the workplace to ensure that the work which takes place results in objectives being achieved. In contrast leadership is concerned with both a leader's ability and approach to influencing the achievement of objectives. Hence different leadership styles and types of power are examined as it is style of leadership and use of power that determine the type of leader a person becomes. There is no one best style of leadership and this chapter seeks to present a variety of views on leadership to enable the reader to formulate their own opinions on leadership.

When you have read this chapter and worked through the associated activities you should be able to achieve the objectives specified opposite.

1 Explain what is meant by 'management'.

2 Discuss different ways of managing staff and resources, and the expected outcomes.

3 Identify the key aspects of management in organisations.

4 Summarise the role of leaders and leadership in organisations.

5 Discuss different approaches to leadership and their suitability for different situations.

Strong leadership which is able to engage staff in taking the business forward can be key to its success. Therefore this entry case study looks at the importance of the role of leadership in organisations.

Industry maps DNA of 21st-century movers and shakers

FT

by Stefan Stern

Management fads come and go but leadership is always in vogue, both as a subject for debate and a priority for business. The once briefly fashionable idea that leadership was somehow questionable in an era of egalitarianism is already a distant memory. The squeamishness of the anti-leaders is a thing of the past. Today, customers, shareholders, employees and voters all say they want to see strong leadership.

But this unanimity does not mean leadership has ceased to be controversial. The point was made in a recent FT Business Education special report. In an exclusive debate were the distinguished business academic Henry Mintzberg, a professor at McGill University in Montreal, and Frank Brown, the new Dean of the INSEAD business school at Fontainebleau. Prof Mintzberg is famous for his critique of conventional business and executive education over its apparent obsession with lonely, heroic leaders who transform vast organisations on their own, through sheer force of will and personality.

This kind of detached leadership is a destructive myth, Prof Mintzberg says, which in the most extreme cases can lead to the sort of malfeasance seen from leaders at businesses such as Enron, WorldCom and Tyco. Dean Brown, on the other hand, seemed happy to salute the role of the leader in more conventional terms. 'Simply said, the last thing the business world needs is more managers,' he observed starkly. 'On the contrary, it is in need of more leaders.' It is this sense that too many businesses and organisations are 'over-managed and under-led' that pro-

vides an added impetus to employers' desire for better leadership training.

What sort of interventions can work, and what are the smartest companies doing about developing more and better leaders? Jonathan Perks, managing director of leadership services at the consulting company Penna, says that more and more businesses are moving away from advocating a traditional 'command and control' style of leadership. 'Businesses want their leaders to grow other leaders,' he says. 'That means having leaders who coach their people and don't just tell them what to do, trusting them to grow and become more empowered.'

Perhaps unexpectedly, Mr Perks, who was trained as an officer at Sandhurst, says that his experiences in the army have helped him to develop a more 'emotionally intelligent' style of leadership with corporate clients. 'When people hear the word "emotional", they do tend to get a bit emotional,' Mr Perks concedes. 'But this is really about dealing better with life and what makes people successful at work.'

Mr Perks cites Northern Foods chief executive Pat O'Driscoll as a leader who is serious about introducing a coaching culture into the business; 'personally leading by example', he says. But down on the shop-floor, PC World has been working with its managers to develop better coaching skills as well. Generation X and Y employees do not take kindly to an authoritarian, overly directive style of leadership, Mr Perks suggests. 'Discretionary effort' is just that; a freely made choice.

→

The 'collateral damage' caused by bad leaders can be huge, Mr Perks adds, at a time when younger employees may feel no particular loyalty to their employer. They will be gone, taking their skills and experience with them. Leaders are vital. As the cliché goes, people join a company but leave to get away from the boss.

The increasingly international nature of business means the pressure is on companies to develop more leaders who are comfortable working in foreign environments, becoming 'cultural chameleons', as Steve Newhall, managing director of consultants DDI, calls them. Businesses know that there are many exciting opportunities to be grabbed, in the emerging markets of the BRIC countries, for example (Brazil, Russia, India and China).

'Firms look at their pipeline of talent and ask "who have we got who can go out there and perform?",' Mr Newhall says. After researching this question with corporate clients, DDI has developed an interesting blueprint of what a global leader needs to look like in the early 21st century. They have identified certain key characteristics that they feel need to be found in the 'DNA' of the global leader.

These include having a fiercely sharp intellect, being a 'black belt' in people skills, being genuinely intellectually curious about the world, while also boasting superb energy levels and a certain personal humility. It is a rare combination, to say the least. Energy is important, Mr Newhall explains, because the international leader may get so few opportunities to see his people face to face. 'You get off the plane in Mumbai or Shanghai and you have really got to be on song,' he says.

But if the list of characteristics seems depressingly daunting we should not despair, Mr Newhall adds. 'No-one emerges fully equipped in this way,' he admits. 'These skills can be developed, through coaching and mentoring, and an effort to understand the cultural issues,' he adds. 'Leaders are first born and then made,' he says.

There has been no ceasefire in the corporate 'war for talent'. But it is expensive to go out into the market and buy in new leaders. Cheaper, and more effective, is to grow your own. The businesses that achieve success establishing this future 'talent pipeline' will be the ones that also achieve greater commercial success in the future.

Source: *Financial Times*, 10 November 2006.

INTRODUCTION

Management is relating to people in defined roles and working within a structured organisation.

Management and leadership exist in organisations and this chapter aims to examine the role of both. Management is often seen as getting things done via other people to achieve organisational objectives. Management is the activity

Business illustration of management – China

Companies in China which rely on adopting US and multinational approaches to provide the basis for management have been unable to identify and develop a distinctive Chinese 'brand' of management. The difficulties with developing managers are reinforced by overseas expatriate managers sent to China to run operations who tend to struggle to adapt and often fail to make the grade.

The other side of the coin is that China is not developing enough global managers of its own to work for Chinese multinationals, which have developed significant overseas operations. The management consultancy McKinskey estimates that China has only 3,000 to 5,000 managers capable of operating globally but needs to develop at least 75,000 such managers over the next 10 to 15 years. The shortage of talent is widespread across disciplines and large salary rises make it difficult for companies to retain skilled and talented staff.

Source: 'China faces crisis among management', Roland Gribben, *Daily Telegraph*, 2 November 2006.

of relating to people in defined roles and working within a structured organisation. Managers will not necessarily occupy leadership roles, particularly if their focus is on operational activities.

Management is, therefore, viewed in terms of supervising, organising, planning and directing the day-to-day work of subordinate staff. In contrast leadership is seen as being concerned with communicating with, motivating and involving staff, which influences interpersonal behaviour in the organisation and the willingness of staff to support and follow a successful leader. Hence there is a perception that managers manage resources and exhibit a limited amount of emotional involvement in the job they perform, while leaders lead people and develop empathy with staff. Leadership can occur due to someone's formal position in the organisational hierarchy, but equally a leader may operate without a formally defined 'leadership role'. This view is supported by Belbin, 'There is a clear implication that leadership is not part of the job but a quality that can be brought to a job ... The work that leadership encompasses in the context is not clearly assigned but comes about spontaneously.'[1] In organisations it is clear that both management and leadership occur and an effective manager is often one who exhibits the ability to lead staff, meaning leadership is often viewed as a management role. This chapter will first look at management and then at leadership in organisations.

WHAT IS MANAGEMENT?

Management is a general term which can be interpreted in many different ways by the varying stakeholder groups in an organisation. We can all be viewed as managers of our own time and work. Hence staff in organisations have some control over the planning and organisation of their work, to either a greater or lesser extent. However, management in organisations is often concerned with exercising formal power and control, within a defined structure, to shape the behaviour and work patterns of staff with the aim of achieving good performance and meeting organisational objectives. This is also illustrated in the cultural web (see Chapter 5).

Management is concerned with 'making things happen' and is a largely practical activity that involves working with and developing people to meet objectives and achieve results. Depending on the situation an organisation finds itself in, management may be about changing behaviour due to the organisation's position in the external environment and key success factors changing (see Chapters 2 and 3). Hence management is concerned with the achievement of objectives via the efforts of other people in an organisational structure with defined roles, using resources and control systems to achieve the outcomes required for success. Peter Druker broadly echoes this view.

Peter Drucker

Peter Drucker was born in Vienna in 1909, trained as a lawyer, worked as a journalist in London between 1933 and 1936, before emigrating to the US in 1937. Today Drucker is widely regarded as a guru of modern management and has written extensively about the significance of management and its development in the twentieth century. He undertook his first management consultancy job for General Motors in 1942 and his direct approach to consultancy was not well received by General Motors. However, Drucker continued both to work as a consultant and to look at what constituted a modern organisation and what the managers running them should do. Drucker's consultancy work grew and in 1954 one of his books, the *Practice of Management* was published which resulted in the theory of Management by Objectives (MBO), being high profile in the 1950s and 1960s. In this work Drucker identifies the seven tasks of a manager of 'tomorrow' (see **Exhibit 6.2**).

Exhibit 6.2 Drucker's seven tasks of tomorrow's manager

He or she should:
- manage by objectives.
- take more risks, over a longer time period and also allow this to happen further down the organisation.
- take strategic decisions.
- build an integrated team, in which members are capable of assessing their own performance in relation to common objectives.
- communicate quickly and clearly and have a motivating influence on staff at all levels such that their participation, in a responsible manner, is obtained.
- see the organisation as a whole and understand his/her role within it.
- understand the external environment and the significant factors, which impact on the organisation, its products and services, and the sector as a whole.

Source: summarised from Clutterbuck, D and Crainer, S (1990) *Makers of Management*, London: Papermac Macmillan.

Drucker views management as being both a group of people with power, knowledge and expertise and the function or activity of managing. 'Management is tasks. Management is a discipline. But management is also people. Every achievement of management is the achievement of a manager. Every failure is a failure of a manager.'[2]

The alternative view is that management is not separate and distinct as there is the problem of identifying which tasks and activities in organisations are management and which are not. Additionally job titles do not necessarily help in identifying staff as being management or not, as in some organisations the use of the title 'manager' is an attempt to enhance the status and improve the morale of staff who do not undertake a full range management tasks. In contrast in some organisations titles such as captain, head teacher, consultant and superintendent are used to denote management positions. The title 'head teacher' suggests an experienced teacher who teaches; however, the reality is head teachers spend much of their time managing the staff, budgets and problems of the schools they work in and do very little teaching. Similarly the superintendent in the police force also fulfils a managerial role.

One question which is often asked is: 'Are managers born or made?'. The obvious answer is a combination of both. A potentially good manager will possess natural talents and innate qualities, but these have to be developed and encouraged via education, training, appropriate experience and proper guidance or mentoring.

The other question which is often asked is: 'Is management an art or science?'. Again the obvious answer is a combination of both. Management requires subject or discipline knowledge of, for example, accounting, HR or product development and the associated skills of how to manage people and resources – which can all be taught and learnt. However, management is also something of art as it involves practice, experience and personal judgement in dealing with different groups of stakeholders, staff, customers, suppliers, financiers and trade unions. It should be borne in mind that managers themselves are people and to that end may often base decisions on their own views, prejudices and opinions rather than the facts which knowledge and analysis present.

Douglas McGregor

Douglas McGregor was born in Detroit in 1906 and was professor of management at Massachusetts Institute of Technology between 1954 and 1964. McGregor is best known for his work *The Human Side of Enterprise*, which presents the arguments for **Theory X** and **Theory Y**, which represent two extremes of management style.

Theory Y assumes people regard work as normal activity and are self-motivated towards the achievement of organisational objectives.

Theory Y assumes people regard work as normal activity and are committed to the organisational objectives, and self-motivated towards their achievement and the associated rewards. Additionally people will accept and seek out responsibility, behaving creatively while resolving problems in the organisation helping it to develop and move forward. People undertake such roles, performing a wide variety of tasks, which involve exercising initiative and judgement and in return seek high levels of intrinsic satisfaction. Hence individuals may satisfy their motivational needs and achieve their own goals through meeting the goals of the organisation.

In practice, however, the actual style of management behaviour adopted will be influenced by the demands of the situation. Hence the task of management is to create the conditions in which staff are motivated and can gain the intrinsic satisfaction that they seek. Do not assume that the Theory Y approach is a 'soft' option, as in practice it can be difficult to achieve high levels of motivation and commitment across all staff all of the time. Therefore at times the Theory Y approach to managing will be time-consuming and frustrating, and mistakes will be made. However, managers successfully adopting the Theory Y approach will develop much more co-operative relationships with their employees.

Theory X assumes that people dislike work and seek to avoid it at all costs.

The other extreme, Theory X, assumes that people dislike work and seek to avoid it at all costs. Hence staff doing jobs which offer little in the way of intrinsic satisfaction, motivation or rewards may perform best if a Theory X or a more dictatorial style of management is adopted. Jobs and roles which are tightly defined and designed, with outputs which can be measured precisely are often like this. These jobs include ones in complex production processes in manufacturing firms, which require a Theory X approach if adequate levels of performance are to be maintained. The Theory X approach is also applied in emergency situations or where shortage of time, or other factors, means authority is needed to direct actions. Examples include dictatorial chefs who appear to bully their staff into undertaking many tasks which need to be co-ordinated over very short timescales to deliver the very best food to diners – and many kitchen staff accept the Theory X style of management as appropriate.

Managers should adopt the Theory Y approach to management when it is appropriate for the staff and their roles. However, on occasions the Theory X approach will be needed to achieve the desired outcomes.

Review questions What is management

1 Write your own definition of formal management.
2 Discuss the role of objectives in management.
3 Explain Drucker's management tasks.
4 In your view are managers born or made?
5 Compare and contrast Theory X and Theory Y.

MANAGERS, EFFECTIVENESS AND EFFICIENCY

Successful managers need to be able to handle people effectively to get the best performance from them for the organisation to successfully meet its objectives. Many organisations have mission statements and corporate objectives which encompass the view that employees are their most valuable assets. However, in many organisations these missions and objectives are poorly pursued and implemented, such that the valuable asset of staff is actually poorly managed in practice. This often occurs because staff are managed via rules, regulations, systems and procedures rather than as people. This occurs in many organisations where employees do not feel valued as an important asset, and their knowledge and expertise are not used and understood. Hence it is critical that managers have a highly developed sense of perception when it comes to understanding the feelings, motivations and expectations of their staff. This should translate into a genuine concern for people and their welfare, which in turn impacts on performance in the workplace.

Freemantle[3] suggests that managers are often not concerned about people until they become a problem and do not deliver an effective performance in the workplace. Hence complex systems of rules, regulations and procedures are developed for managing people. This, in turn, often leads to the view that staff are a cost which needs to be minimised rather than an asset which should be valued. However, there are some organisations, such as Northern Foods and PC World, which view managing people and 'coaching' as key areas in the development of their own managers and leaders (see Entry case study 6.1).

The achievement of objectives by an organisation will determine the likelihood of its survival and its degree of success. Managers are responsible for how well an organisation achieves its objectives, and this is clearly partly linked to both the efficiency and effectiveness of management.

Efficient managers seek to use resources to achieve objectives, while minimising waste.

The **efficient manager** is concerned with using resources to achieve objectives, while minimising waste. Therefore to be efficient a manager must be clear about targets and organise, plan and control to meet the targets without using resources unnecessarily.

In contrast effectiveness is achieved by managers 'doing the right things' to achieve outputs and meet objectives. The effectiveness of managers can be assessed by measuring how well targets are met and the results achieved. However, the manner which a manager adopts to achieve results will impact on staff and can influence the longevity of a manager's effectiveness. An **effec-**

Effective managers 'do the right things' to achieve outputs and meet objectives.

tive manager needs to consider the outputs and seek to achieve the best performance from staff in terms of factors which are important to the organisation, such as quality, cost-effectiveness, increased profitability and meeting customers' needs and wants – which normally relate to the organisation's objectives. These mean managers have a role to play in creating a workplace environment and culture (see Chapter 5) in which staff are also able to operate efficiently and effectively.

It can be argued that effectiveness is more important than efficiency as managers must first do 'the right thing' and then focus on doing it efficiently. The manager doing the 'wrong thing' efficiently will ultimately fail to achieve the desired outcomes and meet objectives.

 Check your understanding

- Do you understand the relevance of the manager's role in an organisation?
- Check your understanding by taking into account efficiency and effectiveness in organisations and explaining the relevance of the following quote from Entry case study 6.1: 'Simply said, the last thing the business world needs is more managers.'

Managers, effectiveness and efficiency

1 Explain why managers should have a highly developed sense of perception.
2 Explain why organisations develop complex rules and regulations for managing staff.
3 Identify the problem(s) of managing staff via rules and regulations.
4 Compare and contrast the efficient manager and the effective manager.

MANAGERIAL STYLE AND THE ROLE OF TRUST AND RESPECT

An effective management style is the result of how a manager uses their authority. The Theory X style of management uses direction and control along with rewards and sanctions, which all depend on the manager's authority. This is in contrast to Theory Y, which assumes people are committed to organisational goals and are self-motivated towards their achievement and the associated rewards. Many people see Theory Y as being the preferred management style for their organisation. Central to a Theory Y management style is the role of trust and respect.

Respect and trust

Employees in an organisation usually respond positively if treated with respect and trust. They will make a positive contribution to the organisation and its achievement of goals and objectives. Managers who offer trust and respect to their workforce gain reputations for being good and fair managers, which, in turn, allows them some leeway with staff when things do not run smoothly.

Offering trust and respect means managers will allow staff to get on with their work and achieve results. Managers providing positive feedback on good results offer a strong motivator to staff. In contrast lack of acknowledgement leads to demotivation and a lack of mutual respect between staff and manager. Managers who fail to create mutual respect with their staff will waste time checking up on their staff and also fail get the best out of the staff; staff in their turn will not trust their manager. Equally the manager who does not acknowledge good performance and is quick to severely criticise poor performance, will not engender respect and trust from his or her staff.

People expect to be treated fairly at work and for rewards to reflect their input to the organisation. Discrimination and inequality in managing staff leads to tension and diverts staff efforts from achieving organisational objectives. People often respond to the way they are treated. If praised and encouraged, staff will generally give a lot back to the organisation, as they have a sense of self worth. Equally, if the opposite is true and staff and their work are not acknowledged, then people will seek to give the organisation the bare minimum in terms of performance.

Respect, trust and management involvement

Successful managers understand the work of their staff and the associated problems and difficulties, and will have established a two-way communication process with staff. The two-way communication process will only be effective if both staff and managers respect and trust each other. The misuse or abuse of the two-way communication process, by either staff or managers, will lead to it becoming ineffective and possibly breaking down all together. Hence the successful manager will need to be both a good listener and effective communicator. Being a successful manager means achieving the right balance between understanding and involvement in the work of the staff, while avoiding excessive interference, which will inhibit the freedom of staff to take decisions and get on with tasks which need completing.

Offer respect, trust and treat staff as individuals

The treatment of staff as individuals avoids a general approach to managing issues which apply only to specific members of staff. For example, in the marketing department two staff routinely miss deadlines for the return of monthly sales figures. The marketing manager sends an email to all staff in the marketing department reminding them of the importance of the deadline for returning sales figures. In this situation the staff who normally meet that deadline are likely to feel resentment at being 'told off' for something they haven't done, and this will undermine any mutual trust and respect between staff and their manager. While the staff who do miss the deadline may feel that the general email doesn't really apply to them because they are not very late with their sales returns. It is also likely that they do not understand they are breaking the trust placed in them to return their sales figures on time. Hence the motivated staff are demotivated and the problem remains. The approach of speaking to the two staff involved and using the two-way communication process in a more targeted way, to make sure they are fully aware of their responsibilities and the importance of them, is more likely to be effective in helping solve the problem.

Respect, trust and an emphasis on outcomes

Organisations may choose to focus on outcomes and the contributions made by individual employees. The organisation which takes this approach places trust in staff to meet the required level of achievement rather than complying with detailed rules and regulations. The university lecturer who comes into work from 9am to 5pm every day, teaches the required classes, and spends the rest of the time drinking coffee and reading the newspaper in his or her office, is likely to be seen as making a minimal contribution to the university department. In contrast, the lecturer who is often not to be found in their office may actually be the most effective contributor to the department. This type of lecturer will either be teaching, doing research in the university library, writing their latest book or paper at home, or be at a conference presenting their latest research findings.

Where set attendance times are a necessary requirement of the job, such as working behind the counter in a bank or building society, it is appropriate for managers to ensure that good timekeeping is observed. However, in many jobs rigid times of attendance are not an essential requirement for effective performance. The office administrator may have a requirement to work 37.5 hours per week. However there may be a degree of flexibility, with core hours being 10am to 12pm and 2pm to 4pm, while the office is open from 8am to 6pm every week day. This allows the use of flexi-time.

If good timekeeping is an important part of the job, then clearly it needs to occur. However, if strict hours of attendance in the workplace are not necessary for effective performance, it can easily be argued that there is nothing to be gained by insisting on them. Applying set attendance times when they are not required can be seen as bureaucratic and unnecessary. Hence, it may turn a well-motivated employee who uses their time flexibly and well into an employee who does as little as possible beyond meeting the attendance criteria. The result is an adverse effect on performance and a downturn in achieving outcomes and results. The movement to flexible working and teleworking, along with demands for greater productivity, place increasing emphasis on staff actually achieving results rather than merely logging the amount of time spent at work. This clearly requires mutual trust and respect to exist between employee and manager.

Respect, trust, staff and customer satisfaction

It can be argued that customer satisfaction is the result of good manager–staff relationships. Working relationships in which mutual trust and respect exist

Business illustration of changing perception – McDonalds

David Fairhurst, the vice president for people for McDonalds in the UK has the task of closing the gap between how McDonalds is perceived, as a 'poor' place to work, and the more positive reality. Emphasising the positive reality is seen as developing an 'employer brand'. His initial task is build confidence amongst the staff, so that the staff, family and friends see and understand the positive aspects of working for McDonalds, such as decent promotion prospects.

Underpinning the building of an employer brand is the development of competent staff. This makes use of McDonald's policy of hiring people for their positive attitude and then providing the right skills and training. More broadly developing the successful employer brand requires a management structure in which marketing, human resources and public relations come together. This allows the company to build its employer brand or reputation as employer of choice.

Source: 'Changing the perception of working in a McJob', Colin Cottell, *Daily Telegraph*, 26 October 2006.

are more likely to generate a working environment in which there are high levels of staff motivation and satisfaction, which in turn result in customer satisfaction and success for the organisation. The follow through is that successful companies tend to attract better employees, who are more motivated to do a good job to satisfy the needs of their customers. Organisations need to manage the relationship between staff, strategy, structure and customers. McDonalds is seeking to develop the relationship between staff, strategy and structure as a result of developing its employer brand (see Business illustration on McDonalds). Hence, the importance of 'people': treat both staff and customers well and success should follow.

Review questions **Managerial style and the role of trust and respect**

1 Explain why trust and respect is central to the Theory Y approach to management.

2 Discuss the benefits of mutual trust and respect between a manager and his or her staff.

3 Identify the likely outcomes if no mutual trust and respect exists between a manager and his or her staff.

4 Describe the role of management involvement in gaining trust and respect.

5 Identify how a general approach to managing staff can undermine mutual trust and respect between a manager and his/her staff.

6 Determine the likely result of insisting that staff meet criteria which are not required for effective performance of their job.

7 How does respect and trust between staff and managers contribute to customer satisfaction?

LEADERSHIP IN ORGANISATIONS

Leadership is the ability to direct staff towards achieving goals.

'**Leadership** is the ability to influence a group towards the achievement of goals.'[4] A person may occupy a leadership role due to their position in the organisation and normally leadership is associated with the role of manager. However, a leader and manager are not necessarily equivalent, as providing a manager with position and certain rights in an organisation is no guarantee that he or she will be an effective leader.

Formal leaders are appointed and exist within the formal structure of the organisation. Equally informal leaders can emerge from outside the formal structure of the organisation (see Business Illustration on HSBC). Both are important and can make a difference in the performance of groups and the organisation. A change in leader can enhance the performance of underachieving groups or organisations, while, equally, a rapid turnover of leaders can be detrimental to performance.

Business illustration of successful leadership –
HSBC

Sir John Bond, the chairman of HSBC, retired in 2006 after a 45-year career with the bank. He started work as an '18 year old gofer' at HSBC in Hong Kong and worked his way up to the chairman's post. Sir John accepts he was lucky and HSBC survived political and financial upheaval to become Britain's biggest bank as a result of taking over the Midland Bank in the 1990s.

Sir John's successful leadership resulted from his solid judgement and timing, along with the avoidance of any big mistakes or corporate scandals, which can ruin organisations.

Source: 'The bad-omen chairman', Jeff Randell, *Daily Telegraph*, 27 January 2006.

Good leadership has strategic vision and is persuasive at implementing strategy to achieve tangible results.

Core competencies are the skills and abilities developed within an organisation with which competitive advantage can be created and maintained.

It could be argued that **good leadership** has strategic vision and is persuasive at implementing strategy to achieve tangible results. The underpinning of good leadership in organisations requires the appropriate **core competencies** and effective working relationships between leaders, managers and staff. Hence leadership is concerned with motivating staff and 'taking them with you' such that they identify with the strategic vision. This can require motivating and persuading staff to take decisions and undertake tasks that otherwise might not have been pursued. This can be particularly important in times of change and good leaders have to be able to manage the change process sensitively and appropriately. Therefore good change leadership drives an organisation successfully through the stages of the change process model and through the associated complexity and uncertainty (see Chapter 5).

Leadership is a dynamic process and, like strategy, it is important that it exists at all levels of the organisation: the corporate, divisional and functional levels (see Chapter 1). This means leaders and their leadership are seen throughout the organisation and if the leadership seen is good, then its high profile throughout the organisation will contribute to the motivation and results that leaders are seeking from the organisation and the staff. Hence the leadership–staff relationship is a two-way process.

Therefore leadership is about a relationship between people working for the same organisation, in which a person or leader seeks to influence the decision-making behaviour or actions of other staff. Thus leadership is not separate from the tasks and activities of groups and teams in the organisation, but an integral part of the organisation. Having established strategic vision and worked towards its achievement, leaders also have to focus on moving the organisation forwards which can include improving the competency of staff and the development of teams. Equally leadership can also play a key role in reducing employee dissatisfaction, which is critical in a failing organisation where leadership is seeking to achieve effective turnaround (see Chapter 12).

Management and leadership are often seen as synonymous and it can be difficult to separate them; indeed one might argue it is not necessary to separate them. The leader who has the grand vision needs to be able to at least manage at the strategic level. This ensures that the strategy is followed and that staff use resources and finance to best effect. Hence management and leadership are closely related and both qualities are need by people who are going to lead their organisation to success.

CLASSIFICATION OF LEADERSHIP STYLES

There are different ways of defining and classifying approaches to leadership. Leadership styles can be thought of as falling into one of three broad categories, namely **autocratic**, **democratic** or **laissez faire** (genuine style). The leadership styles have different approaches to exercising power and dealing with staff (see **Exhibit 6.3**).

Exhibit 6.3 Leadership style and types of power

Leadership style	Type of power
■ Autocratic	■ Centralised power rests with a dictatorial leader
■ Democratic	■ Some power rests with the leader and some is devolved to staff
■ Laissez faire	■ Power is passed on to the staff

The **autocratic leadership style** has centralised power, which rests with a dictatorial leader.

The autocratic style is where the leader or manager exercises power in developing policy and making decisions involving the allocation of work and achievement of objectives. Power in this type of set-up is centralised with the autocratic leader. This type of approach to leadership is suited to the organisation which is in trouble and needs to achieve a rapid turnaround if it is to survive. In contrast this approach would be counter-productive if an organisation was doing well and experiencing significant growth, when a more democratic or laissez faire approach may be more appropriate.

The **democratic leadership style** occurs when power is split between the leader and his/her staff.

The democratic style of leadership involves power being more devolved than with the autocratic style and resting with the group as a whole. The leadership will be shared between group members and the manager or leader, who is often seen as part of team. Hence there is more interaction within the group between staff and managers. The more devolved nature of the power means group members have a greater say in the development of policy, decision making, and in the use of control systems.

The **laissez faire leadership style** occurs when all power is passed to on to the staff.

The laissez faire or genuine style of leadership occurs when the manager or leader can see that members of the group are working well on their own and makes a conscious decision to pass power to group members. This allows the group the freedom 'to do as they think best' without management interference, but with management assistance being readily available if required. The word 'genuine' is used to describe this approach which is in direct contrast to the manager who does not care, does not get involved and deliberately keeps away from difficulties or 'trouble'.

Leadership in organisations

1 Define good leadership.
2 Explain why it is important that leadership exists at all levels of the organisation.
3 Explain why both management and leadership are needed in organisations.
4 Define an autocratic leadership style.
5 Define a democratic leadership style.
6 Define a laissez faire leadership style.

LEADERSHIP STYLES

There are other ways of defining leadership styles and this section examines some of the common leadership styles which are found in organisations (see **Exhibit 6.4**).

Exhibit 6.4 Key characteristics of common leadership styles

Leadership styles	Key characteristics
Charismatic leadership	■ Charismatic leaders will focus on making their team distinctive and build a strong image for the group. ■ Pay attention to scanning their environment and will pick up the moods of both individuals and larger audiences. Hence charismatic leaders will adjust their words and actions to suit the situation.
Participative leadership	■ Participative leaders seek to involve staff and others in the decision-making process. ■ The participation of staff in the decision-making process improves their understanding of the potential problems and issues of implementing the decisions. ■ Hence staff are more likely to be committed to actions.
Transactional leadership	■ Transactional leadership is based on the view that rewards and punishment motivate staff and is concerned with managers establishing authority over the staff. ■ This results from an agreed contract, which gives the subordinate a salary and the company gains authority over the subordinate in the workplace. ■ Transactional leaders work best via a clear chain of command so that it is clear to employees what is required of them and the associated rewards and punishments.
Transformational leadership	■ Transformational leaders are charismatic but have less self-belief than charismatic leaders. Hence transformational leaders recognise that success results from their belief in both themselves and their staff. ■ Transformational leaders sees the strategic view and can develop strategic vision for an organisation, but can often not see the detail. Therefore trusting in others who manage the detail is important. ■ Successful transformational leaders need staff to buy into the future vision and this requires a high level of enthusiasm in selling it to staff.

Charismatic leadership

Charismatic leadership involves judging the moods of individuals and larger audiences, and adjusting words and actions to suit the situation.

Good examples of the **charismatic leadership** style are illustrated by politicians past and present, such as Winston Churchill, Margaret Thatcher and Bill Clinton. Many would argue that Tony Blair has a charismatic leadership style, while his successor as leader of the Labour Party, Gordon Brown, does not. Charisma arises from personality and charm and not from any form of external authority. Politicians use a charismatic style, as they need to gather a large number of followers. They project themselves and their message to their audience or the electorate in a very positive way, and seek to interact with the audience in the same manner.

Charismatic leaders who are building a group, whether it is a political party or a business team, will often focus strongly on making the group very clear and distinct, separating it from other groups. They will then build the image of the group in particular in the minds of their followers as being far superior to all others competing groups. To achieve this charismatic leaders will pay a great deal of attention to scanning and reading their environment, and they will be good at picking up the moods and concerns of both individuals and larger audiences. They will then adjust their words and actions to suit the situation and meet the needs of the audience, be they staff or the electorate.

The values of the charismatic leader are highly significant because if they are well intentioned they can help transform an entire company, which is key if the business is struggling to survive. In contrast if the values of the charismatic leader are selfish and devious they can end up creating a cult or group which people either leave very quickly or remain with out of fear and worry. It is also likely that the selfish charismatic leader will be intolerant of challengers and view themselves as indispensable, so when they eventually leave the organisation there will be no obvious successor.

Participative leadership

A participative leader does not take autocratic decisions but seeks to involve staff, peers, superiors and other stakeholders in the decision-making process. The issue of how much influence others are given depends on the manager's preferences and beliefs and there is a whole spectrum of participation (see **Exhibit 6.5**).

Exhibit 6.5 Spectrum of participation in leadership

Non participative				Highly participative
Autocratic leader makes all decisions	Leader suggests decisions, listens to team's feedback and makes decisions	Team suggests decisions; however, leader has final say	Joint decisions with the team as equal partners	Decisions are fully delegated to the team

Source: www.changingminds.org

The participation and involvement of staff, peers and superiors in the decision making improves the understanding these stakeholders have of the potential problems and the implementation of strategy. This in turn means people are more likely to be committed to actions which they have been involved in shaping and deciding.

The participative style of leadership is often referred to as joint decision making, consultation, empowerment or power sharing. However, while the benefits of this approach to leadership are clear, **participative leadership** can be deceptive if managers ask for opinions and then choose to ignore them; this in turn engenders cynicism and a sense of betrayal among staff.

Participative leadership is to involve staff and others in the decision-making process.

Transactional leadership

Transactional leadership works via a clear chain of command so that it is clear what is required of staff.

Transactional leadership is based on the view that staff are motivated by rewards and punishment. This approach to leadership means employees undertake the job and tasks which their manager tells them to do. The early stage of transactional leadership is concerned with the manager establishing authority over the staff. This is the result of an agreed or negotiated contract which gives the subordinate a salary and in return the company and the manager gain authority over the subordinate in the workplace.

The transactional leader works best via a clear chain of command and a transparent structure, so that it is clear to employees what is required of them and the associated rewards and punishments. Often rewards will be mentioned and highlighted, while punishments may not be mentioned; however, they will be clearly understood and will take the form of action via official discipline systems.

There are clearly limitations in the transactional approach to leadership and it assumes people are motivated by a purely rational approach to work and its rewards. However, people are often motivated by having inputs into decision making and the achievement of objectives (see earlier section on participative leadership).

Transformational leadership

Transformational leadership recognises that success results from their belief in both themselves and their staff.

Transformational leaders are often charismatic but tend not to have as great a self-belief as purely charismatic leaders. Transformational leaders recognise that success will result from their belief both in themselves and in others who work with them. Additionally transformational leaders are able to see the big picture or strategic view, often at the expense of not seeing the detail; hence the importance of believing and trusting in others who can operate appropriately and manage the detail. If this does not happen, then the transformational leader may end up failing to achieve his or her strategic vision and the organisation could end up in a turnaround situation (see Chapter 12).

Transformational leadership often starts with developing a strategic vision for the future of the organisation. A successful transformational leader needs staff to buy into the future vision, and for this to happen the vision has to excite and inspire people. This in turn means the transformational leader is constantly selling his or her vision, which requires high levels of commitment to the vision and enthusiasm in selling it to staff. Additionally it is the transformational leader's high level of commitment to the new vision which enables him or her to continually persevere through the difficult times and dark days, when others are questioning the new vision and its potential success in the organisation.

Initially a few staff will buy into a new vision immediately and others will commit more slowly and over a longer period of time. This means transformational leaders need to continually listen to, motivate and rally their staff behind the new vision, taking every opportunity to encourage staff to engage. The transformational leader should be careful to preserve his or her personal integrity, as they are selling both themselves and their vision for the future of the organisation. This is also necessary as good transformational leaders will be visible in the organisation and hence their attitudes and behaviour will be seen by those staff who are being asked to buy into the vision – and in turn will indicate to staff the behaviour expected of them in the workplace.

Staff will follow a leader who inspires and has a passion to achieve great things. Hence working for a transformational leader can be a positive experience as energy and passion are put into successfully achieving organisational objectives. Transformational leaders, by definition, seek to transform organisations experiencing major upheaval or change and can achieve great results. However, if an organisation is experiencing a period of stability, then a transformational leader is not what is required and indeed he or she will be likely to become frustrated at the lack of any significant challenge.

✔ Check your understanding

- Do you understand the importance of good management and/or good leadership? Which is the most important?
- Check your understanding by reviewing the following quote from Entry case study 6.1: 'people join a company but leave to get away from the boss'.

Review questions | **Leadership styles**

1 Summarise the characteristics of a charismatic leader.

2 Explain the likely outcome if a charismatic leader is devious and holds selfish values.

3 Discuss the advantages and disadvantages of participative leadership.

4 Describe the circumstances which need to exist for transactional leadership to work well.

5 Compare and contrast transactional and transformational leadership.

LEADERSHIP, POWER AND STAKEHOLDERS

In any organisation the styles of leadership present will be linked to the types of power present in the organisation. The exercising of power by leaders influences the behaviour of others, and therefore different types of power will produce different organisational cultures and outcomes (see Chapter 5).

According to French and Raven[5] there are five main sources or types of power a leader or manager may exercise. These are **reward power**, **coercive power**, **legitimate power**, **referent power** and **expert power**. It is important to understand the different types of power which can be exercised, as often the managers or leaders exercising the power have high levels of power and fall into category D in the stakeholder power–interest matrix (see Chapter 5). An understanding of the power a leader or manager exercises will add to the understanding of their relationship with other stakeholders such as employees, who often fall into category B on the stakeholder matrix and hence have low power and high interest (see Chapter 5).

Exhibit 6.6 Subordinate's perception of leadership power

Type of leadership power	Subordinate's perception of leadership power
■ Reward power ■ Coercive power	■ Leader can reward staff who comply with instructions ■ Leader is able to punish staff who do not comply with instructions
■ Legitimate power	■ Leader is able to exercise power as a result of their position in the organisation
■ Referent power	■ Leader is able to exercise power because of their charisma and reputation
■ Expert power ■ Personal power	■ Leader has power because of their expert knowledge ■ Leader has power because subordinates support and trust him/her

It should be remembered that sources of power are in part based on the employee's understanding of the leader's influence and whether it is real or perceived. It is the employee's perception of the leader's power which determines how the employee behaves and contributes to the organisation. Therefore understanding types of power requires that they be viewed from both the point of view of the leader exercising power and the subordinate on the receiving end of the power (see **Exhibit 6.6**).

Reward power is based on the subordinate's perception that the leader has the ability and resources to reward those who comply with instructions. The manager or leader who is perceived to have reward power can give or reward staff with a variety of options including promotion, pay rises, bonuses, praise and recognition.

Coercive power is the opposite of reward power and is based on fear. The subordinate holds the perception that the leader is able to punish staff who do not

Reward power is based on the subordinate's perception that the leader can reward staff who comply with instructions.

Coercive power is based on the subordinate's perception that the leader can punish staff who do not comply with instructions.

comply with instructions. This may take the form of withholding rewards such as a pay rises or promotion as well as the allocation of undesirable work, the withdrawal of support and the implementation of formal disciplinary procedures or dismissal.

Legitimate power, sometimes called 'position' power, is based on the employee's perception that the leader holds the right to exercise power and influence due to their role or position in the organisation. Therefore legitimate power is based on authority and position in the organisation's hierarchy and not on the nature of the relationship between the leader or manager and their staff.

Legitimate power is based on the employee's perception that the leader can exercise power due to their role in the organisation.

Referent power is based on the subordinate's identification with the leader who is able to exercise power and influence because of their perceived charisma and reputation. Leaders or managers with referent power may not be able to reward or punish certain subordinates, but can exercise power over subordinates because they command their subordinates' respect.

Referent power is based on the subordinate's identification with the leader who is able to exercise power because of their perceived reputation.

Expert power is based on the subordinate's perception of the leader as someone who has expertise and specialist knowledge in a certain area. Hence the leader or manager with expert power has to have credibility and their specialist knowledge needs to be clear and transparent if it is to be perceived as such by subordinates. This type of power is often held by 'functional' specialists such as an accountant or IT analyst and as such is often limited to narrow, well-defined areas.

Expert power is based on the subordinate's perception of the leader as someone who has specialist knowledge in a certain area.

In addition to these five types of power defined by French and Raven, Finlay[6] suggests a sixth type of power, **personal power**. Personal power arises from the support and trust of subordinates and colleagues.

Personal power arises from the support and trust of subordinates and colleagues.

Additionally French and Raven[7] suggest that the five types of power are interrelated and that the use of one type of power can affect the likelihood of a manager exercising another type of power. For example, a manager exercising and perceived to exercise coercive power will probably find if difficult to ever be seen as holding referent power, as it is unlikely staff will ever identify with him or her. Equally the types of power can be interrelated as the same manager or leader may exercise different types of power in different situations. For example, the leader or manager with legitimate power may also hold and use expert power, as their expertise and specialist knowledge has resulted in him or her gaining a position of authority in the organisation.

✔ ## Check your understanding

- Do you understand the following quote from Entry case study 6.1: 'Leaders are first born and then made'?
- Check your understanding by explaining if this applies equally to leaders who exhibit coercive power and those who exhibit expert power.

Leadership, power and stakeholders

1 Explain why power should be viewed from the point of view of both the leader and the subordinate.

2 Compare and contrast reward power and coercive power.

3 Define legitimate power.

4 Explain why the leader with referent power is able to exercise power.

5 Define expert power.

6 Explain why a leader holding legitimate power may also hold expert power.

LEADERSHIP, STAGES AND SITUATIONS

A **champion** is a leader who will push a business through the early stages of development and into significant growth.

Clarke and Pratt[8] suggest different styles of leadership may be appropriate at different stages of an organisation's development. The leadership styles identified by Clarke and Pratt are those of **champion**, **tank commander**, **housekeeper** and **lemon squeezer**.

A new and developing business needs a champion as its leader, someone who will push the business through its early stages of development and into significant growth. Hence the champion should have the energy and enthusiasm to drive a small multi-skilled team to win orders and deal with a wide range of external stakeholders such as customers, suppliers and the bank.

A **tank commander** is a leader who can support a team to exploit and gain maximum benefit from all possible market segments.

The business which has started to grow significantly needs a tank commander who can lead and support his or her team. The job of the tank commander and his or her team is to exploit and gain maximum benefit from all possible market segments, as the same opportunity is unlikely to ever arise again as markets mature.

A **housekeeper** is a leader who can ensure the company holds its own against other competitors who may also be mature and established.

The more mature business requires a housekeeper as its leader, to ensure the company holds its own against other competitors which may also be mature and established in the marketplace. It is likely that if market share is lost to such competitors it will be very difficult to retrieve. Additionally, as new profit opportunities will be limited, the housekeeper has to ensure the efficient implementation of control systems to help maintain a reasonable profit margin. This can be difficult as the business is likely to face increasing price competition. The control systems used will have to cover the cost of all resources, including materials, equipment, premises and staff.

A **lemon squeezer** is a leader who can extract the maximum benefit from a business if is to survive and/or achieve turnaround.

A business which is entering a premature decline phase needs a leader who is a lemon squeezer. The role of the lemon squeezer leader is to extract the maximum benefit from the situation if the business is to survive. The lemon squeezer needs to be tough and to cut costs and improve productivity if retrenchment is to be achieved (see Chapter 12). Additionally the lemon squeezer should be innovative if the business is to ever flourish again, as new ideas for products and their sales and marketing need to be forthcoming for true turnaround to be achieved (see Chapter 12).

The skill lies in finding the manager who has the best skills and abilities to meet the needs of the business when it is at a particular stage. Clarke and Pratt[9] suggest that most managers are one type of leader or another, with only a few managers being flexible enough to switch between the different leadership roles.

The right leader for the right situation

Rodrigues[10] argues that organisations exist in dynamic environments and are at different stages of the change and development process, namely the problem-solving stage, the implementation of solutions stage and a stable stage. These could be aligned with the three stages of Lewin's change process model, unfreezing, moving to a new level and re-freezing (see Chapter 5). Organisations at different stages of change and development require leaders with different skills and abilities, and Rodrigues[11] identifies these leaders as **innovators**, **implementers** and **pacifiers**.

An **innovator** is a leader who is bold and able to search for new ideas in a complex and dynamic external environment.

The innovator is a leader who is bold and able to lead the search for new ideas and is willing to struggle with a complex and dynamic external environment. An innovator style of leadership is likely to be most effective when a business needs new ideas and refreshing, such as when starting out or when successful retrenchment and turnaround are required. Hence it is argued that both the champions and lemon squeezers need to be innovators (see previous section).

An **implementer** is a leader who can achieve results via efficient and effective use of staff and resources.

The implementer is the leader with the ability to achieve results through efficient and effective use of staff and resources, and is similar to the housekeeper leader suggested by Clarke and Pratt (see previous section). The implementer leader needs to have influence with staff and the skills to control and manage resources to be effective. When the implementer has brought stability to the organisation, it is argued, there is a need for the pacifier leader.

The **pacifier** is the friendly and sociable leader, who has the ability to decentralise decision making to key individuals.

The pacifier leader is the friendly and sociable leader, who has the ability to decentralise decision making to key individuals. The pacifier is also able to incorporate feedback from earlier decisions into the decision-making process, which should help achieve cohesiveness in the decision-making process. At this stage staff members usually feel pacified, and competent to perform the necessary tasks – and perform well under a democratic or laissez faire style of leadership (see earlier in this chapter).

Review questions | **Leadership, stages and situations**

1 Compare and contrast a champion and a lemon squeezer.
2 Compare and contrast a tank commander and a housekeeper.
3 Explain why both champions and lemon squeezers need to be innovators.
4 Define an implementer.

CONCLUSION

This chapter illustrates different approaches to both management and leadership. It is often claimed that people-orientated and democratic approaches are more likely to result in job satisfaction. However, there are occasions when an autocratic style of leadership is more effective, for example, if the pressure is on for immediate results to ensure success. Managers are often fairly consistent in following one style or approach to dealing with staff; however, different situations or problems may require a different style of management or leadership, and this should be expected.

There are many different approaches to management or leadership which can result in success. However, the critical aspects to consider when deciding on the most appropriate approach to management and leadership in an organisation are the manager or leader, their skills and abilities, their staff, the working environment and the external environment in which the organisation operates. There are also other factors which will influence the appropriateness of a manager or leader's approach to their role. These include personality; power; the nature of the relationships between subordinate staff; the impact of both organisational and sometimes national culture; the structure of the organisation; the extent of hierarchical relationships within the organisation; the impact of technology; and the aims of the organisation.

LEARNING OUTCOMES AND SUMMARY

→ **Learning outcome 1**
Explain what is meant by management.

- Management in organisations is concerned with exercising formal power and control within a defined structure, to shape the behaviour and work patterns of staff. The overall aim will be to achieve good performance and meet organisational objectives.
- Management can also be about changing behaviour, due to changes in both the organisation's position in the external environment and key success factors.

→ **Learning outcome 2**
Discuss different ways of managing staff and resources, and the expected outcomes.

- McGregor's Theory Y assumes people regard work as normal activity, and are committed to the organisational objectives and self-motivated towards their achievement and the associated rewards.
- The other extreme, Theory X, assumes that people dislike work and seek to avoid it at all costs. Hence management may also be based on 'organisational power' derived from status or position within the hierarchical structure, and the use of formal and more dictatorial authority.

- Equally staff in an organisation will respond positively if treated with respect and will behave as responsible individuals wishing to contribute to the organisation and its success. People also expect to be treated fairly and equitably at work, and expect rewards and outcomes to reflect their inputs to organisations.

- In contrast an alternative approach is one where organisations focus on outcomes and the contribution made by individual employees. Therefore if customer satisfaction is important to the organisation then the good manager–staff relationships are those which help achieve customer satisfaction. These tend to be trusting, honest and open working relationships which result in high levels of staff motivation and satisfaction, which in turn result in customer satisfaction.

→ **Learning outcome 3**
Identify the key aspects of management in organisations.

- Managers are responsible for how well an organisation achieves its objectives and this is clearly partly linked to both the efficiency and effectiveness of management.

- The efficient manager is concerned with using resources to achieve objectives, while minimising waste. Therefore to be efficient a manager must be clear about targets and plan to meet the targets, without using resources unnecessarily.

- Effectiveness is achieved by managers 'doing the right things' to achieve outputs and meet objectives. The measurement of effectiveness is concerned with; doing the right things, and relates to outputs of the job and the targets managers actually achieve.

→ **Learning outcome 4**
Summarise the role of leaders and leadership in organisations.

- Leadership is the ability to influence a team towards achieving objectives. Leadership is a dynamic process and like strategy it is important that it exists at all levels of the organisation; the corporate, divisional and functional levels.

- Formal leaders are appointed and exist within the formal structure of the organisation. Equally informal leaders can emerge from outside the formal procedures and structure of the organisation. Both are important and can make a difference in the performance of groups and organisations.

- A change in leader can enhance the performance of underachieving groups or organisations while, equally, rapid turnover of leaders can be detrimental to performance.

→ **Learning outcome 5**
Discuss different approaches to leadership and their suitability for different situations.

- Leadership styles can be thought of as falling into one of three broad categories, namely authoritarian, democratic or laissez faire (genuine style).

The leadership styles have different approaches to exercising power and dealing with staff.

■ The autocratic style is where the leader or manager exercises power in developing policy and making decisions involving the allocation of work and achievement of objectives. The democratic style of leadership involves power being more devolved and resting with the group as a whole than with the autocratic style. The laissez faire or genuine style of leadership occurs when the leader can see that members of the group are working well on their own and makes a conscious decision to pass power to group members.

■ There are alternative ways of defining leadership styles which are found in organisations. Charismatic leaders, who are building a group, will often focus strongly on making the group very clear and distinct from other groups. A participative leader does not take autocratic decisions but seeks to involve staff, peers and superiors in the decision-making process. Transactional leadership is based on the view that staff are motivated by rewards and punishment and, therefore, employees undertake the tasks which their manager tells them to do. Transformational leaders are often charismatic but tend not to have as great a self-belief as purely charismatic leaders. Transformational leaders recognise that success will result from their belief both in themselves and in others who work with them.

■ Within an organisation leadership influence will be dependent upon the type of power that the leader can exercise over the followers. The exercise of power is a social process, which helps to explain how different people can influence the behaviour/actions of others.

EXIT CASE STUDY 6.2

This exit case study looks at Wolfgang Mayrhuber's role as leader of the airline Lufthansa.

Learning outcomes	Check you have achieved this by	
Discuss the tasks of a manager.	Analyse a manager's activities using Drucker's seven tasks of tomorrow's manager.	Answering exit case study question 1.
Explain the relevance of models and frameworks.	Explain the relevance of the framework, Drucker's seven tasks of tomorrow's manager.	Answering exit case study question 2.
Determine the role of respect and trust in managing organisations.	Summarise the role of respect and trust in a particular manager's style of management.	Answering exit case study question 3.
Identify leadership styles.	Determine which leadership style a particular manager exhibits and its characteristics.	Answering exit case study question 4.
Identify sources of power.	Explain which sources of power a particular leader may hold.	Answering exit case study question 5.

Engineer with tools to rebuild an airline

by Gerrit Wiesmann

The dazzling sunshine pierces the sixth floor of Lufthansa's glass-clad headquarters beside Frankfurt airport, making a backlit Wolfgang Mayrhuber seem momentarily like an apparition waiting at the door to the chief executive's office. It is 11.12am and the Austrian should not be here. His flight from Zurich only touched down at 11am, leading his press chief to warn apologetically that the boss would not make it to his desk before 11.30am, half an hour behind schedule.

Instead, he has made it in 10 minutes, and is standing coolly at the reception to the chief executive's suite. The Lufthansa chief executive has a knack for making things look easy. When he arrived in the job in June 2003, amid the industry's post-9/11 malaise, the German flag carrier was under fire for its lack of focus. Styling itself as a broad provider of travel-related services, it did everything from flying passengers on scheduled flights to selling package holidays.

Displaying his characteristic fondness for figurative language, he likens his role at that stage to that of a physician. '[I was] the doctor who is obliged to tell his patient: "You must change the way you live or you can forget about living."' In this case, the patient was on course for losses of €1bn ($1.3bn). Mr Mayrhuber ordered big cost cuts and the sale of non-core units – most recently a half-stake in travel group Thomas Cook in a deal that closed on Friday. He now expects operating profits of €1bn in 2008. As part of the treatment, Mr Mayrhuber acquired Swiss, the national airline, in 2005, and improved Lufthansa's business and first class offerings with better seats and a raft of extra services, including a bespoke first-class terminal at its Frankfurt hub. As a result, premium revenues are up by 50 per cent. He has also introduced low fare offers in Europe in order to compete with no-frills carriers and to react better to volatile demand. And by improving services in its economy class, he says, Lufthansa can now cater to a world in which executive travellers often fly first class on business and economy for pleasure. 'Demand has become so varied: it's trainers and patent leather shoes.'

The tall, trim Mr Mayrhuber gives an impression of polite discipline, but a toughness lurks not far below the surface. The 59-year-old may have had a head start when it came to factual rigour – his father was a journalist, he himself trained as an engineer. But it is also a quality he seeks to encourage in others. When he took charge of Lufthansa's passenger business in 2001, he wanted to gauge the scale of the difficulties facing the airline. So he asked his controller to find out what would have to happen for the company to wipe out €1bn in operating profit. 'He came back a few days later and said: "Five fewer passengers on every flight, five euros less per ticket and a two per cent cost overrun – then we'll be at zero,"' he says. This revelation stuck with Mr Mayrhuber. In conversation, he repeatedly circles back to the 'five people per airplane' as a stark reminder of the delicate environment in which an airline and its chief executive operate. It also helped him clarify what he needed to do. 'I asked myself: "Why did you take the job?"' His smile straightens. 'It struck me that this business needs good sensors and a careful hand on the rudder.'

His subsequent strategy has aimed to bring this complexity under control. First, he hived off non-core businesses. 'Doing aircraft catering has a certain logic for an airline of our size. Running German motorway service stations did not.' Second, he improved transparency. Mr Mayrhuber revised the airline's financial reporting to identify loss-makers as a prelude to remedies, even if this made it easier for investors to grumble about the business mix. The less transparent Air France group faces no such complaints, he notes. But Lufthansa will always remain more complex than British Airways and Air France, he says. They fill flights from populous London or Paris 'by underground', he says. He needs 50 feeder flights within Germany and Europe to fill a plane to Hong Kong, and has not one but three hubs: Frankfurt, Munich and Zurich. So it is no surprise that he has turned the quest for detail into a central plank of his management philosophy. 'While striving for the bigger picture I sometimes bore into details that exasperate my colleagues,' Mr Mayrhuber says. One detail that recently struck him was the fact that many European airlines have not ordered new long-haul aircraft, or are reducing their fleets. This, for him, indicates that smaller players are readying themselves for consolidation into bigger groups. While Lufthansa ordered a raft of long-hauls jets last year, the likes of Austrian Airlines and Scandinavia's SAS, seen as targets of the German airline, did not. But Mr Mayrhuber says he cannot comment on individual rivals.

Despite his attention to detail, he appears to care what people, and particularly employees, think about him. He is, after all, no gunslinger drafted in to raise dust, but a Lufthansa veteran of 37 years with all the friendships this implies. 'Lots of people know me,' Mr

→

Mayrhuber says, summing up a career that started at maintenance unit Lufthansa Technik in Hamburg, then Frankfurt. He helped rescue the passenger unit in the mid-1990s, then led Technik into bumper profits. He sounds almost wistful when remembering that time. 'I built those hangars,' he says pointing at the concrete hulks and their long shadows on the airport fringes. He says his task of the past three years was made easier by success at Technik. As promised, the engineers in Hamburg had kept their jobs even as Mr Mayrhuber transferred more basic work to the Philippines. 'Trust comes from the fact that people know you,' the chief executive says, making things sound easy once again. All hands on the flight deck.

Lufthansa passengers should look out for a tall man a pilot's hat short of two metres next time they fly. It might be the airline's chief executive, Wolfgang Mayrhuber, who has often proved to be a useful person to have aboard. He recalls the time a first-class passenger's expensive cigarette lighter disappeared into the innards of his seat. 'He was quite surprised when I told him to hang on a minute, fetched a screwdriver and dismantled the chair to retrieve the lighter.' Stories of the engineer's skills abound. A colleague recalls how the boss helped a flight attendant get the in-flight entertainment system running. Mr Mayrhuber says he was similarly useful with an air-conditioning unit on another flight.

'Good service is all about detail,' says Mr Mayrhuber. Given that his engineering expertise has allowed him to help his customers on more than one occasion, he should count himself lucky that no airline wanted him as a pilot 37 years ago. After studying in Austria and Canada in the late 1960s, he applied to Austrian Airlines, Swissair and Lufthansa for flight training. The Austrians warned that he would have to pay the full cost of tuition if he did not succeed in getting a job at the end of it. 'I had $6 at the

time, so I had to decline. Swissair said it couldn't employ a foreigner. So that left Lufthansa. It didn't need any pilots, but said it desperately needed engineers.'

He followed the call to Hamburg, home to Lufthansa Technik. 'I thought, "Why not? A couple of years in Hamburg won't hurt you".' says the Austrian. 'But then I went from one thing to the next and it turned into a long stay.' Mr Mayrhuber says he has no regrets over his failure to don the pilot's hat. 'I'm the kind of guy whose interest in things wanes once he has mastered them,' he says. His role in leading the German flag carrier will not leave him short of challenges.

Source: *Financial Times*, 11 February 2007.

Exit case study questions

1 Which of Drucker's seven tasks of tomorrow's manager does Wolfgang Mayrhuber undertake? Are there any he doesn't undertake and should?

2 Do you think Drucker's 'seven tasks of tomorrow's manager' are relevant today? Describe, if any, the contexts in which organisations might use Drucker's seven tasks of tomorrow's manager.

3 Discuss the role of respect and trust in Wolfgang Mayrhuber's style of management.

4 Identify Wolfgang Mayrhuber's leadership style and the characteristics of your chosen leadership style which Wolfgang Mayrhuber appears to exhibit.

5 Identify the sources of power which Wolfgang Mayrhuber could be perceived to hold.

DISCUSSION TOPIC

1 Read the paper 'Covert leadership: Notes on managing professionals' by Henry Mintzberg, Chapter 15, in *The Strategy Process*, Mintzberg, Lampel, Quinn and Ghosal, Harlow: Prentice Hall, 2003.

2 Critically evaluate the analogy of conducting an orchestra for managing professionals. Does the conductor of the orchestra lead or manage?

WIDEN YOUR HORIZONS

1 Widen your horizons by considering Drucker's seven tasks of tomorrow's manager and plan a two-year graduate trainee programme to develop the managers of tomorrow for a large high street retail chain selling a full range of clothing for men, women and children.

2 Widen your horizons by comparing and contrasting the leadership styles of UK and US business leaders.

WEBLINKS

The websites for this chapter provide a look at some further material on management and leadership.

■ Visit the following website and test your management style – see the section at the bottom of the first page.
www.managementvitality.com/msq/4styles.php

■ The following website contains lots of information about approaches to management. Click on one of the grey tabs at the top of the page to find out about 'team building', 'employee motivation' or 'productivity'.
www.accel-team.com/index.html

■ A good website with lots of information about leadership, 'The Art and Science of Leadership'.
www.nwlink.com/~donclark/leader/leader.html

■ The following page is from the Society of Electrical Engineers and is about leadership.
www.ee.ed.ac.uk/~gerard/MENG/ME96/index.html

FURTHER READING

The following are further readings from strategy textbooks.

■ Cameron, E and Green, M (2004) *Making Sense of Change Management*, London: Kogan Page. Chapter 4, 'Leading change'.

■ Dess, G G, Lumpkin, G T and Taylor, M L (2005) *Strategic Management*, 2nd edn, New York: McGraw Hill Irwin. Chapter 11, 'Strategic leadership: creating a learning organisation and ethical organisation'.

■ Jenkins, M, and Ambrosini, V (2002) *Strategic Management: A Multi-perspective Approach*, Basingstoke: Palgrave Macmillan. Chapter 11, 'Leadership perspective'.

■ Pearce, J A and Robinson, R B (2007) *Strategic Management: Formulation, Implementation and Control*, 10th edn, New York: McGraw-Hill International. Chapter 12, 'Leadership and culture'.

■ Pettinger, R (2004) *Contemporary Strategic Management*, Basingstoke: Palgrave Macmillan. Chapter 16, 'Leadership'.

The following are further readings from organisational behaviour textbooks.

■ Huczynski, A and Buchanan D (2001) *Organisational behaviour*, 4th edn, Harlow: Financial Times/Prentice Hall. Chapter 21, 'Leadership'.

■ Martin, J (2001) *Organisational Behaviour*, 2nd edn, London: Thomson Learning. Chapter 15, 'Management within organisations'.

- Martin, J (2001) *Organisational Behaviour*, 2nd edn, London: Thomson Learning. Chapter 16, 'Leadership and organisations'.

- Mullins, L J (2005) *Management and Organisational Behaviour*, 7th edn, Harlow: Financial Times/Prentice Hall. Chapter 6, 'The nature of management'.

- Mullins, L J (2005) *Management and Organisational Behaviour*, 7th edn, Harlow: Financial Times Prentice Hall. Chapter 7, 'Managerial behaviour and effectiveness'.

- Mullins, L J (2005) *Management and Organisational Behaviour*, 7th edn, Harlow: Financial Times Prentice Hall. Chapter 8, 'The nature of leadership'.

- Weightman, J (1999) *Introducing Organisational Behaviour*, Harlow: Addison Wesley Longman. Chapter 8, 'Developing leadership and autonomy'.

- Weightman, J (1999) *Introducing Organisational Behaviour*, Harlow: Addison Wesley Longman. Chapter 7, 'Group working'.

REFERENCES

1   Belbin, R M (1997) *Changing the Way We Work*, Oxford: Butterworth-Heinemann.
2   Drucker, P F (1979) *Management*, Oxford: Butterworth-Heinemann.
3   Freemantle, D (1985) 'The people factor', *Management Today*, December, in Mullins, L J (2005) *Management and Organisational Behaviour*, 7th edn, Harlow: Financial Times/Prentice Hall.
4   Robbins, S P (2000) *Essentials of Organizational Behavior*, New Jersey: Prentice Hall.
5   French, J R P and Raven, B 'The bases of social power', in Cartwright, D and Zander, A F (eds) (1968) *Group Dynamics: Research and Theory*, 3rd edn, Harper and Row, in Mullins, L J (2005) *Management and Organisational Behaviour*, 7th edn, Harlow: Financial Times/Prentice Hall.
6   Finlay, P (2000) *Strategic Management: An Introduction to Business and Corporate Strategy*, Harlow: Financial Times/Prentice Hall.
7   French and Raven, op. cit.
8   Clarke, C and Pratt, S (1985) 'Leadership's four-part progress', *Management Today*, March, in Mullins, L J (2005) *Management and Organisational Behaviour*, 7th edn, Harlow: Financial Times/Prentice Hall.
9   Ibid.
10 Rodrigues, C A (1988) 'Identifying the right leader for the right situation', *Personnel*, September, in Mullins, L J (2005) *Management and Organisational Behaviour*, 7th edn, Harlow: Financial Times/Prentice Hall.
11 Ibid.

CHAPTER 7

Developing competitive and marketing strategy

Exhibit 7.1 Essential strategy model

The model shows a wheel with a central circle and eight surrounding segments:

- 1 What is strategy? (Ch1) — centre
- 2 Environmental analysis (Ch 2)
- 3 Resource analysis (Chs 3 & 4)
- 4 Stakeholders, culture and change (Ch 5)
- 5 Management and leadership (Ch 6)
- 6 Strategy development (Chs 7, 8 & 9)
- 7 Structure culture and groups (Ch 10)
- 8 Strategic control (Ch 11)
- 9 Managing failure and turnaround (Ch 12)

Chapter objectives

Organisations which have analysed their external environment, understand the demands of their stakeholders and resource availability, putting the organisation in a position to make choices concerning its strategy. Developing strategy involves deciding how to compete in different market segments. Competition is usually based either on keeping both costs and prices low or on adding value for the customer. Therefore this chapter looks at the concept of achieving competitive advantage via competitive strategy, and in so doing avoiding failure and strategic mis-match. This is followed by an overview of marketing strategy, segmentation, targeting and positioning.

When you have read this chapter and worked through the associated activities you should be able to achieve the objectives specified below.

1 Identify and discuss Porter's competitive strategies and alternative approaches to competitive strategy.

2 Develop competitive strategies for companies, avoiding competitive strategies, which lead to failure and strategic mismatch.

3 Understand and summarise the relationship between competitive strategy, marketing strategy and competitive advantage.

4 Explain Press's management philosophies and their link with competitive strategy.

5 Determine marketing objectives and strategies for companies.

6 Understand the different types of market segmentation variables, targeting and positioning strategies and where they may be appropriately applied.

There are different ways to enter new markets and this entry case study looks at Viacom's joint venture with the Shanghai Media Group of China as a way of moving into producing TV programmes for the Chinese market.

Viacom agrees China deal

FT

by Mure Dickie and James Kynge

Viacom, the US media conglomerate, yesterday announced plans for a pioneering joint venture TV production company with Shanghai Media Group of China. The venture is the first to be announced following an easing of Beijing's ban on foreign investment in local production companies, revealed by the *Financial Times* in February.

Sumner Redstone, Viacom chairman, said the US group also planned a second joint-venture production operation, with Beijing Television, that would be agreed 'very soon'. The deals underline the eagerness of international media groups to play a greater role in the rapidly growing Chinese market, in spite of the relatively meagre progress made by Viacom and its rivals over the past decade. The venture between Viacom and state-owned SMG will produce programmes for children and young people, initially for the domestic Chinese market.

SMG is expected to take a 51 per cent stake, but the two sides declined to comment on their shareholdings or likely investment before the venture has been formally approved by China's State Administration of Radio, Film and Television. Li Ruigang, SMG president, said content for children was a particularly attractive market segment, with demand not just from the group's own channels but also from regional counterparts. 'In the near future, a lot of provinces will have their own kids' programme chan-

nels,' Mr Li said. 'I think there will be huge market demand for us to explore here.'

The joint venture is the latest in a series of co-operative projects announced by SMG, China's second largest and perhaps most innovative media group. Mr Li said a content-sharing deal with US-owned business channel CNBC Asia Pacific was already profitable.

The venture marks a new direction for Viacom, which has lobbied hard for the right to broadcast directly its MTV music channel in China but remains restricted to audiences in the southern province of Guangdong and to approved hotels and residential compounds. Viacom also syndicates its MTV programmes through cable operators to an estimated 115m households and its Nickelodeon cartoon channel content to about 62m households for a 'peppercorn' fee and access to advertising income, according to executives.

Mr Redstone, unabashed about his ambition to beat international rivals into China, was reticent on how soon it might become a material market for Viacom. 'We still have big ambitions for expanding our presence in China both for MTV and Nickelodeon,' he said. 'Our ambition is for a 24-hour MTV channel nation-wide. It's no secret. Just stay tuned.'

Source: *Financial Times*, 24 March 2004.

INTRODUCTION

Today's consumer is surrounded by marketing in the form of brands, adverts and promotions, which all aim to influence the consumer's behaviour. Adverts may promote everything from the latest G3 Orange phone, through to the NHS 'quit smoking' message. Hence organisations need to understand how to effectively compete in the marketplace and this chapter looks at how organisations can develop competitive strategy. Initially evolving a competitive strategy requires an organisation to understand the basis on which it is competing. This is dealt with by looking at different definitions of **competitive advantage** and different approaches to creating it. This is followed by a review of different approaches to competitive strategy and the critical challenges they present for organisations. The second half of the chapter examines approaches which organisations may use to compete in the marketplace. Marketing objectives are introduced, followed by a detailed look at the key areas of marketing strategy, namely segmentation, targeting and positioning. The frameworks for marketing and competitive strategy together provide ideas, which allow strategies and approaches for operating in the competitive arena to be continually developed.

COMPETITIVE STRATEGIES

Organisations require an effective competitive strategy to operate successfully in a market where there is established and potential competition. This section examines the options companies can pursue to compete in their competitive environment. Michael Porter developed the well-known generic competitive strategies and these are examined here along with the views of Kotler[1] on achieving competitive advantage. Subsequently the difficulties with Porter's strategies, and Bowman and Faulkner's strategy clock are both examined. The Bowman and Faulkner strategy clock looks at feasible competitive strategies as well as those to be avoided due to the likelihood of failure.

Porter's three competitive strategies centre on two issues: the scope of the market to be served and the basis of competition. There are two options for each issue, the scope of market to be served can be broad or narrow. The basis of competition is either cost based or added value based. According to Porter these decisions result in three possible competitive strategies: **cost leadership**; **differentiation**; **focus** (see Exhibit 7.2).

Exhibit 7.2 Generic competitive strategies

		Competitive advantage	
		Lower cost	Differentiation
Competitive scope	Broad target	1. Cost leadership	2. Differentiation
	Narrow target	3a. Cost focus	3b. Differentiation focus

Exhibit 7.3 Porter's generic competitive strategies – a man's suit

		Competitive advantage	
		Lower cost	Differentiation
Competitive scope	Broad target	1. Burton	2. Armani
	Narrow target	3a. Matalan	3b. Savile Row

Cost leadership

A **cost leadership strategy** is used to serve a mass market with standard products.

A cost leadership strategy requires that a broad target or mass market be supplied with standard products or services (see Exhibit 7.3). A successful cost leader in an industry will be the lowest cost producer in the sector and offer the mass-market products and services of a quality comparable to that offered by direct competitors. Cost leadership is likely to be achieved by economies of scale, extremely efficient production or very efficient distribution processes. The supermarket chain Asda-Walmart serves a mass market (see Exhibit 7.5)

Exhibit 7.4 Value chains for cost-based competitive strategies

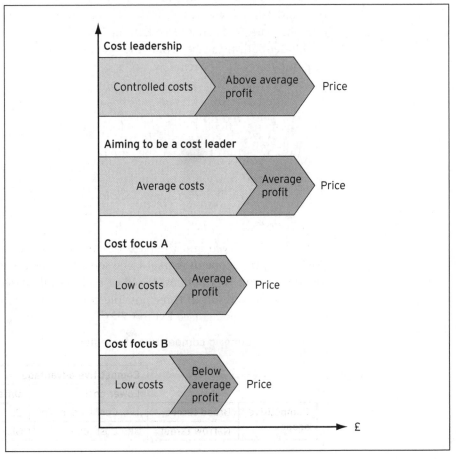

and seeks to be a cost-based competitor by using its buyer power and efficient distribution system. Following a cost leadership strategy and hence operating in a mass market means there will be a number of key competitors and the competitive rivalry is likely to be fierce. There can only be one true cost leader in a sector; the other competitors claiming to follow a cost leadership strategy will have average costs, sell at an average price and make average profits. The cost leader will also sell at an average price, but due to lower costs will make a greater profit (see Exhibit 7.4). It is difficult for the cost leader or any other competitor attempting to follow a cost leadership strategy to charge above average prices as the competitive rivalry in the mass market will make it diffi-cult for such a competitor. This is effectively strategy 6 on the strategy clock, which is one of the strategies likely to lead to failure (as discussed below, see Exhibit 7.7).

Differentiation

A **differentiation strategy** targets a mass market with added value products.

A differentiation strategy, like a cost leadership strategy, targets a mass market. However, there the similarity ends, with a differentiation strategy used to offer the customer added value, rather than the reduced costs and lower prices of a cost leadership strategy. This is the strategy pursued by the food retailing oper-ation of Marks & Spencer (see Exhibit 7.5).

Differentiation can be actual and real or merely perceived by the customer. Real differentiation occurs when a company delivers products or services which are different and distinctive from others on the market. This is likely to be achieved by using higher quality and improved inputs and processes. In contrast perceived differentiation occurs when a company provides products or services which appear different and distinctive compared to competitors' offerings by virtue of the way they are presented to the marketplace. Perceived differentiation arises from the manipulation of price, place and promotion aspects of the marketing mix. This is the same as Kotler's idea of image differ-entiation, as discussed later in this chapter.

Real or perceived, the customer needs to be prepared to pay for the added value, otherwise it is not added value. If customers are not willing to pay for

Exhibit 7.5 Porter's competitive strategies and UK supermarkets

		Competitive advantage	
		Lower cost	**Differentiation**
Competitive scope	**Broad target**	Cost leadership ■ Asda/Walmart ■ Tesco	Differentiation ■ Marks and Spencer ■ Waitrose
	Narrow target	Cost focus ■ Netto ■ Kwik Save	Differentiation focus ■ Fortnum & Mason ■ Harrods Food Halll

added value, resources will have been wasted in providing it and the potential superior profit will not result. Consequently the value chain (see Chapter 3) for a company following a differentiation strategy should be such that costs are average in areas which do not add value, with only the added value incurring extra costs (see Exhibit 7.6).

Exhibit 7.6 Value chains for differentiation-based competitive strategies, compared to cost leadership

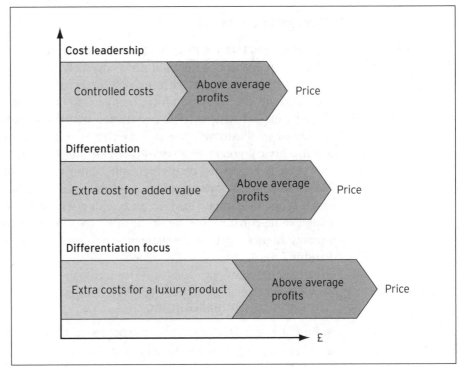

Focus strategies

The focus strategies are clearly used to aim for a niche or a section of the market which is not served well by mainstream competitors in the sector. Consequently a company implementing a focus strategy is most likely to succeed if it centres its efforts on a number of niche market sectors and serves only them to the exclusion of other broad market segments (see Exhibits 7.2 and 7.3). Therefore clear and distinct differences between the segments focused on and the mass-market segments in the sector have to exist.

Cost focus

The **cost focus strategy** targets market niches where customers are very price sensitive.

The **cost focus** strategy is followed by organisations wishing to target market niches where customers are very price sensitive (see Exhibits 7.4 and 7.5). Therefore organisations following a cost focus strategy will aim for low costs, which will allow low-priced products and services to be delivered to price sensitive customers. This strategy is pursued by the supermarket chain Netto in the United Kingdom (see Exhibit 7.5). The value chain required if pursuing a cost focus strategy is to achieve the lowest possible costs by using the cheapest raw materials, manufacturing processes, packaging, delivery and advertising. The low costs mean a price which appeals to the price sensitive customer can be charged and, due to the very low costs, either an average profit or below average profit is made (see Exhibit 7.4).

Differentiation focus

The **differentiation focus strategy** targets niche markets with luxury or added value products.

The **differentiation focus strategy** is similar to the cost focus strategy as both target niche markets. The main difference between the two focus strategies is the basis of competition, with the cost focus strategy being based on very low costs and the differentiation focus being based on lots of added value. The type of niche market which would be targeted with a differentiation focus strategy is one where customers are prepared to spend a lot of money in order to acquire luxury goods or services (see Exhibits 7.5 and 7.6). In food retailing this strategy is pursued by high-class delicatessens and the shop Fortnum and Mason in London, for example (see Exhibit 7.5). The value chain which should ensue is one of standard costs in areas which do not add value, with the luxury added value contributing significantly to the higher costs, in turn, enabling a notably higher price to be charged – resulting in above average profits (see Exhibit 7.6).

✔ Check your understanding

- Do you understand the different competitive strategies companies may pursue?
- Check your understanding by stating which competitive strategy is being pursued with the following products/services.
  1 KFC family sized meal.
  2 14 day coach touring holiday to France.
  3 New red Rolls-Royce.
  4 Thorntons Continental Chocolate Selection.

CHOOSING A SUCCESSFUL COMPETITIVE STRATEGY

Choosing competitive strategies which will deliver competitive advantage is an inexact process. In general terms the achievement of competitive advantage and hence superior profits are central to the strategy of any organisation. Successful achievement of competitive advantage is likely to result if a company is clear about its competitive strategy, which may be one of the following: cost leadership, differentiation, cost focus or cost leadership – or alternatively a combination of competitive strategies (see Business illustration of a combination of competitive strategies). Originally Porter argued that organisations should avoid following a competitive strategy or combination of competitive strategies which results in a lack of clear strategic direction and ineffective implementation, as superior profits would never be achieved.

Business illustration of a combination of competitive strategies - airlines and cars

Many airlines, rail companies and holiday companies pursue a combination of competitive strategies offering a range of different tickets and products to suit different budgets and different markets. For example, airlines like BA, Virgin, Air France or Iberia will compete by offering a range of tickets: first class, business class and economy class. The car company Volkswagen follows a variety of competitive strategies with its Volkswagen, Skoda and Seat cars with different brand names and models.

GILBERT AND STREBAL'S COMPETITIVE STRATEGIES

Gilbert and Strebel present an alternative view of competitive strategies. They argue that there are two constituents of competitive advantage: lower delivered cost and higher perceived value. However, unlike Porter, Gilbert and Strebel go on to argue that lower delivered cost and higher perceived value can be used together to give a company a superior **position** in an industry or sector (see Business illustration on IKEA and John Lewis). The essence of their argument is that to achieve competitive advantage a firm must strive to give the highest perceived value for the lowest delivered cost.

Business illustration of highest value for lowest cost - IKEA and John Lewis Partnership

Examples of organisations that strive to offer the combination of highest perceived value for lowest delivered cost are IKEA and the John Lewis Partnership. IKEA, a chain of Swedish furniture stores, prides itself on offering 'good design at best ever prices'. It achieves this by seeking out and using good design, efficient suppliers, and innovative and rationalised global distribution systems. The commitment of the John Lewis Partnership's retail stores to offering best quality at lowest prices is summarised in its own slogan, 'never knowingly undersold'. John Lewis offers a refund if a customer finds the same item cheaper elsewhere.

Competitive advantage is achieved by creating 'disequilibrium' between the perceived value of the product and the asking price. This is done by increasing the perceived value or reducing the asking price. This alters the terms of competition and could drive competitors out of the market or influence them to offer more perceived value for the same price or the same value for less money. However, Gilbert and Strebel[2] go on to argue that the number of competitive formulas is small, not large. They give two possible reasons for this, the first being that there is an 'internal logic to each business system' that dictates the possible combinations of perceived value and delivered cost that must exist for the whole business system. This number of combinations is clearly finite. The second somewhat obvious reason is that there are only two basic generic competitive strategies: higher perceived added value and lower delivered cost. Depending on a company's industry position and circumstances, there can only exist variations around these two themes, which must therefore limit the number of competitive formulas.

Further to this, Gilbert and Strebel[3] proceed to suggest that strategic advantage can be obtained by the implementation of generic competitive moves in a sequence, such that the implementation of one prepares for the implementation of another. This should of course result in higher perceived value for lower delivered cost.

✔ Check your understanding

- Do you understand that companies may use lower delivered cost and higher perceived value to compete effectively?
- Check your understanding by indicating which companies named below offer lower delivered cost and higher perceived value.

  1 Matalan

  2 Ryanair

  3 Amazon

  4 Starbucks

FAULKNER AND BOWMAN'S STRATEGY CLOCK

Faulkner and Bowman[4] developed the strategy clock, which was further adapted by Johnson, Scholes and Whittington.[5] The strategy clock (see Exhibit 7.7) builds on Porter's three competitive strategies and is an alternative model to Porter for assessing competitive strategy options.

No frills

The **no frills strategy** targets very price sensitive customers who cannot afford higher priced goods.

The **no frills strategy** is used to target very price sensitive customers, who cannot afford or do not wish to pay for higher priced goods or services (see Exhibit 7.7). Success with a no frills strategy is accomplished by offering basic products with no or very limited extra features (see Business illustration on easyJet).

Business illustration of a no frills strategy –
easyJet

easyJet are a good example of a company who have adopted a deliberate 'no frills' strategy. easyJet fly from lower cost airports such as Luton, rather than Heathrow, the flights offer limited extras, and booking is done via the Internet in such a way that tickets do not have to be issued.

Low price

The **low price strategy** is charging reduced prices for products identical to competitors' products, which could result in a price war.

The **low price strategy** is just that, a plan to charge reduced prices for products and services which are identical to those offered by competitors (see Exhibit 7.7) . The risk associated with this strategy is the damaging effects of possible price wars. Success with a low price strategy means a firm must achieve lower costs than its competitors and have the financial might to withstand a price war. However, in the longer term, price wars tend to damage whole industries by severely restricting the ability of companies to reinvest in long-term development. The most likely move by companies which have operated a low price strategy and experienced industry price wars is either a no frills or a differentiation strategy.

However, Bowman and Faulkner do suggest that some companies may succeed with a low cost strategy by focusing on particular market segments where economies of scale can be achieved. A good example of this would be companies that manufacture own label products for supermarket groups. This specialised focus means the cost of seeking new customers is minimal and value systems and value chains can be efficiently tailored to the group of customers being focused on.

Hybrid

A **hybrid strategy** is a combination of differentiation and lower price strategies, to achieve differentiation at a lower price than competitors.

A **hybrid strategy** is a combination of two strategies, namely those of differentiation and lower price (see Exhibit 7.7). The aim is to achieve differentiation from competitors' products and services, while charging lower prices. One example is the car manufacturer Hyundai, which appears to follow a hybrid strategy (see Business illustration on Hyundai). Hyundai offer added value or

Business illustration of a hybrid strategy –
Hyundai

In *What Car*, April 2005, the Hyundai Sante Fe was described as a 'Face-lifted Land Rover Freelander rival', with a five door, two litre model selling for £18,000. Hence it could be argued that the Huyndai Sante Fe seeks to offer some of the perceived value of a Freelander, circa £20,000, but at a lower price.

perceived added value for a lower price, in the hope it will lead to higher turnover than that achievable by differentiation on its own. This is most likely to be achieved by cutting costs (to allow lower prices to be charged) in areas that are not important to the customer.

Differentiation

Differentiation is used to target a mass market and offer customers added value for which they are prepared to pay.

Differentiation is a commonly used generic competitive strategy, which is used to target a mass market and to offer customers added value for which they are prepared to pay. The differentiated or added value products may be of higher quality, provide additional features, or offer better levels of service (see Exhibit 7.7). This strategy is also used by car manufacturers offering more expensive models of cars which have extra features, for example air conditioning, bigger engines, electronic windows, satellite navigation and leather seats. By way of illustration, there were 72 different models/specifications of Renault Megane available in the UK in 2005, ranging in price from £11,000 to £21,000.

Focused differentiation

A **focused differentiation** strategy targets a niche market where customers pay a lot of money for luxury goods.

A **focused differentiation** strategy is similar to differentiation, with the customers being offered more; however, with a focused differentiation strategy a niche or narrow market is targeted (see Exhibit 7.7). As a niche market is being

Exhibit 7.7 The strategy clock

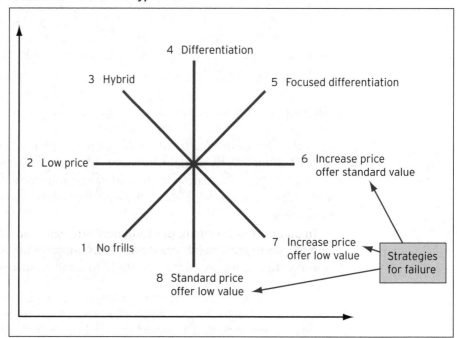

Source: based on Faulkner, D and Bowman C (1995) 'Competitive strategy options', *The Essence of Competitive Strategy*, Hemel Hempstead: Prentice Hall.

Business illustration of a differentiation focus strategy - Porsche

In the car industry, Porsche compete with a focused differentiation strategy with their Porsche 911 GT2 Coupe, which retails for a mere £126,000. The few competitors in the same league as Porsche include Aston Martin, with cars ranging from £103,000 to £174,000 and Bentley with prices from £112,000 to £170,000. The Honda NSX range has more modest prices from £60,000 to £63,000 and the Jaguar XJ range more reserved prices, ranging from £40,000 to £72,000.

targeted there will be very few competitors offering a highly specialised or luxury product or service, for which customers will be prepared to pay a lot of money (see Business illustration on Porsche). Successful differentiation focus requires strong core competencies (see Chapter 3) in areas of importance to the narrow range of customers. Innovation, design and engineering skills will be particularly important core competencies for manufacturers of luxury cars.

Failure strategies - 6, 7 and 8

Strategies for failure include strategy 6 - high price and standard value, strategy 7 - reduced value and increased price, and strategy 8 - standard price and low value.

If a company's competitive strategy should emerge to be number 6, 7 or 8 on the strategy clock and it is pursued for any length of time then failure is highly likely to occur (see Exhibit 7.7).

Competitive strategy 6 is one of high price and standard value. This strategy will only be successful if competitors do not offer a standard product at standard or low price, or if customers cannot access information about where better value could be obtained. If a company continues to offer standard products for high prices, competitors will attract customers from the company by simply offering standard products at standard or low prices. In the same vein strategy 7 (see Exhibit 7.7) will lead to failure as value is reduced and prices increased, hence driving customers to more competitive rivals. Finally strategy 8 (see Exhibit 7.7), is perhaps the most disastrous of all the competitive strategies, charging a standard price for low value products and services. Customers will realise they are being short-changed and move to a competitor offering a better deal.

In addition to Bowman and Faulkners' strategies for failure – numbers, 6, 7 and 8 – there are several other competitive approaches which should be followed with caution as they are unlikely to result in success (see Exhibit 7.8).

Exhibit 7.8 Competitive tactics to avoid

- Follow the leader
- Same as the past
- Competitive race
- Follow all competitive strategies
- Spend too much

Follow the leader

Following the market leader or emulating leading competitors could appear to be a good idea. However, it is likely that the company which does this is ignoring its own strengths and weaknesses, hence not building on its strengths and – even more dangerously – is not minimising its weaknesses. However, occasionally there may be situations when a company is able to benefit from the market awareness raised and lessons learnt from the leader.

Same as the past

Pursuing the same strategy for success because it has worked in the past is dangerous, as the past may not be an accurate predictor of the future. There should be sound business reasoning for pursuing the same strategy again (see Business illustration on Dyson).

Business illustration of a 'Same as the past' strategy – Dyson

The company Dyson is currently flourishing due to the successful development of the Dyson vacuum cleaner. It has followed exactly the same strategy of innovation with the development of its washing machine. The Dyson washing machine washes your clothes faster and more efficiently due to two drums revolving in opposite directions. Only time will tell if the Dyson washing machine will be as successful as the Dyson vacuum cleaner. However, back in 1947 Ken Wood developed the famous Kenwood Chef Blender, and although the company went on to develop a variety of other kitchen electrical appliances over the years, nothing was really quite as successful as the original Kenwood Chef Blender.

Competitive race

A strategy of entering into a competitive race with a competitor for increased market share might raise sales revenue. However, it is likely that increases in revenue will be cancelled out by higher costs in the areas of advertising, promotion, development and manufacturing. Hence following the strategy of entering a race for increased market share is perhaps best avoided.

Follow all competitive strategies

Another option is to follow every competitive strategy and market opportunity presented to the organisation, because one of them must lead down the road to success. This is not a good idea as the resulting overall strategy of the firm is likely to be incoherent and lack direction. Equally the company is unlikely to have enough time, money, or resources to pursue every strategy and project through to its conclusion.

Spend too much

Believing 'too much money has been invested and so quitting is not an option', can be another poor approach to the competitive arena. This approach probably indicates that the organisation is unwilling to accept it is failing and hence the organisation continues to waste money. Organisations need to identify the competitive strategy/strategies they are currently following, and decide if they are likely to lead to success in the future and should continue to be pursued. If it appears that current competitive strategies are leading to failure and strategic mismatch, then competitive strategies should be reviewed and adjusted accordingly.

Review questions

Competitive strategies

1 Which competitive strategies are most appropriate for a mass market?
2 Illustrate the marketing mix which could successfully underpin a differentiation focus competitive strategy.
3 Explain why it is possible to make a profit following a cost focus strategy.
4 Explain the essence of Gilbert and Strebel's approach to competitive strategy.
5 Explain the difference between hybrid and differentiation competitive strategies.
6 Summarise the main danger of a low price strategy.
7 Explain why strategies 6, 7 and 8 on the strategy clock are strategies for failure.
8 Why is entering a competitive race perhaps best avoided?
9 What is the main weakness in pursuing a follow the leader strategy?

DEFINING AND CREATING COMPETITIVE ADVANTAGE

The development of both competitive and marketing strategy is underpinned by the type of competitive advantage an organisation is seeking to create for customers. A review of the literature reveals a variety of different views on how competitive advantage could be created. The views of Coyne[6] and Kotler et al.[7] are examined here.

Conditions for competitive advantage

For **competitive advantage** customers must see a **distinct difference** between a company's product and those of competitors.

Coyne[8] identifies three distinct conditions which must occur for sustainable competitive advantage to exist. First, customers must see a **distinct difference** between a company's product or service and those offered by competitors. The distinct differences need to be in the attributes of the product or service, for example additional features or faster service. A greater number of customers will be attracted if there is a wide range of attributes which provide differentiation. In addition to ensuring differentiation has breadth it also requires depth. If an organisation's differentiation has depth then customers will be less likely to switch to competitors as a result of minor attribute changes by the competitors. Hence ensuring a customer's commitment and loyalty to the business is important and a key strand of managing stakeholders successfully.

Distinct differences are those features of a product or service which distinguish it from a competitor's offering.

For **competitive advantage** there must exist a **capability gap** between an organisation and its competitors.

The second condition Coyne identifies is the existence of a capability gap between an organisation and its competitors. A **capability gap** prevails when the activities which create the differentiated products or services and their delivery can only be performed by the organisation under consideration, while competitors struggle to achieve the same differentiation. A capability gap arises from specific differences in physical resources and operating systems, which are routine and measurable. The organisation must seek to understand the precise and explicit differences in capability between itself and the competition. For example, does the organisation need to either incur or eliminate gaps to perform individual activities more effectively than competitors? The organisation also needs to consider how this can be done, for example via: building reputation; building customer awareness and loyalty; making efficient investment decisions on issues such as plant location, patent protection, quality, and innovation.

For **competitive advantage** products attributes and capability gap must be **enduring**.

Capability gaps arise from specific differences in physical resources and operating systems which are routine and measurable.

Enduring is being sustainable or continuing for a long time.

Finally the competitive advantage must be sustainable, meaning the attributes and gap must both be **enduring**. This can be difficult to achieve, with many differentiated goods, being easily 'copied' by competitors. Producers of patented protected goods or technologies have sustainable competitive advantage, but only until the patent runs out or a new product or technology renders the patent protection worthless.

METHODS FOR ACHIEVING COMPETITIVE ADVANTAGE

Kotler[9] suggests a company can differentiate its offerings to customers in four different areas and potentially achieve competitive advantage in each one. The four areas in which competitive advantage can be achieved are product, service, personnel and image.

Product differentiation

Companies can seek to deliver highly differentiated products to the marketplace or they can offer standardised products with small amounts of

Exhibit 7.9 Sources of differentiation

- Product
- Service
- Personnel
- Image

Source: Kotler, P, Armstrong, G, Saunders, J and Wong, V (1996) *Principles of Marketing*, European Edition, London: Prentice Hall.

differentiation (see Exhibit 7.9). For example standardised products such as chickens can be differentiated. A standard roasting chicken costs £3.49 in Tesco, while a lemon basted roasting chicken costs £3.99 – 50 pence more. In contrast other companies offer highly differentiated products, such as car companies like Ferrari offering upmarket cars, with many top of the range features and styling. Equally Volvo differentiate their cars on safety issues, by offering improved safety with their side impact protection system (SIPS). Hence companies can differentiate products on a range of attributes including performance, safety and reliability.

Service differentiation

Service can be used as a source of differentiation by both manufacturers and service organisations (see Exhibit 7.9). Manufacturers may seek to differentiate their products by offering additional services associated with the products, which may be free or may cost the customer extra. The service can take the form of delivery and/or installation, maintenance and repair, or training in use of the product (mostly provided by organisations supplying sophisticated machinery and equipment to other organisations). A guarantee or extended guarantee with a product is also about service, in this case the reliable provision of repair or replacement. For example, delivery services for furniture may be free or may cost extra. John Lewis shops deliver furniture free of charge to addresses in the local area, but IKEA charges for the delivery of many items of furniture, as customers are expected to take it home themselves. Alternatively companies which provide services can seek to differentiate themselves by the speed of service (see Business illustration on service differentiation). This approach to differentiation is taken by fast food companies, with an emphasis on the 'fast'. A similar approach is also taken by photo processors, opticians and dry cleaners, who all offer to provide the required services in one or two hours maximum, with some, but not all, charging extra for the speedy service. Speed of service is offered by companies like TNT, DHL and Royal Mail, with all offering services which guarantee next-day delivery of that important package.

Business illustration on service differentiation – airports and airlines

Airlines and airports, which are both service organisations, often fail to compete on service in the eyes of the customer. In 2004, a 'You Gov' survey identified the London airports, Edinburgh, Luton, and Nottingham-East Midlands as providing poor services in a variety of ways, including the quality of departure lounges, provision of information and speed of baggage delivery. However, the same survey identified Virgin as the airline providing the best customer service with high levels of cleanliness and comfort on planes, punctual flights and polite staff.

Source: 'Passengers fly into a rage over airports', A King, *Daily Telegraph*, 28 August 2004.

Personnel differentiation

Kotler et al.[10] link personnel differentiation very closely with service organisations, claiming that personnel differentiation requires organisations which provide a service, like McDonalds, GAP and Virgin Airlines, to recruit its customer contact staff carefully, and provide detailed and rigorous training to ensure the staff are extremely competent. Companies such as Barclays, LloydsTSB, HSBC and Orange have moved customer service call centres overseas to India in search of a well-educated English-speaking workforce which enables costs to be cut and employee turnover reduced. Employee turnover can be as high as 30 per cent in UK-based call centres.

In addition the author would argue that personnel differentiation can equally be linked with manufacturing organisations. The absence of appropriately skilled operatives is likely to result in poorer goods being manufactured. In contrast a highly skilled, cohesive workforce with a low turnover is also personnel differentiation, especially if competitors do not posses the same type of workforce.

Business illustration on targeting – Nescafe

In 2001 Nescafe was seeking to target young coffee drinkers with a £20 million global campaign, and in an effort to align the Nescafe brand with the youth market Nescafe became the first global sponsor of the MTV Music Awards, in addition to advertising on MTV's global network of channels. The adverts shown on the MTV channels were shot by Vaughn Arnell, who directed Robbie Williams' Rock DJ video. Also in 2005 and 2006 Nescafe continued with campaigns featuring celebrities such as Martin Clunes of *Men Behaving Badly* fame and Trinny and Susannah. Previous celebrities to feature in the Nescafe adverts include Ian Wright, Chris Eubank, Denise Van Outen and Laurence Llewelyn-Bowen.

Image differentiation

Image differentiation is defined by Kotler et al.[11] as being based on a customer's perceptions of a brand or image (see Exhibit 7.9). Elsewhere this is referred to as perceived differentiation. The image or perception of an organisation and its brands, if strong and lasting, will likely have taken a long time to develop. The strength of the image, its lifetime, its creativity, and how long it is used for promoting and targeting the product or service in different market segments are good indicators of the success of the image and advert (see Business illustration on targeting).

ISSUES TO CONSIDER WHEN DEVELOPING A COMPETITIVE STRATEGY

Organisations cannot predict today the most appropriate competitive strategy for competing tomorrow. Hence it makes sense for a company to have a competitive strategy which acknowledges that the environment in which it is implemented is constantly changing.

Companies often base decisions concerning competitive strategy on assumptions concerning competitors' apparent intentions to operate in particular marketplaces in specific ways and not on hard evidence. Herein lies the danger of a company implementing an expensive competitive strategy based on presumptions about a competitor's behaviour, as the rival may choose to do nothing, maintain an existing competitive strategy, or follow a completely new and different competitive strategy. Furthermore, it should be borne in mind that competitors learn from each other's successes and failures. Consequently it is important for companies to have a robust framework for generating and evolving original ideas which feed into the development of competitive strategy rather than just following the nearest rival. Additionally the development of unique competitive strategy is more likely to lead to a sustainable competitive advantage that is more difficult for rivals to copy.

The aims of generating, evolving and developing a competitive strategy are twofold: first to keep the company ahead of its competitors in the marketplace and second to make it as difficult as possible for rivals copy the competitive strategy. Achievement of these aims should allow a company to stay ahead in the marketplace and benefit from its competitive strategy in the relative long term. Therefore effective competitive strategies are those which are both well planned and adaptable. It could be argued this is at odds with Porter's competitive strategies, which infer that companies should select and follow a specific competitive strategy. However, a constant and flexible strategy should not always be adjusted the moment difficulties and significant environmental change arise. Companies should seek to achieve a balance between continuity of a current strategy and responsiveness to difficulties and change in the external environment. Developing the skills, abilities and judgement to do this, many would argue, is as important as actually developing and implementing a competitive strategy.

ASSESSING COMPETITORS' MANAGEMENT PHILOSOPHIES

Press[12] develops a simple framework for assessing basic different types of **management philosophy** and suggests that any competitive analysis should include an assessment of the management philosophy of competitors, as this will influence the strategies and tactics employed. The framework is developed by considering two dimensions: those of management goals and measurement criteria.

The first dimension considers management goals and at one end of the dimension or continuum, all management goals are orientated towards the internal environment of the business. This end of the continuum will focus entirely on the internal activities of the organisation and include goals relating to employees, rewards, production and control systems. The other end of the continuum will focus on the external environment in which the company operates and covers goals relating to: performance in the competitive environment; the marketplace and economy; and satisfying customers' needs and wants. Obviously organisations fall between these two extremes with a mixture of internal and external goals, which may be accompanied with a tendency to lean towards either internal or external goals.

The second dimension considers measurement criteria, which are concerned with the different ways in which management goals can be evaluated. This is also a continuum with two extremes of measurement criteria at either

Exhibit 7.10 Press's management philosopies

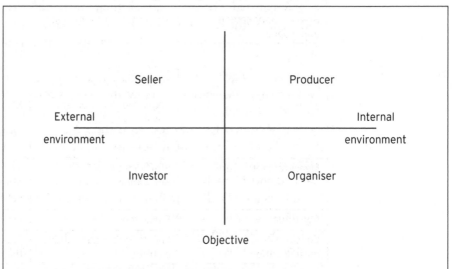

Source: Press, G (1990) 'Assessing competitors' business philosophies', *Long Range Planning*, 23, 5, October.

end, those being objective and subjective measurement criteria. The objective measurement criteria are quantifiable and easily measurable criteria, for example return on investment and profit margin. These quantifiable measures can be general for almost all businesses and can then be used to compare the performance of different businesses with each other. These quantifiable measurements are best achieved by having highly efficient systems for managing people, resources and outputs. In contrast, the subjective measurement criteria take the view that management is an art, not a science, and requires experienced and skilled managers whose role it is to ensure the right people are in the right jobs in the organisation. This ensures effectiveness and no quantitative system can replace the work of experienced and skilled managers.

Press[13] goes on to arrange these two continuums to form a matrix (see Exhibit 7.10), entitled 'management philosophies'. This gives rise to four management philosophies: the manager as a producer, organiser, investor or seller (see Exhibits 7.10, 7.11 and 7.12).

Exhibit 7.11 Items for defining Press's management philosophies

- **Management objectives**: the key aims of managers in the organisation.
- **Tools to achieve objectives**: techniques managers use to help achieve objectives.
- **Measurement criteria**: how efficiency and effectiveness are assessed.
- **Constituency**: whom managers in the organisations see as main stakeholders.
- **Considerations for diversification**: the critical issues to be considered should diversification via acquisition or merger occur.

Source: based on Press, G (1990) 'Assessing competitors' business philosophies' *Long Range Planning*, 23, 5, October.

Exhibit 7.12 Defining Press's management philosophies – the entrepreneurial paradigm

Press's management philosopies	The producer philosophy	The investor philosophy
Management objectives	Seeks co-operation of workers, improve workforce's skills	Maximise shareholders or 'investors' wealth
Tools	Employee development rewards, creating a motivating workplace environment	Budgeting and other management accounting techniques
Measurement criteria	Staff morale and motivation	Return on investment and other measurements of return
Constituency	Employees	Investors
Consideration for diversification	Matching of organisational cultures	The risk involved versus the potential benefits

Source: based on Press, G (1990) 'Assessing competitors' business philosophies', *Long Range Planning*, 23, 5, October.

Exhibit 7.13 Defining Press's management philosophies – the corporate paradigm

Press's management philosopies	The organiser philosophy	The seller philosophy
Management objectives	Improve efficiency of resources used	To be market leader
Tools	Economies of scale and use of systems such as JIT	Manipulation of the marketing mix (product, price, place and promotion)
Measurement criteria	Management accounting techniques, productivity of staff and resource use	Company image, perceived quality and value of products and services
Constituency	Suppliers and other partners	Customers
Consideration for diversification	Synergy of internal activities	Synergy for market position

Source: based on Press, G (1990) 'Assessing competitors' business philosophies', *Long Range Planning*, 23, 5, October.

Press[14] goes onto discuss combinations of some of his philosophies, resulting in two **paradigms** or combinations of philosophies. The entrepreneurial paradigm is defined as a combination of the producer and investor philosophies (see Exhibit 7.12), the thinking being that managers sought to improve the motivation of workers as a way of maximising shareholders' or investors' wealth.

The second paradigm is a combination between the organiser and seller philosophies, which creates the corporate paradigm (see Exhibit 7.13). Press[15] argues that the corporate paradigm is a combination of low-cost production with differentiation, something of the hybrid strategy of Bowman and Faulkner.

Review questions   Competitive advantage and management philosophies

1 Summarise the three conditions needed for sustainable competitive advantage to exist.

2 'Service differentiation is only used by service companies as a source of differentiation.' True of false? Explain your choice of answer.

3 Explain the difference between 'personnel' and 'image' differentiation.

4 Specify the two key aims in developing a competitive strategy.

5 Define the key measurement criteria in the producer philosophy.

6 Who is the main constituency (stakeholders) in the seller philosophy?

7 What are the key aims of the entrepreneurial paradigm?

8 Identify and briefly discuss, with examples, the type of company to which the corporate paradigm could apply.

MARKETING STRATEGY AND OBJECTIVES

Companies which have developed competitive strategy and a clear idea of how competitive advantage is to be achieved, that is via cost or added value, will need to turn their attention to the development of a marketing strategy to underpin and support the chosen competitive strategy. The challenge for any organisation's marketing strategy is for it to enable the organisation to meet its objectives. The skill the strategist must develop is that of selecting the right combination of competitive strategy, marketing objectives and marketing strategy to allow a company to perform more successfully in its competitive arena than its nearest rivals.

Exhibit 7.14 Marketing strategy

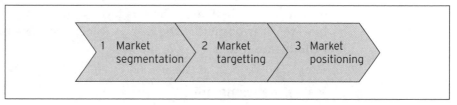

The rest of this section defines and examines marketing objectives which result from combinations of market options and product options, giving rise to four categories of marketing objectives.[16] Later sections in this chapter focus on the key activities of marketing strategy which are segmentation, targeting and positioning (see Exhibit 7.14).

Exhibit 7.15 Marketing objectives

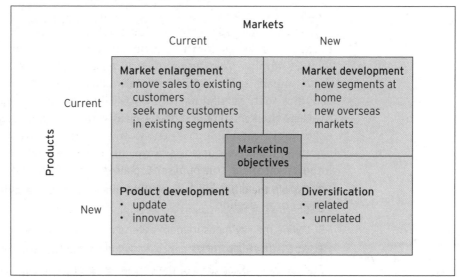

Market enlargement

Market enlargement is the expansion of a company's existing markets.

Market enlargement (see Exhibit 7.15) is simply an expansion of a company's existing markets, which requires manipulation of the price, promotion and place for a product such that existing customers buy and use more. Market enlargement has been pursued by Kellogg's promoting breakfast cereal as a before bedtime snack. Additionally in the UK, Kellogg's have promoted cereals such as Special K and Crunchy Nut Cornflakes in their 'Drop a jeans size' campaign. Consumers are encourage to a have one balanced meal a day and replace two meals with a bowl of cereal as a way of losing those extra pounds gained at Christmas.

Market enlargement is easiest in a growing market as there is plenty of new demand and most difficult, if not impossible, in a declining market due to decreasing demand. In a static or mature market, enlargement will normally be fairly difficult due to there being few or no new customers available; however, it is possible if the market leader becomes complacent and allows performance to slip.

Market development

Market development is the creation of new markets or market segments.

Market development (see Exhibit 7.15) is the creation or exploitation of new markets or market segments. Market development requires either the market to be re-segmented and new profitable segments identified or new geographic markets to be identified and entered into for the first time. McDonalds have re-segmented the market for fast food and sought to meet the customer's requirement for healthier options by introducing new menu items, such as porridge and raisin toast on to the breakfast menu, salads on to the main menu and fruit bags on the children's menu.

Market development via new geographic markets often requires a company to expand or engage for the first time in international business activities. These include simply exporting products to an overseas market or internationalising the company's activities. Internationalising operations involves locating activities such as manufacturing, distribution and promotion in or close to overseas markets. While this is clearly more complex and expensive than exporting, greater financial benefits in the form of lower costs often result – for example, lower labour costs, lower distribution costs and the overcoming of import controls. A company may choose to internationalise its operations if its new geographic market is growing, while at the same time home markets are mature or in decline.

Product development

Product development is the generation of new products via innovation, research, design and development.

Product development (see Exhibit 7.15) is usually undertaken by companies which are successful at innovation, research, design and development (see Business illustration of product development). It is the generation of brand new products and updated versions of existing products in an effort to keep and acquire customers. Companies which choose product development as a marketing objective are likely to be structured around product divisions and create new or updated products. Virtually all car manufacturers update successful cars by bringing out new models which involves a change of shape and improvements to mechanical features; examples include companies and their products such as the Ford Fiesta, Vauxhall Corsa and the Nissan Micra.

Business illustration of product development – consumer electronics and pharmaceuticals

Consumer electronic companies, such as Sony and Apple, develop new products which perform a similar function to an existing product, for example DVD players to replace video players, MP3 players to replace personal CD players. Another industry in which companies seek to achieve successful product development is the pharmaceutical industry. Pharmaceutical companies employ money and resources in seeking to produce new drugs which treat patients in better ways than existing treatments, for example developing insulin which can be taken orally rather than by injection.

Entering new markets with new products

In order to develop a balance between product ranges and market locations, some organisations may decide to enter a variety of new markets with new products. Large diversified companies or conglomerates are the best examples. The new markets and new products can be related to current products and markets or be in completely different areas from current business (see Exhibit 7.15). For example, the ice cream manufacturer Walls entered the market for non-frozen deserts with its newly developed Magnum chocolate and white chocolate deserts in 2006.

✔ Check your understanding

- Do you understand the different marketing objectives companies may pursue?
- Check your understanding by stating which marketing objectives are sought by the following activities.
  1. B&Q open in Beijing.
  2. Jamie Oliver appears in a new Christmas Sainsbury TV advert.
  3. Richard Branson's Virgin Group to sell jeans and casual clothes on UK high street.
  4. Coca Cola launch 'Lime Coke'.

Marketing objectives

1 Describe the type of marketplace in which market enlargement is a difficult marketing objective to achieve.

2 How is market development achieved?

3 Why might a company pursue market development?

4 What type of structure do companies pursuing product development often have?

5 Explain the reasons for a company undertaking product development.

MARKET SEGMENTATION

Market segmentation is dividing up a diverse market into small groups of customers with similar needs.

Market segmentation is the dividing up of a large and diverse market into small groups or sub-markets which consist of customers with the same or similar requirements from a product or service. Segmentation results from analysis of a large and diverse market, followed by defining the market segments or sub-markets. If the segmentation is carried out correctly each market segment will be clearly and distinctly different from other market segments. If this is not the case, then the market segmentation is inefficient, as two or more market segments will have the same requirements. In addition for market segmentation to be effective each segment must be of a size (for example, measured by number of customers) to generate sufficient revenue and profit.

Successful market segmentation allows companies to target the most viable segments, giving them the best chance of making the greatest profits. Alternatively effective segmentation may highlight market segments which are being ignored by current competitors, hence providing an opportunity for potential new entrants to join the marketplace. This is due to effective market segmentation allowing companies the opportunity to develop products or services which have different marketing mixes and are segment specific. Depending on the segment to be targeted, different marketing mixes can be developed to provide a product or service which offers either cost or value added differentiation. Market segmentation also allows opportunities and threats to be identified, with new niche market segments which have not been spotted by the competition providing potentially profitable opportunities.

Segmentation variables

There is a wide range of variables which can be used to segment consumer markets and they fall into two groups (see Exhibit 7.16). First there are those segmentation variables which describe the consumer and potential customers, including variables such as age, income and type of housing occupied by the consumer. The second category of segmentation characteristics are those which relate to the product and the customer's reasons for buying it.

Exhibit 7.16 Market segmentation variables

Customer characteristics	Behavioural characteristics
■ Demographics	■ Customer loyalty
■ Socio-economic traits	■ Purchase occasion
■ Lifestyle	■ Benefit segmentation
■ Geographic location	■ Product usage

Customer characteristics

Customer characteristic variables can be broken down into sub-groups: demographics; socio-economics; lifestyle; geographic location.

Information on **customer characteristics**, such as age, sex and occupation, is easy to obtain and measure. Hence this results in such characteristics being widely used as variables to segment markets for consumer products and services. The customer characteristic variables can be broken down into a variety of sub-groups and these include four sub-groups: demographics, socio-economics, lifestyle and geographic location.

Demographic segmentation variables include age, sex, family size and family lifecycle. **Customer needs and wants** change with age, for example different CDs and videos are targeted at different age groups. The latest CD by Atomic Kitten is largely targeted at the teenage market; the latest Cliff Richard album aimed at women aged 50 and over, many of whom will have been fans since the 1960s; while the CD of Bob the Builder was marketed for young children and at their parents. Equally, in China (see Entry case study 7.1) Viacom aim to focus on children's television programmes as this is seen as a growing and extensive market segment across China.

Socio-economic variables include income, occupation, terminal education age and social class. Clearly people with higher incomes are more likely to have higher disposable incomes. The logical argument is that those with higher incomes have better jobs, are better educated and are therefore of a higher social class. In contrast lifestyle variables (see Exhibit 7.16) are not as easy to measure as demographic and socio-economic variables. Lifestyle variables involve three main elements which reflect a person's lifestyle, namely activities, interactions with others, and opinions. However, an option for Viacom (see Entry case study 7.1) may be to define a market segment for TV home makeover programmes in the China by use of lifestyle and socio-economic variables as home ownership is rising quickly in China.[17]

Geographic segmentation is the dividing of a marketplace into different geographical units such as countries (Denmark, Germany, Italy), regions (Highlands and Islands of Scotland, Northern France, Sicily and Southern Italy), counties (South Yorkshire, Staffordshire, Cornwall), cities (Berlin, Sheffield, Lille) or local neighbourhoods. Companies may choose to operate in one or few geographic areas, for example the Waitrose chain of supermarkets operates mainly in the south of England.

Behavioural characteristics related to products

Behavioural characteristics define the customers' behaviour and attitude to the product, including customer loyalty, occasion and frequency of purchase.

Behavioural characteristics are used to segment markets according to variables such as the loyalty of customers, the benefits sought from the product, attitude to the product, the occasion, and frequency of purchase. In contrast to the customer characteristic variables, which describe customers, these variables clearly define the customers' behaviour and attitude to the product or service.

Markets can be segmented by customer loyalty and different marketing approaches used on customers with different degrees of loyalty to the product. The outcome of segmentation by loyalty normally produces three categories of customer. The few hard core loyal customers who always buy the same brand, a significant number of customers who will change between a number of brands on an occasional basis, and a significant group of customers who will frequently switch between the full range of brands available.

Market segmentation by purchase occasion groups buyers according to the occasion which triggers the idea to buy or use the product or service. Interflora and flower shops use this approach by targeting customers and suggesting the sending or buying of flowers for a special occasion, for example birthdays, Mother's Day, Valentine's Day.

Benefit segmentation uses causal rather than descriptive variables to segment the market. Therefore benefit segmentation is segmentation of the market according to the major benefits consumers are seeking from the product. The major toothpaste manufacturers segment the market according to the benefits their products offer, for example protection against decay; whiter teeth; fresher breath; reduced plaque build up. Viacom (see Entry case study 7.1) may seek to promote their children's programmes to parents as educational and of benefit to children's development.

Product usage can be used to segment the markets into light, medium and heavy user groups. Frequent users of a product are the small number of buyers accounting for a high percentage of sales and may be rewarded for their repeat purchases, for example by some airlines offering frequent flyers extra discounts and services.

In conclusion the benefits which are sought via market segmentation include: greater sales and profitability; closer match of products and services to customer requirements; greater consumer satisfaction; and a focus on segments with the greatest potential. Additional benefits include further market opportunities, and the development of new market segments and better competitive positions for existing products and services. If benefits of the type described above do not result for either the company or customer then the segmentation process has not been performed correctly.

✔ Check your understanding

- Do you understand the concept of market segmentation?
- Check your understanding by indicating how Viacom (see Entry case study 7.1) could segment the marketplace in China for television programmes and channels.

Evaluation and selection of market segments

The evaluation of market segments requires both the segments themselves to be evaluated and the external environment in which the organisation is situated to be analysed and understood. The external environment in which the segments exist can be evaluated by analysis of the external environment and the competitive environment (see Chapter 2). Therefore chapter 2 and this chapter provide an understanding of the environment in which companies operate and the strategies which may be used to compete effectively within it.

Different organisations will regard different types of market segments as attractive, for example, in terms of size, large segments tend to be more attractive since potential sales are greater and economies of scale more likely. The large size of the market and market segments in China is undoubtedly one of the reasons for Viacom expanding into China. In contrast some companies will view large segments as less attractive due to their highly competitive nature and the large number of competing companies. This will be particularly

Exhibit 7.17 The product lifecycle

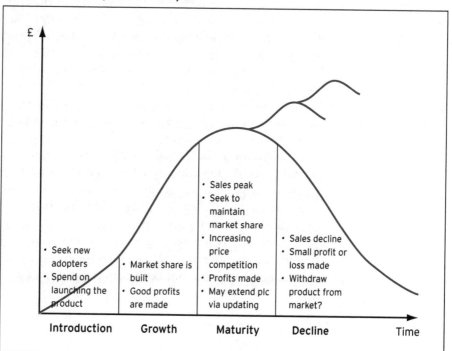

true for small companies, which, due to their limited resources, can find it difficult to compete in large segments against large competitors. Therefore some companies will find smaller or niche segments attractive, as they can compete effectively and make a profit.

Growing market segments are usually viewed as attractive because it is easier to build market share and pick up new customers, because there is often no previous loyalty to a particular company or brand. In contrast in mature markets the rate of product purchase is not growing and for some customers their loyalty to existing brands will have to be broken if a competitor is to attract them. In conclusion, careful analysis and assessment of the growth rate of a segment and the competition within it should be undertaken. Declining markets may offer an opportunity if competitors are pulling out of the market and releasing market share. However, this should be not be viewed as a sustainable long-term strategy. Products and market segments which are in the introduction, growth, maturity and decline sectors of the **product lifecycle** display the characteristics shown in Exhibit 7.17.

Accessibility is the ease with which a company can communicate with a market segment.

Market segments can be evaluated by assessing their **accessibility, measurability** and **viability**. Accessibility requires an evaluation of how easy or difficult it is to reach and communicate with the different market segments, in a cost-effective manner. Do customers or potential customers in a market segment shop in the same type of shops? Do they access the same type of media (newspapers, television, Internet). If the answer to both questions is yes for a particular market segment, then it is likely to be cost effective to target the segment with advertising and **sales promotion** campaigns.

Measurability is quantifying the potential size and buying power of the segment.

Measurability is quantifying the potential of the segment by measuring the size and buying power of the segment. For example, how many customers are there in the segment? How much will customers spend? How often will customers buy? Will customers make repeat purchases? Viacom (see Entry case study 7.1) could measure the size of its Chinese market segments by the number of viewers or potential viewers.

Viability of a market segment is determined by assessing if a segment is profitable enough to be treated separately.

The viability of a market segment is determined by assessing whether the segment is commercially lucrative enough to be treated as a separate sub-market. The returns expected from the market need to be quantified and therefore the costs involved (development, launch, production, advertising and promotion) in delivering the product or service to the marketplace will need to be taken into account.

In conclusion research covering the product or service, the market and the company's marketing will need to answer the questions raised in assessing a segment's accessibility, measurability and viability. Hence, the market segments selected by an organisation should be those which have been evaluated as providing the best opportunity for the company to meet its marketing objectives.

Market segmentation and evaluation

1 Define market segmentation.

2 Describe the two main groups of segmentation variables.

3 Discuss the difference between demographic and socio-economic variables.

4 Explain benefit segmentation.

5 Why are growing market segments more attractive than mature segments?

6 Explain how market accessibility can be evaluated.

7 How can the size of a market segment be measured?

8 How can the viability of a market segment be assessed?

MARKET TARGETING

Once the market segments have been selected and evaluated, development of appropriate market coverage strategies needs to occur, allowing the chosen segments to be targeted. There are four market coverage strategies,[18] namely, undifferentiated marketing, differentiated marketing, focused marketing and **customised marketing**, with each allowing the targeting of different or specific market segments.

Undifferentiated marketing

An **undifferentiated market coverage strategy** targets the whole market with one product or service.

Companies that follow an **undifferentiated market coverage strategy** will target the whole market with one product or service (see Exhibit 7.18). This approach is used in a number of different situations. First, the undifferentiated approach can be used if there are no strong differences between possible market segments. In this case the product or service offered will focus on the commonality of customer requirements rather than differences. Second, the undifferentiated approach may be used if it is believed that the appeal of the product or service transcends all segment boundaries. Next, evaluation of possible market segments may indicate that the cost of serving different segments is greater than the revenue and profits which would be generated; therefore the undifferentiated approach will be the most economically viable.

Exhibit 7.18 Market coverage strategies – undifferentiated marketing

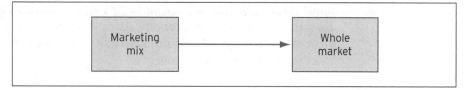

Promotion work undertaken by water companies such as Severn Trent Water will focus on the commonality of customer requirements for constant clean water and non-wasteful use of the resource, as the product – water – is undifferentiated. Finally, an undifferentiated approach may be followed by default. A company may not have a marketing orientation and will therefore lack the customer knowledge required for a targeted approach to the marketplace.

The benefits of an undifferentiated market coverage strategy arise from the opportunity to limit or reduce costs in the areas of product development, production, storage, distribution and delivery. Additionally, savings can be made in the sales and marketing, as only one or very few products or services have to be offered. Organisations gaining the majority of their business from large market segments will be likely to use an undifferentiated approach. However, they may face fierce competition and reduced profit margins, which may mean the organisation ultimately chooses to follow a more targeted approach and employ a differentiated, focused or customised market coverage strategy.

Differentiated marketing

A **differentiated market coverage strategy** targets a number of market segments, all with an individually tailored marketing mix.

A **differentiated market coverage strategy** is applicable where a number of market segments have been identified and the company develops individual marketing mixes for two or more of the market segments identified. The main benefit derived from this approach is that more sales revenue is generated than if the undifferentiated approach was adopted.

Exhibit 7.19 Market coverage strategies – differentiated marketing

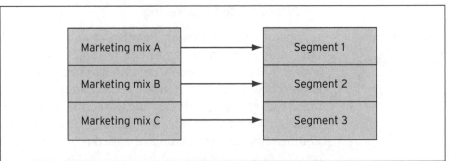

The differentiated approach (see Exhibit 7.19) is that which is typically used by airlines, railways and package holiday operators. For example, an airline offering flights across the Atlantic from Paris to New York can fill its planes in a number of different ways, but needs to select an approach which will both fill the plane and make the greatest profit (see Business illustration of differentiated marketing). An airline could adopt an undifferentiated approach and fill all seats by charging an economy fare. However, this will not generate the greatest profits, indeed it is unlikely that costs would be covered, hence the need for a differentiated strategy.

Business illustration of differentiated marketing - airlines

Airlines sell economy class tickets on a flight (circa 300 passengers) to those passengers who know exactly when they want to travel in advance of doing so and they will have bought a ticket well in advance of travelling. Also in economy class will be those passengers who booked late in the day and those who are not sure about their exact travel dates. These passengers will all receive the same type of seat, service and baggage allowance, but those who booked later will have paid significantly more for their flight compared to passengers who booked well in advance. Additionally there will be some passengers who try to book a flight very late in the day and consequently may get a very cheap flight, as the airline would rather fill the seat, than it remain empty.

In business class (circa 60-80 passengers) there will be passengers who will have paid three to five times more than the economy passengers. In many cases the passenger's employer will have paid the fare. Finally there are first class passengers (circa 10-20 passengers) who will have paid around twice that paid by the business class passenger. This type of approach to differentiating tickets for long haul flights is well known to be that which is likely to produce the greatest revenue, while filling the plane. Hence it is followed by many airlines on long haul routes all over the world.

Focused marketing

The **focused marketing strategy** targets only one market segment, despite having the choice of several market segments.

The **focused marketing strategy** (see Exhibit 7.20) occurs when a company decides to focus on only one market segment, despite having the option to focus on several market segments. This approach makes sense for smaller companies, which will be stretched in terms of resources and effort if competing in many segments. Focused marketing strategy is in contrast to the differentiated approach to marketing, which suggests a company serve a number of market segments with the aim of generating a maximum amount of revenue and profit.

The best segment or niche to serve is one which is neglected by the larger companies operating in the big market segments; in this scenario the smaller

Exhibit 7.20 Market coverage strategies - focused marketing

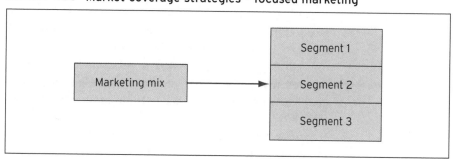

company aims for a big share of a small segment, rather than a small share of a large segment. This allows resources, knowledge and expertise to be focused on the market niche, with a fair chance of success.

Customised marketing

Customised marketing (see Exhibit 7.21) occurs when a unique marketing mix is developed for each customer. Advertising agencies, management consultancies, lawyers and builders of customised hand-built kitchens all vary their offering depending on each client and their requirements. The requirements and how they can be met will be discussed in person on a one-to-one basis with each individual client. The purchasing power of the customer makes this approach worthwhile for the company.

Exhibit 7.21 Market coverage strategies – customised marketing

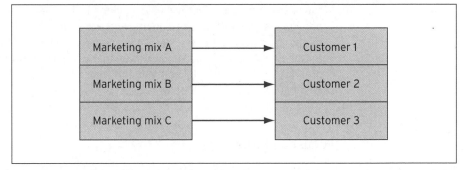

Selecting a market coverage strategy

In choosing a market coverage strategy several factors need to be taken into account. First, company resources; if they are limited, then a focused marketing strategy is best, otherwise any of the other approaches which is appropriate can be used.

Second, the amount of variability in the product or service; if uniform – such as table salt or kiwi fruit – then an undifferentiated approach will suffice. If there is great variation in the products or services offered, as with cars, mobile phones and interior design, then one of the other market coverage strategies would be more suitable.

Next, consider the product's (or service's) position on the product lifecycle (see Exhibit 7.17). A product or service in the introduction or growth phase will benefit most from an undifferentiated or focused approach. This means one offering or marketing mix is developed and is aimed at the whole unsegmented market or at one significant market segment. This approach should enable the product or service to build up market share during its early days on the market.

Finally, variation in the market needs to be taken into account. Clearly if the market is such that all customers behave in the same or a similar manner with regard to taste, buying habits and advertising, then an undifferentiated approach will be fine. However, it is more likely there will be variation in the market, with clear differences between identifiable market segments; hence the differentiating approach would be better.

In conclusion the market coverage strategies being employed by competitors need to be considered. If competitors are following a differentiated strategy and have clearly segmented the market, then an undifferentiated approach would result in failure. The differentiated, focused or customised approach would have to be used to compete directly with the competitors or to compete in a market niche which other competitors had chosen to ignore. In the reverse situation, if competitors are using an undifferentiated approach, then market segmentation and a more targeted approach are likely to result in greater success.

✔ Check your understanding

- Do you understand the different market coverage strategies organisations may use?

- Check your understanding by indicating the market coverage strategies Viacom (see Entry case study 7.1) may use in China.

MARKET POSITIONING

Position defines how customers perceive a product in comparison to products offered by competitors.

Once the targeted segment(s) have been selected, the product(s) or service(s) must be positioned in order to create a clearly defined image in the minds of customers. The term **position** defines how customers perceive a product or service in comparison to products or services offered by competitors. The key positioning aims for companies are to position products or services such that they are perceived differently compared to competing products and services. Positioning requires a company to understand: how customers think about and view their products or services; how the product (or other aspects of its marketing mix) can be modified to meet customer perceptions; and how the customer's perceptions can be altered to fit the product or service.

Companies operating in a number of segments, which could include different foreign markets, need to assess the status of each product or service in each marketplace. First the extent of the product's appeal should be assessed; does it have mass market appeal or niche market charm? Second the advantages of the product or service should be obvious and credible, with any similarities and differences in how those advantages are perceived in different countries clearly understood. An appreciation and awareness of cultural differences can be helpful in achieving such understanding (see Chapters 5 and 9). Additionally knowledge concerning the degree of substitutability of a product or service is also required. In an overseas market some substitutability may arise from locally produced brands, which may provide clues as to how the features of a product or service could be altered to achieve success.

Developing a marketing mix for position

The four aspects of the marketing mix (product, price, place and promotion) can be manipulated such that the product or service and customer perceptions match, hence creating a perceived difference between a company's offerings and those of its competitors. However, it is unlikely the perceived difference between a company and its competitors will be in all areas of the marketing mix. Normally companies choose to match or underscore a competitor on some aspects of the marketing mix and to outperform it on others, to create a perceived difference or competitive advantage. However, organisations should be wary of a common mistake, which is to keep the same marketing mix for each market segment. Customer requirements and buying behaviour vary from segment to segment, and hence, so should the marketing mix. The choice companies have is to compete head-on and manipulate the same aspects of the marketing mix as competitors, or to manipulate and compete on other aspects of the marketing mix and create competitive advantage that way.

Product

In manipulating the marketing mix, a company will seek to make as much of a product for as along as possible, with the minimum of development, while keeping sales and profits high. However, should sales of a product begin to decline, it is not inevitable that a brand new product needs to be found straight away. Sales of an existing product can be kept buoyant by manipulating certain aspects of that product, at little cost, in order to offer a newer, fresher face to the product. The aims of this approach are clear: to attract new customers or persuade existing customers not to switch to a competitor's product. Product aspects which can be manipulated include style, performance, quality, branding, packaging and after-sales service.

Price

The price aspect of the marketing mix can be used to influence sales of new and existing products. Products being introduced to the market can be offered at a 'special introductory price' or 'introductory offer' to entice customers to try the product or service. Orange 3G mobile phones where introduced to the marketplace in the UK during the first half of 2005 with the offer of buy one phone, get one free, to give to a loved one. This would allow the purchaser to communicate verbally, in text and on video with someone whose phone had the same technical capability as their own, and hence encourage new adopters of the product and technology to buy and use it.

Promotion

Promotion is a combination of advertising and sales promotion, which are both needed to create and support a successful product. Advertising media such as the press, magazines, television, radio and the Internet are used to attract customers and inform them about products or services. In store or point-of-sale promotional activity, in the form of 'a free taste' for food products or a test drive for a new car, are designed to tempt the potential customer even further and hopefully persuade the undecided to buy.

Place

The location of the interface between customers and the product or service is manipulated by altering the 'distribution' of the product or service. The aim is to get the right amount of product to the right place at the right time, and this is essential whether from manufacturer to wholesaler; wholesaler to retailer; retailer to customer; or manufacturer direct to the customer. This is particularly so for those organisations that are reacting to customer demand for more products which can be delivered direct to the home, without the need to go out shopping, for example Internet shopping.

Marketing objectives and their relationship with marketing strategy are examined prior to consideration of the key activities of marketing strategy, namely segmentation, targeting and positioning. Segmentation variables, the selection and targeting of segments and positioning are examined. An understanding of marketing strategy will complement and support the development of competitive strategy, which was covered in the first half of this chapter.

Review questions   Market targeting and positioning

1 Why is a growing market segment attractive?

2 Explain how a market segment could be evaluated.

3 How many products or services will a company following an undifferentiated market coverage strategy have in the marketplace?

4 What is the main benefit of a differentiated market coverage strategy over an undifferentiated one?

5 Explain the difference between a focused and customised market coverage strategy.

6 To position a product correctly, what needs to be clearly understood?

CONCLUSION

This chapter has sought to examine aspects of competitive and marketing strategy. Porter's work on competitive strategies is well known and is covered in this chapter. However, in addition, the chapter seeks to present some alternative approaches to competitive strategy and the achievement of competitive advantage. The chapter concludes by considering marketing strategy, which underpins and supports competitive strategy.

So, do companies follow the approaches to competitive and marketing strategy discussed in this chapter? Yes, many undoubtedly do. For example, the car manufacturer Daihatsu clearly follows a cost focus strategy and strives to keep costs low. In contrast companies such as BMW and Mercedes seek to add value to their cars and pursue a differentiated marketing strategy.

LEARNING OUTCOMES AND SUMMARY

The learning outcomes for this chapter are specified and a brief summary of the material relating to the learning outcomes is provided.

→ **Learning outcome 1**
Identify and discuss Porter's competitive strategies and alternative approaches to competitive strategy.

- According to Porter there are four competitive strategies: cost leadership, differentiation, cost focus and differentiation focus. Cost leadership is selling a standard product to a mass market and differentiation is selling an added value product to a mass market. The cost focus strategy is selling a low cost product to a niche market; and differentiation focus is selling a high added value or luxury product to a niche market.
- Gilbert and Strebel suggest that in competitive strategy there are only two constituents of competitive advantage, lower delivered cost and higher perceived value, which can be used in combination to give a company a superior position in an industry or sector.
- Bowman and Faulkner have developed the strategy clock as an approach to competitive strategy. The no frills strategy is used to target very price sensitive customers. The low price strategy offers identical, but low cost products and services compared to competitors' offerings. The hybrid strategy achieves differentiation from competitors by offering both added value and lower prices. The strategy of differentiation is offering added value and expecting customers to pay for it, while differentiation focus is a strategy of differentiation in a niche market.

→ **Learning outcome 2**
Develop competitive strategies for companies, avoiding competitive strategies which lead to failure and strategic mismatch.

- The aims of generating, evolving and developing a competitive strategy are twofold: first to keep the company ahead of its competitors in the market-place and second to make it as difficult as possible for rivals to copy. Additionally companies should seek to achieve a balance between continuity of a current strategy and responsiveness to difficulties and changes in the external environment.
- Strategies to avoid are numbers 6, 7 and 8 on the strategy clock, which offer standard value for high price, low value for a higher price, and low value for a standard price respectively. Other competitive tactics which are likely to

result in failure and should be avoided are 'follow the leader'; 'same as the past'; 'competitive race'; 'follow all competitive strategies'; and 'spend too much'.

→ **Learning outcome 3**
Understand and summarise the relationship between competitive strategy, marketing strategy and competitive advantage.

■ The development of competitive and marketing strategy is underpinned by the concept of competitive advantage. Coyne identifies three distinct conditions for competitive advantage to exist. First, customers must see a distinct difference between a company's product and those offered by competitors. Second there must be a capability gap between an organisation and its competitors. Finally, the competitive advantage must be sustainable, that is the distinct difference and capability must be long lasting.

■ Kotler suggests competitive advantage can be achieved via four different areas, individually or in combination. The four areas are product, service, personnel and image.

→ **Learning outcome 4**
Explain Press's management philosophies and their link with competitive strategy.

■ Press's framework for assessing competitors' management philosophies has two dimensions: those of management goals and measurement criteria. These two dimensions give rise to four management philosophies: the manager as producer, organiser, investor and seller.

■ Press defines the entrepreneurial paradigm as a combination of the producer and investor philosophies, with the view being that managers seek to improve the motivations of workers as a way of maximising shareholders' or investors' wealth. The second paradigm is a combination of the organiser and seller philosophies and is called the corporate paradigm. The corporate paradigm can be viewed as low cost production and differentiation.

→ **Learning outcome 5**
Determine marketing objectives and strategies for companies.

■ Marketing strategy and competitive strategy together allow organisations to develop approaches for operating in the external environment.

■ Marketing objectives include market enlargement, market development, product development and entering new markets with new products. Market enlargement is expansion of a company's existing markets. Market development is the creation or exploitation of new markets or market segments. Product development is the creation of brand new products and updating of existing products. Entering new markets with new products is diversification, which can be related or unrelated.

→ **Learning outcome 6**

Understand the different types of market segmentation variables, targeting and positioning strategies and where they may be appropriately applied.

■ Market segmentation is the dividing up of a large and diverse market into small groups or sub-markets, which consist of customers with the same or similar requirements from a product or service. Segmentation variables include customer characteristics such as demographics, lifestyle, socio-economic traits and geographic location, and behavioural characteristics such as customer loyalty, purchase occasion, benefit segmentation and product usage.

■ There are four market-targeting strategies which can be used once market segments have been selected and evaluated. The targeting strategies are undifferentiated marketing, differentiated marketing, focussed marketing and customised marketing.

■ Position is defines as how customers perceive a product in comparison to products offered by a competitor and the marketing mix can be adjusted to make the product more appealing than the competitor's offering.

This exit case study looks at Nike and its expansion in the football business and can be used to assess the learning outcomes below.

Learning outcomes	Check you have achieved this by	
1 Developing competitive strategy.	Explaining and choosing which competitive strategies a company could follow.	Answering Exit case study question 1.
2 Developing marketing strategy.	Applying the concepts associated with marketing to a company.	Answering Exit case study questions 2, 3, 4 & 5.

Nike overtakes Adidas in football field   **FT**

by Matthew Garrahan

Nike has overtaken Adidas as Europe's leading football brand for the first time in the history of the US group, according to new research. NPD, a market research company, said Nike commanded 34 per cent of the market in football-related footwear for the 12 months to March. Adidas, which has long dominated European football sales, had 30.2 per cent, NPD said.

Euan McLaughlin, head of Nike's European business, said the group had only been taking football seriously for the past 10 years. The 1994 World Cup, staged in the US, was the spark. Back then, Nike was only the seventh most popular brand. But in the past decade, the company has strived to generate more revenues from football, signing endorsement deals with some of the most glamorous teams: Brazil, the World Cup holders, and Manchester United, one of the leading English sides.

The sports group has also agreed sponsorship deals with star players, such as Ronaldo of Brazil, Luis Figo of Portugal and England's Wayne Rooney. Sales from football-related products accelerated from 1994 to the World Cup in 2002. But the group's growth since the tournament in Japan and South Korea has been significant, with Nike doubling its football business in the two years to $1bn of sales.

Nike now makes more money from its international business than from its core US market. Its football division is a key driver of its non-US success. 'Basketball is growing for us hugely in the US, and our women's business is also up,' Mr McLaughlin said. 'But football is still the fastest-growing part of the business.'

He added that football was key to the future growth of the group's European business. 'The US is 260m people, the new Europe as you look at it today is over 600m–700m people. So in terms of market power and spend, Europe is now a bigger market opportunity than the US,' said Mr McLaughlin.

Nike is also involved in the Olympics, where it has sponsored athletes chasing medals, such as Paula Radcliffe in the marathon.

Source: *Financial Times*, 19 August 2004.

Exit case study questions

1 Determine which competitive strategies Nike could employ in the football business.

2 Specify possible marketing objectives for Nike.

3 Explain which segmentation variables Nike may use.

4 Identify which market coverage strategies Nike could employ.

5 Discuss how Nike might use the concept of the marketing mix in selling its products.

DISCUSSION TOPIC

1 Read the paper 'A guide to strategic positioning' by Henry Mintzberg, Chapter 4, in *The Strategy Process*, Mintzberg, Lampel, Quinn and Ghosal, Harlow: Prentice Hall, 2003.

2 Consider the following quote from the end of the paper.

'The truly creative strategist, however, shuns all of these categories, or at least recombines them in an innovative ways to develop a novel strategy, for which there is no diagram, since no one can tell what it might look like!'

3 Recombine the strategies discussed in Mintzberg's paper to develop a strategy for an organisation with, which are familiar.

WIDEN YOUR HORIZONS

1 Widen your horizons by researching and summarising the marketing strategy of Avon Cosmetics, whose global annual turnover was $6.8 billion in 2003. Accessing and reading the article 'A ding dong battle to keep ahead of the pack' by Jerry McDonald, *Daily Telegraph*, 2 December 2004, will help.

2 Widen your horizons by identifying and discussing the marketing and competitive strategies which have lead to the current decline of the French wine industry. Accessing and reading the article 'Why the finest vineyards in France are tipping away 266 million bottles' by Charles Bremner, *The Times*, 27 January 2005, will help.

WEBLINKS

The websites for this chapter provides some short articles on marketing and competitive strategy.

- This website contains a series of short articles on marketing strategy.
  www.knowthis.com/internet/strategy.htm
- This website contains an article on developing marketing strategy.
  www.businessplans.org/Market.html
- This website contains a series of short articles on competitive strategy.
  www.refresher.com/archives2.html

FURTHER READING

Competitive strategy

- Capon, C (2004) *Understanding Organisational Context*, 2nd edn, Harlow: Financial Times/Prentice Hall. Chapter 10, 'The competitive environment'.
- Dess, G G, Lumpkin, G T, and Taylor, M L (2005) *Strategic Management*, 2nd edn, New York: McGraw Hill Irwin. Chapter 5 'Business level strategy'.
- Johnson, G, Scholes, K and Whittington, R (2005) *Exploring Corporate Strategy*, Harlow: Financial Times/Prentice Hall, Chapter 5, 'Business-Level Strategy', pp 235-79.
- Lynch, R (2006) *Corporate Strategy*, 4th edn, Harlow: Financial Times/Prentice Hall. Chapter 4, 'Analysing markets, competition and co-operation'.
- White, C (2004) *Strategic Management*, Oxford: Oxford University Press. Chapter 8, 'Creating and maintaining competitive advantage', pp 266-301.

Competing using the Internet

- Hoffman, D L and Novak, T P (2000) 'How to acquire customers on the web', *Harvard Business Review*, May/June.
- Kenny, D and Marshall, J F (2000) 'Contextual marketing: the real business of the internet', *Harvard Business Review*, November/December.

How low-cost airlines competed in the wake of 9/11

- Saunders, A (2002) 'The new skymasters', *Management Today*, September.

Ethics of competing

- Jones I W and Pollitt M G (1998) 'Ethical and unethical competition: establishing the rules of engagement', *Long Range Planning*, 31, 5, October 1998.

REFERENCES

1 Kotler, P, Armstrong, G, Saunders, J and Wong, V (1996) *Principles of Marketing*, European Edition, Harlow: Prentice Hall.
2 Gilbert, Xavier and Strebel, Paul (1988) 'Developing competitive advantage', in *The Strategy Process*, eds Quinn, J B, Mintzberg H and James, R M. (1988) Boston: Prentice Hall.
3 Ibid.
4 Faulkner, D and Bowman, C (1995) *The Essence of Competitive Strategy*, Hemel Hempstead: Prentice Hall.
5 Johnson, G, Scholes, K and Whittington, R (2005) *Exploring Corporate Strategy*, Harlow: Financial Times/Prentice Hall.

6   Coyne, K P (1988) 'Sustainable competitive advantage – what it is, what it isn't', *Business Horizons*, January–February.

7   Kotler et al., op. cit.

8   Coyne, op. cit.

9   Kotler et al., op. cit.

10 Ibid.

11 Ibid.

12 Press, G (1990) 'Assessing competitors' business philosophies', *Long Range Planning*, 23, 5.

13 Ibid.

14 Ibid.

15 Ibid.

16 Jobber, D (2004) *Principles and Practice of Marketing*, 4th edn, London: McGraw Hill.

17 Thorniley, T (2003) 'B&Q opens Beijing store as Chinese embrace "BIY"', *Daily Telegraph*, 20 October.

18 Jobber, op. cit.

CHAPTER 8

Growth for success

Exhibit 8.1 Essential strategy model

The circle diagram contains:

1 What is strategy? (Ch1)
2 Environmental analysis (Ch 2)
3 Resource analysis (Chs 3 & 4)
4 Stakeholders, culture and change (Ch 5)
5 Management and leadership (Ch 6)
6 Strategy development (Chs 7, 8 & 9)
7 Structure culture and groups (Ch 10)
8 Strategic control (Ch 11)
9 Managing failure and turnaround (Ch 12)

Chapter objectives

The strategic decisions companies make often involve deciding how to grow and develop the business using the resources and opportunities available. To ensure best use is made of resources and opportunities, an understanding of the different ways a company can grow is needed. Companies can spend their money on undertaking internal growth or put money into developing via external growth, which can include licensing, franchising, alliances and acquisitions. Each method of growth has its own advantages and disadvantages, and it is an understanding of these which will enable managers to make effective strategic choices when developing strategy.

When you have read this chapter and worked through the associated activities you should be able to achieve the objectives specified below.

1 Discuss the benefits and potential disadvantages of organic growth.

2 Explain exporting and licensing as methods of international expansion.

3 Explain franchising, its advantages and disadvantages.

4 Discuss the advantages and potential disadvantages of each type of strategic alliance and how the suitability of strategic alliance partners should be assessed.

5 Discuss acquisitions as a method of growth.

6 Identify actions which a company can take to resist a hostile takeover bid.

The entry case study looks at Proctor & Gamble's acquisition of Gillette. It illustrates the market access and benefits the newly merged company will have in competing with Proctor & Gamble's main rival, the Anglo-Dutch consumer group, Unilever.

Procter & Gamble strengthens its clout with retailers

FT

by Jeremy Grant and James Politi

Procter & Gamble's decision to buy Gillette for $57bn could unleash fresh consolidation in the consumer products industry. The planned merger signals the sector's desire to boost growth through global scale and higher margins, and by winning back pricing power from big retailers. Industry margins have been forced down by rising raw material costs and increasingly powerful retailers such as Walmart, Carrefour and Tesco.

Jim Kilts, the chief executive of Gillette who initiated the merger talks, said: 'The consumer products industry needs to consolidate and I would rather lead that consolidation than get stuck with the leftovers at the end.' Mr Kilts is to stay on for a year to oversee the integration. The combined company would become the largest in the industry, overtaking Anglo-Dutch rival Unilever by market capitalisation and revenue. It would have about $60bn in revenues and 21 brands with revenues of $1bn or more, from Pampers diapers to Mach 3 razors and Duracell batteries. Gary Stibel, chief executive of the New England Group consultancy, said: 'It leaves many [rival] companies

up against the wall. They must now figure out ways to become one of the two or three major global players.'

A. G. Lafley, who has engineered a four-year turnround at P&G and will remain chief executive, said both groups could grow together 'at levels that neither could sustain on its own'. The new company would raise operating margins from P&G's current 19–20 per cent to 24–25 per cent by the end of the decade, he said. The deal, if completed, would mean that half of P&G's portfolio will be made up of healthcare, personal care and beauty products, all high-growth sectors. Mr Lafley said the women's hair care sector alone was worth $10bn in annual sales, and was growing at 8 per cent.

Consumer products markets in emerging economies in China and Russia would grow at 5–6 per cent for the next few years. 'If you project a growth rate to the end of the decade this company will be about $75bn in size. We need another $750m [in sales] a year. We believe at least half of that will come from developing markets by simply plugging in Gillette and playing with broader distribution,' he said.

The companies expect to save $14bn–$16bn of costs over three years by co-ordinating purchasing and logistics and cutting 6,000 jobs, 4 per cent of combined headcount.

The deal, the largest US transaction since JPMorgan bought Bank One for $58.6bn last January, sent Gillette's shares up 12.9 per cent to close at $51.60 in New York.

Gillette	Procter & Gamble
Duracell	Old Spice
SensorExcel	Head & Shoulders
Oral-B	Always
Complete Skincare	Crest
Braun	Max Factor
Right Guard	Pringles

P&G shares closed down 2.1 per cent at $54.15, a relatively positive reception for such a large deal. Shares in Colgate-Palmolive, the personal care group, slipped 2 per cent to $51.66. The bid was blessed as 'a dream deal' by Warren Buffett, chief executive of Berkshire Hathaway, Gillette's largest shareholder, who pledged to increase Berkshire's holding in the merged group.

Source: *Financial Times*, 28 January 2005.

INTRODUCTION

In seeking to achieve their mission and objectives organisations may choose to grow and expand (see Exhibit 8.2). Growth takes a variety of forms, including increasing market share and expanding the range of products or services offered to the customers. Businesses may achieve expansion by undertaking the development themselves, this is known as **organic growth** and the UK clothes retailer Next has grown by spending £100 million on the expansion of outlets in the UK in 2002. This organic growth saw pre-tax profits for Next rise to £353 million in 2003; additionally, the final dividend payment rose by 13 per cent to 35 pence per share.[1] Alternative methods of growth include **exporting**, licensing, franchising, **strategic alliances** and acquisition. Acquisition is the purchase of another company and the aim of the buying company is often to expand their product and market portfolio. In contrast a strategic alliance is growth via collaboration with one or more external partners (see Business illustration on Tesco and the BBC). Finally expansion by franchise is when the right to operate a business is bought from a franchiser. Growth by franchise outlet is common among fast food chains, including McDonalds, Burger King and KFC. These are all ways in which organisations may expand and grow to become more effective competitors in the marketplace.

Acquisition is when one company buys another or a significant shareholding in another company.

Business illustration of acquisitions and alliances – Tesco and the BBC

■ The UK food retailer Tesco has grown considerably in recent years by acquisition in the UK and abroad. Tesco's acquisitions have provided geographic expansion abroad and growth in the UK. The acquisitions have included HIT of Poland for £383 million in July 2002; T&S stores in the UK for £530 million in January 2003; the C2 Network in Japan during July 2003; and Kipa of Turkey in November 2003.

■ In April 2004 BBC Worldwide entered into a strategic alliance with Bennett and Coleman, India's biggest publishing group, to publish mass market magazines, including a *Radio Times* style listing magazine as 82 million households in India own television sets.

Source: 'Tesco seeks cash to expand local stores', S Butler, *Times*, 14 January 2004 and 'BBC in joint venture with Indian media group', K Merchant, *Financial Times*, 8 April 2004.

Exhibit 8.2 Growth for organisations

■ Organic growth	■ Franchises
■ Exporting	■ Alliances
■ Licensing	■ Acquisitions

ORGANIC GROWTH

Organic growth involves a company using its resources to establish new operations.

Organic or internal growth involves an organisation using its own resources and competencies to expand the business. The expansion, depending on the business, may include opening new retail outlets, new call centres, new distribution systems and new manufacturing facilities. In January 2005 it was estimated that 8,000 new manufacturing jobs were created in the UK as a result of the new Airbus A380 being launched. The start of production of the A380 resulted in several hundred UK suppliers gaining contracts and expanding via organic growth.[2]

A key benefit of internal growth is the lower risk of such a strategy compared to external growth. The reduced risk arises from the adoption of an incremental approach to development, which allows ongoing learning to be achieved by the organisation, its managers and employees. This in turn means a strategy of internal growth allows the organisation to develop via: its strongest skills and capabilities; specialised products; being close to the customer; and building a reputation based on some or all of these. This is how Rolls-Royce expand, resulting in January 2005 in the company gaining around half of the market for the new Airbus A380 engines, which sell for up to £30 million for a set of four engines.[3] This internal approach to development allows the managers and decision makers to have greater control over the direction and speed of growth of the company and the associated rate of expenditure, meaning cash flow is more likely to be uniform. This is in contrast to acquisition where things occur more rapidly and the full price for the acquired company has to be paid when the acquisition occurs. Additionally a strategy of internal growth means mismatches of organisational cultures are less likely to occur than with an acquisition or alliance.

The potential disadvantages of organic growth centre on slow organisational expansion, and a lack of expertise and knowledge leading to misjudgement and costly mistakes. Slower organisational growth becomes a critical disadvantage if the industry and/or markets in which the company operates are growing or declining rapidly, as flexibility and quick responses are required to adapt to a fast-changing external environment. This was clearly not the case with Rolls-Royce supplying aeroplane engines for the Airbus A380; hence a strategy of organic growth was appropriate for Rolls-Royce.

EXPORTING

Exporting is selling goods to overseas customers from a domestic base.

Exporting is selling goods to overseas customers from a domestic base. Exporting is often used by manufacturing companies to start their international expansion before switching to one of the other methods of growth such as licensing, franchising, alliances or acquisition. A key advantage of exporting is the avoidance of the substantial cost of establishing manufacturing operations overseas. Additionally manufacturing in one or more centralised locations, initially the home country, and exporting goods to other countries may allow the company to achieve economies of scales in manufacturing which are only possible because of the substantially greater global sales achieved through exporting.

If manufacturing costs overseas are lower and improved economies of scale can be achieved by relocating production abroad, then exporting from a company's home country is not appropriate. However, the company may choose to export from its overseas production facility to other countries, including its home country. It should be noted that the cost of exporting can be significantly increased by transport costs if the goods are bulky; hence moving production to regional bases overseas, close to markets, can make sense as economies of scale in production are achieved and transport costs limited. Moving production overseas can mean that tariffs and the threat of tariffs, which can limit the returns from exporting, are avoided.[4] Other actions, which may increase the likelihood of success in an export market are outlined in Exhibit 8.3.

Exhibit 8.3 Increasing success in an export market

- Enter the export market on a small scale and add more product lines once initial exporting success has been achieved.
- Use local staff and agents to promote the company's products.
- Commit managerial resources and time to build strong and enduring relationships with local agents, distributors and customers.

The level of success in an export market can be further enhanced by using an export marketing company (EMC) or an experienced export consultant to help identify relevant market segments and assist in navigation through the regulations and paperwork involved. Success can also be improved by focusing on one or a few markets to learn the lessons of exporting and building the business up before moving on to more or different export markets. Entering many export markets at once, particularly if they are all very different, can result in resources and expertise being spread too thinly; hence the business doesn't establish itself well in any export market and the lessons of successful exporting are not learnt.[5]

Exporting can be viewed as a sensible method of foreign market entry, without making a significant capital investment. However, once the export market has been successfully established, companies may wish to consider local or regional production via organic growth, licensing, franchising, alliance or acquisition.

The pitfalls and disadvantages of exporting can be minimised by the use of an export management company (EMC),[6] a specialist export company which takes on the role of export marketing department for the client company. An EMC may be used in one of two ways, the first of which is to set up the exporting operations for the client company, with the agreement that they will take over their own export activities once established. The other approach is that the EMC has continuing responsibility for selling the company's products in the export market(s). The advantage of using a competent EMC is their relevant experience in the export market. The expertise of a good EMC will centre on good knowledge and experience of the local market, and the local importing, exporting and business regulations. The EMC should also have a good network of contacts and employ local multilingual staff. This should mean the EMC could assist the client company in identifying the right market segments and avoiding common pitfalls in the export market. However, any exporter should check the track record of any agent or EMC with whom business is to be undertaken and references should be thoroughly checked. A possible major downside of using an EMC is that a company fails to develop its own in-house exporting capabilities.

Finally, problems with exporting can arise if a company outsources its overseas marketing to a local agent, or even an EMC, who also carries competitors' products and hence has divided loyalties. A possible way to avoid this situation is to establish a wholly-owned subsidiary in the export country to handle local marketing. The establishing of a subsidiary will allow tight control over marketing in the export country while also reaping the economies of scale from having one or a minimal number of manufacturing locations.[7]

LICENSING

International licensing is an arrangement where a foreign licensee buys the rights to produce a company's products in the licensee's country.

International licensing is an arrangement where a foreign licensee buys the rights to produce a company's products in the licensee's country, with the licensee supplying the capital to set up the overseas marketing or manufacturing operation (see Business illustration on drugs and soft drinks). There is a negotiated fee payable to the licensor and usually a royalty based on the number of units manufactured and/or sold. This development process is often viewed as an attractive option for companies that lack the capital or are unwilling to commit capital to markets which are unstable and risky, or just difficult to enter. Additionally the licensing company does not have to bear the development costs and risks associated with opening up a new market.

> ### Business illustration of licensing – drugs and soft drinks
>
> In July 2004 the UK drug company Vernalis licensed the US company Endo Pharmaceuticals to sell its migraine treatment, Frova, in North America. The licensing deal will see Vernalis gain at least $400 million, including royalty payments of 20 per cent on Frova sales. The licensing process is also used by soft drink manufacturers and brewers, to allow their products to be manufactured in the country or region where they are sold.
>
> Source: 'Vernalis soars on US licensing deal', D Firn, *Financial Times*, 15 July 2004.

During September 2004 the Indian pharmaceutical company Glenmark[8] signed a licensing deal with the American company Forest Laboratories for $190 million over five years. In contrast with the Vernalis deal (see Business illustration on drugs and soft drinks) this was a product rather than a market development agreement, which will allow Forest to develop Glenmark's new asthma drug through clinical trials and hopefully to the marketplace. Glenmark chose to license the future development of the new asthma drug as the risk profile increases as a new drug goes through clinical trials, and hence a larger partner with greater capabilities was needed to share both the risks and costs involved.

The disadvantages of licensing are the licensor does not have close and tight control over manufacturing and marketing in the foreign countries and hence there is a risk associated with licensing technological know-how to foreign companies. For many multinational companies technological know-how forms the basis of their competitive advantage and they want to maintain control over the use to which it is put; by licensing its technology, a company can quickly lose control over it. However, this risk can be reduced by the companies involved agreeing to enter into a cross licensing agreement, that is each company licenses some valuable process, technology or know-how to the other. In such cases negotiated payments and royalties are still payable. The likelihood of one company using the knowledge obtained to compete directly with the licensor is reduced. Also, if the overseas licensing arrangements are not successful and profitable, then the licensing company may find it difficult to gain its negotiated royalty payments.

FRANCHISES

A franchise is a contractual agreement where the franchiser provides the franchisee with the right to sell the franchiser's products or services.

A **franchise** is a contractual agreement between a franchiser and franchisee. The franchiser provides a number of small businesses or franchisees, with the right to sell the franchiser's products or services. In selling the franchise, the franchiser accepts an initial signing on payment and royalties, usually based on turnover not profit, from the franchisee. In return for these payments the franchiser agrees to provide the franchisee with a variety of items to enable the franchise to operate (see Exhibit 8.4). The geographical area of a franchise may be several counties or a few streets in a city centre. The geographic area of a franchise for the distribution of greeting cards may cover a whole county, for example all of Hampshire. In contrast a franchise for a fast food outlet such as McDonald's may cover one part of a city centre, with another McDonald's outlet covering the rest of the same city centre. The up-front investment needed to buy a franchise typically starts from around £10,000 upwards. The cost of a franchise depends on the type of franchise and the items, equipment, advice, training and support provided by the franchiser.

Exhibit 8.4 Items provided to operate a franchise

- Advice and know-how.
- Equipment.
- Training.
- National support advertising.
- Exclusive rights to supply in a designated geographic area.

Exhibit 8.5 Companies which have grown by franchise

■ McDonald	■ Tie Rack
■ Thorntons	■ Fast Frame
■ Body Shop	■ Pronta Print
■ Texaco	■ Costa Coffee

Franchising is just one method of growth which many well-known companies have used (see Exhibit 8.5 and Business illustration on Easy Group). Companies are careful with their cash and find the idea of expanding their brand without spending capital appealing. Hence in 2004 Whitbread were franchising Costa Coffee outlets, Texaco was transferring 100 petrol stations to franchisees, and Boots was seeking to franchise its optician shops.[9] High street names provide the franchisee or outlet operator with an established name, its perceived continuity and stability along with the necessary resources and support to make the franchise work. However, other less well-known companies have also grown by franchising and these include Post26, which manufactures carved wooden posts that, for example, can be used as gate posts, and the Global Travel Group, which offers franchises as independent travel agents.

The obvious advantages of franchising are, first, the franchiser does not have to put up the capital and bear the risks of entering a new geographic market. This can make franchising an attractive option when entering an overseas market. Second, franchising allows the company to expand at low cost.

The disadvantages of franchising include the franchiser's potential inability to maintain strategic co-ordination across several regions or countries and quality control. A company which has grown by franchising, for example McDonald's, Thorntons, Boots Opticians, is conveying via the brand name the

Business illustration of growth by franchising –
Easy Group

In 2004, the Easy Group having established its brand name was seeking to grow by franchising and the view of Stelios Haji-Ionnou of the Easy Group was 'You can only franchise something that you have done yourself, when you have learnt from your mistakes'. To illustrate this point Stelios was developing the first Easy Hotel in London, with only 9 cubic metres of space per room, and was asking the question 'Are windows essential? On cruise ships there are many cabins without windows.'

Source: 'Bewildering choice awaits would be franchisees', M Becket, *Daily Telegraph*, 29 March 2004.

message to customers that the products, services and their quality are of a particular standard and this is expected by the customers. Hence a significant disadvantage of franchising is the potential lack of quality control. This issue is key in franchising as the customer whose expectations are not met in one franchised outlet will be likely to behave as a dissatisfied stakeholder and as such may shop elsewhere for the same goods. If this type of customer experience is repeated in many franchised outlets in a country or region then lost sales and a decline in overall worldwide reputation is possible. In global companies which have grown by franchise, such as McDonald's, KFC and Hilton International, the geographic distance separating the franchiser from overseas franchisees and the large number of franchised outlets makes both monitoring quality and detecting poor quality difficult.[10]

Companies which have grown a global empire by franchising can tackle the disadvantages by seeking to avoid them in the first instance. This can be done by establishing a subsidiary in each country or region of franchised growth. The subsidiary might be wholly-owned by the company or have been set up via a joint venture with an operator experienced in the overseas area of expansion. This should make strategic co-ordination easier and allow quality to be maintained. The subsidiary takes on the role of setting up the franchises in the overseas area of expansion. This reduces the number of franchises any company or subsidiary has to set up or monitor and hence should minimise any quality control problems. Additionally the parent company will own or partly own the subsidiary and will therefore be able to place its own managers in the subsidiary to help ensure quality standards are upheld.[11]

✔ Check your understanding

- Do you understand why consistency is critical to successful growth by franchising?
- Check your understanding by explaining how companies which have grown by franchising such as Thorntons, Costa Coffee and Texaco maintain consistency across a large number of outlets.

Organic growth, licensing and franchises

1 Define organic growth.

2 How risky is organic growth compared to external growth?

3 Why is exporting a good way for a company to start international operations?

4 How can a company increase the likelihood of its exporting succeeding?

5 Summarise the advantages and possible disadvantages of using an EMC.

6 Explain licensing.

7 Define a franchise.

8 Discuss the advantages and disadvantages of franchising.

STRATEGIC ALLIANCES

A **strategic alliance** occurs when two or more businesses agree a contract to operate a joint project.

A strategic alliance occurs when two or more businesses agree a contract to operate a joint project. Organisational growth can be achieved via a strategic alliance. The motives for organisations choosing growth by strategic alliance are many and varied and include access to markets, competitive pressures, technology and resources. The joint venture between the airlines BA and Iberia, provided access to each other's geographic markets, hence avoiding the need to grow organically in already competitive markets, that is BA gained access to the Latin American routes and Iberia to BA's North American, Asian and African routes.[12]

Other justifications for strategic alliances relate to securing favourable access to supplies of raw materials and components, according to Lorange and Roos.[13] This view is supported by Hill[14] who describes strategic alliances as a possible method for organisations to facilitate entry into foreign markets. Additionally strategic alliances can allow companies to share fixed costs and the associated risks of product and technology development, while also providing a platform on which organisations can bring together complementary skills (see Business illustration on General Motors and Ford). Alliances can be

---

Business illustration of an alliance – General Motors and Ford

In April 2004, General Motor and Ford announced their strategic alliance, which was to share product and technology development via the development of a new six-speed automatic transmission system. General Motors and Ford agreed to invest S350 million and $370 million respectively in the new transmission system, which will be in production by 2006. This joint venture arose due to cost and competitive pressures in the global motor industry driving companies to pool resources in the areas of product and technology development.

Source: 'Car rivals invest $720m in gearbox joint venture', J Grant, *Financial Times*, 20 April 2004.

risky and, unless a firm is careful, it can give away more than it receives. Conflict within the alliance may arise from battles between the partners for control of the project, which can occur as the objectives of the partner firms change over the lifetime of the venture.

Strategic alliance types

Lorange and Roos[15] go on to to examine the types of alliances organisations undertake and define four different types of strategic alliance: ad hoc pool; consortium; project-based joint ventures; **full-blown joint ventures** (see Exhibit 8.6). These are based on the nature of the resource input into the alliance and retrieval of resources and profits from the alliance. In deciding the type of strategic alliance to pursue the parent companies of the alliance have to decide and agree on the level of resources to commit to the project. Decisions should also be made concerning if and when withdrawal of resources from the project is to occur. If the parents take a limited and prescriptive view of the alliance they are pursuing and commit limited resources in the areas of staff, technology and money, then the alliance is unlikely to have the means to counteract unforeseen strategic change. The opposite situation occurs when alliance parents commit a large range of resources, including the aforementioned resources, along with greater skills in terms of strategic capability and flexibility. This provides an alliance with an improved ability to adapt to a changing environment. Lorange and Roos also make the point that the type or form of a strategic alliance is dictated by the views of the parent companies on timescales, resource input and retrieval. This obviously means that for the alliance to work the parents must hold the same or similar views on the alliance type, its resources and timescales. The likelihood of an alliance working is remote if one views it as an ad-hoc pool and the other as a full-blown joint venture.[16] This point is also made by Hill[17] who views strategic alliances as a range of agreements between companies, from formal joint ventures in which all partners have an equity or capital stake through to short-term contractual agreements. Hill also makes the point that partners in an alliance should have complementary capabilities and a shared vision, and that the best alliance partners are those with a reputation for 'fair play' and the worst those with a reputation for exploitation.

Lorange and Roos also consider the end of a strategic alliance and the future of the resources in the alliance. The future of alliance resources and their possible retrieval by the parent companies runs through a spectrum from everything to nothing. The initial option is the complete retrieval by the parents of all resources and output generated by the alliance. Therefore all profits, staff, and technical knowledge revert to the parent companies. The opposite end of the spectrum occurs where all outputs created via an alliance remains with the alliance itself and a separate organisation eventually results from the alliance. There are variations between these two extremes, as is illustrated by the different types of alliance discussed in the work of Lorange and Roos.[18]

Exhibit 8.6 Types of strategic alliances

		Parents' input of resources	
		Sufficient for short-term operations	Sufficient for long-term operations
Parents' retrieval of output	To parents	1 Ad hoc pool	2 Consortium
	Retain	3 Project-based joint venture	4 Full-blown joint venture

Source: Lorange and Roos (1993) *Strategic Alliances*, Oxford: Blackwell Publishers.

Ad hoc pool

An **ad-hoc pool alliance** occurs when parents contribute limited resources on a short-term basis and expect to reap the profits.

An **ad-hoc pool alliance** occurs when the parents contribute limited but complementary resources on a short-term basis, with resources returned and benefits accrued to the parent companies.

Consortia

A **consortium alliance** occurs when parent companies contribute resources on a long-term basis and expect to reap the profits.

The **consortium alliance** occurs when the parent companies contribute resources on a long-term basis and expect to see the profits and benefits created distributed back to the parent companies. In the UK consortia are often used in capital investment projects in the public and private sector, such as building a new office block, a shopping centre, a new bridge, a hospital or a school.

Project-based joint venture

In a **project based joint venture** parent companies contribute limited strategic resources to the alliance to create strategic value for all parents.

In **project based joint ventures** the parent companies contribute limited strategic resources to an alliance, which will create strategic value for all parents in the venture. The resources generated remain with the alliance except for payments such as dividends and royalties, which are distributed to the parent companies. There are many examples today of strategic alliances between Western companies and companies in China, with the Western company gaining access to the Chinese market and the Chinese company gaining access to Western business ideas. For example, in June 1999 the B&Q Decorative Warehouse Store opened in a Shanghai suburb to gain access to the Chinese market. The B&Q Decorative Warehouse Store was the result of a project based joint venture between B&Q, the largest DIY operator in Europe, and a local Shanghai business, Home-Dec Building Materials. B&Q have a 30 per cent holding and full operational control of the purpose built 735,000 sq. ft shop. This foray into China was well timed by B&Q as increasing home ownership, encouraged by the Chinese government, has led to the development of a growing decorating and home furnishings market.[19]

Full-blown joint venture

The **full-blown joint venture** occurs when parents contribute significant resources and allow the alliance to retain the profits.

The full-blown joint venture occurs when all parents submit significant resources and allow the alliance to retain the resources it generates. The full-blown joint venture is the long-term co-operation between the parents which results in the creation of a new freestanding business. For example, in February 2004 the new container shipping company Royal P&O Nedlloyd was created when P&O withdrew from its joint venture with the Dutch company Royal Nedlloyd, called P&O Nedlloyd. The financial transaction was complex but, in summary, P&O disposed of its 50 per cent stake in P&O Nedlloyd for 215 million euros and a 25 per cent stake in the new company, Royal P&O Nedlloyd.[20]

✔ Check your understanding

- Do you understand when growth by a strategic alliance is appropriate?
- Check your understanding by explaining why strategic alliances can be appropriate in mature industries, such as the airline industry in Europe and the car industry.
- You may find it useful to review the Business illustration on General Motors and Ford and the in-text discussion on BA and Iberia.

Selecting alliance partners

When deciding to grow via an alliance a company has to assess its own ability and that of any prospective partner very carefully if the alliance to succeed. Medcof[21] presents five criteria for selecting an alliance partner (see Exhibit 8.7). The first criteria assess the business rationale of the alliance and how good a **strategic fit** the prospective alliance partner is. If the rationale and strategic fit are sound, then it is appropriate to examine the other four criteria, called the Four Cs: **capability; compatibility; commitment; control**, which appertain to the operational functioning of the suggested alliance. Assessing the five criteria can be undertaken by considering the questions shown in Exhibit 8.7.

Exhibit 8.7 Assessing alliance partners

- Is the strategic fit with the alliance partner good?
- Is the prospective partner capable of carrying out its role in the alliance?
- Is the prospective partner compatible enough to work effectively in day-to-day collaboration?
- Is the prospective partner committed to the alliance and its strategic aims?
- Are the control mechanisms of the alliance appropriate?

Source: based on Medcof (1997) 'Why too many alliances end in divorce', *Long Range Planning*, 30, 5, October.

Strategic fit

Strategic fit occurs when an organisation's use of resources and strategy give rise to success in the external environment.

The key objectives of an alliance involve furthering the strategic objectives of the parents of the alliance. For this to occur potential alliance partners have to offer each other good strategic fit. The assessment of this strategic fit is based upon a shared understanding of the business rationale for the alliance, with alliance partners clearly understanding each other's strategic reasons for entering into the alliance. This requires that an extensive exchange of views and debate have occurred prior to the alliance, such that a shared understanding of the alliance and its strategic rationale is achieved. This involves an organisation understanding its own and its prospective partner's rationale for entering into the alliance (see Exhibit 8.8 and the Business illustration on STMicroelectronics).

Exhibit 8.8 Key factors to understand concerning alliance partners

- The importance of the alliance to the partners.
- The current competitive position of the partners in the industry in which the alliance will operate.
- The relevance of the alliance to the partners' current core business.

Business illustration of strategic fit via an alliance – STMicroelectronics

In 2004 the strategic alliance between STMicroelectronics, Europe's largest chip producer, and South Korea's Hynix Semiconductor was to allow both companies to share the cost of entering the Chinese market. The deal would allow both companies to enter the Chinese market via building a manufacturing plant in Wuxi, an industrial city in the Yangtze delta region around Shanghai. This was seen as a suitable location due to there being a growing cluster of chip manufacturers in the region. This strategic logic was also supported by an upturn in the world market for microchips and China was seen as an ideal location due to the country's demand for microchips rising by 37 per cent annually against a global increase of 23 per cent. This new alliance would also deepen an alliance forged between the two companies, in 2003, to develop Nand flash memory chips, which are used in digital cameras and MP3 players.

Source: 'STMicro in line for China joint venture with Hynix', A Ward and R Milne, *Financial Times*, 23 March 2004.

Capability

Capability is the ability to deliver required outputs.

The first of the four Cs assessing operational functioning is capability. The capability criteria asks the question: is the prospective partner capable of carrying out its role in the alliance? An organisation should ask this question of a potential alliance partner and itself. Assessing capability should involve examining the common issues for all alliances, including: the management team and its contribution to the alliance; ability of each partner to deliver promised outputs on time; ability of each partner to understand the benefits and costs of contributing to the alliance. Each alliance will have further specific issues, which will need to be examined.

Compatibility

Compatibility is the ability to collaborate effectively.

The next of the four Cs is compatibility and examines if the prospective alliance partners are operationally compatible: can the partners collaborate effectively on a day-to-day basis? In addition, for an alliance to succeed, the partners have to be capable of fulfilling their own role in an alliance. In any relationship which is to succeed, the partners have to be compatible with each other, therefore self-examination is important. Consequently positive vibes between the organisations and staff involved are critical, particularly between those at the top who initiated the alliance and are expected to keep it on course. The positive relationship between people at the top of the partner organisations has to be duplicated further down the organisations at the operational level of the alliance if it is to succeed. Organisational culture plays a crucial role in determining and influencing the behaviour, beliefs and values of those involved at all levels of the alliance. Expected and unintentional differences in behaviour, beliefs and values have to be anticipated and managed, otherwise they will damage the alliance and its chances of success.

Commitment

Commitment is the ability to contribute resources or effort.

The third of the four Cs is commitment and there are two issues to consider here. The first is the commitment of resources and effort by each partner to the alliance on a continuing basis. The second is the commitment or staying power of a partner to the alliance. How likely is a partner to leave the alliance when unexpected difficulties arise? Partners who commit only minimally to the alliance may expect the other partner to do more than their fair share of the work. Alternatively if a partner who has committed minimally leaves an alliance, the remaining partner is left without the commitment which will enable them to gain the expected strategic benefits of the alliance or will leave them with unexpected liabilities. Hence organisations need to evaluate their own commitment as well as that of prospective alliance partners. This kind of evaluation should disclose whether the partners are genuinely able and willing to commit the required resources, time and effort. If the required commitment cannot be made the alliance should be discontinued, for the benefit of both alliance partners.

Control

Control is the ability to hold on to and co-ordinate resources and staff.

The last of the four Cs is control and considers if the control and co-ordination arrangements of the alliance are pertinent and strengthen its effectiveness. In some alliances where strong, focused leadership occurs and interests of all members are very similar to those of the leading partner, dominance by that partner is likely to be opportunistic and agreeable. Alternatively dominance by the leading partner may be undesirable. The crucial question is, will the systems of control implemented 'allow one's own firm to achieve its strategic objectives in the alliance'?

In deciding if a strategic alliance is the 'right' method of growth for itself, a company should evaluate the potential advantages and disadvantages of the proposed collaboration. The work by Medcof, which is discussed in this section, can provide a useful framework for assessing a possible strategic alliance.

Alliance contracts

Finally, should organisations enter into an alliance, the contract between the partners will cover much specific detail governing the proposed alliance and how it will operate. The main areas of the contract are shown in Exhibit 8.9.

Exhibit 8.9 Key areas of an alliance contract

- Rules and restrictions on transferring knowledge and competencies between the parties.
- Ownership of intellectual property rights arising from the alliance.
- Accounting arrangements.
- Dispute settlement.
- Exit arrangements.

The contract should cover both the use of intellectual property contributed to the alliance by the partners, and how any intellectual property developed in the alliance is used and its ownership is to be allocated. Disputes between alliance partners can be settled via external arbitration or involvement of very senior managers from the parent companies. The exit arrangements should specify if the remaining alliance partners get first refusal should an alliance partner wish to withdraw from the alliance. Some alliance contracts seek to minimise the likelihood of partners leaving the alliance by requiring resources to be contributed for a minimum period of time. The accounting and financial standards need to be agreed and to cover decisions including the currency to be used, the professional accounting standards to apply, and the frequency of accounts, review and audit arrangements.

Strategic alliances

1 Define an alliance.

2 Why do companies chose to grow by pursuing an alliance?

3 Identify the defining characteristics of an alliance.

4 What is the key difference between a short-term alliance and a long-term alliance?

5 Define consortia.

6 How are prospective alliance partners assessed?

7 What should be considered in assessing the compatibility of potential alliance partners?

8 Explain the two aspects of commitment which are key in assessing the suitability of a prospective alliance partner.

9 Summarise the main areas any alliance contract should cover.

ACQUISITIONS

Acquisition is when one company buys another or a shareholding in another company. Acquisition is widely used to achieve organisational growth more rapidly and/or at lower cost than that achievable via internal growth, which can be difficult if markets are mature. Examples of growth by acquisition include the easyJet takeover of its competitor Go in 2002 and in December 2004 Lenovo China's largest computer manufacturer purchased a controlling stake in IBM's personal computer business for $175 billion.[22]

Companies undertake acquisition with the aim of gaining improved access to markets and reducing the number of competitors. This enables a current competitive position in a growing market to be maintained, or expansion in a mature market, and can make it more difficult for competitors to achieve the same aim. Acquisition is often the preferred strategy for companies seeking to expand internationally, as it can be implemented fairly swiftly. Increasing market share internationally via acquisition can be crucial if home markets are mature, growth rates are low or non-existent, and hence, internal growth is not feasible and merger or alliance partners are difficult to find. It is for these reasons that many Western brewing companies have sought to expand in the Far East and in January 2005 the Dutch brewer Heineken was seeking to expand its 21 per cent stake in the Chinese brewer Kingway to a controlling stake.[23]

Acquisition can provide rapid access to both the home and international marketplace. Another attraction of growth via acquisition is the possible access to a strong and established brand name, which would take years to establish via organic growth. This is one of the reasons for Lenovo undertaking the IBM acquisition, as it would take many years for Lenovo to convince consumers outside China that it was a reliable computer manufacturer and establish a brand name like IBM, which competes with Dell and Hewlett Packard.

Alternatively a company may target, by acquisition, specific businesses already trading in markets it wishes to enter and/or businesses possessing certain specialist employees and equipment which could be a useful vehicle for future commercial development. As a result of acquisition organisations aim to improve competitive position, diminish the power of a competitor or remove a competitor from the market. Overall the company resulting from related acquisition will aim to have a bigger market share, a more secure market position, better defences against competitors, and a greater likelihood of achieving market leadership or dominance. A potential benefit of undertaking growth via acquisition is that the likelihood of retaliation from other competitors is reduced as the acquisition only changes the ownership of a company and not the capacity of the marketplace. In contrast successful internal growth would attract customers from all competitors in the marketplace and hence would be more likely to produce a competitive reaction from all players in the market. It was primarily for reasons of improving market share outside its home US market and access to a strong brand name that Walmart acquired the British supermarket chain Asda in July 1999. In addition an acquisition may bring into the company's portfolio, products which are currently question marks and stars and potentially profitable in the future. If cash cows are procured via acquisition, they may be used to fund research and development, innovation or new product development.

Equally an acquisition may provide improved access to knowledge, technology, skills and competencies. Acquisition is also a source of different and sometimes better relationships and work practices. These can take the form of economies of scale made possible via more extensive operations, expert use of resources, and better management and control of raw materials and suppliers. Additionally an acquisition can allow a company to pre-empt their competitors and achieve a better market position, which can be a significant benefit in an increasingly international marketplace. This occurred in 2004 when Anheuser-Busch, the world's market leader in the brewing industry, outbid number two in the marketplace, SABMiller, and paid $718 million for Harbin, the largest brewer in north east China.[24]

CHOOSING GROWTH BY ACQUISITION

The decision to grow by acquisition needs to be supported by careful tracking and analysis of possible acquisition targets. Hence the strategic leaders in the acquiring company have responsibility for assessing possible acquisitions and their compatibility with the company's growth strategy. The issues to be considered include: whether the acquisition is to be integrated or managed as a standalone subsidiary; the bidder's decision on how much can afford to be spent on the acquisition; and identifying the potential benefits of the acquisition. The benefits of a particular acquisition have to be clearly established and high-lighted to all stakeholders, including staff and shareholders in both businesses.

There are two possible views regarding acquisition as a method of growth for organisations. The first view is that acquisition is risky and if the difficulties associated with acquisition are to be minimised then the acquiring company needs to initially tolerate the resources and attributes of the acquired organisation. The attributes include location of premises, their physical layout and conditions, and contracts with buyers and suppliers. This contrasts with organic growth where the most convenient location can be selected and purpose-built premises constructed if required. The problems of acquisition often occur because of differences between the two organisations – the bidder and the acquired – therefore the success of an acquisition depends on the careful management of these differences.

The second or opposing view is that acquisitions are less risky than organic growth. A company making an acquisition purchases a business and its resources, which are delivering a known turnover and profit. This contrasts with organic growth in which the turnover and profits of an unestablished venture are perhaps more uncertain. Additionally an acquisition in an overseas market will not only provide the business and its tangible resources, but also the all-important valuable intangible resources which include local branding and the knowledge local managers have of the marketplace. Such local knowledge could significantly reduce the likelihood of errors resulting from a lack of understanding of the needs, wants and buyer behaviour of local customers.

In January 2005 the takeover of Gillette by Proctor & Gamble for $57 billion was announced. Proctor & Gamble own brands such as Head and Shoulders, Crest, and Max Factor; and Gillette owned brands such as Duracell, SensorExcel, and Braun. The takeover was done with the very specific aims of boosting global growth in the healthcare, personal care and beauty sectors, and increasing profit margins by gaining improved prices from retailers, such as Wal-mart, Carrefour and Tesco (see Entry case study 8.1). It was also estimated that growth in China and Russia would run at 5–6 per cent per annum, giving the company over half of its desired international growth in a relatively straightforward way (see Entry case study 8.1).

In selecting an acquisition target, the predator company has to appraise the long-term prospects of the target company. A company experiencing short-run financial problems will pay poor dividends and in consequence the market price of its shares will fall. Nevertheless the business may be fundamentally sound and represent a lucrative takeover opportunity, with its share price rising as its short-run difficulties are resolved. The response of the target's management team, and whether or not they recommend the takeover bid to shareholders, will also influence the challenge the takeover presents to the bidding company. Equally the number of shareholders in the target company needing to be convinced of the benefits of the takeover is also part of the challenge facing the bidding company. Hence a business with a small number of dominant shareholders, anxious to sell their large shareholdings will be easier to take over than a company with powerful shareholders who don't want to sell their shares.

However, a successful bid and completion of the acquisition is not the end of the process. In most acquisitions there will be initial work to be done to ensure the integration of the acquired business and its staff. Alternatively the decision may have been taken to keep the acquisition as a separate subsidiary if integration is not regarded as suitable. However, the decision to integrate the acquisition or keep as a separate subsidiary requires the collection, analysis and interpretation of large amounts of data and information, and should have been undertaken as part of the process to take the initial decision to undertake the acquisition. If the acquisition is to be integrated into the bidding company, the culture, structure, work processes and activities have to be assessed as compatible with those of the bidder. If they were not compatible the rational decision would be to manage the acquisition as an autonomous subsidiary.

The issue of staffing in the target business has to be considered. Difficulties will arise if key employees in the target business feel unable to work for the new parent company and resign following the acquisition. Equally the opposite problem may arise with managers in the target firm not possessing the skills and abilities required by the new parent company. Hence redundancies and the associated costs have to be taken into account when planning for managing new acquisitions.

Problems with acquisition may also arise from the external environment, with market conditions suddenly changing shortly after an expensive acquisition has been made. This may result in new competitors emerging or, in the case of BMW-Rover, over-capacity in the world car market made it difficult for BMW to become a successful volume producer via its Rover acquisition.

✔ Check your understanding

- Do you understand the reasons why organisations grow by acquisition?
- Check your understanding by reviewing Entry case study 8.1 and summarise:
  1 the reasons for growth by acquisition;
  2 the advantages and disadvantages of growth by acquisition for Proctor & Gamble.

Resisting acquisition

Strategies for avoiding a hostile acquisition or takeover bid inevitably revolve around making the company unattractive to prospective bidders. If the company is successful, profitable, pays good dividends and has the support of principal shareholders then the strategy, while not necessarily easy, is clear. Continue to maintain the same degree of success relative to competitors and the industry in which the company operates. This makes the company expensive for any likely bidder. However, if a company is struggling to achieve success and meet the needs of key stakeholders, it is more difficult to avoid a takeover bid and different tactics have to be employed, with no guarantee that a takeover will be avoided. Tactics which companies have used to resist an acquisition are outlined in Exhibit 8.10. The impact of all these tactics is potentially positive in the short term for the target company. However, in the longer term the impact of these tactics is overwhelmingly negative, with either the target company or the successful bidder having to live with and manage the consequences of such tactics. The consequences include being tied into unattractive contracts, high gearing and a lack of required assets.

Exhibit 8.10 Tactics to resist an acquisition

- Entering into long-term contracts with suppliers and buyers which will not be attractive to a potential bidder.
- Restructuring the company's finances; borrowing cash, so that higher dividend payments can be made to current shareholders, causes the share price and cost to the bidder to increase.
- Disposing of fixed assets to generate cash to pay higher dividends, which also causes the share price and cost to the bidder to increase.

Other actions that the management of the target company can undertake include promising and delivering improvement in the company's performance; this could include restructuring and divesting non-core areas and non-profitable areas. Equally the focus could be on long-term achievements and successes, with expected future successes being highlighted. These should include future profitable opportunities and may encompass innovation and product developments along with market opportunities. The target company may also revise forecasts on profit and performance upwards, with the aim of making the company appear more attractive and consequently more expensive.

A predator can be discouraged if the target company seeks an alternative friendly bidder to take over the company or purchase a large number of its shares, hence making the acquisition of a controlling interest by a predator difficult. Friendly bidders of this type are called white knight bidders. Another tactic target companies can employ is to have the takeover referred to the competition authorities. A full investigation by the competition authorities into the suggested monopoly or anti-competitive aspects of the takeover can last from six to nine months in total, giving the target company more time to fight the hostile takeover bid. Overall, resisting a hostile takeover bid is hard work with no guarantee of success and characteristically requires the appointment of a whole host of expert advisers including lawyers, merchant banks and public relations companies.

✔ Check your understanding

- Do you understand the reasons why organisations resist hostile takeover bids?
- Check your understanding by comparing and contrasting the possible outcomes of a hostile takeover bid and a white knight takeover.

Successful management of an acquisition

Once a suitable acquisition has been made, its future success depends on its effective management. The effective management of an acquisition starts with decisive action, as delays prolong speculation and uncertainty about the future of the business; and in particular rationalisation and job losses should be dealt with swiftly. Communication is important at this stage and the message should be explicit. The future of the acquired company, the benefits of its acquisition and the expectations of the acquiring company all need to be made clear to people in both businesses.

Synergy is often one of the desired results from an acquisition and occurs at different levels of the organisation. If synergy is to occur at the level of individual employees and managers, their skills and abilities have to be transferable from one group of activities to another, and between the successful bidding company and acquired company. This type of transferability aids and supports the combination of knowledge, ideas and experience from individuals of both organisations which, ideally, results in staff working as a team towards the achievement of the objectives of the new organisation.

In complementing synergy at the individual level, divisional level synergy requires the seeking out of activities undertaken for one product or area of the business which can benefit other products or areas of the new organisation. For example, in a related acquisition the same distribution channel being used for several products or services is synergy. Equally efficiency in operations can be achieved by spare capacity being reduced when the parent company and the acquired company integrate production processes. The opportunities for such benefits and synergy have to be sought out, actively managed and made

---

Business illustration of related acquisition – **Bayer & Schering**

In April 2006 Germany's largest drug company, Bayer, made a white knight bid of €16.5 billion for Schering another German pharmaceutical company. This take-over will create a company with total sales of €14.9 billion, with €9 billion from prescription drugs. The new larger merged company will specialise in drugs for cancer, blood and heart diseases and hormone treatments. This acquisition complements Bayer's existing products and boosts Bayer's specialist healthcare business

Source: 'Bayer bid is shot in arm for Germany', K Griffiths, *Daily Telegraph*, 14 April 2006.

to happen. Equally corporate level benefits and synergy have to be identified and managed. Corporate level synergy could relate to more effective market or product development or to an improved overall cash flow position (see Business illustration on Bayer & Schering). Money generated in some areas of the new combined business could be used to finance areas which are currently short of cash, with the overall aim of strengthening the corporate image of the new organisation.

Review questions   **Acquisitions**

1   Explain why companies may choose to grow by acquisition.
2   Summarise the benefits of successful growth by acquisition.
3   Briefly compare and contrast expansion by acquisition and organic growth.
4   Summarise the problems which may arise once an acquisition has occurred.
5   Discuss the tactics a company can follow to resist a hostile takeover bid.

CONCLUSION

The growth and expansion undertaken by organisations can take a variety of formats and there are no hard and fast rules about which methods of growth a company has to employ. Companies undertake expansion in what they see as a profitable arena. This can include market development or product development and can be achieved via organic growth or collaboration with a third party. The collaboration can take the form of licensing, franchising, strategic alliance or acquisition and may occur in the domestic marketplace or overseas. The key issues to consider with any method of growth are the level of resources and finance which have to be committed up front and the retrieval of the resources and capital. The key issues under consideration should also include the benefits and profits which the company achieves from the expansion, and the associated risks of losing resources and money and of not seeing the expected benefits and profits.

LEARNING OUTCOMES AND SUMMARY

The learning outcomes for this chapter are specified and a brief summary of the material relating to the learning outcomes is provided.

→ **Learning outcome 1**
Discuss the benefits and potential disadvantages of organic growth.

- Organic growth, also called internal growth, occurs when a company invests money in expanding its activities from scratch, that is setting up new outlets or manufacturing activities by itself. This means the company can closely control the rate of growth, but it can be a slow method of growth if the environment and market are fast moving.

→ **Learning outcome 2**
Explain exporting and licensing as methods of international expansion.

■ Exporting is often the first way in which companies start international activities. Goods are manufactured in one country, shipped abroad and sold in a foreign country. Exporting is a way of entering a foreign market without having to commit significant capital expenditure to expensive overseas operations.

■ An alternative to exporting is for a company to license an overseas company to manufacture its products in return for a fee. This approach is often used by soft drinks manufacturers and brewing companies. This means a company can enter into overseas production without having to bear the capital cost, as this is borne by the licensee.

→ **Learning outcome 3**
Explain franchising, its advantages and disadvantages.

■ Franchising is also a contractual arrangement in which a fee is paid to the franchiser in return for the right to run a particular business, for example a hotel or restaurant, in a defined geographical area. The franchiser provides equipment, know-how and advertising in return for the fee and royalty payments.

■ The advantages of franchising are that the franchiser does not have to put up the capital and bear the risks of entering a new geographic market. Hence the company can expand at low cost. The disadvantages of franchising include the franchiser's potential inability to maintain quality control and strategic co-ordination of the business.

→ **Learning outcome 4**
Discuss the advantages and potential disadvantages of each type of strategic alliance and how the suitability of strategic alliance partners should be assessed.

■ A strategic alliance occurs when two or more businesses agree a contract to operate a joint project. Different partners in an alliance will be likely to reap different benefits, for example access to new markets, and access to new technology or access to skills and abilities.

■ The ad-hoc pool alliance is when partner companies contribute limited resources for a short period of time, with resources and profits returning to the parent companies. A consortium occurs when partners contribute resources on a long-term basis, but expect to retrieve resources and profits eventually. A project-based joint venture occurs when the partner companies put in resources, which remain with the alliance, and the parent companies take a royalty payment. The full-blown joint venture occurs when the partner companies commit enough resources to allow a new free-standing business to be developed.

- When selecting alliance partners, companies need to assess strategic fit, capability, compatibility, commitment and control. Any alliance contract entered into should cover restrictions on knowledge transfer and intellectual property rights; dispute settlements; exit arrangements; and accounting procedures.

→ **Learning outcome 5**
Discuss acquisitions as a method of growth.

- Acquisition occurs when one company buys another company or a shareholding in another company, often with the aim of gaining new markets and reducing the number of competitors. Acquisition can provide rapid growth. Selecting an acquisition target requires careful appraisal of the target's long-term prospects and potential performance. Consideration also needs to be given to how the acquired company will be managed; will it be integrated or managed as a subsidiary?

→ **Learning outcome 6**
Identify actions which a company can take to resist a hostile takeover bid.

- A company which is the target of a hostile acquisition takeover bid may seek to resist the bid by making itself unattractive to the bidder by, for example borrowing cash, and tying the company into long contracts with suppliers and buyers. The company could also seek to make itself more attractive to its shareholders by promising improvements in performance of the business and divesting non-core areas and unprofitable activities.
- Alternatively if the target company can persuade the competition authorities to launch a full investigation then a final decision on the take-over will be delayed for six to nine months, until the final report on the acquisition is published. Hence this gives the target company more time to fight the hostile takeover bid.

Exit case studies 8.2a and 8.2b look at Napster and MTV respectively and the issues surrounding the licensing of music products. They can be used to assess the learning outcomes below.

Learning outcomes	Check you have achieved this by	
1 Explain how an industry will develop in the long term.	Identify and discuss how a specific industry will grow over a 10-year period.	Answering Exit case study question 1.
2 Evaluating methods of organisational growth.	Identifying the advantages and disadvantages of licensing as a method of expansion.	Answering Exit case study question 2.

Napster attacks delays in European music licensing

FT

by Tim Burt

Napster, the Internet service that was behind the explosion in online music, has accused European licensing groups of hampering the growth of legitimate web-based music companies across the continent. The US-listed company, which rescued the Napster brand from bankruptcy 14 months ago, yesterday claimed that failure to reach agreement on licensing music had exacerbated illegal Internet piracy in Europe.

Napster and Apple, the US technology group that developed the iTunes online service, have been forced to delay the launch of European services by complex negotiations with so-called national collection societies, which hold the licensing rights to music in each country. Apple – which had been hoping to launch its iTunes service last year – has declined to set a date for its introduction in Europe. Chris Gorog, the chairman and chief executive of Napster, said: 'As each day passes that Napster isn't operating in Europe, substantial amounts of money is lost to pirates because there is no legal alternative available.'

On a global basis, analysts estimate that online piracy cost the music industry some $2.4bn (£1.3bn) during the past year. But Mr Gorog's comments are likely to irritate European music trade associations and rival online services such as OD2, the British web-based music retailer, which last week claimed significant growth in online demand. Napster and Apple have been frustrated by the slow pace at which collection societies have been signing licensing deals.

Eddie Cue, Apple's vice-president of applications and Internet service, said it hoped to launch its iPod devices and iTunes download service in Europe this year. But he admitted the launch depended on resolving different pricing and music release schedules in the EU. 'We said we'd be here this year and we're working very hard on that,' he added. Apple has sold over 30m songs on its US service since its launch last year, while Napster – formerly an illegal file-sharing operation – has more than 500,000 tracks on its subscription service.

Speaking at the annual Midem music conference in Cannes, Mr Gorog said: 'Administratively, there are some real challenges [for licensing societies] to keep up with our requirements. We would like to debut with more than half a million tracks in Europe, but we are months away from a resolution.'

Source: *Financial Times*, 26 January 2004.

MTV in European video licensing row

FT

by Tim Burt

Europe's leading independent record labels on Wednesday accused MTV, the music channel owned by Viacom, of market abuse and price gouging in a bitter war of words over licensing rights for music videos. Artists including Travis, Craig David, Prodigy and So Solid Crew could be pulled off MTV's pan-European TV network amid a stand-off between the labels and MTV over video royalty payments.

Impala, the European trade association representing 2,400 independent record companies, accused MTV of threatening to stop broadcasting videos from independent labels unless they agreed to a 55 per cent reduction in royalties. 'MTV is trying to impose a US rights model on the rest of the world,' said Alison Wenham, vice-president of Impala. 'They're are offering a flat fee equivalent to the rate before 1995.'

According to the independents, MTV's US parent has ordered the company to cut the annual royalty fees paid to independents in Europe from a total of £1.9m ($3.5m) a year to £845,000. The Viacom subsidiary rejected the allegations, which centre on the re-negotiation of a four-year contract terms with Video Performance (VPL) – the licensing association action on behalf of the independent labels. MTV executives argue that Video Performance is seeking a deal worth more than twice as much as the last contract, which expired at the end of last year but has been extended to March 31. Simon Guild, chief operating officer of MTV Networks Europe, said: 'We want to make proposals that the independent labels are happy with, but VPL is effectively a monopoly on video rights and we want to explore different things.'

MTV is already in talks with several independent labels about agreeing new direct terms, as it already does with the five music majors: Universal, Warner, EMI, Sony Music and BMG. But European independent labels claim that they are not being offered the same global terms as the majors, while arguing that MTV is offering less money for videos shown on many more channels and digital outlets than in the past. The £1.9m royalty payments for the past four-year contract were, however, only a fraction of the music sales enjoyed by the independents. In Europe, the independent sector accounted to 21 per cent of the market in 2002, the last year for which figures are available, worth $2.5bn.

In an open letter to MTV from almost 300 labels, the companies said: 'The terms being offered by MTV are totally unacceptable.' Mr Guild said collective licenses were inflexible but pledged to seek a resolution with VPL. MTV has questioned the independent's claims of price-cutting, but predicted that the two sides could reach an accommodation before the end of the month that would avoid music videos being pulled off the air.

Source: FT.com site, 24 March 2004.

Exit case study questions

1 Identify and discuss ways in which you think the recorded music industry will grow and develop over the next 10 years.

2 Manufacturing companies such as soft drink producers and brewing companies have traditionally used licensing. Identify similarities and differences in licensing a music video or online song compared to soft drinks.

DISCUSSION TOPIC

1 Read the papers 'Why create alliances' by Stephen B Preece and 'Creating knowledge through collaboration' by Andrew C Inkpen, both in Chapter 10, of *The Strategy Process*, Mintzberg, Lampel, Quinn and Ghosal, Harlow: Prentice Hall, 2003.

2 Research the global telecommunications industry and discuss how the ideas concerning collaboration presented in these two papers apply to the world wide telecommunications industry.

WIDEN YOUR HORIZONS

1   Widen your horizons by visiting the British Franchise Association website, www.british-franchise.org, and identify the questions which should be asked and answered prior to a franchisee purchasing a franchise.

2   Widen your horizons by visiting www.sakshairandbeauty.com and reading the article 'Salon lets its hair down' by Cindy Duffield, *Sunday Times*, 27 June 2004. Saks is a chain of hair and beauty salons which has grown by franchise. Identify and evaluate possible future growth options for the company.

3   Widen your horizons by determining the HR and cultural issues B&Q will face in China and how they might be overcome. Accessing the following articles will help: 'B&Q opens Beijing store as Chinese embrace "BIY"' by Tessa Thorniley in the *Daily Telegraph*, 20 October 2003 and 'Year of the DIY enthusiast in China' by Kate Rankine in the *Daily Telegraph*, 2 December 2004.

WEBLINKS

The websites for this chapter provides some information on acquisitions or takeovers and franchising.

- This website contains a short article about issues to consider in making a takeover a success.
  www.thinkingmanagers.com/management/takeovers.php
- This website looks at large UK takeovers including the NATWEST deal, which was initially launched by the Bank of Scotland before the Royal Bank of Scotland actually took over NATWEST.
  news.bbc.co.uk/1/hi/business/the_company_file/456429.stm
- This website contains lots of information about franchising.
  www.british-franchise.org
- This Business Link page has lots of information about joint ventures, sometimes known as strategic alliances and how to get the most out of joint ventures.
  www.businesslink.gov.uk/bdotg/action/layer?topicId=1073864682

FURTHER READING

The following readings provide an overview of how organisations grow and develop.

- Abdou, K and Kliche, S (2004) 'The strategic alliances between the American and German companies', *European Business Review*, 16, 1, pp 8-27.
- Dess, G G, Lumpkin, G T and Taylor, M T (2005) *Strategic Management*, 2nd edn, New York: McGraw Hill. Chapter 7, 'International strategy'.
- Hill, W L and Jones, G R (2001) *Strategic Management*, 5th edn, New York: Houghton Mifflin. Chapter 10, 'Corporate strategy: diversification, acquisitions and internal new ventures'.
- Johnson, G, Scholes, K and Whittington, R (2005) *Exploring Corporate Strategy*, 7th edn, Harlow: Financial Times/Prentice Hall. Chapter 7, 'Methods of development'.
- Darling, J R and Seristo H T (2004) 'Key steps for success in export market', *European Business Review*, 16, 1, pp 28-43.
- Haggle III, J and Singer, M (1999) 'Unbundling the corporation', *Harvard Business Review*, March/April.

- ■ Hilton, A (2003) 'Unzipping the merger myth', *Management Today*, February, pp 48–51.
- ■ Shaw, V and Kauser, S (2000) 'The changing patterns of international strategic alliance activity by British firms', *Journal of General Management*, 25, 4, Summer.
- ■ Smith, D J (2003) 'Strategic alliances and competitive strategies in the European aerospace industry the case of BMW Rolls-Royce GmbH', *European Business Review*, 15, 4, pp 262–76.

REFERENCES

1   Keers, H (2004) 'New store sales help Next show off some stylish profits', *Daily Telegraph*, 26 March.
2   Marsh, P (2005) 'Airbus brings 8000 jobs to Britain', *Financial Times*, 21 January.
3   Ibid.
4   Hill, C (2004) *Global Business Today*, 3rd edn, New York: McGraw-Hill.
5   Ibid.
6   Ibid.
7   Ibid.
8   Merchant, K (2004) 'Glenmark in record licencing deal', *Financial Times*, 27 September.
9   Becket, M (2004) 'Bewildering choice awaits would be franchisees', *Daily Telegraph*, 29 March.
10   Hill, C W L and Jones, G R (2001) *Strategic Management*, 5th edn, Boston: Houghton Mifflin.
11   Ibid.
12   Done, K (2004) 'BA and Iberia link up on flights', *Financial Times*, 16 December.
13   Lorange, P and Roos, J (1993) *Strategic Alliances*, Oxford: Blackwell.
14   Hill, op. cit.
15   Lorange and Roos, op. cit.
16   Ibid.
17   Hill, op. cit.
18   Lorange and Roos, op. cit.
19   Thorniley, T (2003) 'B&Q opens Beijing store as Chinese embrace "BIY"', *Daily Telegraph*, 20 October.
20   Wright, R (2004) 'P&O quits container joint venture', *Financial Times*, 3 February.
21   Medcof, J W (1997) 'Why too many alliances end in divorce', *Long Range Planning*, 30, 5, October.
22   Smith, D and Rushe, D (2004) 'Devoured by the dragon', *Sunday Times*, 12 December.
23   Financial Times Reporters (2005) 'Heineken in talks to take over China's Kingway', *Financial Times*, 21 January.
24   Ibid.

CHAPTER 9

Developing international strategy

Exhibit 9.1

Chapter objectives

When you have read this chapter and worked through the associated activities you should be able to achieve the objectives specified below.

1 Discuss reasons for companies choosing to operate overseas.

2 Identify and evaluate the impact of key aspects of the external environment likely to impact on a company operating worldwide.

3 Identify and discuss strategies which a company operating in a worldwide environment may pursue.

4 Indicate possible HR strategies for companies pursuing different worldwide strategies.

5 Discuss the advantages and disadvantages for home and host countries of pursuing FDI.

6 Summarise the characteristics of FDI in the major world economies, for example China, India, Europe and USA.

The entry case study looks at Disney's strategy for international expansion in a number of different markets, both geographical (Asia and Europe) and sectors (for example children's television and sports television).

Disney to unveil international strategy

FT

by Tim Burt

Walt Disney, the US entertainment and media group, will on Wednesday unveil ambitious plans to expand its international TV business with significant investment in branded channels from its ABC network, the ESPN sports and Disney TV operations. Bob Iger, Disney president and chief operating officer, is expected to tell an industry conference that the US group is planning to launch new Disney channels in India and China, while expanding its ESPN presence in Europe and Asia.

Mr Iger is also likely to take a swipe at Comcast, the cable group which abandoned a $60bn hostile bid for Disney earlier this year, by suggesting that better exploitation of new channels and technology makes more strategic sense for Disney than merging content and distribution.

In a speech to the Royal Television Society in London, the Disney president plans to say that fierce competition among distribution companies risks turning that sector into a commodity business. By contrast, Mr Iger will outline a content strategy based on 'greater personalisation' in Disney programming allowing more viewers to select schedules on personal video recorders, mobile devices, the Internet and pay-per-view channels. The company hopes to reverse losses and rebuild ratings at ABC, its flagship network, through a combination of new dramas, family comedies and imported reality programmes.

Disaffected Disney shareholders, however, have demanded more radical changes at both ABC and in the group's overall strategy. Stanley Gold and Roy Disney the former directors behind a campaign to oust Michael Eisner as chief executive have warned of stagnation if Mr Eisner is not replaced before his planned retirement in September 2006.

Last week, the Disney board named Mr Iger as the sole internal candidate to succeed Mr Eisner. Mr Iger is not expected to refer to the controversy in his speech today. But he will point to signs of ratings improvement at ABC and growth among overseas channels. This week Disney launched ABC1 in the UK, the first ABC-branded channel outside the US, and is to invest $100m over the next several years in new programming aimed at children.

Mr Iger, a keen advocate of developing TV programmes as franchises for other Disney divisions, is likely to predict knock-on benefits for the group's theme parks, theatrical, DVD and consumer products businesses. In addition to new channels, he will point to the launch of ESPN-branded mobile phone services, the launch of 'classic sport' programming in the UK and an ESPN magazine in China.

Industry analysts regard potential contributions from such activities as marginal, set against forecast revenues of about $31bn and earnings of $4.2bn for the 12 months ending September 30. Nevertheless, Mr Iger will hail such services as important potential revenue streams for the future.

Source: *Financial Times*, 28 September 2004.

INTRODUCTION

Companies choose to internationalise for one or a combination of reasons (see Exhibit 9.2). The pressure from stakeholders such as shareholders, the stock markets and financiers to raise sales and profits will drive the need for growth and expansion. Hence overseas expansion is likely to be the best option when opportunities in the home market are limited. Domestic opportunities for growth and expansion will be limited when home markets are saturated, small and highly competitive, as there will be many competitors chasing a limited number of customers. The home market of the United Kingdom is saturated for both Tesco and B&Q, which is why both companies now operate overseas, for example Tesco have expanded overseas to countries such as Hungary and Taiwan and B&Q have gone into China.

When operating internationally many of the aspects concerning the use of resources (see Chapters 3 and 4) and the development of strategy and growth (see Chapters 7 and 8) will obviously apply. Hence, this chapter seeks to focus on additional aspects of strategy which are relevant to operating internationally.

Exhibit 9.2 Why go international?

- Saturated home markets
- Small home markets
- Slow growth home markets
- Competition
- Costs

Key areas of the **international environment** to understand when trading worldwide are political, economic and cultural.

Companies which choose to internationalise due to difficult home markets should evaluate their position carefully. Failure to evaluate and anticipate the wider **international environment** will increase the likelihood of a lack of success with international operations. A company's home market should be secure before going abroad, as companies that are struggling to survive at home are very unlikely to successfully compete in a fierce international marketplace. Tesco and B&Q both achieved success in their home markets before undertaking substantial overseas expansion.

Equally slow growth or recession in a home market may drive a company to consider going international. The successful South African diamond company De Beers realised it was going to experience limited growth with its South African operations as new discoveries of diamonds in the country were unlikely. Hence in 1997 De Beers started working towards establishing its own diamond mines in Canada, which were expected to start producing stones in 2007.[1]

Before going international a company must weigh up the risks and evaluate its ability to operate overseas. This evaluation should consider the impact of foreign regulations and political environments, and whether the company has managers with the required international skills and experience to operate in such a foreign environment. Will the company and its managers be able to adapt to other countries' societal, business and individual cultures?

THE INTERNATIONAL ENVIRONMENT

The company looking to venture abroad must develop an understanding of its international environment (see Exhibit 9.3). The key areas of the international environment which companies trading worldwide need to understand are political, economic and cultural.

Exhibit 9.3 The international environment

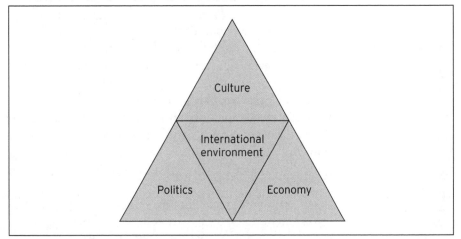

Politics

The political situation in any potential overseas market needs to be carefully considered. This means the company should consider the political system – whether **democracy** or **autocracy** – the level of political stability, and how receptive the government is to foreign investment and trade.

> **Democracy** is the system of government via fairly elected representatives.

Democracy is the system of government where people are able to choose, through a system of voting, who represents them in the corridors of power and in the decision-making process. As it is impossible for every individual in society to be completely free from the rules of the state, democratic systems are the mutual agreements under which people are able to live together collectively and yet express a collective opinion on periodic change via fair and proper elections. Democratic systems divide broadly into those that have evolved and those that are the product of a sudden and extreme change, such as a popular revolution.

For example, the UK is called a constitutional monarchy and has a parliamentary system. The current system has evolved through concessionary changes throughout history. Today in the twenty-first century the UK has a hereditary monarch as figurehead, a popularly elected House of Commons, and mix of hereditary and appointed peers in the second chamber, the House of Lords. This is used as a blueprint of democratic government. There are now only 92 hereditary peers in the House of Lords, elected by their colleagues and this is likely to reduce pending further reform. In contrast countries such as the USA, France and Germany have all had occasion to invent their political systems from scratch after revolution or war. These systems are based on written constitutions and codes of conduct, and feature elected government at all levels, including chambers and head of state – usually a president. One of the newest democracies which emerged in 2004 was the Ukraine with Viktor Yushchenko successfully winning the election – despite being poisoned, and having to use protests and the courts to have his election victory recognised by the opposition. Democracies tend to be relatively politically stable, as the people's will has determined which political party should govern and it is accepted by the population.

Autocracy is where government is unelected and one person or few people retain all power.

The exact opposite of a democratic system is an autocratic system where one person or few people retain all power. During the Cold War, this lack of democratic process was most keenly observed under communism in countries such as Poland, East Germany and Russia. Therefore in the old communist countries the people were unable to choose the political party to represent them and had little or no personal liberty. These systems were known as oligarchies, as a powerful elite dominated them. Today autocratic governments exist in Zimbabwe under the dictatorship of Robert Mugabe and in Cuba under Fidel Castro.

Governments change hands, sometimes violently. Even without a change, a government may decide to respond to new popular feelings. The foreign company's property may be taken, its currency holding may be blocked, or import quotas or new duties may be set. International marketers may find it profitable to do business in an unstable economy, but the unsteady situation will affect how they handle business and financial matters.

✔ Check your understanding

- Do you understand that countries are either democratic or autocratic?
- Check your understanding by stating whether the following countries are democratic or autocratic.
  1 Ukraine
  2 Iceland
  3 Alaska
  4 North Korea
  5 Lebanon

Countries and governments which are receptive to overseas companies will often experience economic growth. The receptive nature of many SE Asian governments, in the 1980s and 1990s, to foreign companies manufacturing and selling goods in their country led to the growth of the Asian 'Tiger' economies. In the early twenty-first century the same type of growth and expansion is being seen in the economies of China and India. China has retained its communist political system, but has chosen to open up economically, and has seen rapid economic growth. This economic growth is illustrated by the city of Shanghai, which is experiencing a huge amount of expansion and reconstruction; such development is also occurring in Beijing as the city prepares to host the 2008 Olympics. In contrast India has been a democracy with a highly protectionist stance for many years, but in recent years has chosen to relax the regulations covering currency movements and overseas companies operating in India. The result has been a surge in overseas companies operating in India in all sorts of industries, including pharmaceuticals and financial services.

Hence, the attitude of a government towards international trade will determine how receptive or unreceptive the country is to foreign investors. A government which is unreceptive to foreign companies and trade will impose a variety of restrictions, which will make it difficult for overseas companies to operate in their country. The restrictions can take the form of import quotas, currency restrictions, foreign staffing restrictions and government bureaucracy. It is also a possibility that a culture of bribery, and inefficient and difficult customs and excise handling will exist, adding to the problems of operating in the country.

A **tariff** is a tax levied by a foreign government against certain imported products.

Restrictions against overseas companies include **tariffs**, **quotas** and **embargoes**. The most common is the tariff, which is a tax levied by a foreign government against certain imported products. The tariff may be designed either to raise revenue or to protect domestic firms. The exporter also may face a quota system, which sets limits on the amount of goods the importing country will accept in specified product categories. The purpose of a quota is usually to conserve and protect local industry and employment. An embargo is the strongest form of quota and is a total ban on some imports. Companies may also face exchange controls that limit the amount of foreign currency or profits which can be exchanged and moved back to a company's home country. This may be done by limiting the amount of currency which can be moved or by government control of the exchange rate.

A **quota** is a limit on the amount of goods the importing country will accept.

An **embargo** is a total ban on some imports.

Trading blocs are groups of countries that act collectively in regard to trade and commerce.

In contrast, the creation of **trading blocs** may make it easier for companies to trade within the trading bloc. Trading blocs are geographic blocs made up of a number of countries that agree to act together in some way with regard to trade and commerce. The countries may, for example, agree to allow special concessions on the taxing and movement of goods within the trading bloc or merely support each other with regard to economic issues. Examples of trading blocs include the European Union (EU), North American Free Trade Area (NAFTA) and The Association of South East Asian Nations (ASEAN).

The EU (see Chapter 2) is a large trading bloc stretching from Eire in the west to Poland in the east, allowing free movement of goods and citizens between all member states. Although the EU's Single European Market came into operation in 1993 and allows free movement of goods between member states, rates of taxation on goods have yet to harmonised across the EU.

NAFTA was established in 1994 by agreement between the governments of Canada, USA and Mexico, which sought to establish larger and more secure markets for the goods and services their countries produced. The aim was to improve the competitiveness of companies from NAFTA countries in global markets, while also generating improvements in working conditions, living standards and employment levels in the NAFTA countries.[2]

ASEAN was formed in 1967 in Bangkok with five founding members and a further four members joining between 1984 and 1997 (see Exhibit 9.4). In July 1997 Burma and Laos were admitted, but Cambodia's entry was postponed due to violence that threatened to escalate into civil war.[3] Cambodia's entry to ASEAN finally occurred in 1999. ASEAN seeks to promote the economic, social and cultural development of the region; to safeguard the region's political and economic stability; and to serve as a forum for the resolution of intra-regional differences.[4]

Exhibit 9.4 Members of ASEAN

Year of entry	Countries		
1967	• Indonesia • Singapore	• Malaysia • Thailand	• Philippines
1984	• Brunei		
1995	• Vietnam		
1997	• Laos	• Myanmar (Burma)	
1999	• Cambodia		

Source: www.asean.org

Review questions The international environment

1 Why do companies choose to trade internationally?

2 Explain the differences between a democracy and autocracy.

3 Indicate factors which make a country receptive to foreign investment and trade.

4 Define the term trading bloc and explain their relevance to the international and global environment companies operate in.

The economy

*A country's **industrial structure** determines its employment levels, income levels and products required.*

When considering operating overseas a company should ensure it understands the economic environment into which it is venturing. Three economic factors reflect the country's attractiveness as a market: the country's **industrial structure**, its income distribution, and the type of economy operating.

Industrial economies trade goods with each other and with raw material economies and industrialising economies.

Industrial structure

A country's industrial structure determines its employment levels, income levels and the types of product and services required. The **industrial economies** of the West and Asia are large exporters of services and manufactured goods, for example UK, Germany, USA, Malaysia and Thailand. Industrial economies trade goods between each other and with raw material exporting economies and **industrialising economies**. The service and manufacturing activity in industrial economies creates wealth and in many industrial economies there will be a significant middle class who are a relatively wealthy market for goods and services produced by the industrialised and industrialising economies.

Industrialising economies are those countries which are experiencing rapid growth in manufacturing and exporting.

Industrialising economies such as China, India, Brazil and South Africa are experiencing rapid growth in manufacturing and exporting. As manufacturing increases, these countries require greater imports of materials and equipment, including oil, steel and construction equipment. Industrialisation normally creates a new rich class and a small but growing middle class, with both demanding new and more sophisticated imported goods (see Business illustration on Porsche and Rolls-Royce).

Business illustration of sale of luxury goods in India and China – Porsche and Rolls-Royce

In India the changes in the spending power of people is illustrated by two trends. The first is the sale of expensive cars such as Porsches and Rolls-Royces, both luxury goods and therefore attracting a tax of 100 per cent. The first Porsche Boxter was sold in India, during 2005, for £80,000, to Suhel Seth, a successful businessman from the world of advertising. In addition Rolls-Royce has returned to India after an absence of new car sales for around 50 years and recently a Rolls-Royce Phantom was sold to a stud farm owner for £435,000 or 35 million rupees.

Equally at the bottom end of India's economy, the second trend is evident, in that the poorest 20 per cent of families now spend 65 per cent of their income on food. This is in contrast to 20 years ago, when the same people spent 80 per cent of their income on food. Hence poor families have on average seen their non food expenditure increase by 15 per cent, much of which will be spent on other goods and services.

In China a similar demand exists for Rolls-Royces, with the cost of a Phantom being £200,000 plus £200,000 in import tax. In 2003 Rolls-Royce opened sales rooms in Beijing, Shanghai and Guangzhou and met its sales target of between 50 and 60 Rolls-Royces in the first year of trading in China.

Sources: 'Porsche dream driving India's new rich', P Foster, *Daily Telegraph*, 12 February 2005, 'Rolls-Royce makes new inroads into India', P Foster, *Daily Telegraph*, 22 April 2005, and 'China's super-rich salute the Red Flag's return', R Spencer, *Daily Telegraph*, 22 April 2005.

Raw material exporting economies are rich in natural resources, but have a poor manufacturing economy.

Raw material exporting economies is the term used to describe countries which are rich in one or more natural resource, but poor in terms of a manufacturing economy. Raw material exporting economies create most of their wealth from exporting their natural resources such as oil, natural gas, copper, iron ore, gold, diamonds; for example, both Saudi Arabia and Brunei are oil producing economies. These countries are good markets for specialised plant and equipment and luxury goods as there is a wealthy upper class and foreign residents earning significant salaries.

*In **subsistence economies** most of the population undertake simple and small scale agriculture.*

Finally few market opportunities are available in **subsistence economies** where the largest proportion of the population is involved in simple and small scale agriculture. The individual farmers and their families will consume most of their output, with the remainder being sold or bartered.

Income distribution

The second economic factor helping determine a country's attractiveness is its income distribution. Income distribution patterns vary from country to country, but will generally fall into one of the following categories: predominately low incomes; very low and very high incomes; low, medium and high incomes; or mostly medium incomes. The attractiveness of a country as a potential market for a company's goods and services will to a large extent be determined by the country's industrial structure and income distribution.

Subsistence economies will provide few market opportunities, as most of the population will undertake small scale agriculture, consume most of the output themselves, and barter or sell any surplus. In contrast raw material exporting economies are good markets for industrial equipment and luxury goods, while in industrialising countries there is a market for luxury goods and a growing middle class, which is why the market for imported consumer goods will be expanding rapidly. In 2006, China and South Africa were countries that fell into the category of industrialising countries. Industrial economies are those which are large exporters of semi-finished and manufactured goods and investment funds. These countries trade between themselves and with industrialising and raw material economies. In terms of population and wealth, these countries tend to have a large middle class.

Type of economy operating

The third factor determining a country's attractiveness as a market is the type of economy operating. There are three basic types of economy (see Exhibit 9.5) the **free market economy, the planned economy** and the **mixed economy.**

Exhibit 9.5 Types of economy

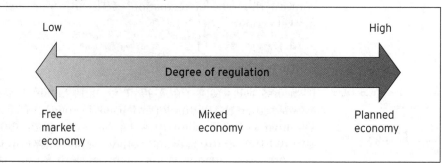

In a **free market economy** there is little or no regulation of commercial activity.

The free market economy is one in which there is little or no regulation of commercial activity by political entities (see Exhibit 9.5). In a free market, the market forces of demand and supply will lead to perfect competition, providing all that the people need or want at a price they can afford. If there is no demand for a product or service in a free market, then that product will not sell, no matter how cheaply it is priced.

In the **planned economy** jobs, housing, production, services and food are organised and regulated by the state.

The planned economic approach was taken by many former communist countries such as the USSR, Poland and East Germany. In communist countries, attempts were made to eradicate the free market and its differences between rich and poor, by planning and orchestrating all economic activity from central government. Thus people were not free to seek whatever job they wished, and organisations could not recruit whomever they wanted. All jobs, housing, production, services and food were organised and regulated by the state via its work units or state-owned organisations (see Exhibit 9.5). Market forces were denied, as consumers were only able to purchase products or services from the state-owned factories and companies, whether they were good or bad. No decision was left to the individual, no matter how small. Thus individuals' every need was catered for in a basic way, but individualism, innovation and creativity were stifled.

Today the planned economic approach is still taken in a few places such as Cuba and North Korea. However, China remains an odd case in point, as it retains a communist government but has become a member of the WTO and allows some economic, but not political freedom.

In the **mixed economy** choice of employment and trade exist, but there is some regulation.

The mixed economy, as the name suggests, falls between a planned and free market economy. Industry is not tightly controlled by government, as in the planned economy, nor is near total freedom allowed in business (see Exhibit 9.5). In a mixed economy freedom of employment and trade exist, but there will be regulations governing employment and business. Since the fall of communism many more economies are mixed economies. Countries with mixed economies include the USA, France, Germany, Poland and the Czech Republic. In mixed economies there will be some regulation of businesses, employees and consumers. For example, employees and consumers alike are at risk of being exploited and in the UK legislation protects employees at work through legislation covering health and safety at work and discrimination, while the consumer is protected by the Sale of Goods and Trades Descriptions Acts. In contrast this type of regulation occurs to a minimal extent in a more free market economy.

Culture

If success overseas is to be achieved, and failure and embarrassing mistakes avoided, then the culture of any overseas marketplace and how it differs from a company's home country need to be understood. **National culture** is the way society in a country acts and behaves, and is determined by a country's politics, economy, education systems, religions, language and social structure.

National culture is the way society in a country acts and behaves.

Hence Hill's model (see Exhibit 9.6) is valuable in considering what a national culture is and how it affects who we are and how we behave as individuals in society, as members of our own national culture, and as visitors to another national culture. It is this understanding of national culture which will allow managers to build cultural empathy with countries and markets where they wish to do business.

Exhibit 9.6 The determinants of culture

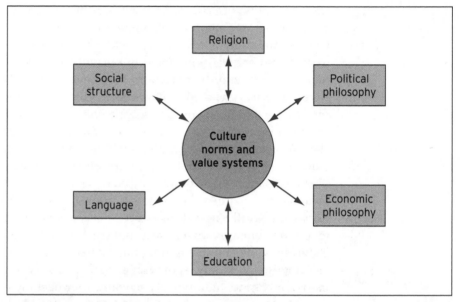

Source: Charles W L Hill, *International Business: Competing in the Global Marketplace*, 2nd edn, 1994, Irwin, reproduced with the kind permission of The McGraw-Hill Companies.

Politics

Political systems and the political environment have been defined and discussed earlier in this chapter. It is clear that the nature of the political system contributes to national culture, and to the norms and values of individuals living in the country.

Economics

The type of economy which operates in a country will provide a set of economic norms and values that affect the way people behave and what they consider to be right or wrong behaviour. See the earlier section in this chapter on the economy.

Education

The type of education people in any society receive depends on its availability, accessibility and value, which influences the understanding people have of the world around them. Education exists at three generic levels – primary (primary school), secondary (secondary school), and tertiary (university) – and societies make decisions about how accessible the education system is going to be. Equally parents make decisions concerning their children's education and, if professional success and security are highly valued, considerable effort and money will be used to ensure the best level of education possible for their children.

For example, in the UK primary and secondary education are free to all and provided by the state, with university education in a transition phase whereby fees are being introduced but accessibility is being increased. There is of course also the option of private education at primary and secondary levels. In some societies parents may choose an education which has a religious element for their children or there may be no such choice if the state education system is completely secular, as is the case in France. Equally the ability to pay may determine the type of education one's children receive or indeed some societies view the education of men and women differently.

Language

The most common first language in the world is Chinese, followed by English and Hindi. However, English is the most widely spoken language, followed by French, Spanish and Chinese, as many people speak English as a second language.

Language influences the way people perceive the world, contributing to the development of national culture and how people to communicate with others from the same and different cultures. This is illustrated by countries in close geographic proximity speaking different languages and having different national cultures. Additionally in countries where more than one language is spoken there will often be two cultures and sometimes there will be a tension between the two. For example, Canada has English speaking and French speaking cultures; Belgium has both Flemish and French speaking cultures (with a small vocal population of Walloon speakers); and Spain has Spanish and Basque speaking cultures. However, in Switzerland there are four national languages, namely French, German, Italian and Runantsch, with English also being widely spoken, and are there are no cultural tensions within the country.[5]

Social structure

Social structure is the basic social organisation of a society. The two major and important dimensions of social organisation are the basic unit of social organisation and the degree of **social stratification**. These two dimensions are key in explaining differences between cultures.

Social stratification is based on hierarchical social categories such as family background, occupation and income.

The basic units of social organisation are the individual and the group. Western societies tend to emphasise the individual, while other societies such as Japan, for example, tend to focus much more on the group. However, groups are found in all societies, with individuals belonging to groups such as families, work teams, social groups and sporting teams; but the degree to which societies differ is determined by the degree to which the group is viewed as the main means of social organisation. In some societies, individual attributes and achievements are viewed as being more important than group membership and achievement, while in other societies the reverse is true.

The second important dimension of social organisation is the degree of social stratification. All societies are stratified on a hierarchical basis into social categories or strata. These social strata are defined on the basis of characteristics such as family background, occupation and income. Individuals are born into a particular stratum and become a member of the same social category as their parents. In general terms people born into high social strata tend to have better opportunities in life with regard to education, work, healthcare, housing and overall standard of living, than people born into a low social category. All societies are stratified to some extent although differences occur in the degree of **social mobility** between strata, and the significance attached to social strata in work and business.

Social mobility is the extent to which a person can move out of the social stratum into which they were born and it varies significantly among different societies. The most rigid systems of social stratification are caste systems, which are closed systems. This means the social stratum into which one is born is determined by one's family and it is unlikely to change during an individual's lifetime. India's rigid caste system was officially abolished in 1949, although it remains a powerful influence in rural India where occupation and marital options are still to a significant extent determined by caste. In contrast a class system is a less rigid and open form of social stratification and social mobility is possible. Therefore the social position of a person at birth can change and those born at the bottom of the class hierarchy can work their way up, often by hard work and through education, while individuals born into higher social classes can slip down to the bottom of the social hierarchy. The extent to which social mobility in a class system can occur may vary from society to society, with some arguing, for example, that Britain has a more rigid class system than other Western societies such as the USA.

Religion

Religions can influence social behaviour and shape attitudes towards society. The issues which religion can influence include crime and punishment, sex, the family, the position of the elderly in society and how society cares for them. In turn, these views influence societal or national culture. Many people have some kind of religious faith or have been brought up following the edicts of one of the world's major religions, be it Christianity, Islam, Judaism, Hinduism, Buddhism. At the level of personal culture, the norm for many, but not all, families is to mark the significant events of life, birth, marriage and death with ceremonies that are religious in nature.

Therefore an understanding of another national culture requires an insight into many aspects of its society. This understanding will inform how the business world in a country operates, including the behaviour of two critical

Social mobility is the extent to which a person can move out of the social stratum into which they were born.

stakeholder groups – namely employees and customers. These need to be understood if a company is to operate successfully in a foreign country.

The economy and culture

1 Explain the differences between planned, mixed and free economies.

2 Describe the impact an industrialising economy has on the sale of basic goods and luxury goods in the economy.

3 How does the education system present in a country impact on business and the economy?

4 Why is language important in defining a country's culture?

5 Explain two major dimensions of social structure.

DEVELOPING AN INTERNATIONAL STRATEGY

In addition to choices concerning its domestic markets and operations, a company may have chosen to operate internationally and therefore its strategic choices will include decisions concerning overseas operations and activities.[6] Companies use four basic strategies to enter markets and compete internationally, namely, **international strategy**, **multi-domestic strategy**, **global strategy** and **trans-national strategy**,[7] with each strategy having its own advantages and disadvantages. The appropriateness of each strategy is determined by the level of the pressures for **cost reductions** and **local responsiveness** present in the overseas marketplace.

Pressures for cost reductions

Cost reductions arise from the marketplace demanding lower prices, which in turn can only be met via a reduction in cost.

Pressures for cost reductions require a company to lower its unit cost, possibly by using low-cost locations for manufacture or producing a standard or undifferentiated product. If a company is supplying a commodity type product – such as iron ore, steel, sugar, oil, or semi-conductor chips – then price is the

Business illustration of pressures for cost reductions – Samsung

Samsung, the world's largest producer of plasma screens, reported a 77 per cent drop in its first quarter net profits for 2005 because of tumbling flat screen prices. Samsung has struggled to cope due to fierce competition in the market for plasma screens and a supply glut sent plasma screen prices plunging by 30–40 per cent in 2004. This was then followed by profit margins being very tightly squeezed as the market experienced the effects of oversupply. Hence there is pressure on suppliers of plasma screens to reduce costs and prices.

Source: 'Samsung reckons the only way is up for plasma', Jung-a Song, *Financial Times*, 27 April 2005.

main basis of competition as differentiation is difficult to achieve when customer needs and wants are almost identical across the whole market. Additionally excess capacity in a commodity industry where there is little differentiation and low switching costs will provide the customer with the opportunity to shop around, and hence increase the pressure on suppliers for reductions in cost and price (see Business illustration on Samsung).

Pressures for local responsiveness

Local responsiveness arises from variation in consumer tastes, different infrastructures and regulation requirements.

The demand for companies operating internationally to tailor their products in response to local markets and conditions can vary from very little to significant demand. The demand for local responsiveness can arise from differences in consumer tastes and preferences.

The infrastructure in a particular geographic market can determine the local responsiveness required. Aspects of a country infrastructure which cannot be modified by companies include provision of mains electricity, which is 110 volts in US and 240 volts in many European countries, and driving on the left-hand side of the road in the UK and Eire. These sorts of variations in country infrastructure mean companies supplying electronic goods and cars have to have a high level of local responsiveness to supply appropriate products. There may also be differences in the commercial infrastructure which have developed over time and are difficult to change in the short term, for example distribution systems. In the UK the distribution channels for food are to a very large extent controlled and owned by the large powerful supermarkets, while in Italy the food market is more fragmented.

Other types of infrastructure which companies will need to respond to include the political and economic demands which governments place on public sector organisations, such as in the healthcare sector, where governments control much of the expenditure. In the United Kingdom the National Health Service is overwhelmingly funded by central government from taxation and the government sets the legislation covering the clinical testing, approval and registration of new drugs. In the UK, the National Institute for Clinical Excellence (NICE) evaluates the cost-effectiveness of treatments, and those deemed expensive and ineffective cannot be prescribed or offered by

Exhibit 9.7 Hill's worldwide strategies

		Local responsiveness	
		Low cost	High
Pressures for cost reductions	Low	1. International strategy	2. Multi-domestic strategy
	High	3. Global strategy	4. Trans-national strategy

Source: based on Hill, C W L (2004), *Global Business Today*, New York: McGraw-Hill.

NHS doctors. Therefore pharmaceutical companies need to have a high level of local responsiveness to comply with the legislation and regulation which will be different in each country in which they operate.

In contrast some companies will require only a low level of local responsiveness, examples include McDonalds, Kellogg's and Toys R Us. These companies create value by transferring differentiated products developed for home markets to new markets overseas, with little or no variation in the products.

International strategy

An **international strategy** is used where pressures for cost reduction and local responsiveness are both low.

An international strategy[8] is most appropriate where low pressures for both cost reduction and local responsiveness in the marketplace occur (see Exhibit 9.7). This is in addition to the company having strong core competences (see Chapter 3) which competitors in overseas markets lack. Companies in this situation can follow an international strategy by transferring those strong core competences to the overseas markets, which will allow the differentiated products developed in the home market to be sold successfully in the foreign market. This can be very successful if there is minimal local competition.

Companies pursuing an international strategy will usually establish manufacturing and marketing functions in each main overseas country in which they operate. This does give rise to the downside of an international strategy, which is the expense of the duplication of activities overseas. Additionally an international strategy is inappropriate if the overseas market exerts a high level of pressure for cost reductions.

The corporate headquarters in the home country will retain tight control over product development and marketing, with only minor local customisation of products and marketing for the foreign market. Research and development and product development activities are normally centralised in the home country. Hence an international strategy can be very profitable in the right circumstances where the pressures for cost reduction and local responsiveness are low. However, if the pressure for local responsiveness is high, an international strategy could become a strategy for failure as the company loses out to competitors offering products tailored to local conditions. Therefore in this situation a multi-domestic strategy would be more appropriate.

Multi-domestic strategy

A **multi-domestic strategy** is used where pressures for cost reductions are low and high for local responsiveness.

A multi-domestic strategy[9] is best suited to locations where low cost reduction pressures and high pressures for local responsiveness exist, if success to be achieved (see Exhibit 9.7). Maximum response to local conditions is achieved by locating production, marketing and product development activities in each overseas market (see Business illustration on B&Q, IKEA and Obi). Hence an expensive cost structure and a multi-domestic strategy are not the route to success in a marketplace with high pressure for cost reductions.

Business illustration of entering China – B&Q, IKEA and Obi

In entering China B&Q, IKEA and Obi have adapted their product offerings and prices to compete in the local marketplace. For example, B&Q do not sell garden sheds in China, as much of the new housing being built is apartments. The prices B&Q charge are lower than in the UK, but are in proportion to wages, land, and building costs, which are all lower in China. B&Q expect to make a profit in China in 2004.

Source: 'B&Q opens Beijing store as Chinese embrace 'BIY'', T Thornley, *Daily Telegraph*, 20 October 2003 and 'Year of the DIY enthusiast in China', K Rankine, *Daily Telegraph*, 2 February 2004.

The need to undertake extensive customisation of both products and marketing to obtain a strategic match with different national conditions means companies are generally unable to realise economies from the experience curve and efficient location of facilities. Additionally a major weakness of the multi-domestic strategy is that overseas operations become decentralised and largely autonomous operations, hence links with corporate headquarters become weak and meaningless.

Global strategy

A **global strategy** is used where pressures for cost reductions are high and low for local responsiveness.

The global strategy[10] makes most sense where there is high pressure for cost reductions and low demand for local responsiveness (see Exhibit 9.7). These conditions are often found in the markets for industrial goods. In contrast the market for consumer goods often has a high level of demand for local responsiveness, hence the global strategy is usually inappropriate for consumer goods. Therefore companies following a global strategy are often those producing industrial goods and services, such as Intel, Motorola and Adobe.

The lack of a need for local responsiveness and high pressure for cost reductions means centralised production, long production runs and a very competitive pricing strategy are undertaken by such companies – that is, a low-cost competitive strategy is pursued. The key activities, such as production, marketing and product development, of companies pursuing a global strategy are concentrated in a few favourable locations. Companies employing a global strategy prefer to market a standardised product worldwide so maximum economies of scale can be achieved. Therefore efficiency and cumulative experience lower the unit cost and allow the cost advantage to be used to underpin aggressive pricing in world markets.

Trans-national strategy

An **trans-national strategy** is used where pressures for cost reduction and local responsiveness are both high.

A trans-national strategy[11] is suitable for a marketplace where there is high pressure for both cost reductions and local responsiveness; hence, the customers are seeking a lot of product and value for low cost (see Exhibit 9.7). This makes the trans-national strategy difficult to implement successfully as the company will be seeking to lower costs, while being locally responsive, which increases costs. Not surprisingly, Bartlett and Ghoshal[12] argue that achieving success with a trans-national strategy is a difficult and complex process as it requires the company to simultaneously achieve both cost and differentiation advantages. Hence, in some industries companies can successfully adopt a trans-national strategy and create sustainable competitive advantage, while in other industries global, multi-domestic and international strategies remain the most viable.

The argument is that the worldwide competitive arena faced in many industries is extremely fierce and, in order to survive, companies need to pursue a trans-national strategy. Examples of industries where the fierce worldwide competition requires a trans-national strategy include markets for cars and consumer electronics. General Motors pursue a trans-national strategy and a common global platform or basic technical framework for cars is used and costs kept down, while the local responsiveness is achieved via the tailored features and additions for each market. The company Caterpillar, which manufactures heavy earth-moving equipment, has centralised manufacturing of basic frameworks, parts and components to help achieve a cost advantage, but seeks local responsiveness by assembling parts and components in the combination required by the local marketplace. In contrast, in worldwide industrial markets where competition is based almost solely on cost, such as the semi-conductor industry, a global strategy will be most suitable.

Exhibit 9.8 Multi-directional flow of core competences

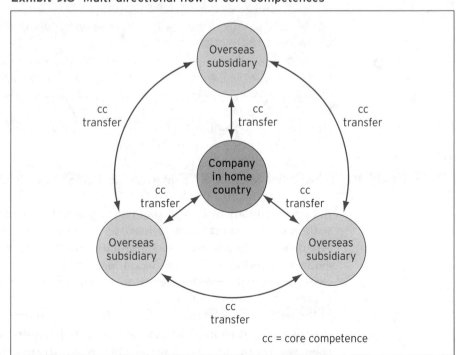

In seeking to successfully pursue a trans-national strategy a company should exploit economies of scale and the experience curve benefits, use centralised locations and exploit all core competences (see Chapter 3) while paying close attention to the pressures for local responsiveness. In the worldwide environment companies will have developed core competences in their home country and in their worldwide operations. This allows the process of global learning to occur, which is the flow and transfer of core competences from home and overseas subsidiaries to each other – that is, all subsidiaries learn from each other (see Exhibit 9.8). Hence the flow of products, skills and abilities should not all be one way, from home company to overseas subsidiary, as is the case when pursuing an international strategy; rather the flow should be two-way between all home and overseas subsidiaries (see Exhibit 9.8).

✔ Check your understanding

- Do you understand the circumstances in which each of the worldwide strategies – international, multi-domestic, global and trans-national – could be successfully used?
- Check your understanding by identifying which of the worldwide strategies Disney follows, given their expansion, which is described in Entry case study 9.1.

Review questions Developing an international strategy

1 Summarise the aspects of infrastructure in a country which can influence how companies do business in the country.

2 Describe the circumstances in which it would be appropriate for a company to pursue an international strategy.

3 Explain the changes to circumstances which would need to occur for a company to pursue a multi-domestic instead of an international strategy.

4 Discuss the circumstances in which a company should pursue a global strategy.

5 Explain why a trans-national strategy is difficult to implement.

INTERNATIONAL HUMAN RESOURCE MANAGEMENT

Achieving success in foreign markets requires the appointment of managers with relevant international experience, who can adapt to operating in a different culture, hence the need to understand different cultures, as is discussed earlier in this chapter. This section is concerned with international HR strategy (see Exhibit 9.9) and the selection of employees for particular jobs in a company's worldwide markets.

International HR strategy is similar to domestic HR strategy in that staff and managers recruited need to have the skills required to do the job for which they are recruited. HR strategy will for some companies also be about recruiting staff who have beliefs and values which are similar to those under-pinning the corporate culture. This means employees should have the type of personality which will produce a good performance, meeting both the individual's aspirations and the corporate objectives. The corporate culture in such companies is strong and likely to be reinforced by such a recruitment strategy. This means major change could be difficult to implement.

Exhibit 9.9 International human resource strategies

Geo-centric strategy	■ Seeks best people for job
Poly-centric	■ Key roles occupied by home country nationals ■ Subsidiaries managed by host country nationals
Ethno-centric	■ All management roles occupied by home country nationals

A **geo-centric** HR strategy seeks the best people for the job.

However, there are different international human resource strategies (see Exhibit 9.9). The HR strategy which seeks the best people for the job is the **geo-centric** HR strategy.[13] A geo-centric staffing strategy is the recruitment of the best people for key jobs throughout the international company regardless of nationality. The main advantage of the geo-centric staffing strategy is that it allows the company to make the best use of its staff and enables the building of a pool of international staff who feel at home working in a number of countries and cultures. The creation of such a pool of managers is key in building a strong and unified corporate culture and informal management network, both of which are required in companies pursuing trans-national and global strategies. However, the downside of building a strong unified corporate culture is the emergence of a lack of creativity and a tendency for the whole management team to think in the same way. This can be problematic as there will be circumstances when different views of problems or issues will be helpful. Finally, companies pursuing a geo-centric approach to staffing will be in a stronger position to create value from the experience curve, location economies and the multi-directional transfer of core competences, than companies following a **poly-centric** or **ethno-centric** HR strategy.

Difficulties can arise which may limit a company's ability to pursue a geo-centric HR strategy. Many countries, including Western countries like the UK and US, want foreign companies to employ their citizens. To achieve this gov-

Immigration is the flow of people entering a country to live and work.

ernments establish employment and **immigration** laws, which require the employment of host country nationals where they exist with the necessary skills. Companies wishing to employ a foreign national instead of a local national will be required to provide extensive documentation, which is time-consuming, expensive and often futile. In addition a geo-centric HR strategy is expensive to implement due to the higher and additional employment costs. There will be increased training costs, the additional costs of relocating managers from country to country, and the increased salaries for international managers, which are often higher than for domestic managers, as the base pay level is higher and allowances will be payable on overseas postings.

A **poly-centric** HR strategy sees key roles occupied by home country nationals and subsidiaries managed by host country nationals

The poly-centric HR strategy is the recruitment of host country nationals to manage subsidiaries with parent country nationals occupying key roles at corporate headquarters.[14] The poly-centric HR strategy will be less expensive to implement than a geo-centric HR strategy as the costs associated with relocating and remunerating expatriate managers are not payable to the same extent. Additionally a company pursuing a poly-centric HR strategy is less likely to fail due to a lack of cultural understanding, as host country managers are not vulnerable to making mistakes arising from cultural misunderstandings in the same way as expatriate managers. Hence a poly-centric HR strategy would normally support a multi-domestic strategy in the global marketplace, as cost pressures are low but there is high pressure for local responsiveness.

The main disadvantage of a poly-centric HR strategy which can emerge is a gap between host country managers and parent country managers. The parent country managers and headquarters' managers may become isolated from overseas operations and subsidiaries due to cultural differences, including language barriers. This lack of integration can arise from parent country managers not working overseas and from host country managers not having the opportunity gain experience outside their own country, meaning lack of career progression beyond their own subsidiary, possibly causing resentment. This often results in largely independent national units with only nominal links to corporate headquarters, and means that the benefits of the experience curve, location economies and the transfer of core competencies are difficult to achieve. Hence, while the poly-centric HR strategy is appropriate for a company pursuing a multi-domestic strategy, it is less suitable for companies pursuing international, trans-national or global strategies.

An **ethno-centric** HR strategy occurs when all management roles are occupied by home country nationals.

An ethno-centric HR strategy is the recruitment of parent country nationals to fill key management positions in overseas operations and subsidiaries. This practice was very widespread at one time by multinationals such as Philips, Proctor & Gamble, and Matsushita.[15] Companies pursue an ethno-centric HR strategy for three main reasons. First, it is believed that the host country lacks qualified individuals to fill senior management positions and will most often be used when a company is operating in developing countries. The next reason in support of an ethno-centric HR strategy is that it assists in maintaining a unified corporate culture. In general terms an ethno-centric HR strategy is compatible with an international strategy where pressures for cost reductions and local responsiveness are both low.

Finally, if the company is seeking to transfer core competencies to an overseas operation, it may be best achieved by transferring parent country managers with knowledge of that competency to the overseas operation. This will allow the tacit knowledge and experience of home country managers to be transferred to the overseas operation and ensure the core competencies materialise in the overseas operation.

✔ Check your understanding

- Do you understand the difference between geo-centric, poly-centric and ethno-centric HR strategies?
- Check your understanding by reading the short example below and explain which HR strategy you think Reed Elsevier are pursuing in China.

Short example

Reed Elsevier is a leading information, scientific and educational publisher and generates approximately 10 per cent of its turnover from the Asia Pacific region. In seeking to expand its business and increase turnover in the Asia Pacific region Reed have created a post for and appointed native entrepreneur Shan Mei to become chairman of Reed Elsevier in China. The appointment of Mei is unusual for Reed, as they don't currently have country managers for any parts of the business. However, Mei will operate from Beijing and is expected to grow and develop Reed in the areas of its current joint ventures, exhibitions, business to business, and publishing in the Chinese language.

For the previous twenty years Shan Mei has worked as Chinese adviser to former US Secretary of State Henry Kissinger and it is the contacts and knowledge of how things get done in China that Reed expect Mei to use to help them expand in the country. At the same time Reed recognise they have to work with the Chinese and provide what they ask for and require in terms of information and publishing.

Source: 'Reed targets China for expansion', Frank Kane, *The Observer*, 11 December 2005.

Review questions | International human resource management

1 Discuss the reasons why a company pursuing a geo-centric or ethno-centric HR strategy might be forced to operate a poly-centric HR strategy.

2 Why might a company pursuing a multi-domestic worldwide strategy employ a poly-centric HR strategy?

FOREIGN DIRECT INVESTMENT

If a company decides to pursue an overseas strategy there will be decisions to be made concerning the establishment of overseas operations. If the overseas strategy involves the investment of funds to produce goods or services in a foreign country, then this is known as **foreign direct investment** (FDI). Inward FDI is the investment of money in a country by overseas companies; for example, African countries received investment of $15 billion from overseas companies in 2003. Outward FDI is the investment made overseas by companies from one country; for example, in 2003 US companies invested $151.9 billion overseas.[16]

FDI can occur via a greenfield operation, a joint venture, licensing, or acquisition. Generally acquisition of a shareholding in excess of 10 per cent in a foreign company is accepted as FDI. Companies such as Nissan and Toyota

Foreign direct investment (FDI) is investment overseas to produce goods or services in a foreign country.

have set up in UK and France with greenfield ventures, whereas Volkswagen acquired Skoda in the Czech Republic. In 2003 45 per cent of companies chose acquisition as the preferred method of FDI; however, by 2004 this had fallen to 39 per cent.[17] Companies were choosing to restrict acquisition to their home markets due to greater problems with overseas acquisitions, such as regulatory problems, poor performance of the acquired company, and the resulting large debts. There is some variation across different geographical regions, however, with European companies (46 per cent) being keenest to undertake overseas acquisition, North American companies (36 per cent) being less keen, and Asian companies (24 per cent) being least keen.[18]

In developed countries such as the USA and Western European countries FDI is usually undertaken by a company making an overseas acquisition, as it is possible to identify a suitable acquisition target in a developed economy. This is viewed as being quick to implement and the strategic assets such as local resources, managers, knowledge; customers; and access to distribution systems are gained. In contrast, in developing countries such as India, Brazil and the former Eastern Bloc countries there will be fewer suitable acquisition targets, as the economy is less developed, hence companies wishing to under-take FDI are more likely to establish a greenfield operation. This is illustrated by Ford and a German engineering company, Getrag, undertaking a joint venture to enter Slovakia. In December 2004 Ford and Getrag announced they would be investing in excess of £398 million in Slovakia in a new plant to produce gearboxes. The new plant was to be located in eastern Slovakia and welcomed as unemployment in the region was running at more than 20 per cent.[19]

Why FDI?

Entering an overseas market by FDI allows companies to maintain tight control over manufacturing processes, marketing, knowledge, innovation, retained earnings and profits, while extending their markets and sphere of operation. Additionally companies undertaking FDI may be seeking to over-

---

Business illustration of import tariffs - US steel industry

In March 2003, under pressure from US steel manufacturers, George Bush introduced a 30 per cent tariff on imported steel. This import tariff was designed to protect America's ailing steel industry from cheaper imports produced by European countries, Japan and other steel producing nations. The tariffs were viewed as unfair and a case was taken to the World Trade Organisation (WTO) by the EU, Japan, South Korea, Switzerland, Norway, New Zealand and Brazil. The WTO ruled the tariffs had been implemented unjustly.

Source: 'US Steel tariffs break WTO rules', *BBC Online*, 11 July 2003.

---

come possible import quotas, trade barriers and import tariffs. Import quotas limit the goods which can be imported into a country; trade barriers prohibit the import of goods from another country and are often put in place to protect home producers; and import tariffs protect home producers by making imported goods more expensive (see Business illustration on US steel industry).

Companies considering undertaking FDI will examine the value to weight ratio of goods before deciding to export or manufacture overseas. Goods which are expensive to export and transport are often manufactured overseas close to the market of consumption. Such goods normally have a low value to weight ratio; examples include soft drinks and beer, which are often manufactured under licence in the foreign market. Goods which have a high value to weight ratio are easier to transport and will often be manufactured in one location and exported to the marketplaces where they are to be sold and used. Examples include microchips, computers, communications and medical equipment. Other FDI projects can include services and, as in the case of Disney (see Entry case study 9.1), the distribution of TV programmes overseas. Disney as part of their international strategy is planning to launch new Disney channels in both India and China, and expand ESPN sports in Europe and Asia.

THE BENEFITS AND COSTS OF FDI

FDI benefits for the host country

If a country is receptive to overseas companies and allows FDI to occur, then a positive contribution is made to the economy via FDI as local staff are employed, providing them with income which is spent in the local economy

---

Business illustration of FDI benefits to host country – Nissan in the UK

In February 2005 the UK car industry received a boost when Nissan announced an investment of £223 million to build a new model, which will help take UK car production to 1.65 million vehicles a year.

The new model was seen as the Qashqai concept vehicle at the 2004 Geneva motor show. Its production starts in 2006 at Nissan's Tyne and Wear factory and 130,000 cars per annum will be built, taking total plant production to 400,000 vehicles. This inward FDI in the UK will create 200 new jobs at Nissan and safeguard the company's existing 1,000 workers and 4,000 staff employed by suppliers.

Source: 'Nissan invests £223m to build new car in Britain', Andrew English and Christopher Hope, *Daily Telegraph*, 2 February 2005.

(see Business illustration on Nissan in the UK). If the FDI is a greenfield project further employment is created as a result of any construction projects associated with the FDI and extra new jobs are created when the FDI project starts operating, all contributing to economic growth.

Depending on the HR strategy – ethno-centric/poly-centric/geo-centric (see earlier section in this chapter) – there will be the development of skills in the labour market. Overall FDI will have a positive effect on the balance of payments of the country which allows FDI to occur, as the goods produced will be sold and some are likely to be exported. This limits the impact of imports, which have a negative impact on the country's balance of payments.

FDI costs for the host country

Countries may be at a disadvantage as a result of allowing FDI to occur as the competition from multinationals may be too strong for local companies and they may be priced out of the marketplace. The profits made by the multinational company may flow out to the multinational's home country, hence the profit is not spent in the local economy. The multinational may import supplies and inputs, hence local suppliers and the local economy do not benefit from doing business with the multinational.

FDI benefits for the home country

The benefits to the home country of companies operating overseas and undertaking FDI are that an inflow of foreign earnings is generated, for example Starbucks' earnings in SE Asia are returned to the US, adding to Starbucks' home country's balance of payments. Employment is created in the home economy if home suppliers are used and in turn the home country benefits, whereas the host country does not benefit if capital equipment and consumable supplies are imported by foreign companies. Additionally skills and knowledge developed overseas by companies which have undertaken FDI can be transferred back to the home economy, for example Ford's acquisition of Mazda was used to transfer knowledge of the Japanese car industry back to Ford's US manufacturing plants.

FDI costs for the home country

A home country's trade position deteriorates if FDI is used by companies to serve their home market from a low-cost location. For example, US companies transferring manufacturing to Mexico where labour cost are low and then exporting finished goods back into the US has a negative impact on the US economy, as employment and the spending of wages earned all occur in Mexico, not the US – so it is the Mexican economy that benefits. This strategy is used by companies like Levis who no longer manufacture in the US (see Business illustration on Levi Strauss). Overall there will be a negative impact on the US economy and balance of payments. Similarly Toyota's FDI in the US is a substitute for exporting from Japan, hence having a negative impact on Japan's economy and balance of payments, with the impact being greater if unemployment is high in the home country. A country's balance of payments is reduced if FDI is a direct substitute for exporting and if FDI is a substitute for home production, then unemployment levels may rise in the home economy.

Business illustration of FDI costs for the home country – Levi Strauss

In 2003 Levi Strauss announced it was to close its last two remaining manufacturing plants based in the US at San Antonio and the last two manufacturing plants in Canada would close by March 2004. This meant a total loss of 2,000 jobs in North America. However, the production of Levi jeans was to continue via contract manufacturers in the Far East. Levi-Strauss maintains its headquarters in San Francisco and simply markets the jeans.

Source: 'The all-American Levi's jeans ride into the sunset', Oliver Poole, *Daily Telegraph*, 27 September 2003.

Review questions | Foreign direct investment

1 List the different methods for undertaking FDI and highlight which is the most popular method for FDI among European companies.

2 Why is FDI by acquisition most common in developed countries?

3 Summarise the barriers to trade which can be overcome by a company undertaking FDI.

4 Summarise the advantages and disadvantages of FDI for both home and host countries.

CHARACTERISTICS AND APPROACHES TO FDI

The major economies of the world all participate in FDI and all countries have their individual characteristics as destinations for inward FDI and as investors overseas (see Exhibit 9.10). The following section seeks to provide a brief overview of each country's situation with regard to FDI.

North America

North America comprises the US, Canada and Mexico, the three countries which make up the North American Free Trade Association (NAFTA). The US is the second most attractive location for inward FDI in the world, China is first.[20] In 2003 inward FDI in the US was $30 billion and in 2004 it was in

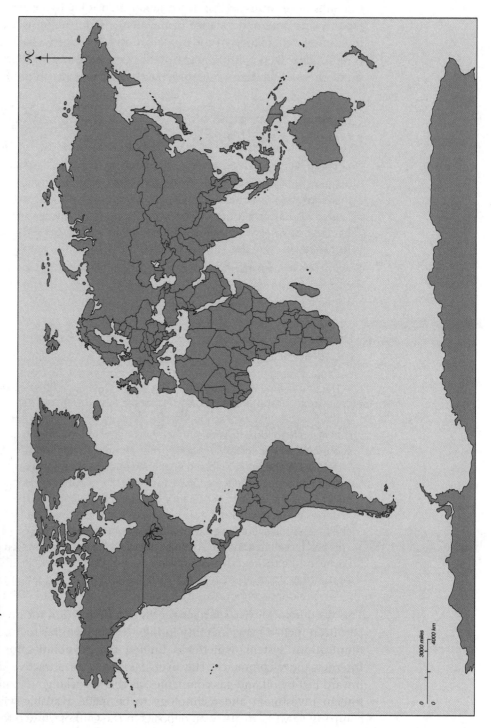

Exhibit 9.10 Map of the world

excess of $85 billion. This is clearly illustrated by the large number of foreign companies operating in the US, e.g. BP, RBS and Tesco. Countries which are receptive to and attract FDI commonly have a stable economy, are politically stable, and are a large geographic market in which many consumers have moderate to high levels of income. Equally, for the US outward FDI is significant and was $152 billion in 2003 – more than twice that of the next largest outward FDI investor, France, but still below the peak of $209 billion of outward FDI from the USA in 1999.[21]

In 2003 Canadian outward FDI fell to $6.6 billion from $21 billion the previous year, along with a reduction of inward FDI from the UK, Canada's largest European investor. However, Canada remains an attractive investment opportunity for heavy manufacturing sectors, and oil and gas companies. Additionally Canada has a growing population of working age and this results in a greater demand for consumer goods and financial services.[22]

Mexico was seen as an attractive location for overseas investment in the 1990s, but this has now changed with the emergence of China, Brazil, India and Poland as countries which are successful in providing low-cost labour and high production volumes. One major example concerns the manufacturing of socks (see Business illustration on sock manufacture).

Business illustration of the impact of FDI – sock manufacture

In the mid 1970s Mrs Hong lived in the village Datang, which is about four hours drive south west of Shanghai. Mrs Hong was fed up with Mao Tse-Tung's doctrine and her lack of pay as a school teacher, so she started making socks which she sold illegally to lorry drivers at a nearby junction on the main road. This proved successful, as her socks were better than those available via the state shops. Then in 1978 the Deng Xiaoping economic reforms allowed Mrs Hong to set up a small factory and produce and sell socks legally. In 2005 Mrs Hong's sock factory was the largest sock factory in Datang and along with the other sock factories in the town, around six billion pairs of socks are manufactured per annum and the average salary of a factory worker is around £65 per month. This has threatened the American sock producing industry centred on Fort Payne, as the US imported 265 million pairs of Chinese socks in 2003!

Source: 'Woman who makes 12 billion socks a year', R Spencer, *Daily Telegraph*, 17 November 2004.

This decline in Mexico's attractiveness as a destination for inward FDI has in part been fuelled by its inability to fully reform its infrastructure and telecommunications system, which has limited the possibilities for access to the Internet and e-commerce. However, Mexico is an attractive destination for inward FDI by oil and gas companies, as the Mexican government is keen for foreign investment and technology to be made available, via the state oil company PEMEX, to allow oil deposits in the Gulf of Mexico to be accessed.[23] Finally Mexico, not surprisingly, attracts inward FDI from both Canada and the USA, which provide more than half of inward FDI in Mexico.

China and India

China and India are currently two of the most popular destinations for FDI investment by overseas companies and this is expected to continue for at least the next ten years. China is viewed as providing manufacturing and assembly activities, which means FDI in China is capital intensive. In contrast India is viewed as providing IT, research and development, and business processing activities. This means FDI in India is less capital intensive than in China, but is education and skills based to a greater degree than in China. The most attractive features of India to investors are its: well-educated workforce; management talent; legal systems and the rule of law; transparency in undertaking transactions; and manageable cultural barriers. In contrast the most attractive characteristics of China for overseas investors are its: market size; potential for market growth; ease of access to export markets; government incentives; and the cost of labour.[24]

The risks of investing in China and India are perceived as being different for each country. In China the greatest risks of investing are deemed to be: the levels of regulation, piracy and corruption, along with foreign exchange controls and political reform. In India the greatest risks to overseas investors are perceived to be: the amount of bureaucracy, political stability and the geo-political risk (that is the Pakistan and Kashmir situation), along with the limited infrastructure development and the likelihood that low labour cost advantages cannot be maintained in India.[25]

Australia and Pacific Rim countries

The rapid growth of the Pacific Rim economy in the 1980s and 1990s has been due to countries such as Singapore, Malaysia, Thailand, Indonesia and the Philippines being relatively politically stable. The limited regulation of the economy has made such countries attractive to multinationals, such as McDonalds, IKEA, B&Q, Starbucks, Coca-Cola, Gap and Nokia. The economic development of China, and its membership of the World Trade Organisation (WTO) in January 2002, has meant major markets such as the USA are permanently accessible to companies from China. This is further illustrated by the lifting of the global Multi-Fibre Agreement on 1 January 2005, which lifted export quotas from China and other Asian countries, giving them unlimited access to America's clothing market. The side effect of this has been serious damage to the textile industry in Lesotho and other African countries.[26]

Australia receives significant FDI from British companies (for historic reasons) and from American companies. American companies make the largest amount of FDI in Australia and this looks set to grow by the introduction, in 2005, of the Australia–United States Free Trade Agreement (AUSFTA), providing greater and easier access to Australian markets for US companies. Additionally Australia seeks to develop and improve its trade links with the Association of South East Asian Nations (ASEAN) and in particular Singapore, which views Australia as an attractive FDI destination.[27]

Equally Australia views Singapore as an attractive FDI destination and significant amounts of inward FDI investment in Singapore are provided by Australian and French investors. Additionally the US–Singapore Free Trade agreement is designed to encourage further amounts of American FDI. Singapore is viewed as a financial hub in Asia and has an IT-driven economy. There are very high levels of IT infrastructure, mobile phone and Internet use underpinning industry, banking and retailing.[28]

Hong Kong, although now part of China, is often viewed as an FDI destination in its own right. Hong Kong's economy, which grew 12 per cent in the second quarter of 2004, is the second most popular destination for outward FDI by Asian companies after mainland China. This is due in part to Hong Kong's low taxes, good infrastructure and strong legal system. In 2003 the Closer Economic Partnership Agreement (CEPA) between Hong Kong and mainland China came into force and will further develop the trading relationship between the two 'countries'. This agreement should improve the flow of investment from Hong Kong to China, for both Hong Kong companies and overseas companies which have already invested in Hong Kong, along with improved access to markets.[29]

Malaysia

The largest amounts of FDI investment in Malaysia come from Australian and Singaporean investors, in both heavy and light manufacturing sectors, which include electronics, computer equipment, industrial equipment and fabricated metal products. Malaysia has high reserves, low inflation and a government which is keen to tackle corruption, thereby making Malaysia an attractive destination for FDI. The potential threats to Malaysia as an attractive FDI location arise from the emigration of its graduates and skilled labour to better paid jobs in the West and Singapore, and militant Islamic terror groups operating in neighbouring Thailand close to the Malaysian border.[30]

Indonesia

Indonesia struggles to maintain positive inflows of FDI and although in 2002 the FDI balance was $145 million this dropped to a negative balance of $597 million in 2003, as companies find Indonesia a difficult business environment in which to operate. The problematic business environment faced by overseas companies investing in Indonesia arises from the following challenges and threats: the high levels of bureaucracy, poor infrastructure, unstable financial systems, high national debt, widespread corruption, and terrorism. Examples of high profile incidents include the Bali bombings, and pirate attacks on international shipping in the Straits of Malacca.[31]

However, with oil prices hitting $100 a barrel in January 2007, and China's ever growing demand for energy, oil and gas companies are prepared to face the challenges of operating in Indonesia. Indonesia is a member of the

Organization of Petroleum Exporting Countries (OPEC) and as well as the state-owned Indonesian oil company Pertamina, Chinese, Italian, Australian, British and American energy companies all operate in Indonesia.[32]

Europe

In Europe the UK, which is viewed as having a innovation and technology driven economy, is the most attractive destination for FDI by US companies, accounting for 15 per cent of total US outward FDI. The UK along with Eire also provides what is seen as an 'offshore' Celtic fringe with locations such as Belfast and Glasgow able to offer well-educated workforces and a developed infrastructure, with costs being significantly lower than in London and the South East. Additionally there is also clearly the same low level of risk with regard to political and economic stability and security of intellectual property as exists in London and the South East. The UK is also a large provider of FDI outward flows, investing $55 billion overseas in 2003, behind only the US and France.[33]

In overall terms France receives three times more inward FDI than either the UK ($14.5 billion in 2003) or Germany ($13 billion in 2003), with much of the FDI being in high value sectors such as pharmaceuticals, telecoms, IT, chemicals and automotives. Germany has become a marginal outward FDI country, with inward FDI falling from $36 billion in 2002 to $13 billion in 2003, while outward FDI has fallen from $109 billion in 1999 to only $2.6 billion in 2003. Germany has good manufacturing, innovation and technical expertise; however, the German tax system is expensive with non-wage costs such as social benefits, healthcare and pensions all set to rise due to an ageing population.[34]

In Spain inward FDI is most likely to come from companies in the chemical and transportation sectors. Inward FDI in light manufacturing sectors has reduced in recent years as Spain no longer has a low labour cost advantage; wages in Spain are three times higher than in Poland, the Czech Republic and Hungary, which are now all EU members.[35]

Italy saw an increase in inward FDI from $14.5 billion in 2002 to $16.4 billion in 2003; however, Italy has a very rigid labour market, inefficient government, and in parts of the country has a relatively poor infrastructure, which together make the country relatively unattractive as a destination for inward FDI. This is illustrated by only 5.8 per cent of gross capital formation coming from inward FDI compared with an average of 14.7 per cent for EU countries overall.[36]

In Europe in 2004 ten new member states joined the EU: the Czech Republic, Estonia, Latvia, Lithuania, Hungary, Cyprus, Malta, Poland, Slovenia and Slovakia. These countries are seen as attractive markets for consumer goods; however, in some cases, poor infrastructure and corruption limit their attractiveness as a location for inward FDI. Membership of the EU and economic reforms will allow these and other factors such as inefficient supply chains and inflexible labour markets to be tackled. However, resolving the inefficiencies of these economies will eventually reduce the cost advantages of operating in countries like Hungary and Latvia and hence their attractiveness as a location for inward FDI will be reduced.[37]

Poland is viewed as a lower risk location for inward FDI than China, India, Brazil and Mexico; however, 20 per cent of employment in Poland is in agriculture, which accounts for only 3 per cent of GDP. Therefore the Polish economy faces a difficult transition period as it industrialises further.[38]

Russia, while not part of the EU, is a close neighbour of an enlarged EU and is attractive as a destination for inward FDI. Inward FDI in Russia occurs mainly in the oil and gas sectors, although there is a fast-growing market for consumer goods, catering, food and beverages, and a significant amount of demand is catered for by inward FDI. However, the Yukos affair, terrorist attacks, and limited reform of the Russian economy all diminish Russia's attractiveness as a destination for inward FDI.[39]

South America

In the 1990s South America attracted increasing amounts of FDI as markets opened up, and deregulation and privatisation occurred; by 1999 South America attracted 27 per cent of the world's FDI in developing countries. However, by 2003 this had fallen to just 11 per cent due to Eastern Europe and Asia attracting ever-increasing amounts of FDI. However, high economic growth is expected in South America as China continues to demand ever-increasing amounts of the commodities which are produced in South America, such as oil, minerals and soya beans.[40]

South Africa

Inward FDI in South Africa is largely provided by British, French, Swiss and Italian investors, with a strong focus on the transportation and automotive sectors. The attractiveness of South Africa as an FDI destination arises from its decent infrastructure and macro-economic policies; however, crime and the prevalence of HIV and Aids both lessen the country's competitive position. Therefore FDI in South Africa is less than in other developing economies such as China, India and Brazil.[41]

Review questions Characteristics and approaches to FDI

1 Identify the main FDI trends in European countries.

2 Explain the impact of economic growth in China on the American market.

3 Specify the differences between India and China as FDI destinations.

CONCLUSION

This chapter has sought to examine aspects of strategy which relate to organisations operating in the worldwide arena. Hence reasons for operating worldwide including the state of a company's domestic market and evaluation of the proposed international marketplace are covered. This is followed by discussion of the strategic choices companies have to make concerning worldwide strategy, which will be influenced by the pressures for cost reductions and local responsiveness in the worldwide marketplaces. Additionally, the staff required and the staff it is possible to employ in a particular country influence the type of HR strategy it is possible to pursue. Finally the worldwide marketplaces or different countries companies may choose to operate in are examined, by looking at advantages and disadvantages of being a home or host country for FDI and by reviewing particular FDI destinations such as China, India, US and Europe.

LEARNING OUTCOMES AND SUMMARY

The learning outcomes for this chapter are specified and a brief summary of the material relating to the learning outcomes is provided.

→ **Learning outcome 1**
Discuss reasons for companies choosing to operate overseas.

- Companies choose to internationalise for a variety of reasons, which are often connected to difficulties in the domestic markets. Difficulties in the home market could include cost pressures and competitive pressures, as well as small, slow growing and saturated home markets.
- Prior to going international a company must weigh up the risks and evaluate its ability to operate overseas and evaluate its chosen overseas environment. The international environment should be assessed in terms of its politics, economy and culture.

→ **Learning outcome 2**
Identify and evaluate the impact of key aspects of the external environment likely on a company operating worldwide.

- In evaluating the political environment of an overseas market, the following should be examined: the political system – democracy or autocracy; the level of political stability and the receptiveness of the host government to foreign trade and investment.
- The economy of an overseas market should be looked at in terms of the country's industrial structure, its income distribution and the type of economy operating (planned, mixed or free).
- The culture of a different country requires some knowledge of different aspects of that country and its society. The aspects which should be under-

stood are politics; the economy; the education system; language; social structure; religion.

→ Learning outcome 3
Identify and discuss strategies which a company operating in a worldwide environment may pursue.

- A company operating internationally should understand the pressures from the overseas market for cost reductions and local responsiveness, as these factors will determine the most appropriate worldwide strategy.
- Possible worldwide strategies are the international strategy, which is used when the pressures for cost reductions and local responsiveness are low. In contrast a trans-national strategy is used when pressures for cost reductions and local responsiveness are both high, making a trans-national strategy difficult to implement.
- The other two worldwide strategies are a multi-domestic strategy and a global strategy. The multi-domestic strategy is appropriate when the pressures for cost reductions are low and the pressure for local responsiveness is high. The global strategy is used when the pressure for local responsiveness is low and the pressure for cost reductions is high.

→ Learning outcome 4
Indicate possible HR strategies for companies pursuing different worldwide strategies.

- When operating worldwide, companies have to staff the overseas ventures. There are three international HR strategies, namely geo-centric, poly-centric and ethno-centric. A geo-centric strategy is the seeking of the best person for the job. The poly-centric strategy is where key roles overseas are occupied by home country nationals, while subsidiaries are managed by host country nationals. The ethno-centric strategy is where home country nationals occupy all management roles.

→ Learning outcome 5
Discuss the advantages and disadvantages for home and host countries of pursuing FDI.

- A country allowing FDI to occur will see a positive contribution to its economy, as local staff will be employed, jobs created, and incomes spent locally. The downside for a country of allowing FDI to occur is that multinationals may price local competitors out of the marketplace. Additionally the local economy will not benefit if multinationals import supplies and export profits.
- The benefits to a home country of allowing companies to undertake FDI are that home suppliers have more business, if supplies are exported overseas, while skills and profits created overseas may flow back to the home country. The disadvantages to a home country occur when FDI is used to export jobs to low-cost locations, which then enables low-cost goods to be imported back into the home country.

→ **Learning outcome 6**
Summarise the characteristics of FDI in the major world economies, for example China, India, Europe and USA.

- All the major economies of the world participate in FDI and all countries have their individual characteristics as destinations for inward FDI and as investors overseas. The USA, China and India are some of the largest participants in FDI activity. In stark contrast Africa does not participate extensively in FDI.

This exit case study looks at Burberry and its business in Japan and can be used to assess the learning outcomes below.

Learning outcomes	Check you have achieved this by	
1 Analyse an international business environment.	Explaining the attractiveness of a particular international business environment.	Answering Exit case study question 1.
2 Understand the concept of the marketing mix.	Identifying or developing the marketing mix for a product.	Answering Exit case study question 2.
3 Identify the impact of pressures for cost reductions and local responsiveness in markets.	Discuss how pressures for cost reductions and local responsiveness impact on how a company operates in a particular market.	Answering Exit case study question 3.
4 Develop a worldwide strategy.	Examining and discussing how companies use their international and competitive strategies to operate worldwide.	Answering Exit case study question 4.

Burberry tailors a fresh image in Japan   **FT**

by Mariko Sanchanta

The ephemeral sakura blossoms that are Japan's harbinger of spring have faded and last Friday the weather had turned in Tokyo. Just before 10am, a few curious customers were queuing in front of the new Burberry shop in Ometesando, a shopping street in Tokyo reminiscent of Paris's Champs Elysées.

Inside, black-clad Burberry staff buzzed about attending to last-minute details before the shop opened to the public for the first time. Their urgency was exacerbated by the imminent arrival of several company officials, including chief executive Rose Marie Bravo. The opening was the climax in a week of Burberry-related marketing events in Tokyo, including a fashion show of

the exclusive Prorsum fall line, the first time the collection has been shown outside Milan. For Burberry, a British brand with a history that dates back more than a century, the success of the shop is critical. The Japanese market contributes half the company's brand sales, but growth there has been stagnant owing to a competitive market and the maturity of the Burberry brand.

Ms Bravo, an American who was previously at the helm of Saks Fifth Avenue, has been widely credited with enlivening Burberry's staid image. On her arrival in 1997, she set about reining in the company's licences, which had led to a proliferation of its trademark check-patterned goods that diluted the cachet of the brand.

A new advertising campaign featured models such as Kate Moss in an effort to target a younger audience. Ms Bravo has overseen adaptations of the trademark check: sometimes loud but often extremely subtle.

In Japan, Burberry renegotiated licence agreements with its two partners, Sanyo Shokai, a clothing manufacturer, and Mitsui, the trading house, which are responsible for producing nearly all the company's merchandise in the country. The licences are valid until 2010, with a 10-year renewal clause based on volume growth. The agreement includes a 'step-up clause' that increases the royalty fees Burberry receives until 2005. After then, there are no increases in royalty fees until 2010. The company also set up a Burberry representative office in Japan in 2002 in an effort to work more closely with its partners.

The Burberry brand appeals to a wide range of customers in Japan, from high-school students to middle-aged housewives. Sanyo Shokai has produced a Blue Label line for Burberry in Japan which targets younger Japanese women, and a Black Label for young men. For consumers who prefer the quality of Burberry products made abroad, the company carries imports under its Burberry London and Prorsum labels at both its Ginza and Ometesando flagship stores. 'We are very happy with what our licensees have created, with an appeal to the younger consumer,' says Ms Bravo, seated on a plush banquette in the shop. 'We believe that in a market as big as Japan, one can speak to many different customer groups. Our positioning has always been about accessibility. [The locally produced labels] can exist in harmony with what we are bringing in here on an imported basis.'

Under Ms Bravo, Burberry acquired brand licensees and distributors in Spain, South Korea and elsewhere in Asia, thereby tightening its grip on production, distribution and marketing – a strategy that Gucci undertook in the 1990s under the leadership of Domenico De Sole, its president. 'There was a moment in the 1980s where everything was licensed and the idea was: just take my name, pay me a royalty and I'll see you next year when the cheque comes in. And then we went very dramatic and said absolutely no licensing in the industry,' says Ms Bravo. 'Now I'm hearing and feeling that there is more of an openness to the approach; that maybe a licence can be done on a different basis. In general, people are forming partnerships in a more proactive way, where the brand has more input and is not solely interested in the royalty.'

Nonetheless, Japanese licensing agreements accounted for 38 per cent of Burberry's earnings before interest, tax and amortisation (ebita) in the 2002 fiscal year, according to Credit Suisse First Boston. Growing licensing activities requires a low capital investment and has high ebita margins; however, if demand increases, Burberry's gain is limited to the increase in royalties, which represent a small percentage of sales under its brand name.

In Japan, where sales have been more or less flat in recent years, the licensing agreements make sense as they provide Burberry with a steady stream of royalty income. Next year, the licence on the Burberry London line will expire in Japan, providing the company with considerable leverage to develop the brand, primarily through accessories – an area with a weak presence in Japan.

'Volume growth going forward for Burberry in Japan is virtually flat, as the company does not have the ability to pass on huge price increases to the consumer with its focus on apparel,' says Antoine Colonna, a luxury goods analyst with Merrill Lynch in Paris. 'But designer handbags, with their high profit margins, are a huge category in Japan. This is an area in which Burberry has a very high potential to increase growth.'

Investors and analysts hold Ms Bravo in high regard, and to many she is the chief engineer behind the brand's rebirth. Charismatic and a straight talker, Ms Bravo is very much the public face of the company: rumours that she might leave for Gucci in the wake of Mr De Sole's departure sent Burberry's share price lower. But Ms Bravo is quick to say that she thinks the attention she has received has been undeserved. 'I've been unfairly credited with the success of the brand. It has been a team effort and it is never about just one person,' she says. 'I think the "star CEO" concept has been overrated.' Ms Bravo says Burberry will focus on continuing to grow in the Japanese market and will more clearly define each label in the country, while differentiating its imported products from locally made goods.

As the clock strikes 11am, a Japanese Burberry employee slides over and whispers that the store is about to open: Ms Bravo is to be downstairs to greet the Ometesando customers for the first time. She jumps up and scurries down the stairs. Outside, the original handful of customers has multiplied and soon a long line snakes up and around the shop's stairs. In a few minutes these Japanese consumers will sample for the first time the wares of the new 6,000 sq ft shop which houses an 'Art of the Trench' corner where shoppers can acquire imported, made-to-order trenchcoats for a base price of ¥200,000 ($1,857).

→

It is Ms Bravo's hope that they will not just browse, but buy.

The quest for staying power in a world of passing fancies

It was hard in the late 1990s to escape the ubiquitous plaid Burberry scarf in Japan. Seemingly every other high-school student topped off his or her outfit with the accessory, which was considered an affordable luxury product, writes Mariko Sanchanta.

Demand was so high that Ito-Yokado and Aeon, Japan's leading mass retailers, offered them at between Y3,900 and Y7,800 ($36–$73). But they had to recall the scarves and pay refunds after an investigation by an industry watchdog and Burberry determined that most were knock-offs. Burberry subsequently re-examined its licensing agreements in Japan and renegotiated several contracts in 2000. Although counterfeiting is not a big problem in Japan compared with China and other Asian countries, the fake scarves highlighted how too many licensing and distribution agreements can tarnish a brand.

Today, Burberry scarves in Japan are not as visible as they once were, and the fad that spread among teenagers has passed. The challenge for many luxury brands in Japan is just this: how to ensure products are not merely passing trends, particularly among fickle young consumers.

Michael Causton, publisher of *Japan Consuming*, the trade magazine, says overall consumer spending on luxury brands is increasing, but the amount of money spent per consumer on a single brand is falling as shoppers diversify their spending. The proliferation of luxury brands over the years means consumers have more options. The sheer amount of advertising, in-store promotions and advertorials in women's fashion magazines attests to the severe competition among luxury goods makers. Often, having one signature product can distinguish a brand from its rivals.

Burberry was well-placed to ride the trenchcoat's wave of popularity this spring, as it invented the product. 'We've found in doing business here the past several years that there is no higher appreciation for quality than in Japan,' says Rose Marie Bravo, chief executive. 'They love the credibility of a brand that has been around for centuries. That's something we try to cater to as much as we can.'

Source: *Financial Times*, 15 April 2004.

Exit case study questions

1 Explain why Japan is an attractive international business environment for Burberry to operate in.

2 Identify the marketing mix for Burberry's products, for example trenchcoats, scarves and handbags.

3 Discuss the pressures for cost reductions and local responsiveness in the Japanese market for Burberry.

4 Considering your answers for questions 2 and 3, identify and summarise Burberry's international and competitive strategies, and comment on their success.

DISCUSSION TOPIC

1 Read the paper 'Global strategy . . . in a world of nations' by George Yip, Chapter 11, in *The Strategy Process*, Mintzberg, Lampel, Quinn and Ghosal, Harlow: Prentice Hall, 2003.

2 Using the paper by George Yip, and Chapter 9 of this book, compare and contrast multi-domestic and global strategy.

WIDEN YOUR HORIZONS

1 Widen your horizons by visiting the EU website (www.europa.eu.int) and naming three candidate countries and indicate when they may become EU members.

2 Widen your horizons by visiting the ASEAN website (www.aseansec.org) and summarising the nature of ASEAN's relationship with China. Do you think China will become a member of ASEAN?

3 Widen your horizons by reading the article 'Why ethical sourcing means show and tell' by Lauren Foster and Alexandra Harvey, *Financial Times*, 22 April 2005. Then summarise the main ethical considerations for a Western manufacturer in China.

4 Widen your horizons by reading the articles 'Near shoring brings companies closer to home' by Peter Marsh, in the *Financial Times* on 10 June 2005 and 'Smaller markets "better bet than China"', by Richard McGregor in the *Financial Times* on 6 December 2004. Define 'near shoring' and summarise its benefits over FDI.

WEBLINKS

The websites for this chapter are for some of the key bodies impacting on organisations operating in an international arena.

- The following website is for the European Union.
  www.europa.eu
- The following website is for the North America Free Trade Association.
  www.nafta-sec-alena.org
- The following website is for the Association of South East Asian Nations.
  www.aseansec.org
- This is the website of Burberry, the company looked at in Exit case study 9.2. Visit the website and click on 'About Burberry' to see a brief history from 1856 to 2006.
  www.burberry.com
- This website was established by MIGA, a member of the World Bank Group, and provides lots of information on FDI in different countries.
  www.fdi.net
- This website allows access to interesting articles on FDI without subscription
  www.fdimagazine.com

FURTHER READING

Worldwide strategy and FDI

- Hill, C W L (2004) *Global Business Today*, New York: McGraw Hill.
- Lasserre, P (2003) *Global Strategic Management*, Basingstoke: Palgrave.
- Rugman, A M and Hodgetts, R M (2003) *International Business*, Harlow: Financial Times/Prentice Hall.

Foreign direct investment

- Global Business Policy Council and A T Kearney (2004) 'FDI Confidence Index', Volume 7, October, Alexandria, Virginia.
- Pooley, R (2005) 'The model alliance of Renault and Nissan – how to work successfully

with overseas partners', *Human Resource Management International Digest*, 13, 2, pp 29-32.

■ Smith-Hillman, A V, and Omar, M (2005) 'FDI, international business and regulation', *European Business Review*, 17, 1, pp 69-82.

■ Suh Taewon, and Khan, O J (2003) 'The effects of FDI inflows and ICT infrastructure on exporting in ASEAD/AFTA countries', *International Marketing Review*, 20, 5, pp 554-71.

■ Thomas, M and Hill, H (1999) 'The impact of ethnocentrism on devising and implementing a corporate identity strategy for new international markets', *International Marketing Review*, 16, 4/5, pp 376-90.

■ United Nations Conference on Trade and Development (2004) *The Shift Towards Services*, New York and Geneva.

■ Wint, AG, and Williams, D (2002) 'Attracting FDI to developing countries – a changing role for government', *International Journal of Public Sector Management*, 15, 5, pp 361-74.

REFERENCES

1   Smy, L (2002) 'Amec and De Beers in Canadian diamonds deal', *Financial Times*, 18 November.
2   www.nafta-sec-alena.org
3   Bardacke, T (1997) 'Cambodia rebuffed by Asean', *Financial Times*, 11 July.
4   www.aseansec.org
5   www.swissworld.org
6   Bartlett, C A and Ghoshal, S, 'Managing across borders', in Hill, C W L (2004) *Global Business Today*, New York: McGraw Hill.
7   Ibid.
8   Ibid.
9   Ibid.
10 Ibid.
11 Ibid.
12 Ibid.
13 Hill, C W L (2004) *Global Business Today*, New York: McGraw Hill.
14 Ibid.
15 Ibid.
16 United Nations Conference on Trade and Development (2004) *The Shift Towards Services*, New York and Geneva.
17 Global Business Policy Council and A T Kearney (2004) 'FDI Confidence Index', Volume 7, October, Alexandria, Virginia.
18 Ibid.
19 Anderson, R (2004) 'Ford, Getrag venture heads for Slovakia', *Financial Times*, 1 December.
20 Global Business Policy Council, op. cit.
21 Ibid.
22 Ibid.
23 Ibid.
24 Ibid.
25 Ibid.
26 Blair, D (2005) 'Lesotho facing ruin after textile trade rules change', *Daily Telegraph*, 12 February.
27 Global Business Policy Council, op. cit
28 Ibid.
29 Ibid.

30   Ibid.
31   Ibid.
32   Ibid.
33   Ibid.
34   Ibid.
35   Ibid.
36   Ibid.
37   Ibid.
38   Ibid.
39   Ibid.
40   Ibid.
41   Ibid.

CHAPTER 10

Structure, culture and groups in organisations

Exhibit 10.1 Essential strategy model

Chapter objectives

The key purpose of structure is to help a company organise itself for effective implementation of its strategy. There are a number of generic structures for organisations to adopt, although many will adapt these structures to suit their specific business or adopt a combination of different structures. The other topic to consider is culture and how culture and structure can echo each other, with both determining the type of place an organisation becomes. This is also reflected in how groups and teams are put together and developed in the organisation. Organisational culture, its determinants and development are covered in detail in Chapter 5.

When you have read this chapter and worked through the associated activities you should be able to achieve the objectives specified below.

1 Explain the types of structures which new and small businesses may adopt to trade domestically and overseas.

2 Discuss the types of structures which larger businesses may adopt to trade domestically and overseas.

3 Specify the types of structures which global businesses may adopt.

4 Determine the relationship between structure and organisational culture.

5 Summarise the types of teams and groups in organisations and their development.

This entry case study looks at Sony and the decisions it takes to alter its structure, reduce costs and improve profits.

Sony takes first step towards leaner structure | FT

by David Pilling

Sony on Monday began the process of ridding itself of non-core operations, saying it would sell a 51 per cent stake in five retail-related businesses to Nikko Principal Investments, a private equity company. Neither Sony nor Nikko Principal would discuss the price of the deal, but one person familiar with the agreement said it was likely to be set at around ¥50bn.

The sale is a tentative first step towards paring down Sony's sprawling empire, a strategy announced by Sir Howard Stringer, who became the first foreign chief executive of the iconic Japanese electronics company last June. Sir Howard said in September that he wanted to offload 15 unprofitable business units as a first step, though he did not name them for fear of further damaging company morale.

Nikko Principal will buy a 51 per cent stake in a holding company to be established by Sony, comprising Sony Plaza, B&C Laboratories, Lifeneo, Sony Family Club and Maxim's de Paris. The businesses span a wide range of activities including cosmetics, health spas, mail order company and retail outlets selling imported lifestyle goods. Maxim's, whose signature restaurant is in Sony's landmark building in the upmarket Ginza shopping district, was a trophy possession of Akio Morita, Sony's co-founder. It has since expanded to 18 outlets, including less exclusive pasta restaurants and cafes. The sale, though largely symbolic, is likely to be seen as a signal that Sony's new management team is serious about turning the company around even if that means axing sacred cows.

Nikko Principal said it aimed to float the business off in three to five years. Management would be left largely untouched, it said, but would be encouraged to find synergies, for example marketing cosmetics through its own outlets. Nikko did not expect big redundancies among the 3,000 or so employees of the five businesses, including part-timers. The transaction is due to be completed in May or June when a final price will be agreed.

Sony said it would 'gradually reduce its stake in the holding company' in order to promote the independence of the businesses. People familiar with the transaction said Sony was reluctant to sell the assets all in one go for fear of unnerving staff in other units that might also be spun off.

Separately, Sony said on Monday it had finalised plans to establish a joint venture with NEC for optical disk drives. To be called Sony NEC Optiarc, the venture, which will start operations from April, will control about one-fifth of the market with annual sales of about ¥220bn. Sony will hold a 55 per cent stake.

Sony last month raised its full-year profit forecast after a strong third quarter, saying it would make operating profits of ¥100bn rather than a loss of ¥20bn. The improvement came on the back of strong sales of flat panel TVs and handheld game consoles. The electronics division staged a strong recovery, with a 56 per cent rise in operating profits.

Source: *Financial Times*, 27 February 2006.

INTRODUCTION

This chapter will cover the key implementation issues for developing a successful organisation. Decisions taken and arrived at concerning structure, culture and communication will determine the type of business an organisation becomes, which in turn is linked to the strategic choices the company is able to make concerning its competitive, marketing, growth and international strategies (see Chapters 7, 8 and 9). The principles of structure apply to all organisations, whether commercial, charitable or in the public sector (see Business illustration on Zoological Society of London).

Business illustration of structure - Zoological Society of London

The Zoological Society of London (ZSL), with its best known operation being London Zoo, is an organisation with a clear structure to help manage its diverse range of activities and meet the key aim of 'worldwide conservation of animal and their habitats'. ZSL has five divisions, covering London Zoo; Whipsnade Wild Animal Park in Bedfordshire, north of London; the Institute of Zoology (covers education, including postgraduate Zoology degrees); conservation programmes; and fellowship services (covers fundraising).

Source: www.zsl.org

First, different approaches to structure are looked at, including how to develop structure for domestic and international activity. Domestic structures once established can be adapted to take account of international activity, for example by establishing an export department. However, larger multinational enterprises (MNEs) will require an international structure to help achieve their goals successfully. There are many options including establishing international divisions and subsidiaries, which deal with all overseas operations or developing strategic alliances (see Chapter 8) or undertaking foreign direct investment (see Chapter 9). Next, the impact of culture on structure is covered, before finally examining how this influences communication between people in the structure and culture that have become the organisation.

GENERIC ORGANISATIONAL STRUCTURES

The structures that organisations adopt are usually aligned to one of the five generic organisational structures. These are the **simple structure**; the **functional structure**; the **divisional structure**; the **holding company structure**; and the **matrix structure**.

THE CENTRALISED STRUCTURES

In **centralised structures** top management take all the important and long-term decisions.

The simple and functional organisational structures are **centralised structures** and are suitable for smaller businesses wishing to maintain their current size or those seeking growth, development and eventual restructuring. The centralised structures allow smaller businesses to operate their competitive, marketing, international and growth strategies effectively, with one owner or a small board of directors steering the company towards profit and growth. Hence, the senior management will take the important and long-term decisions in the company. Rules, regulations and procedures will be used to closely govern and direct the jobs and tasks of managers further down the organisation. The managers further down the organisation will be responsible for the departments, products, services and markets on a day-to-day basis and this centralised direction should enable close control and co-ordination. This means maximum benefit from **economies of scale**, elimination of duplication and uniformity of strategy across the company should result. In contrast the potential disadvantages are a loss of centralised control through **diseconomies of scale**, which can lead to communication breakdown, possible insensitivity to local conditions and the vulnerability of the organisation to unexpected events due to the limited range of centralised business activities.

Economies of scale are the improved efficiency gained from undertaking an activity on a large scale

Diseconomies of scale are the loss of efficiency due to poor control and management of a business.

In determining structure, the extent of international activities will have an impact. Companies manage their international activities in at a variety of different ways, with the extent of an organisation's international activity determining the structural arrangements put in place to accommodate that international activity.

The first formal international structure that companies often establish is an export department, as part of a functional structure. In the international functional structure with an export department, management and control will be centralised with the board of directors. As international activities grow international divisions will become more appropriate and restructuring involving the closure of export departments occurs, with international activities being accommodated in newly formed divisions or subsidiaries (see later section on decentralised structures).

The simple structure

The **simple structure** allows the owner to manage a small number of employees in a small business.

The simple structure (see Exhibit 10.2) is centralised, with all short-, medium- and long-term power and decision-making responsibility resting with the managing director, who is also likely to be the owner of the business. The managing director/owner controls and oversees all aspects of the company's operations. Therefore, the simple structure is suitable for a small business in the early stages of growth and development. This allows the managing director/owner to have control over the future growth and development of the business. This makes sense as the managing director/owner will have a financial stake in the business, usually along with expertise relating to the products or services sold by the business and the markets to which it sells. This type of business will often have a **sole trader** or partnership legal structure.

The company YO! Sushi was started in 1997 by Simon Woodroffe with the last of his savings. YO! Sushi restaurants are Japanese sushi conveyer belt restaurants, adapted for Western markets. The first restaurant will have operated with a simple structure with Simon Woodroffe overseeing its setting up, launch and initial day-to-day running. Businesses which start as small businesses usually have a simple structure, and as they grow and develop the structure is likely to change as described below. It is also possible that, as in the case of Simon Woodroffe and YO! Sushi, the founding entrepreneur of a small business which has been successful will sell his or her stake in the company. Simon Woodroffe sold his controlling interest in YO! Sushi to a private equity company for £10 million in 2003. Simon Woodroffe retains a 22 per cent stake in YO! Sushi.[1]

Exhibit 10.2 The simple structure

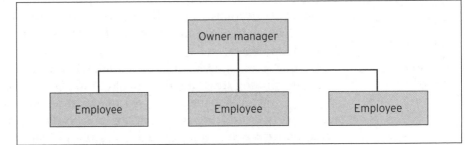

The growth and development of a business means the simple structure becomes less suitable. The managing director/owner finds it more and more difficult to control and oversee the greater number of tasks and activities undertaken by a larger and growing business – or larger number of restaurants as in the case of YO! Sushi. However, the likelihood also exists that the founding entrepreneur, managing director or owner has the skills, knowledge and abilities to run a small business, but may be lacking some of those necessary to run a larger and growing business. This situation usually requires the business to restructure if it is to survive and increase further in size. Simple structure businesses that grow in size commonly develop **functional structures**. If it has not already been considered, at this point in the development of a sole trader or partnership business the owner(s) should look to creating a limited company. This will limit financial liability to the assets of the business.

The functional structure

The **functional structure** is structured around departments and is rigid and centralised.

The functional structure (see Exhibit 10.3) is rigid and centralised with efficient management control systems, and is common in both companies that have outgrown the simple structure and in well-established public-sector organisations. Such organisations are medium sized and have a limited range of related products and services delivered to clearly defined and clearly segmented markets. Variations on the functional structure are looked at below, including the export functional structure and the **global functional structure**.

The functional structure also sees the introduction of specialist functional managers who head the different departments, for example marketing manager, operations manager, finance manager and human resource manager. In the case of growing private companies, these new managers provide the specialist skills, knowledge and abilities that may have been missing under the simple structure.

Exhibit 10.3 The functional structure

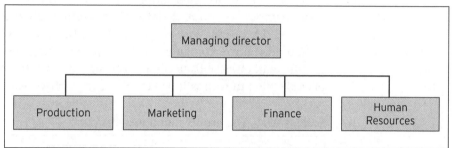

Business illustration of functional structure – Thorntons

The chocolate company Thorntons has elements of the functional structure, with five areas of operation, namely, finance, human resources, trading and marketing, supply chain and retailing. Each area of operations is headed up by a director, with all five directors (finance director, HR director, trading and marketing director, supply chain director and retail director) reporting directly to the chief executive. The directors are all clearly responsible for functional activity, which Thorntons undertakes to manufacture and sell chocolates and other confectionery.

Source: www.thorntons.co.uk

The structuring of the organisation around the different functions or tasks that have to be carried out by its employees results in job roles that are clearly defined and understood by everyone in the organisation (see Business illustration on Thorntons). Short-term decision-making power and responsibility tend to rest with the departmental heads, who have to work together with the board of directors to ensure that what is happening at an operational level also reflects and feeds back into the long-term and medium-term decision-making process. Long- and medium-term decision-making power and responsibility, however, rests very much with the board of directors.

The export functional structure

A company with a functional structure seeking to diversify into an international market can do so by making minor adjustments to its functional structure. The first international sales a company makes are likely to be small additions to domestic operations and initially dealt with as they occur, with no real co-ordination of the overseas activities. Formal incorporation of international transactions will occur via the establishment of an export function or department with its own manager and staff (see Exhibit 10.4). A small export department can either be part of the marketing department or report directly to the managing director. However, it should be noted that any company planning to increase its international activities should ensure that the export department or section undertakes all marketing activities for overseas markets and does not operate just as a sales office. These arrangements if put in place should enable the company to develop marketing specialists who learn the specific marketing skills needed to operate successfully in the overseas marketplaces, which in turn will be key in expanding overseas activity.

Exhibit 10.4 The export functional structure

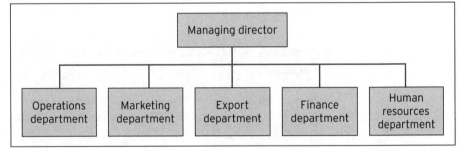

If initial attempts at exporting are successful, the nature of the work undertaken by the export department will develop to include staff actively seeking out overseas opportunities. If the company chooses to move into overseas joint ventures or direct investment, then the export department will cease to be adequate. An expansion of international activities will see more extensive arrangements made to manage overseas business, as the functional structure does not accommodate diversity of product or markets well. Hence the divisional and holding company structures are more suitable for dealing with diversity of markets or products.

The global functional structure

The **global functional structure** allows tight centralised control by a small group of directors over a worldwide organisation.

The global functional structure is similar to the functional structure used in domestic markets and is built around the basic tasks the organisation undertakes. The departmental heads are responsible for domestic and international activity, that is the head of the production department is responsible for all domestic and international manufacturing and the head of marketing is responsible for worldwide sales and marketing (see Exhibit 10.5). The global functional structure allows tight centralised control by a small group of directors or senior managers over a worldwide organisation, with the **centralisation** meaning there will be little duplication of functional activity.

Companies with a narrow product range that have a stable level of both global coverage and demand and have no potentially aggressive competitors often use the global functional structure. The global functional structure is found among raw materials extractors with heavy capital investment.[2] Examples include energy companies – oil, gas, coal – and diamond mining companies. However, it is not a structure that is suitable for very many businesses, as many global markets require at least some level of local responsiveness (see Chapter 9).

Exhibit 10.5 The global functional structure

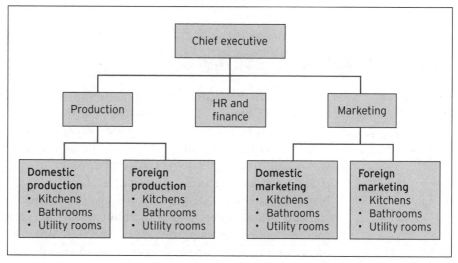

The downside of the global functional structure arises from the potential difficulty in co-ordinating across functions that operate independently of each other, for example production and marketing. Additionally the centralised nature of the structure means responsibility for profits rests primarily with the board of directors as there is little delegation of operating authority to further down the organisation, which can stretch the directors as the business expands and develops.

✔ Check your understanding

- Do you understand when it is appropriate to use the simple and functional structures?
- Check your understanding by showing which structure would be best adopted for each of the following companies.

  1 A plumbing business employing the owner, three qualified plumbers and one apprentice.

→

2 A British company producing high quality commemorative porcelain with most export sales going to the US and Japan.

The simple and functional structures

1 In what type of company is the simple structure most likely to be found?

2 Why does the simple structure become unsuitable for some companies?

3 Explain why the functional structure is often a suitable alternative when the simple structure has become inappropriate for a company.

4 How would a company with a domestic functional structure adjust that structure to enable the start of international business?

5 Briefly discuss the situation in which the global functional structure would be suitable for a company.

THE DECENTRALISED STRUCTURES

In **decentralised structures** decision-making power and responsibility are spread throughout the organisation.

In contrast to the centralised simple and functional structures, the divisional, holding and matrix organisational structures are decentralised and contain operating units, which may be divisions, subsidiaries or project teams.

The decentralised nature of these structures allows companies to spread the decision-making power and responsibility to the middle managers in charge of operating units. This means the company's strategic direction is likely to be established by its senior management, but the company's strategy will be developed with input from these middle managers. Their role in helping develop strategy is crucial, as they will have the responsibility for implementing strategy in the operating units they manage and lead.

Key aspects of any company's strategy will include its approach to competitive, marketing, international and growth strategies, and it is these areas that middle managers should know and understand. In addition good communication and working relationships must exist between middle managers and the board of directors, as decisions made at all levels in the company need to relate to each other and link together if the whole company is to move forward coherently in the same direction. Successful **decentralisation** is necessary to allow flexibility and a quick response to changes in local conditions, which is key if international activity is expanding.

The disadvantages of a decentralised structure are: longer lines of communication between units; potentially harmful competition between decentralised units; and less co-ordination resulting in a lack of uniformity in strategy and actions.

The divisional structure

Companies which adopt a divisional structure will contain separate divisions based around individual product lines or services, for example vehicle rental, pubs and cafes, and garden centres (see Exhibit 10.6). Alternatively, if a company provides a single product or service, divisions can be based on the geographic areas of the markets served, for example Europe, Asia and North America (see Exhibit 10.7). This is the approach to structure taken by the company LexisNexis, which provides news, business and legal information services. LexisNexis has four divisions: North American Legal markets, with headquarters in New York; US Corporate and Federal Markets, with headquarters in Dayton, Ohio; LexisNexis Europe/Canada/Latin America/Africa, with headquarters in London; LexisNexis Asia Pacific with headquarters in Singapore.[3]

This section of the chapter looks at the use of the divisional structure by companies in a variety of situations, for example operating domestically, internationally, with a market focus or with a product focus. Hence the divisional structure (products), the divisional structure (markets), the international divisional structure, the **global area structure** and the **global product structure**, which all contain divisions, are looked at in this section.

Exhibit 10.6 The divisional structure (products)

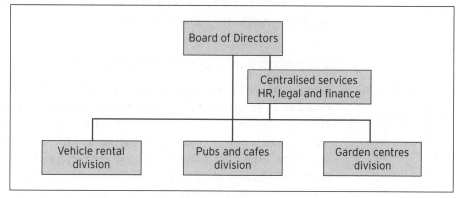

Exhibit 10.7 The divisional structure (markets)

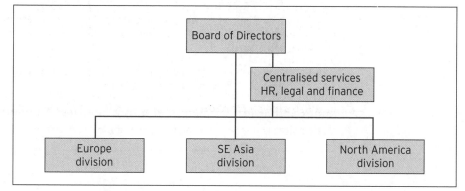

<table>
<tr><td>

Business illustration of divisional structure – Deutsche Bank

Deutsche Bank has a product divisional structure, with three divisions: Corporate and Investment Bank; Corporate Investments; and Private Clients and Asset Management. These divisions are overseen by a Group Executive Committee and are supported by the centralised services (which Deutsche Bank call functional committees) which cover human resources, IT and operations, compliance, assets/liabilities, alternative assets and investments.

Source: www.db.com

</td></tr>
</table>

The divisional structure is decentralised and, as such, a company with a divisional structure usually offers diversity in terms of products or markets (see Business illustration on Deutsche Bank). This is in contrast to a company operating with the more rigid and centralised functional structure. The key benefit of a wide and diverse portfolio is the ability to spread risk and profitability. The divisions in a divisionalised company will be profit centres in their own right, having to manage budgets and satisfy performance criteria relating to profitability and asset use, with profit margins and return on assets likely to be the key measures applied to individual divisions. The company will aggregate the financial information on each division's performance to produce the overall annual company report and accounts.

The international division structure

The **international division structure** centralises all the international operations and lessens the managing director's burden of dealing directly with overseas operations.

A company with successful domestic product or service divisions may expand overseas by establishing an international division (see Exhibits 10.8 and 10.9). Establishing one or more international divisions to deal with all overseas operations is a significant challenge for a company. However, this approach allows for the growth and development of managers with international experience.

Exhibit 10.8 Establishing international divisions

- Ensure strategic fit between structure and international environment to maintain leverage of the company's technologies, economies of scale, and current position in local markets.

- Centralise all international operations to lessen burden on the managing director of dealing directly with overseas operations.

- Raise the profile of overseas operations to that of domestic divisions.

- Centralise decision-making responsibility for overseas operations in one division.

Exhibit 10.9 The international division structure

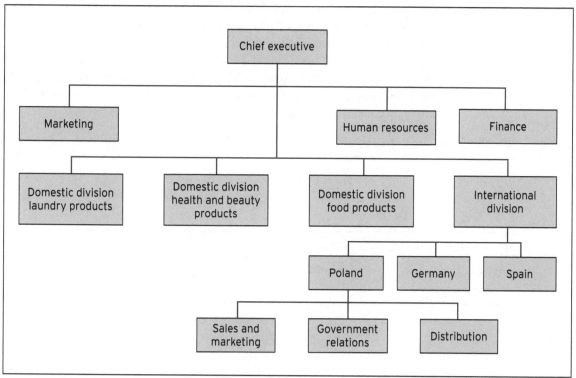

The international division structure has some potential disadvantages. Separating operations into domestic and international may create rivalries, putting pressure on domestic divisions to think in international terms, which can be difficult for a division that has been domestically focused and made most of its sales in home markets. Additionally there can be a tension between centralisation and decentralisation, and agreement will need to be reached as to how much autonomy local managers and staff will have to make decisions which are relevant to local conditions. This will depend on how high the pressures for local responsiveness are (see Chapter 9), and the company's structure will vary according to circumstances and international activities. Regardless, the **international division structure** remains a popular way of formalising the presence of international activity in a company.

The global area structure

The global area structure allows a company to both sell and manufacture locally in various international markets.

A global area structure is based around geographic divisions and allows divisional managers to have primary responsibility for a specific geographic region and all functions within the region – namely production, marketing, HRM and finance (see Exhibits 10.10 and 10.11). Hence the manager in charge of operations in South America will be responsible for all product lines sold in that region.

Companies which both sell and manufacture locally in various international markets will have a global area structure, and will be likely to pursue a multi-domestic strategy (see Chapter 9). In this situation a global area structure will be appropriate, as the pressures for local responsiveness are high and cost pressures are low. Additionally companies that are mature businesses, and have narrow product lines and which are not differentiated by geographic area, commonly use the global area structure which is a poly-centric (host country orientated) structure.

Exhibit 10.10 The global area structure

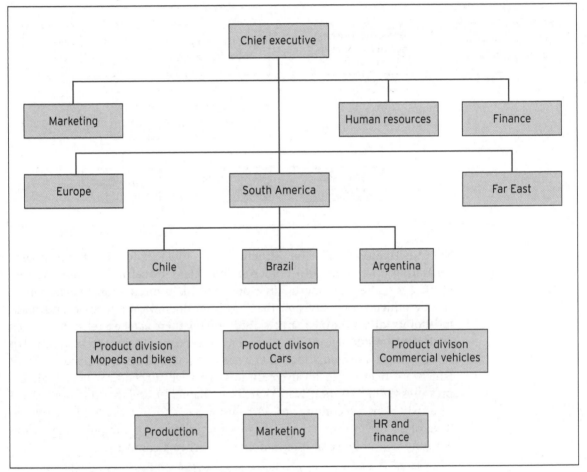

The main disadvantage of the global area structure arises if the products need adapting for local tastes, as the divisional manager is responsible and will need both product and market expertise. Other disadvantages include the expensive duplication of functional activities with, for example, each region having its own production and marketing activities; and the difficulty of co-ordinating the geographically diverse divisions into the company's overall strategy.

Exhibit 10.11 Operating a global area structure

- Divisional managers are able to make rapid decisions and be responsive to local tastes and regulations.

- Company can gain experience of overseas markets and competitive advantage in these markets.

- Suitable where regional manufacturing is undertaken and some economies of scale can be achieved.

- Helps eliminate expensive transportation and distribution costs.

The global product structure

The **global product structure** accommodates manufacturing in a limited number of favourable low cost locations.

The global product structure is based around product divisions and its development allows the divisions to be given worldwide responsibility for product groups (see Exhibit 10.12). Hence each product division sells its goods throughout the world and will therefore operate in a number of countries (see Business illustration on Bayer). The manager of a product division will have control of internal functional support for the whole product line, with all production, marketing, personnel and finance activities managed within the division, and with activities operating from the most cost-effective locations. This means, for example, that manufacturing will be in a limited number of low cost locations. Therefore the global product structure is often adopted by companies pursuing a global strategy (see Chapter 9) as the pressures for cost reductions are high. This is in contrast to a company adopting a global area structure and pursuing a multi-domestic strategy (see previous section on the global area structure and Chapter 9).

Business illustration of global product structure – Bayer Group

The Bayer Group has three self-contained product divisions, Health Care, Material Sciences and Crop Sciences, with each having 'global responsibility for their business and their own management teams'. Hence the Health Care division is responsible for worldwide business in the areas such as animal health, diabetes care, diagnostics and pharmaceuticals. The company also has another division called Service Areas, which provides administrative, engineering and site services, which can be purchased by other Bayer divisions or by external customers. The other key piece of the structure is the 'HQ department' (see Exhibit 10.12) and at Bayer these are part of the corporate centre and include corporate support services and governance.

Source: www.bayer.com

Exhibit 10.12 The global product structure

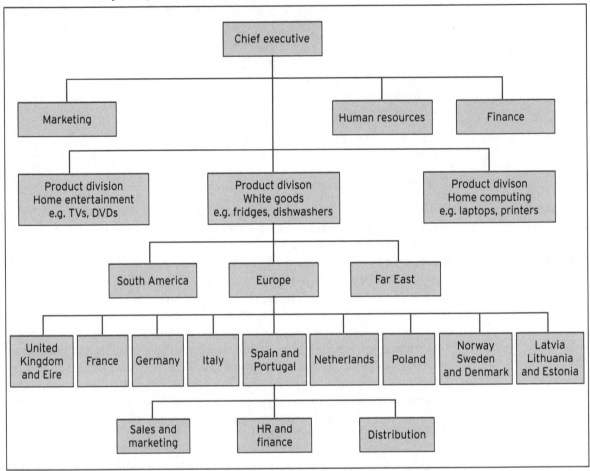

The global product structure relies on the 'profit centre' concept, with each product line expected to meet profit and return on investment targets. Hence the divisional manager has the decision-making power and responsibility to ensure each product line in the division operates as an autonomous business. Providing the product lines meet their financial targets, the division will usually be allowed to operate with limited involvement from head office, although there will often be budgetary constraints imposed by head office.

In a country which a product division has recently entered, the product will be in the introduction or growth phase of the product lifecycle, while in other countries the product may be more established and in the maturity or decline stage of the product lifecycle. The costs and profits associated with different stages of the product lifecycle means different competitive and marketing strategy will be needed. Therefore a global product structure allows the competitive and marketing strategies to be tailored for customers in a particular geographic region, which would be difficult to implement with a functional structure and one centralised marketing department. Additionally the global product division allows the development of well-trained and experienced product managers by providing opportunity in a variety of countries and markets. In contrast, disadvantages of the global product structure are shown in Exhibit 10.13.

Exhibit 10.13 Disadvantages of the global product structure

- The duplication of staff and activities in each division, which is costly and can result in a lack of co-ordination across divisions.

- High selling products attract more resources, while other profitable products end up being sidelined, resulting in a loss of profits.

- A lack of co-operation among the global product divisions can result in decreased sales as, although each division may have information that can be of value to the other, each product division operates independently and communication and co-operation are often discouraged.

✔ Check your understanding

- Do you understand when it is appropriate to use the forms of the divisional structure?
- Check your understanding by showing which structure would be best adopted for each of the following companies.
  1 A chain of department stores selling clothing (for men, women and children), homewares, furniture, carpets, electronic goods, cosmetics and perfume, seasonal gifts (e.g. Christmas, Easter, Valentine's day).
  2 A frozen food producer selling food via supermarkets for domestic use, and frozen food to the catering industry, which has just started to undertake some international business.
  3 A publishing company producing magazines, fictional books and educational books which are sold in Europe, the USA and South America.

Review questions The divisional structure

1 What is a division?
2 Briefly discuss the key advantages of the divisional structure.
3 Identify the advantages and disadvantages of a company having an international division.
4 Explain the type of international strategy a company with a global area structure is most likely to be pursuing.
5 Summarise the advantages and disadvantages of a global area structure.
6 Explain the type of international strategy a company with a global product structure is most likely to be pursuing.
7 Summarise the advantages and disadvantages of a global product structure.

The holding company structure

The **holding company**
structure is found in large
conglomerates with a
parent company owning
smaller subsidiary
companies.

The holding company structure (see Exhibit 10.14) is usually found in large conglomerates with a parent company acting as an investment company acquiring and divesting smaller subsidiary companies. A company operating as a holding company will usually have a small corporate headquarters from which the parent company will conduct business. This means that central overheads will be low because of the economies of scale that this company-wide co-ordination achieves. The finance and legal sections are part of the parent company (see Exhibit 10.14) and their purpose is to provide the expertise needed centrally in the acquisition and divestment of subsidiary companies.

Exhibit 10.14 The holding company structure

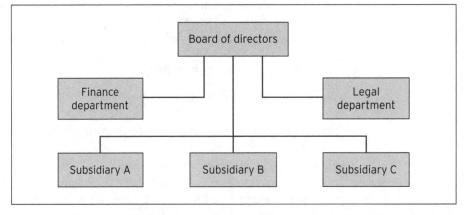

Business illustration of a holding company structure – Gucci

The Gucci Group is a French holding company and it focuses on one main area of activity, that of luxury branded goods. The areas the Gucci Group operate in are ready to wear collections from designers like Alexander McQueen and Stella McCartney; accessories; shoes; fragrances and cosmetics including Yves Saint Laurent and Roger & Gallet; watches and jewellery including Boucheron and Gucci.

Source: www.guccigroup.com

In the holding company structure subsidiary companies normally continue to trade under their own names, with the parent company either wholly owning its subsidiaries or acting as a majority shareholder in them (see Business illustration on Gucci). Subsidiary companies will operate fairly independently of the head office, with all decision-making power and responsibility for their own performance resting with their management. Therefore conglomerates adopting the holding company structure are very decentralised. However, the control systems implemented by head office will tend to centre on the subsidiary companies meeting tight financial targets with regard to profit forecasts, profit margins and return on assets, or risking swift divestment by the holding company.

The ownership of a large number of subsidiary companies in a variety of different industries spreads the risk and profit for the parent company as a whole. The use of subsidiary companies to obtain diversity may ease divestment, especially in the light of poor performance, as that performance can be viewed as being ring-fenced in one or more companies and therefore contained. For example, Gucci could choose to axe its Stella McCartney range and this decision would leave its other businesses – such as its Alexander McQueen collection and Yves Saint Laurent products – unaffected.

The main potential disadvantage of a holding company structure relates to the subsidiary companies, which may view themselves as continuously up for sale. This type of situation invokes a high degree of uncertainty and the likelihood of change can be difficult for the subsidiary companies to manage on a permanent basis. The other potential disadvantages relate to diversity being more difficult to co-ordinate and manage overall than simplicity, and so the holding company management faces a more complex task. The Virgin Group illustrates huge diversity in terms of products and services that it sells and markets, including mobile phones, trains, radio stations and bank accounts, and requires specialist managers and companies in those diverse areas to operate the businesses.

✔ Check your understanding

- Do you understand which type of structure Sony could adopt after it has finished 'the process of ridding itself of non-core operations' (see Entry case study 10.1)?
- Check your understanding by identifying and discussing the characteristics the company managers should take into account when deciding on a structure.

Review questions — **The holding company structure**

1 Describe which type of company often adopts the holding company structure.
2 Explain why the holding company structure is decentralised.
3 Summarise the advantages and disadvantages of the holding company structure.

The matrix structure

The **matrix structure** merges decentralisation with co-ordination across all areas of the business where there are two distinct areas which need to be managed.

The matrix structure has two arms, which represent two areas of activity that need co-ordinating and managing in order to deliver the organisation's products and services. The matrix structure attempts to merge the benefits of decentralisation with co-ordination across all areas of the business. Matrix structures are often found in large multinational companies, educational establishments and small sophisticated service companies.

Exhibit 10.15 The matrix structure: multinational company

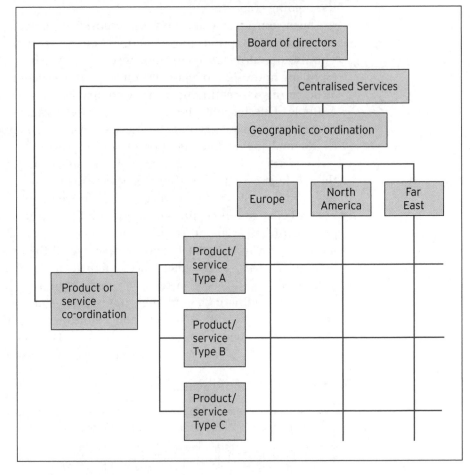

In a large multinational company (see Exhibit 10.15), the two arms of the matrix structure represent the product or service areas and the geographic areas in which the company operates. The product or service arm is responsible for the delivery of a diverse range of products and services, while the geographic arm of the matrix is responsible for the advertising, marketing, sales and distribution of those products or services to the end users in the geographic area for which they are responsible. The geographic arm becomes the customer of the product or service arm, as they purchase the products or services from them, before selling them on to their geographically defined customer base.

In a university business school (see Exhibit 10.16) one arm of the matrix structure is responsible for delivering the products, higher education courses, to their internal customer, the other arm of the matrix. This second arm manages course administration and is therefore responsible for delivering the product on to the end users – the students. The internal customers, the course administrators, can be organised in terms of the type of external customer they serve: full-time or part-time students; undergraduates or postgraduates; funded or fee-paying students. Whatever their provenance, each student grouping is enrolled on one of a number of courses or products, for example BA (Hons) Business Studies, HND Public Policy and Management, Master of Business Administration, or MSc in Human Resource Management. In order for this arm of the matrix to be able to run its courses and satisfy its external customers, it needs the services of the other arm of the matrix, which represents the staff – usually organised in groups that reflect their academic expertise and the subject they teach.

Exhibit 10.16 The matrix structure: educational establishment – university business school

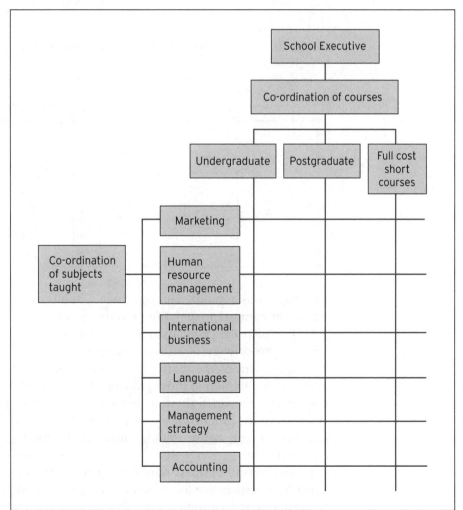

This arm of the matrix is responsible for supplying tutors to classes and for all staff development issues to ensure that individual tutors are competent enough in terms of academic expertise and teaching methodology to deliver the services their internal customers require of them. Hence communication and co-ordination between the two arms of the matrix should centre on subject groups and the course leaders reaching agreement over who will teach what subject to which classes on specified courses – teaching being the main activity occurring in the matrix. The direct contact between people from both arms of the matrix allows decisions to be made by the staff at the sharp end with direct responsibility for running courses and teaching students, which should avoid hierarchical bureaucracy. Decentralisation of responsibility for decision making to people from both arms of the matrix structure should increase the motivation of the staff involved, provided that job tasks and responsibilities are clear. A lack of clarity in people's roles, responsibilities and accountability is a potential disadvantage of the matrix structure.

Exhibit 10.17 The matrix structure: sophisticated service company – design consultancy

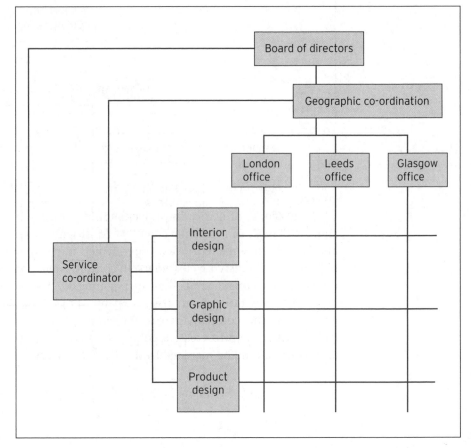

The matrix structure for a small sophisticated service company will contain professional expertise groupings on one arm of the matrix and may contain geographic groupings on the other arm. A design consultancy (see Exhibit 10.17) would operate by having offices in various different regions of Britain to handle the accounts and initial enquiries from clients, as well as having design staff working out of that office. The nature of the project from the client would determine if a team of local design staff could handle it or if a team of designers from across the company's different offices would be required.

Bringing together a team to work on a specific project and then **disbanding** it once the project is complete, only to bring together another team for the next project, is a key feature of the matrix structure and is able to occur due its decentralisation and flexibility.

Making the matrix structure work

Clarity requires ease and transparency with regard to communication and co-ordination.

Consistency requires continuing success with regard to achieving objectives.

Continuity requires the company to remain committed to the same objectives and values to create a cohesive organisational culture.

Whatever the context, whether multinational, private sector, public sector, manufacturing or service, the success of the matrix structure depends on meeting three key criteria, namely **clarity**, **consistency** and **continuity**.[4] Clarity is needed with regard to communication and co-ordination between the two arms of the matrix for any one product or service in any one market. This requires teams consisting of people from both arms of the matrix to work together well at the points where they meet in the matrix and engage in their internal customer relationship. This means job roles and reporting relationships need to be clearly communicated to the workforce. The quality of the end-user or external customer experience depends heavily on the quality of this internal customer relationship between arms of the matrix. Therefore, the main potential difficulty with implementing the matrix structure occurs when people from both arms of the matrix fail to work together and co-ordination and communication break down, thus impeding decision-making processes and adversely affecting the experience of the external customer.

The outcome of clarity in understanding job roles and reporting relationships will assist in the achievement of consistency across operating divisions and in how they relate to each other, which further contributes to achieving objectives and satisfying customers. In contrast a lack of consistency across the operating divisions suggests they are pursuing different objectives, maybe their own objectives rather than the company's objectives. Finally, continuity is achieved if the company remains committed to the same objectives and values, which help to create a coherent and cohesive organisational culture, and which should be matched by a coherent strategy.

GLOBAL ORGANISATIONS

The **global organisation** develops beyond the international organisation in terms of all activities.

Companies that develop beyond being international organisations become **global organisations** and cease to be national companies selling overseas. Global companies plan and develop worldwide activities including manufacturing facilities, global marketing policies, worldwide logistics and distribution, financial systems, and relevant HR policies and procedures which cover expatriate staff. Managers are recruited from many countries and have training and experience in worldwide operations, not just domestic or international operations. Hence a geo-centric HR policy will be pursued as the best people for the job will be sought (see Chapter 9). A global company will also source and purchase components and supplies from where they cost the least and invest in manufacturing where costs are lower, staff skill levels appropriate and expected returns greatest. The global operating units will report directly to the managing director or board and not the head of an international division.

Companies will become more global to compete as foreign companies successfully invade domestic markets. To become a global competitor, the domestic company selling overseas will need to view the whole world as a single borderless market when competing in foreign markets. The increasing levels of competition in global marketplaces means global companies place a premium on organisational flexibility.

✔ Check your understanding

- Do you understand how to apply the matrix structure to an organisation?
- Check your understanding by showing how the following company would look with a matrix structure. The company is a construction company building houses, commercial property and infrastructure projects in China, the US, Canada, Brazil, Mexico and Argentina.

Review questions   The matrix and global structures

1. In what types of organisations is the matrix structure found?
2. Discuss the benefits of a decentralised matrix structure.
3. Name the three key criteria in making the matrix structure work.
4. Explain why the three criteria identified in your answer to question 3 are important in successful implementation of the matrix structure.
5. Define a global organisation.

DETERMINING ORGANISATIONAL STRUCTURE AND CULTURE

The size of an organisation will influence which structure is most suitable. The most suitable structure is that which allows the best and most effective communication and co-ordination within the organisation, which should in turn result in successful implementation of strategy. Hence the size and structure of the organisation dictate the ways in which the people within it are able to operate and the culture the organisation adopts. Organisational culture, its determinants and development are covered in detail in Chapter 5.

Simple structure, power and person cultures

A small, entrepreneurial company with a simple structure will inevitably see and hear the leader regularly, and so staff will have close contact with the original entrepreneur whom they are expected to emulate. The centralised simple structure is that most often adopted by small companies and it offers a number of advantages and disadvantages, but these cease to be appropriate once an organisation has expanded significantly (see earlier in this chapter). In terms of legal structure many small businesses will adopt a sole trader or partnership structure.

The **power culture organisation** is where the owner controls all aspects of the business, represented by a spider at the centre of its web.

The simple structure and the **power culture** echo each other in terms of characteristics, and small companies with a simple structure where the owner works closely with few employees will often exhibit the power culture. This company is a club where the colleagues or employees have been chosen by the owner/manager for their similarity to himself or herself. The centre of power and all crucial decision making is the owner/manager, who either is in personal charge of every aspect of the work or can trust colleagues and employees to do things instinctively the way he or she would have done them. This is depicted by the model (see Exhibit 10.18) which resembles a spider at the centre of its web.

Exhibit 10.18 The power culture

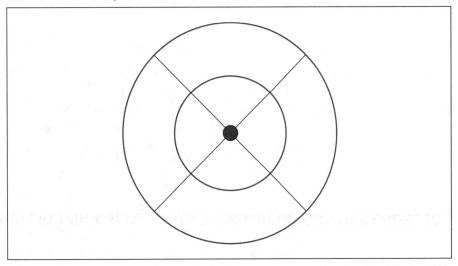

Source: *Understanding Organizations* by Charles Handy (Penguin Books 1976, Fourth Edition 1993). Copyright Charles Handy 1976, 1981, 1985, 1993.

The choice of 'cloned' employees can be deliberate or subconscious on the part of the entrepreneur. Whether explicitly sought or not, an internal culture develops that is intimate and comfortable for those on the inside. This creates further issues for anyone different who tries to join the company, and this is possibly the culture that is least open to equal opportunities issues, as the club members do not wish to admit new members not in their likeness. The power culture is exciting because of the risks involved in its operation, as colleagues at the centre of power make decisions in an unauthorised but implicitly supportive environment. They operate the way they think the entrepreneur would, are rewarded and congratulated when they are correct, but risk disapproval if a mistake is made.

Without the leader, the power centre is lost and the club can break down. Should the leader become ill or die, the organisation grieves and can only recover from its loss with difficulty. This illustrates a danger of the club culture, in that the company becomes over-reliant on the founding entrepreneur who is all too literally the heart and soul of the company.

The **person culture** occurs when professionals collaborate to offer their services and is represented by a number of dots in a circle.

The other type of culture exhibited by small organisations is the **person culture** (see Exhibit 10.19) where a set of professionals agree to collaborate to perform a specific service. The structure adopted in the small organisation with the person culture will not be a simple structure in the traditional sense. There will not be an owner manager, but there may be a senior partner and a practice manager. The senior partner will take responsibility in broad terms for the professional direction of the practice and the practice manager will take responsibility for the day-to-day administration of the practice. In the person culture the role of the practice manager is to organise support staff, receptionists, office staff, nurses and technicians, whose role is to process clients

Exhibit 10.19 The person culture

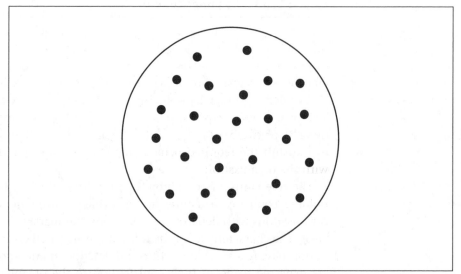

Source: *Understanding Organizations* by Charles Handy (Penguin Books 1976, Fourth Edition 1993). Copyright Charles Handy 1976, 1981, 1985, 1993.

through whatever systems are in place to ensure that the flow of work to the professional is appropriate. This type of arrangement is often found in family doctors' practices, solicitors' practices, barristers' chambers, dentists' practices, architects' offices, management consultancies or design practices.

The professional staff in such practices are likely to be self-employed, or at least would have little notion of being employees of the organisation in the traditional sense. Rather, they see the practice as offering the opportunity to practice their profession in return for payment. They may even avoid the word 'organisation', preferring, as Handy states, terms such as 'practice' to describe the collective activities in which they engage. The person culture centres on the particular professional skills that the individuals possess and without which the organisation could not operate. The individuals consider themselves to be highly valued, unique and often creative. Accountability is often to a professional standards body such as the Law Society for solicitors or the General Medical Council in the case of family doctors in the United Kingdom.

Functional, divisional, holding structures and the role culture

Small companies which successfully grow and develop will alter their structure to accommodate the expanding business. The new structure is often a functional or divisional structure. If the range of products or services remains limited then the functional structure is that most likely to be adopted. If the business grows such that there is increased diversity in its products or markets then one of the divisional, global area or global product structures is more likely to be chosen.

An organisation with a centralised structure, such as the functional structure (including international and global functional structures), will be rigid and mean the company is less able to respond rapidly to major change. In contrast, an organisation with a decentralised structure (including divisional, global area or global product structures) will be able to react more quickly to major change if required to do so. The disadvantage of a decentralised structure is the greater difficulty in co-ordinating an organisation-wide response to change. However, both types of larger, more established companies with clearly defined jobs, departments and divisions will exhibit the **role culture**. This means new recruits will be expected to learn their particular job and tasks quickly for two reasons: to enable them to fit into their position or role; and to transmit the required behaviour to any new people they meet connected with the organisation.

The **role culture** is found in established companies with clearly defined jobs, departments and divisions and is represented by an organisational chart.

The role culture (see Exhibit 10.20) mirrors the functional, divisional and holding company structures and is evident within more mature and larger organisations with departments, divisions and markets in different geographic areas. The characteristics of the role culture are based on everyone in the organisation having a specific job title and description and knowing what it is they are expected to do in their contribution to the organisational mission. Role culture organisations are functional, bureaucratic and highly systematised, with clearly documented, routine procedures and well-organised and efficient operations. Because of their size and the routine nature of their operations, these organisations develop into solid and predictable institutions, which operate the way they do because they have always done things that way. These cultures find an increase in the rate and speed of change a great threat and are thus not adaptive to change.

Exhibit 10.20 The role culture

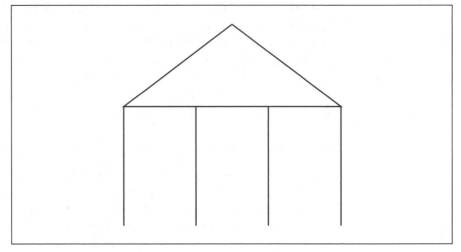

Source: *Understanding Organizations* by Charles Handy (Penguin Books 1976, Fourth Edition 1993). Copyright Charles Handy 1976, 1981, 1985, 1993.

The matrix structure and task culture

Companies often adopt a matrix structure when the work is project based, as it is seen as the most effective arrangement for delivering goods and services to customers. Teams form to undertake specific projects, before disbanding once the project is finished, with the staff then moving on to the next project – as is found in a management consultancy, for example. Handy's **task culture** (see Exhibit 10.21) is flexible and is often displayed in organisations that frequently undertake work for different of customers in a variety of fields. The task culture has close connections with the matrix structure.

The **task culture** is flexible and is often displayed in organisations that frequently undertake work for different customers in a variety of fields.

Organisations with a task culture undertake very specific problem-solving or troubleshooting tasks as projects for internal or external clients, usually on a consultancy basis. The culture is extremely team-oriented, since each task or project requires a fresh team to be constituted containing the required skills and knowledge that will enable the project to be completed successfully. Such a culture is highly flexible, but also expensive. This troubleshooting culture is often brought into an organisation to solve problems that others have found intractable. Members of the project team will exhibit their skills and competence through an extravagant use of resources, as they are used to being able to command anything that they need to get the job done.

Exhibit 10.21 The task culture

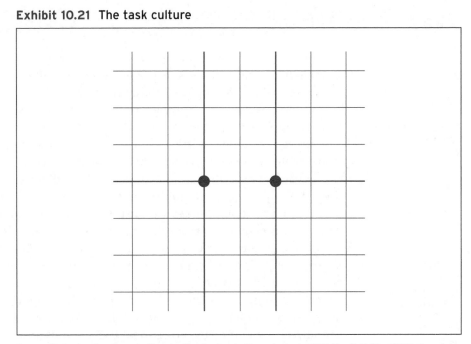

Source: *Understanding Organizations* by Charles Handy (Penguin Books 1976, Fourth Edition 1993). Copyright Charles Handy 1976, 1981, 1985, 1993.

✔ Check your understanding

■ Do you understand in what type of organisations different cultures are likely to occur?

■ Check your understanding by stating which of Handy's cultures applies in each of the following organisations.

1 The civil service.

2 A business of osteopaths and physiotherapists.

3 A corporate training business.

4 A multi-national such as Sony.

Review questions Organisational structure and culture

1 Summarise the relationship between size, structure and culture of an organisation.

2 Identify and discuss the types of structure and cultures small organisations may adopt.

3 If an organisation has a functional structure, what type of culture is it likely to have and how will employees be expected to behave?

4 Summarise the structure and type of work often undertaken by organisations with a task culture.

GROUPS IN ORGANISATIONS

All organisations, however they are structured – with departments, divisions or subsidiaries – will contain groups and teams of staff. The staff in the groups and teams will work towards helping their department, division or subsidiary achieve its goals and in turn the company its objectives.

A **group** is two or more people who come together to achieve objectives. Groups can be formal or informal in nature. A formal group, is for example, a department, team or division, which is defined by an organisation and the group will have specific activities and tasks to undertake. The objectives of the formal group will be determined by the organisation's goals. Formal groups can be command and/or **task groups**, which are determined by the organisation.[5] **Command groups** are determined by an organisation's structure, for example a production department in a TV factory will include the production manager and his or her team of supervisors and assembly workers. Task groups are determined by the organisation, but do not depend on the obvious hierarchical relationships which are present in command groups. Task groups come together to complete a particular job, task or project, and will contain employees with different professional backgrounds and a variety of skills and abilities. An example of a task group could be a product development team containing staff from a variety of backgrounds – those with specific technical ability, marketing staff and production staff. This variety of skills and abilities is also echoed in the matrix structure and task culture. It should also be noted that command groups are task groups, but task groups are not necessarily command groups as task groups cut across levels and departments in the organisation.

Informal groups are **interest groups** and friendship groups and both are informal in nature. People in an interest group may or may not belong to a particular command or task group, but may band together to achieve a common goal. **Friendship groupings** are formed from people who have a social allegiance. Staff in a friendship group may lunch together in the middle of the working day. Additionally friendship groups may extend beyond the workplace and be based on a shared or social activity which is not related to work, for example gardening, going to the theatre, or supporting a particular football team. Friendship and interest groups serve members' social needs and, although informal, do affect the behaviour and performance of individuals in the workplace.

*A **group** is two or more people who come together to achieve objectives.*

Task groups are determined by the organisation, but do not depend on the obvious hierarchical relationships.

Command groups are determined by an organisation's structure and depend on hierarchical relationships.

*An **interest group** contains people who seek to achieve a common goal.*

Friendship groupings are formed by people who have a shared social interest.

Group development

Task achievement is one the key reasons for creating groups and this is obviously important for organisations and the achievement of objectives. A group may collectively have greater knowledge, skills and abilities to complete the job than any individual acting alone. Hence in organisations the use of formal groups to achieve goals can be effective. However, it needs to be recognised that groups and the associated behaviours change over time, and this is shown by the five stages of development suggested by Tuckman and Jensen.[6,7] The first stage is one of '**forming**' in which group members are finding out about each other, making an impression on each other, seeking structure and direction from a leader, and orientating themselves in relation to the task. At this stage there will be a degree of uncertainty, while relationships within the group and ground rules are established. There may also be confusion surrounding the tasks and goals facing the group. Stage 2, '**storming**', is one of conflict in which individuals will jockey for position in the group in terms of leadership, control, priorities, and goal difference between members. Not surprisingly, hostility and conflict will rise to the surface. If the group is to move on to the next stage of '**norming**', then the management and resolution of conflict and differences of opinion are critical.

> **'Forming'** occurs when group members are making an impression on each other and seeking direction from a leader.

> **'Storming'** is the stage of conflict, with individuals jockeying for position in the group.

> **'Norming'** occurs when consensus is achieved and tasks are allocated.

Stage 3, norming, is a much more cohesive stage than stage 2. By stage 3 groups will have moved on to a consensus over leadership, rules, behaviour and tasks. Allocation of tasks will be undertaken with co-operation, as the group has 'gelled' and the conflict of stage 2 has been successfully resolved. Stage 4, '**performing**', builds upon the cohesiveness and co-operation established in stage 3. In a successful group effective structures, flexibility, openness and a clear understanding of goals and successful performance are required to meet those goals and ensure that stage 4 is completed. Less successful groups can become 'bogged' down in the earlier stages and for example remain in continual conflict (stage 2) or remain in stage 3, fulfilling roles but never moving on to completing the tasks and final achievement of objectives (stage 4). Finally, stage 5 is the **disbanding** of the group because the task is complete and/or individual members move on to different projects.

> **'Performing'** occurs as the consensus of 'norming' is built upon and the tasks are successfully completed.

> **Disbanding** occurs when the group has completed the task and staff move on to different projects.

Group performance

Group size impacts on the performance of both the individual and the group. In large groups the total resource and effort is greater, but the impact and contribution of an individual is diluted. There are a number of characteristics of large groups and the behaviour of their members. Individuals are most tolerant of authority and very direct leadership in large groups (or departments, divisions or subsidiaries), as group members recognise the difficulties in managing a large team. Hence there are usually more formal rules and procedures in large groups to enable them to be managed effectively with largely centralised control. However, even with clear rules and procedures large groups usually take longer than small groups to make decisions. It is also likely that job satisfaction in a large group will be less, as individuals have fewer opportunities to participate, and receive less attention from the group and its leader. Hence, with large groups, a level of diminishing return is reached in terms of the outcomes of the group, due to the greater difficulties of co-ordinating and managing a larger group. In contrast in smaller groups, departments or organisations, individuals are more likely to view their participation as critical and are therefore more likely to involve themselves in the organisation, and its tasks and activities. This means there is likely to be a greater element of decentralisation in controlling and managing how activities and tasks are performed. This is echoed in Handy's task and person cultures.

The quality of the work undertaken by a group is directly related to the relevance and diversity of members' characteristics, knowledge, skills and abilities. Teams which are composed of members with very similar traits and skills are likely to view a task or problem from a single perspective, as in the case of the power culture organisation. This can result in the group being both efficient and effective in terms of completing the task or solving the problem. However, it is also the case that a single perspective approach lacks critical awareness of the task, problem and possible solutions. Therefore this leads to the argument that groups with diversity in characteristics, knowledge, skills and abilities are more likely to consider a wider and more innovative range of approaches. This does also require that the more diversified characteristics, knowledge, skills and abilities are relevant to the group task; merely increasing the size of the group alone will not improve the group performance. Hence the matrix structure and task culture allow this diversity to occur in putting a team together to tackle a particular project.

✔ Check your understanding

- Do you understand the stages of Tuckman and Jensen's model?
- Check your understanding by explaining how a company like Sony could use Tuckman and Jensen's model to evaluate the progress of product development teams.

Review questions   **People and communication in organisations**

1 Summarise the differences between command and task groups.

2 Which stage of Tuckman and Jensen's model has been reached in each of the following situations: the group is working well together; the group is starting to compete tasks set; the group is arguing all the time about the project?

3 Explain why in stage 2 of Jensen and Tuckman's group development model, effective management of the group is critical for its success.

4 Discuss how group performance can be influenced by the size of the group.

5 Support the argument that diversity in a group produces a better performance.

CONCLUSION

Companies and organisations have to adopt structures to allow them to operate and implement strategy. Many factors influence possible structures, these include company size; growth and development of the company; range of products; diversity of markets and the external environment. The simple and functional structures (see Exhibits 10.2 and 10.3) are best suited to small companies with limited products and markets. While the divisional, holding and matrix structures (see Exhibits 10.7, 10.14 and 10.15) are most commonly found in larger companies with diversity in products and markets. The nature of markets and external environments influence some companies to adopt structures such as the international divisional structure (see Exhibit 10.9); the global area structure (see Exhibit 10.10) or the multinational matrix structure (see Exhibit 10.15).

The structure a company adopts influences and is linked to organisational culture. Small companies with a simple or functional structure will adopt a power or task culture as these cultures allow small numbers of staff to be managed successfully. Larger companies will contain elements of the role culture, as larger companies tend to have clearly defined jobs, roles and departments. If companies operate teams which disband after the completion of projects, then a task culture will be adopted.

However, all organisations contain groups and teams – some temporary, some permanent – whatever structure has been adopted. How well groups and teams develop and perform depends on appropriate structures and cultures in organisations.

LEARNING OUTCOMES AND SUMMARY

The learning outcomes for this chapter are specified and a brief summary of the material relating to the learning outcomes is provided.

→ **Learning outcome 1**
Explain the types of structures which new and small businesses may adopt to trade domestically and overseas.

- The simple structure is suitable for a small business in the early stages of growth and development, where the owner manager will have control over the growth and development of the business.
- The functional structure has efficient management control systems and is commonplace in companies which have out grown the simple structure. Such organisations offer a limited range of products and services.
- A company wishing to trade overseas by the establishment of an export department can use the functional structure.
- The global functional structure is achieved by having departmental heads responsible for both domestic and international activity; for example, the marketing manager is responsible for domestic and overseas marketing.

→ **Learning outcome 2**
Discuss the types of structures which larger businesses may adopt to trade domestically and overseas.

- The divisional structure contains divisions based around individual product lines or services. A company with successful domestic divisions may expand overseas by establishing an international division.

■ A global area structure is one in which divisional managers have responsibility for geographic divisions. In contrast the global product structure sees product divisions being given worldwide responsibility for product groups.

■ The holding company structure is found in conglomerates, where a parent company owns a number of subsidiary companies, seeking good financial returns.

■ The matrix structure seeks to merge the benefits of decentralisation with co-ordination across all areas of the business. Matrix structures are often used in organisations where there are two distinct areas of diversity which need to be managed and co-ordinated in order to deliver a full range of products or services.

→ Learning outcome 3
Specify the types of structures which global businesses may adopt.

■ The company that develops beyond the international organisation becomes a global organisation. The global company plans and develops worldwide manufacturing facilities, and relevant polices and procedures to cover all activities and staff.

→ Learning outcome 4
Determine the relationship between structure and organisational culture.

■ Small organisations tend to exhibit either the power culture, where a key manager or owner is in charge, or the person culture, where a number of professional staff work together in a practice.

■ Larger companies will often exhibit the role culture, which mirrors the functional, divisional and holding company structures. The key characteristics of the role culture are everyone having a specific job title and description and being clear what it is they are expected to do.

■ The task culture mirrors the matrix structure, which both allow flexibility, and are therefore often found in organisations which undertake project work.

→ Learning outcome 5
Summarise the types of teams and groups in organisations and their development.

■ Groups can be formal or informal. Formal groups can be command or task groups. Command groups depend on a hierarchical relationship in the organisation, that is a manager and his or her subordinates. Task groups do not, and will cut across departments and levels in the organisation. Informal groups include interest groups in which members have a common goal and friendship groups are based on social activities.

■ Groups develop through five stages: forming – coming together; storming – roles are established; norming – tasks are undertaken; performing – tasks and the project are completed; stage 5 – group disbands and members move on to new projects.

These exit case studies look at the different ways Unilever and Shell have dealt with a dual structure and can be used to assess the learning outcomes below.

Learning outcomes	Check you have achieved this by	
Identify the factors which influence decisions concerning an organisation's structure.	Explaining why a company has chosen a particular structure.	Answering Exit case study question 1.
Summarise why and how companies use the generic organisational structures to determine a specific structure for themselves.	Discussing the hybrid structures organisations can adopt.	Answering Exit case study question 1.

Unilever to keep dual structure

FT

by Jenny Wiggins

Unilever, the UK-Dutch consumer goods company, said yesterday it would keep its dual corporate structure, including separate stock listings in London and Rotterdam.

An eight-month review, part of a corporate governance overhaul that began three years ago, found a single structure would have adverse tax consequences for investors and the company. Antony Burgmans, Unilever's chairman, said: 'Unitary structures did not have compelling benefits.' The decision, which comes after Unilever replaced its dual chairman/chief executive structure with a single executive to make faster decisions, disappointed investors looking for more changes to Unilever's corporate culture.

'Change is not as powerful an engine within the company as they might have you believe,' said a fund manager at a large institutional investor that holds Unilever plc stock. John McMillin, analyst at Prudential Equity Group, said the move to a single listing could have added momentum to the 'slow-moving' company. Unilever owns brands including Persil washing powder and Flora margarine but has struggled to compete with food producers Nestlé and Danone in recent years.

Unilever's decision differs from that of another UK-Dutch group, Royal Dutch Shell, which united its holding companies in July with a primary listing in London.

Unilever plc shares fell 1.7 per cent to 572½p. Unilever NV shares fell 1.2 per cent to €58.05. Investors say that a dual listing makes it more difficult for the company to buy back stock and raise money for acquisitions. However, Unilever said moving to a single listing would have been disruptive and made it more difficult for the company to arbitrage its corporate tax liabilities between the UK and the Netherlands. It said investors would also have been affected. UK taxpayers receive tax credits on UK-sourced dividends and Dutch shareholders can reclaim or avoid withholding tax on Dutch-sourced dividends. Mr Burgmans said the present structure gave investors the flexibility to choose between stock in different currencies, and complemented Unilever's status as a multicultural organisation.

Patrick Cescau, Unilever's chief executive, said the current structure did not affect his ability to run the business. 'Performance is what matters – not the niceties of the corporate structure,' he said. The group is to make some changes, however, including alterations to the way it allocates assets between Unilever plc and Unilever NV. It is also splitting NV shares and consolidating plc shares to give the shares an equivalent economic value, and will allow all shareholders to nominate board candidates.

Source: *Financial Times*, 20 December 2005.

→

Royal Dutch/Shell to unify structure and move HQ **FT**

by Gordon Smith

Royal Dutch/Shell, the Anglo-Dutch oil group, on Thursday announced one of the biggest restructurings in its 97-year history in a move that will combine the separate Dutch and English groups into a single entity. The new group, to be called Royal Dutch Shell plc, will be incorporated in the UK and headquartered and tax resident in the Netherlands with a single board, chairman and chief executive.

Separately on Thursday, the group also released third quarter results that were overshadowed by the admission that it was once again reviewing the equivalent of 'approximately 900m' barrels of oil reserves following an extensive audit. It said the results of the review and final figures would be released early next year.

The changes come after a difficult year for the group in which it was forced to restate more than a fifth of its reserves, which resulted in lawsuits from investors in the UK, the Netherlands and the US. The group was also forced to pay fines totalling more that $150m to the market regulators in the UK and the US.

The new ownership structure will reflect the split of the previous two companies with Royal Dutch shareholders owning 60 per cent of the share capital and Shell Transport & Trading shareholders owning the remaining 40 per cent. Commenting on the changes Jeroen van der Veer, who will become the first chief executive of the new group, said, 'I believe these proposals will help propel this group forward.'

Shareholders have blamed the complicated corporate structure, which involved a supervisory board overseeing the activities of the two separate operating companies, for the group's poor performance compared to its rivals. Last month, the group said it would increase capital spending by up to $15bn a year for the next three years to replace ageing production operations, and dispose of between $10bn and $12bn worth of assets.

Shell's financial results showed net income more than doubled in the third quarter to $5.4bn, helped by record oil prices, compared to $2.7bn the previous year. CCS earnings, which are estimated on the current cost of supplies, for the three months were $4.4bn, at the top end of expectations of between $3.6bn and $4.4bn.

Source: FT.com site, 28 October 2006.

Exit case study questions

1 Compare and contrast the outcomes of the different decisions made by Unilever and Shell regarding structure.

DISCUSSION TOPIC

1 Read the paper 'The design of new organizational forms' by Jennifer Herber, Jitendra V Singh and Michael Useem, Chapter 8, in *The Strategy Process*, Mintzberg, Lampel, Quinn and Ghosal, Harlow: Prentice Hall, 2003.

2 Critically comment on the suitability of each of the six organisational forms for both manufacturing and service organisations.

WIDEN YOUR HORIZONS

1 Widen your horizons by visiting the British Library website at www.bl.uk. Explain the difference between the Executive Team at the British Library and the British Library Board. Identify and discuss the type of structure the British Library operates and the role of Executive Team and the British Library Board in developing and implementing strategy.

2 Widen your horizons by visiting the website of FPI, a Canadian seafood company at www.fpil.com. The company has changed and developed as an organisation since it was first established in 1984. Identify the key events in the company's development. Do you think the company's current structure is suitable for its present day operations? Explain your answer.

WEBLINKS

The websites for this chapter provides some further information about Exit case studies 10.2a and 10.2b.

- To find out more about Unilever, visit the website and click on 'Investor relations' and then on 'About Unilever'.
  www.unilever.co.uk

- To find out more about Royal Dutch Shell visit the website.
  www.shell.com

FURTHER READING

Mainstream strategic management books and their views on structures

- Johnson, G, Scholes, K and Whittington, R (2005) *Exploring Corporate Strategy*, 7th edn, Harlow: Financial Times/Prentice Hall. Chapter 10, 'Organising for success'.

- Lynch, R (2006) *Corporate Strategy*, 4th edn, London: Financial Times/Prentice Hall. Chapter 16, 'Organisational structure, style and people issues'.

- Dess, G G, Lumpkin, G T and Taylor, M L (2005) *Strategic Management*, 2nd edn, New York: McGraw Hill Irwin. Chapter 10 'Creating effective organisational designs'.

- Haberberg, A and Rieple, A (2001) *The Strategic management of organisations*, Harlow: Financial Times/Prentice Hall. Chapter 10, 'Structure, information, control and reward systems'.

International and contemporary management books and their views on structure

- Mellahi, K, Frynas, J G and Finlay, P (2005) *Global Strategic Management*, Oxford: Oxford University Press. Chapter 10, 'Global structures and designs'.

- Pettinger, R (2004) *Contemporary Strategic Management*, Basingstoke: Palgrave Macmillan. Chapter 12, 'Strategic management and organisation structure'.

- Rugman, A M and Hodgetts, R M (2003) *International Business*, Harlow: Financial Times/Prentice Hall. Chapter 9, 'Organising strategy'.

- Mead, R (2005) *International Management: Cross-cultural Dimensions*, 3rd edn, Oxford: Blackwell. Chapter 8, 'Formal structures'.

Organisational behaviour books and their views on structure

- Mullins, L J (2005) *Management and Organisational Behaviour*, 7th edn, Harlow: Financial Times/Prentice Hall. Chapter 6, 'Organisational structures'.

- Huczynski, A and Buchanan D (2001) *Organisational Behaviour*, 4th edn, Harlow: Financial Times/Prentice Hall. Chapter 16, 'Organisational strategy and design'.

Groups in organisations

- Mullins, L J (2005) *Management and Organisational Behaviour*, 7th edn, Harlow: Financial Times/Prentice Hall. Chapter 14, 'Working in groups and teams'.

- Huczynski, A and Buchanan D (2001) *Organisational Behaviour*, 4th edn, Harlow: Financial Times/Prentice Hall. Chapter 9, 'Group formation'.

REFERENCES

1 www.yosushi.com
2 Rugman, A M and Hodgetts, R M (2003) *International Business*, 3rd edn, Harlow: Financial Times/Prentice Hall.
3 www.lexisnexis.com
4 Rugman and Hodgetts, op. cit.
5 Robbins, S O (2000) *Essentials of Organisational Behavior*, New Jersey: Prentice Hall.
6 Tuckman, B C (1965) 'Development sequence in small groups', *Psychological Bulletin*, 63, 6, pp 384-99, in Huczynski, A and Buchanan D (2001) *Organisational Behaviour*, 4th edn, Harlow: Financial Times/Prentice Hall.
7 Tuckman, B C and Jensen, M A C (1977) 'Stages of small group development revisited', *Group and Organisation Studies*, 2, 4, pp 419-27, in Huczynski, A and Buchanan D (2001) *Organisational Behaviour*, 4th edn, Harlow: Financial Times/Prentice Hall.

CHAPTER 11

Strategic control

Exhibit 11.1 Essential strategy model

Chapter objectives

Strategy is concerned with an organisation recognising where it sits in the external environment and using its resources to benefit the organisation and its stakeholders. In seeking to benefit the stakeholders organisations make many varied decisions concerning the plans, tasks and activities it undertakes. Strategic control is concerned with providing all organisations with ways of evaluating and assessing its results and performance at different levels.

When you have read this chapter and worked through the associated activities you should be able to achieve the objectives specified below.

1 Summarise the role of strategic control in organisations.

2 Discuss the importance of a balanced approach to strategic control.

3 Explain the strategic control of the primary activities in the value chain.

4 Explain the strategic control of the support activities in the value chain.

5 Explain the strategic control of the value system.

6 Develop effective strategic control systems.

Control of the supply chain is often a source of competitive advantage and this entry case study looks at how Dyson sought to retain control of the supply chain for spare parts for its vacuum cleaners and washing machines.

Designers win the right to control spare parts

FT

by Nikki Tait

Original designers and manufacturers of consumer items are likely to be able to hang on to the market for spare parts for their products after the decision in the Court of Appeal yesterday. Three judges upheld a High Court ruling that found that Qualtex, Europe's largest manufacturer and distributor of domestic appliance spare parts, had infringed Dyson's design rights in respect of a dozen different spare parts and accessories for its vacuum cleaners.

The case was the first to test the extent to which manufacturers can control the market for spare parts in recent years – and is likely to have ramifications across a wide range of industries, some of which are substantial. The European spare parts market for the automotive industry alone is worth €4bn (£2.7bn) annually, for example.

'The overall lesson here is that unregistered design rights ... do not give "carte blanche" for pattern spares. Those who wish to make spares during the period of design right must design their own spares and cannot just copy every detail of the OEM's [original equipment manufacturer's] part,' said Lord Justice Jacob. 'To be on the safe side they will have to make them different as far as is possible,' he added.

Unregistered design rights arise automatically in the case of original designs of the shape or configuration of a product. The right is one to prevent copying, and lasts until 10 years after the first marketing of product made to the design. Intellectual property lawyers said afterwards that the decision was a win for original manufacturers. 'The law is designed to strike a balance between allowing consumers to get spare parts as cheaply as possible, and rewarding original designers,' said Brian Cordery, partner at Bristows law firm. 'This tips the balance quite firmly in favour of the OEMs.' Prices of parts to consumers could be higher as a result, he suggested.

Mr Cordery added that the comments by Lord Justice Jacob, who is one of Britain's most experienced patent and IP judges, appeared to be very good practical advice for spare parts makers to follow. In its decision, the Court of Appeal pointed out that there had been a long history

to the battle between OEMs and independent manufacturers over spare parts, and that differing approaches to legal protections had been taken in the US, continental Europe, and the UK.

Here, OEMs began to assert copyright protections in the 1970s – prompting the independents to defend themselves by calling on competition law. In 1988, the Copyright, Designs and Patents Act was introduced but, as Lord Justice Jacob pointed out yesterday, the drafting of the section on design rights attracted a fair amount of subsequent criticism, partly because of its lack of clarity.

'Neither the language used nor the context of the legislation give any clear idea what was intended. Time and time again one struggles but fails to ascertain a precise meaning,' he said.

Yesterday Dyson heralded the court's decision to dismiss Qualtex's appeal and uphold the High Court decision as a victory for designers generally. 'We're very pleased to have won this case. It shows how important design right is, especially for small design companies and individual designers who don't necessarily have the means to protect themselves legally against people who copy their designs,' said James Dyson, who invented the [Dyson] vacuum cleaner. 'If a musician or a writer can claim copyright, why shouldn't a designer be allowed to have design rights on his or her hard work?'

Dyson added that it was now in negotiations with Qualtex over a final settlement for costs, damages and licence arrangements – having already been paid £130,000 towards the costs of the appeal by Qualtex. It said that it would donate any winnings for the case to the Royal College of Art, to help young designers protect their own work.

'Many individual designers and small agencies cannot afford to defend their design rights and tend to be exploited as consequence,' said Sir Christopher Frayling, rector of the RCA.

Source: *Financial Times*, 9 March 2006.

INTRODUCTION

Strategic control is the ongoing monitoring of staff, managers and activities of an organisation to evaluate **efficiency** and **effectiveness** in both the short and long term. As part of developing strategy an organisation will have adopted the most appropriate structure (see Chapter 10) to allow the organisation to use its staff and resources to achieve competitive advantage. The monitoring and control systems allow managers to determine whether the strategy and structure are working as intended and, if necessary, how they could be improved.

Strategic control can also be concerned with putting the right monitoring systems in place for new activities and ventures as they are fully implemented. This use of monitoring and control in this situation can help to identify teething problems with new activities and ventures, and allow adjustments to the implementation to be made and poor implementation and potential failure of new activities and ventures avoided.

Hence strategic control is about both monitoring how well an organisation and its staff are currently performing, and on developing and implementing strategy in new areas for the business.

LEVELS OF STRATEGIC CONTROL

Strategic control systems can be used to measure performance at four levels in an organisation: the corporate, business, operational and individual levels. The organisation and its managers at all levels must develop and use the most appropriate set of measures to evaluate corporate, business, operational and individual performance. The measures should be closely linked to the goals which have been set at the various levels and should not conflict with other levels.

Strategy implementation requires the right combination of structure (see Chapter 10) and control for a company's strategy to succeed. Organisational structure places people into organisational roles and assigns tasks, which can vary over time, and specifies how the staff are to be co-ordinated and managed. However, the presence of managers and staff in organisational structures does not provide the means to control and manage staff, resources and money. Therefore methods of control are needed to evaluate how the organisation is performing at the different levels and to provide pointers to improvements and possible changes.

A BALANCED APPROACH TO STRATEGIC CONTROL

A balanced approach to **strategic control** is via efficiency, quality, innovation and responsiveness to customers.

Strategic control is not only concerned with monitoring performance, resource use and the achievement of goals, it is also about motivating employees and focusing on how current and future challenges can be met to help ensure the organisation performs better over the long term. Effective strategic control will help the organisation achieve sustained competitive advantage. Kaplan and Norton in Hill and Jones[1] identify four basic building blocks to consider as part of a balanced approach to strategic control, namely efficiency, quality, innovation and responsiveness to customers (see Exhibit 11.2). Hence strategic controls are concerned with both monitoring actions and work already undertaken by the organisation, and with helping it gain and sustain competitive advantage in the future.

Exhibit 11.2 A balanced approach to strategic control

Measure	Assessment made	Value chain area commonly assessed by this measure
Efficiency	■ Cost of inputs ■ Hours needed to produce a product or deliver a service ■ Staff skills, costs and motivation ■ Structure, culture and systems	■ Inbound logistics ■ Operations ■ Procurement ■ HRM ■ Infrastructure
Quality	■ Number of rejects manufactured ■ Number of defective products returned by customers and to suppliers ■ Product reliability over time	■ Inbound logistics ■ Operations ■ Outbound logistics ■ Procurement
Innovation	■ Number of new and improved goods & services launched ■ Time to develop new and improved goods & services compared with competitors ■ Cost of improvement and development of goods & services	■ Technology development
Responsiveness to customers	■ Number of repeat customers ■ Accurate and on-time delivery to customers ■ The level of customer service	■ Marketing and sales ■ Service ■ Outbound logistics

✔ **Check your understanding**

- Do you understand how to take a balanced approach to strategic control?
- Check your understanding by identifying the assessments which a company producing chocolates and confectionery would need to make if undertaking a balanced approach to strategic control.

Review questions **Level and balance of strategic control**

1 Explain why strategic controls at different levels of the organisation are required.

2 Summarise the importance of a balanced approach to strategic control

CONTROLLING THE VALUE CHAIN – THE SUPPORT ACTIVITIES

The support activities of the value chain are examined in detail in Chapter 3. The support activities of infrastructure, human resource management, technology development and procurement define the organisational set up in which the primary activities are performed. All value chain activities, both primary and support activities, contributed towards the achievement of competitive advantage via lower costs or added value and as such the control of these activities is crucial to the effective implementation of strategy. The assessment and evaluations commonly made, and where in the value chain they apply, are shown in Exhibit 11.2 and are discussed below.

Infrastructure

Infrastructure includes structure, culture and systems, and for a specific organisation will reflect what is important for the organisation to control and manage. At the corporate level directors need to select the best structure for organisational effectiveness. An organisation operating in a turbulent environment will require a decentralised and flexible structure (for example, one of the divisional structures) if it is to develop an agile value chain, which provides continual strategic fit between the organisation and its environment. Consideration also needs to be given to any diversity in the organisation which can arise from products or geographic markets, and while each division will have its own requirements in terms of support systems and activities, expensive duplication of these needs to be avoided for effective control.

Integrating mechanisms are systems and relationships which link different parts of the organisation.

Therefore thought needs to be given to the **integrating mechanisms** and control systems which can be used to make the structure work efficiently. Hence organisations tend to implement systems which allow control and management of resources, staff and processes which are important in the achievement of competitive advantage.

Human resource management

HRM is concerned with recruiting, managing, training, developing and rewarding staff to help the organisation achieve competitive advantage. The type of structure the organisation adopts will determine how the human resource management activities are performed. An organisation with a flexible and decentralised structure, such as one of the divisional structures, will seek to recruit staff who are able to work effectively both on their own and in teams. In contrast if the organisation has adopted a more rigid structure, such as the functional structure, staff will tend to be recruited to very specific roles where less flexibility is required and high levels of efficiency are important.

Bureaucratic control and cultural control

There are two approaches to controlling and managing staff, namely **bureaucratic control** and **cultural control**.[2] The approach of bureaucratic control is heavily dependent on rules and regulations and reflects the Theory X approach to management (see Chapter 6). This reflects that the relationship between company and employee is based on a legal contract and that job performance is measurable. The other approach of cultural control is control negotiated and based on trust, loyalty and mutual respect and is sometimes referred to as the psychological contract between employer and employee. The approach of cultural control reflects the Theory Y approach to management (see Chapter 6).

Bureaucratic control is via rules and regulations.

In a company taking the approach of bureaucratic control, corporate headquarters will implement and enforce rigid and impersonal rules which govern selection, recruitment, training, rewards of staff and the individual's workplace performance. The aim of this bureaucratic control is to develop and implement impersonal and bureaucratic approaches to controlling work and measuring performance throughout the company's subsidiaries and divisions. The individual's workplace performance is determined via monitoring and evaluation of work tasks and activities. The monitoring and evaluation is undertaken by managers using rules, regulations, manuals, and one-way communication – often done electronically via text or email.

If bureaucratic control succeeds, the company, its divisions and subsidiaries develop into efficient operating units. The disadvantage of this arrangement is that loyalties to the corporate headquarters are often weak. Relationships with headquarters conducted impersonally and via emails do not create a loyal working relationship based on trust. This is perhaps particularly true if the relationships in the division or subsidiary are not based on bureaucratic controls, but on trust and cultural controls. In a decentralised company corporate headquarters can be unaware of the approaches to controls which exist in sub-

Cultural control is control negotiated and based on trust, loyalty and mutual respect.

sidiaries and divisions and this can threaten the company.

Cultural control seeks to develop loyalty to the company at the level of corporate headquarters and for this to be repeated at divisional or subsidiary level.

Cultural control arises from a company's norms and values that employees implicitly agree to take on board when they join the organisation. Formal guidelines and rules covering processes, procedures and technical operations may be used in training employees to do a job of work. However, at least an equal amount of time will be dedicated to creating an awareness of the organisation's norms and values and integrating a new member of staff into the shared culture (see cultural web in Chapter 5). This can be achieved by ensuring the new employee has personal interactions with established members of staff who are aware and accepting of the organisational culture.

Effective cultural control requires a two-way relationship to develop between the headquarters and the division or subsidiary.

Ensuring that the cultural control developed at the level of the corporate headquarters is repeated at the divisional or subsidiary level requires a two-way relationship to develop between the headquarters and the division or subsidiary (see Exhibit 11.3). The earlier in a division or subsidiary's life cultural control can be introduced, the easier and more successful it is likely to be. Gaining the trust, loyalty and commitment of staff will always be easier and more straightforward when there has not been a history of poor bureaucratic control in the past.

Exhibit 11.3 Developing cultural control at division or subsidiary level

- Second HQ staff to division or subsidiary to act as role models.
- Regular and frequent visits by HQ staff to division or subsidiary and vice versa (e.g. training and meetings not always held on same site).
- Joint social events.
- Company seminars.

The advantages of cultural control are that it can lead to the development of a strong and fruitful relationship between headquarters and the division or subsidiary. However, the cost of frequent visits, social events and seminars can be high in terms of money and time, particularly if there is a significant distance between offices. Additionally subsidiary or divisional staff can be demotivated if the values of corporate headquarters do not sit comfortably with local operations, as the loyalty of divisional or subsidiary employees will be split. This is where bureaucratic control has an advantage over cultural control as the loyalty of employees is not required; it is their compliance with rules and procedures which is needed.

Technology development

Technology development is the use of technology to improve products, services and their delivery to customers. This area of the value chain considers technology in the broadest possible sense – that all activities in the value chain have a related technology or 'know how' (see Chapter 3). Hence technology can underpin research and development, product improvements, and the marketing and selling of goods and services via the Internet; including taking orders and bookings over the Internet to delivery of the service electronically, such as with Internet banking.

The control and management of technology depends on its use. The work of a research and development team would be managed and controlled in a different way to Internet marketing and selling. The work of the research and development team would be evaluated in terms of its final success in the form of commercially viable products and in terms of meeting mid-term goals. A development team in a pharmaceutical company may be evaluated in terms of successfully completing certain stages of the project, for example development of the drug, laboratory trials, hospital trials and clinical approval. In contrast the use of technology for sales and marketing would be evaluated for reductions in costs and increases in revenue and profit.

Procurement

Procurement is the process for acquiring and purchasing goods and materials of appropriate quality for all areas of the business (see Chapter 3). Controlling and managing the procurement process requires various areas of the buying process to be evaluated. The success of the procurement process contributes to competitive advantage, as it is here that money is spent and significant costs incurred. Spending money on the cheapest inputs where differentiation is not key and spending money effectively where differentiation is key to competitive advantage are critical for successful competitive strategy. Therefore examining suppliers, their power and the service they offer, along with alternative sources of supply and substitute products or services (see Chapter 2), is important for gaining the best deal on cost or quality, as required.

Also crucial is the consideration which should be given to a key supplier going out of business, and jeopardising a company's ability to supply its customers in turn. Checks which can be carried out include credit agency checks, claimed membership of any professional or trade body, examination of sources of finance and profitability, a visit to premises and questions about delivery, quality and complaint handling. Contracts with suppliers should specify in writing the length of time (for example, 1 year, 2 years, 6 months), prices and pricing policy (for example, whether there is seasonal variation). In addition the delivery schedule (for example, every day, every week, or at 24 hours' notice), penalties for missed or late deliveries, and volume of goods supplied (such as any minimum order size qualification) should also be specified in the contract.

Review questions Control of support activities in the value chain

1   Explain how the infrastructure of an organisation is controlled and managed.
2   Discuss the difference between bureaucratic control and cultural control.
3   Summarise the different approaches to controlling and managing technology and their appropriateness.
4   Explain why good control and monitoring of procurement is important.

CONTROLLING THE VALUE CHAIN – THE PRIMARY ACTIVITIES

Inbound logistics, operations and outbound logistics

The first three primary activities in the value chain – inbound logistics, operations and outbound logistics – are very much concerned with ensuring a product or service of the right quality is produced and delivered to the customer (see Chapter 3). Control of these value chain activities is very much held at the operational level of the organisation. Determining how efficiently the organisation is using resources requires managers to be able to accurately measure inputs, **productivity** and outputs. Good control systems allow accurate measurement of inputs, productivity and outputs and an assessment of how well the system is working. If changes or improvements have been made, they also enable assessment of whether they have been successful or not.

The linking of the purchase of inputs to production or service delivery is often done via just-in-time (JIT) systems, which allows inputs to the systems to be adjusted to meet capacity and current **utilisation** of the company's facilities. The capacity of the operations depends on a number of factors such as how hard people work, the number of disruptions, the quality of products manufactured, and the **effectiveness** of equipment. An organisation's **forecasting** determines expected demand and this dictates capacity needed to satisfy the demand. Capacity is a basic measure of performance. If a system is operating to capacity then it is producing the maximum amount of a product in a specified time. Decisions concerning capacity are made at the location and process design stage of an organisation's operations management activities. Ideally, an organisation should aim for the capacity of the process to match the forecast demand for products.

> Forecasting determines expected demand and this dictates capacity needed to satisfy the demand.

Mismatches between capacity and demand will result in unsatisfied customers or under-utilised resources. If capacity is less than demand, the organisation cannot meet all the demand and it loses potential customers. Alternatively, if capacity is greater than demand, then the demand is met, but spare capacity and under-utilised resources result. In contrast, if the capacity utilisation hovers around 100 per cent during certain time periods, then on those occasions bottlenecks or queues will occur. A common example of capacity being less than demand is when you are left standing in a long queue in a shop. You may exercise your consumer choice and go to another shop with no queues and staff waiting to serve you. Here capacity is greater than demand, but the cost of paying these under-employed staff will be reflected in your bill.

Utilisation measures the percentage of available capacity that is actually used.

Productivity is the quantity manufactured in relation to one or more of the resources used.

Efficiency is the ratio of actual output to possible output, usually expressed as a percentage.

Effectiveness is how well an organisation sets and achieves its goals.

Utilisation is directly related to capacity. Utilisation measures the percentage of available capacity that is actually used, and productivity is the quantity manufactured in relation to one or more of the resources used. For example the airline with a fleet of a hundred planes, including 15 Boeing 737s, is operating at 100 per capacity when all hundred planes are operating as normal. If a suspected mechanical fault is found in Boeing 737s and all Boeing 737s have to be checked before they can fly again, then the airline will be operating at only 85 per cent capacity until the checks have been carried out. Another measure of how well operations are proceeding is **efficiency**. Efficiency is the ratio of actual output to possible output, usually expressed as a percentage. For example, the plane with 200 seats which flies with 200 passengers on board is operating at 100 per cent efficiency; however, if only 150 passengers pay and fly, then efficiency is 75 per cent.

Efficiency should not be confused with **effectiveness**. Effectiveness is how well an organisation sets and achieves its goals. For example, the airline which is operating at 85 per cent capacity may still achieve goals relating to customer care if it handles the disruption caused by the fall in capacity well. In considering capacity, utilisation, efficiency and effectiveness, thought should be given to how these measures combine. For example, efficient production is of no use if the quality of products or services delivered is poor or quite simply not delivered to the customer.

Business illustration of poor control - train companies

In March 2005 rail passengers continue to experience delays, disruption and poor service due, at least in part, to poor control by the train companies. A train journey from London to Glasgow could take eight and a half hours, a full 20 minutes longer than in the 1930s, when steam trains operated on the network.

The purchase of an economy ticket for travel over Easter 2005 was also made difficult as the train companies chose to release cheap advance tickets only a fortnight before Easter. A journey or holiday requiring more forward planning meant passengers would have to pay the full cost fare. If travelling between London and Manchester, this meant a ticket would cost £187, significantly more than the cheapest advance ticket of £24. Rail user groups also raised concerns over the actual number of cheaper tickets offered by the train companies.

Passengers raised other concerns regarding the accuracy of information provided by rail information services, with travellers being told pets were not allowed on replacement bus services when in fact pets can travel on rail bus services.

Source: 'Trouble on the tracks as delays hit Easter getaways', Mark Townsend, *The Observer*, 27 March 2005.

Marketing and sales

Marketing and sales is about attracting customers and selling them the company's products or services. The methods which can be used to do this are many and varied. The control and management of marketing activities requires them to be assessed for being in budget and effective. Therefore evaluating the return on a marketing campaign is key, as it needs to generate more revenue and profit than it cost to undertake, and normally a target for the extra revenue and profit will need to be met. The control of sales will centre on dealing with and processing orders efficiently in order to support the effective marketing campaign. The Business illustration on the train companies shows poor control of the sales function, which results in confusion for customers.

Service

The service section of the value chain is concerned with additional services, which the organisation may choose to offer customers (see Chapter 3). Controlling and managing these services requires targets setting and monitoring to ensure targets are met. The targets often relate to how many customers use or buy the service and the speed with which it is accurately delivered. For example, customers will not leave their car at a garage which takes a week to perform a routine service.

✔ Check your understanding

- Do you understand how to develop a strategic control system?
- Check your understanding by showing how each of the following could be controlled and managed.
    1 A coffee shop chain and its franchised outlets.
    2 A local taxi company doing local journeys and airport runs.

Review questions Control of primary activities in the value chain

1 Summarise the measurement often taken to ensure good control of inbound logistics, operations and outbound logistics.
2 Explain which measurements should be the focus for controlling and managing marketing, sales and service activities.

STRATEGIC CONTROL OF THE VALUE SYSTEM - RELATED DIVERSIFICATION

A strategy of related diversification is used to build up linkages in the value system (see Chapter 3), which is an important source of competitive advantage. Related diversification can be backwards, forwards or horizontal and can

Exhibit 11.4 Possible related integration in the value system prior to full control by company A

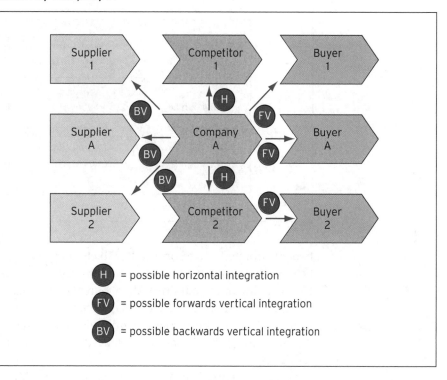

be achieved via organic growth, franchising or acquisition (see Chapter 8). **Backwards vertical integration** occurs when a company establishes or acquires its own sources of raw materials, components or inputs (see Exhibit 11.4). The UK supermarket chain Morrisons has undertaken backwards vertical integration via establishing its fruit and vegetable business Wm. Morrison Produce, Farmers Boy which produces pies and pizzas, and two meat processing facilities. **Forwards vertical integration** occurs when a company establishes or acquires its own distribution channels or outlets for its goods and services (see Exhibit 11.4). On the UK high street the shoe company, Clarks and the chocolate company, Thorntons have both grown via forwards vertical integration, starting as manufacturers and then moving into retailing. **Horizontal integration** occurs when a company starts to expand its existing range of goods and services in order to take on direct competitors.

A strategy of related integration requires that the flow of resources and goods from one 'company' or 'divisions of the same company' need to be controlled and managed (see Exhibit 11.5). A value system in which much related diversification has occurred will be likely to become a company with a divisional type structure (see Chapter 10).

The divisional structure contains a corporate headquarters and part of their role is to manage the devolvement of resources, money and staff to the divisions and between the divisions in a manner such that the organisation

Backwards vertical integration occurs when a company establishes or acquires its own sources of inputs.

Forwards vertical integration occurs when a company establishes or acquires its own distribution channels or outlets.

Horizontal integration occurs when a company starts to expand its existing range of goods to take on direct competitors.

Exhibit 11.5 The integrated value system

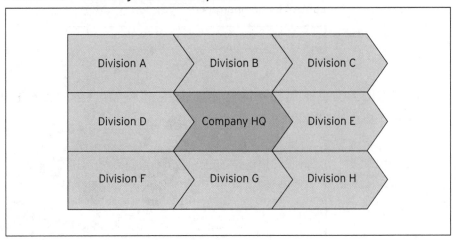

benefits from effective control. It is likely that a set of rules and procedures will be developed to manage these interdivisional transfers and relationships, and this will incur an administrative bureaucratic cost. This is where conflict among divisions and managers may occur as each division will be a cost centre in its own right. The corporate and divisional managers all have a role to play in minimising divisional conflict as this is an inefficient use of time and resources.

However, centralising control at corporate headquarters in a vertically integrated company should be done such that the right balance between corporate and divisional control occurs for strategy to be successfully implemented and the decentralised structure allowed to operate effectively. The wrong sense of balance between corporate headquarters and the divisions means corporate managers become involved in running the divisions and their business. This will result in the division losing its autonomy, which arises because of the decentralised nature of the structure; and the divisional managers and staff will lose motivation if there is unnecessary interference from head office. The autonomy of divisions allows them to decide on the scheduling and control mechanisms regarding the transfer of resources and goods between divisions. The quality of one division's output will determine the quality of the inputs and outputs of a division to which resources and goods are transferred. The integrating and control mechanisms between divisions require effective communication, co-ordination and liaison for divisions to work together successfully. Hence a strategy of vertical integration is best managed via a combination of corporate and divisional controls.

When a level of integration and sharing occurs between related divisions, however, measuring the performance – including financial performance of individual and separate divisions – is difficult. Therefore if a company operates as related and integrated divisions, it needs to find a way of evaluating the contribution of cross-divisional teams to both divisional and corporate goals. The importance of the right balance between divisional and corporate control and management is mentioned above, and this should be mirrored in the mix of incentives and rewards for successful co-operation and integration. Remember that corporate success will be achieved via divisional success.

STRATEGIC CONTROL OF THE VALUE SYSTEM - UNRELATED DIVERSIFICATION

Unrelated diversification is a move into completely different goods and services to those currently sold.

In the case of **unrelated diversification** there are no linkages between divisions, and therefore control and co-ordination are easy and the cost low. The key requirement is that the structure and control systems allow corporate managers to evaluate divisional or subsidiary performance easily and accurately. This is often achieved by the use of financial controls such as profit margins and return on investment, and this allows corporate managers to compare the performance of different divisions or subsidiaries.

Divisions or subsidiaries which meet their financial targets usually retain considerable autonomy, as normally corporate headquarters are not interested in the business level strategy pursued. However, if financial targets and returns are not met then corporate headquarters often acts, and takes steps to remedy the problems and avoid a serious failure or turnaround situation. If corporate headquarters cannot see how the problems can be solved and the performance of the division or subsidiary improved, then the decision may be taken to divest. This is possible if the divisions or subsidiaries are unrelated, as there will be no knock-on effects for other parts of the business.

✔ Check your understanding

- Do you understand how Dyson has extended control of its value system?
- Check your understanding by comparing and contrasting Dyson's strategic control prior to and after the judgement referred to in the Entry case study 11.1 comes into effect.

Review questions — Control of the value system

1 Identify the expansion activities which will allow an organisation to control and manage the value system in which it operates.

2 Explain if complete centralisation is a good way for an organisation to manage its value system.

3 Explain how strategic control is achieved if an organisation's value system is diversified and unrelated.

EFFECTIVE STRATEGIC CONTROL SYSTEMS

Strategic control systems are the means by which managers evaluate whether a company is achieving efficiency, quality, innovation and customer responsiveness – and hence competitive advantage.

Effective strategic control systems should give a true picture of organisational performance, provide accurate information, and be flexible enough to allow managers to respond as required to unexpected events. Control systems which do not do this will lead to decisions being based on out-of-date information and these will be likely to lead to a failure or turnaround situation.[3] The stages of effective control systems are shown in Exhibit 11.6. The companies Matsushita and Sanyo have both changed their strategic control via changes in ownership (see Business illustration on Matsushita and Sanyo).

Exhibit 11.6 Stages of effective strategic control systems

- Set performance targets.
- Create the control systems.
- Compare actual performance against targets.
- Take corrective action when targets not achieved.

Business illustration of changes in control – Matsushita and Sanyo

France's Vivendi Universal paid Japan's Matsushita Electric Industrial $1.15 billion to take full control of the Universal Music record label and increase its stake in the broadcasting and film making company NBC Universal. The acquisition by Vivendi would simplify its corporate structure and improve its net earnings by at least $30 million in 2006.

In contrast Sanyo Electric relinquished control and handed control of its board to a consortium of investors, the three banks, Goldman Sachs, Daiwa Securities and Sumitomo Mitsui Financial Group. Satoshi Iue, a director and member of the company's founding family and two other directors resigned from the board in January 2006 when this occurred. Directors chosen by the investing banks replaced them.

Control was handed over in return for an injection of cash, ¥300 billion, to help reduce crippling debt and a steep decline in earnings. In return Goldman Sachs and Daiwa Securities each received 42 per cent of the new shares and Sumitomo Mitsui Financial Group the remaining 12 per cent of shares.

Source: 'Vivendi takes full control of Universal', David Turner and Adam Jones, *Financial Times*, 3 February 2006 and 'Sanyo Electric relinquishes board control', David Turner, *Financial Times*, 25 January 2006.

Set performance targets

Organisations should set and establish meaningful targets and use strategic control systems to monitor them. The control systems should be both directly and clearly linked to the organisation's key success factors (see Chapter 3) which, if met, determine the organisation's results and performance. Strategic control systems should require and use only the minimum amount of information needed to give a reliable picture of organisational performance. The use of excessive control systems and information creates confusion. Additionally both long-term and short-term controls should be used, as if only short-term measures are implemented then only short-term operational performance will be evaluated and long-term performance will be ignored.

Create the control systems

Strategic control systems should be created to monitor only meaningful activities and results, regardless of measurement difficulty. If co-operation between divisions is important to corporate performance, some form of qualitative or quantitative measures should be established to monitor co-operation.

Strategic control systems can be created to monitor general performance targets based on achieving efficiency, quality, innovation or customer responsiveness and can be used along with specific performance targets. Specific performance targets may include, for example, 'a 20 per cent increase in turnover for a company following a cost leadership strategy' or 'maximisation of profit margins for products in maturity phase of product lifecycle'. If the organisation has developed via related integration (see earlier in this chapter) co-operation between divisions will be important for good results and successful performance, and some form of qualitative or quantitative measures should be established to monitor co-operation.

Compare actual performance against targets

Implementation and monitoring of control systems and the information they yield should be timely to enable corrective action to be taken before failure is the outcome. Equally it should be emphasised that meeting or exceeding realistic targets is linked to rewards, rather than linking failure to meet targets with punishment. In an organisation, and particularly one with cultural control (see previous section), punishment for failure to meet targets typically leads to lack of motivation and a displacement of targets. Displacement of targets will occur as managers fudge the results of the control systems, and push for weaker control systems and lower targets.

If the organisation's performance is better than the targets set, then consideration should be given as to if the right targets were set initially. Were targets set too low? Alternatively if performance is poor and targets not met, then consider if there are any symptoms of failure present? Can causes of failure and poor performance be identified? (See Chapter 12.)

Take corrective action when targets not achieved

If corrective action is required, then the steps taken should allow targets to be met. Corrective action may be at any level – corporate, business, operational or individual – to improve competitive advantage.

✔ Check your understanding

- Do you understand how to develop effective control systems for companies which have developed by either related or unrelated diversification?
- Check your understanding by explaining the difference between effective strategic control systems for a business which has grown by related diversification and for one which has developed via unrelated diversification.

Review questions　Effective strategic control systems

1 Explain the disadvantages of an organisation not having an effective strategic control system.

2 Discuss how an organisation could develop an effective strategic control system.

CONCLUSION

The measuring and monitoring processes and procedures which organisations put in place to establish strategic control at different levels will be many and varied. Generally organisations seek to control, manage and evaluate those things which are important in enabling the organisation to achieve success and meet key success factors.

Measurement, monitoring and control are ongoing processes in both the short and long term and, as such, periodic review is needed to ensure that the right things (for example, sales, staff and costs) are still being evaluated effectively. This is especially true if major changes have occurred in the organisation in terms of structure and expansion.

LEARNING OUTCOMES AND SUMMARY

The learning outcomes for this chapter are specified and a brief summary of the material relating to the learning outcomes is provided.

→ **Learning outcome 1**
Summarise the role of strategic control in organisations.

- Strategic control is concerned with organisations monitoring and evaluating results at different levels of the organisation, namely the corporate, business, operational and individual.

- The controls should be closely linked to the goals which have been set at the various levels and should not conflict with one another.

→ **Learning outcome 2**
Discuss the importance of a balanced approach to strategic control.

- A balanced approach to strategic control can be achieved by considering efficiency, quality, innovation and responsiveness to customers.
- Different measures are commonly used in different areas of the value chain; for example, efficiency is often important for inbound logistics and operations, while responsiveness to customers is important in assessing marketing and sales, service and outbound logistics.

→ **Learning outcome 3**
Explain the strategic control of the primary activities in the value chain.

- Control of inbound logistics, operations and outbound logistics is concerned with ensuring a product or service of the right quality is produced and hence much of the control will be at the operational level of the organisation.
- The control of marketing will centre on the effectiveness of marketing, and the control of sales and service will centre on efficiency and meeting quantitative targets.

→ **Learning outcome 4**
Explain the strategic control of the support activities in the value chain.

- The support activities in the value chain cover infrastructure, HRM, technology and procurement.
- Infrastructure is controlled and managed by use of systems which allow the structure to work effectively and efficiently.
- Technology used to assist in marketing and selling would be controlled and evaluated by the money saved and the increases in revenue and profit produced.
- Technology used to produce and develop new products would be controlled and evaluated in terms of added value and achievement of longer-term goals.
- Procurement is controlled and evaluated by how well money is spent. Good deals negotiated with suppliers and savings made allow the company to offer low-cost goods or most value for least cost.
- In the case of HRM in the value chain, there are two basic approaches to controlling and managing staff, namely bureaucratic control and cultural control.
- Bureaucratic control depends on rules and regulations, while cultural control relies on building trust, loyalty and mutual respect. Cultural control seeks to develop loyalty to the company at the level of corporate headquarters and for this to be repeated at divisional level.
- This requires a two-way relationship and communication to develop between the corporate HQ and the division.

→ **Learning outcome 5**
Explain the strategic control of the value system.

- Strategic control of the value system is gained via related diversification, which allows linkages in the value system to be developed and exploited. Related diversification can take the form of backwards or forwards vertical integration or horizontal integration.

- Backwards vertical integration occurs when a company acquires its own sources of inputs, while forwards vertical integration occurs when a company establishes its own outlets. Horizontal integration is the acquiring of an outlet selling or producing the same or related goods.

→ **Learning outcome 6**
Develop effective strategic control systems.

- Effective strategic control sets and establishes meaningful targets and uses control systems to monitor the performance. This allows actual performance to be compared to targets and rewards and corrective action to be used as appropriate.

EXIT CASE STUDY 11.2

This exit case study looks at control in a private company and can be used to assess the learning outcomes below.

Learning outcomes	Check you have achieved this by	
Identify control activities in organisations	Listing the thing done by the business to keep control	Answering Exit case study question 1.
Explain the contribution of control to business success	Linking control activities to business outcomes.	Answering Exit case study question 2 .

We believe in being in control

FT

by Andrew Bolger

Stewart Milne, chairman and chief executive of the Aberdeen-based house-building company that carries his name, is easily Scotland's best-paid businessman. The £5m remuneration package he received last year was double the amount earned the previous year by Sir Fred Goodwin, chief executive of Royal Bank of Scotland, which employs 137,000 people worldwide and has just reported pre-tax profits of nearly £8bn. The difference is that the former electrician founded Stewart Milne Group and transformed it into a multimillion-pound national operation, and he and his family trust own all the shares in the private company. It employs 1,200 people and made pre-tax profits of £20m on sales of £217m in the year to June. Mr Milne recently announced ambitious plans to expand into England through acquisition and to double the turnover of his business, which specialises in timber-frame housing, by 2010.

Interviewed in the Glasshouse, the modern five-star Edinburgh hotel, 55-year-old Mr Milne recalls the modest circumstances in which he was raised in Aberdeenshire, where his father was a farm worker. A dapper figure, he speaks with quiet intensity about how he launched his business empire. He left school at 15 but, while serving a five-year apprenticeship as an electrician, he developed a taste for business by doing jobs in evenings and at the weekend. He handed in his notice as soon as he finished his apprenticeship. His boss was extremely annoyed: 'He told me how stupid I was, that I didn't know the first thing about business and had no prospect of surviving.'

'So that became a key driver: one way or another, I was going to prove him wrong. I was also dreading telling my father that I'd packed in my job and was setting up on my own. He took me by surprise by saying: "Well, if that is what you have decided, just make sure you make a real go of it – throw yourself into it." And as I was leaving, he gave me a couple of hundred pounds – which was a lot of money to him. I was determined to prove my boss wrong and justify my father's faith in me.'

Mr Milne focused on the fact that most tenement flats in Aberdeen in the early 1970s did not have modern bathrooms or kitchens, for which 75 per cent conversion grants were available. 'The traditional approach to doing a kitchen/bathroom conversion was that the main contractor took on the role, subcontracting the plumbing, electrical and decoration work. A typical conversion took anything from four to six months.'

Mr Milne's business developed a speedy alternative approach, which involved developing a small team that quickly became multi-skilled. 'We were completing two conversions every week, with everything done apart from the decoration. The following week, decorators moved in, so within a 10-day period a complete conversion was finished.'

'The business eventually took over responsibility for the design side, applying for grants for the clients and taking on the whole project. In doing it that way, 75 per cent of the money was coming in a grant. Because we did the grant application, we set it up in a way that the client effectively handed that over to us, so guaranteeing the cash flow.' Clients were prepared to pay a small premium to get the work done quickly.

The experience taught Mr Milne 'the importance of tackling things with an open mind – the traditional route is not necessarily the only route – and the importance of operating as a team, with no demarcation between trades. There was also the importance of planning and organising. When we hit a job on a Monday morning, it had been loaded up over the weekend. When a team arrived at a job they could start and just go right through it. These were the fundamental things that have been at the core of the company's approach over the past 30 years.'

Mr Milne established a limited company in 1975. He moved into house building as the Aberdeen conversions were starting to come to an end and the city's housing market was taking off, thanks to North Sea oil. 'We looked around and saw what was being done with timber frame – in this country, but particularly in Scandinavia. We decided that was the way we would go.'

The Stewart Milne Group expanded throughout Scotland and is now poised to acquire house builders in England. With a timber frame manufacturing plant in Aberdeen already established, the group decided four years ago to spend £15m on building one of Europe's most advanced timber frame factories in Oxford. It intends to build another such factory in England on a greenfield site. The company has not made a loss in 30 years of trading, and has been able to fund all acquisitions from retained profits and borrowing, supported by Bank of Scotland.

Mr Milne says: 'We do probably 85 per cent of the things we would be doing if we were a quoted company. But we are great believers in being in our own control. We can dictate the pace of growth or change we want to make. The main reason for going public is to get access to funds. If you have a good, sound business with good management that is well run financially there is money out there.'

'Being private allows us to take long-term views on things. We are convinced that land control is the secret to a good house building operation. Being private allows us to make judgements and commitments on things that might be a lot more difficult for a public company.' Being private also explains Mr Milne's chunky pay packet. 'Rather than seeking an exit strategy by disposing of the company or of shares externally – and bearing in mind the profits we have declared were after what I had taken out – I thought it was a sensible route to go down, so I can become less dependent on the company when I reach a stage when it is right for me to be taking a back seat and handing over the reins to others.'

Two of Mr Milne's sons work in the business, and he says he would 'dearly love' them to play a key role in the future. 'But they know it is not there to be just taken or given – they are there to prove themselves, that they are equal to the very good management that we have coming up through the business.'

Source: *Financial Times*, 8 March 2006.

Exit case study questions

1 Summarise the way Stewart Milne's business keeps control.

2 Discuss the importance of good control to the success of Stewart Milne's business

DISCUSSION TOPIC

1 Read the paper 'From competitive advantage to corporate strategy' by Michael E Porter, Chapter 17, in *The Strategy Process*, Mintzberg, Lampel, Quinn and Ghosal, Harlow: Prentice Hall, 2003.

2 Discuss how strategic control may assist or hinder an organisation in moving from competitive advantage to corporate strategy.

WIDEN YOUR HORIZONS

1 Widen your horizons by comparing and contrasting the strategic control measures which would be needed in a high street business such as a retailer or bank and an online business.

WEBLINKS

The websites for this chapter provide some further information on Dyson, which is the subject of Entry case study 11.1. The other website looks at the strategic control of human resources.

■ This is the website of Dyson; there is a section about the company and its history.
   www.dyson.co.uk

■ This website looks at the strategic control of human resources in organisations.
   www.management-training-consultants.com/management-control.htm

FURTHER READING

The following chapters in different strategy textbooks offer a variety of views on strategic control.

■ Dess, G G, Lumpkin, G T and Taylor, M L (2005) *Strategic Management*, 2nd edn, New York: McGraw Hill Irwin. Chapter 9, 'Strategic control and corporate governance'.

■ Haberberg, A and Rieple, A (2001) *The Strategic Management of Organisations*, Harlow: Financial Times/Prentice Hall. Chapter 10, 'Structure, information, control and reward systems'.

■ Johnson, G, Scholes, K and Whittington, R (2005) *Exploring Corporate Strategy*, 7th edn, Harlow: Financial Times/Prentice Hall. Chapter 9, 'Enabling success'.

■ Lynch, R (2006) *Corporate Strategy*, 4th edn, London: Financial Times/Prentice Hall. Chapter 17, 'Resource allocation, strategic planning and control'.

■ McGee, J, Thomas, H and Wilson, D (2005) *Strategy: Analysis & Practice*, Maidenhead: McGraw Hill. Chapter 18, 'Analysing and measuring strategic performance'.

■ Mellahi, K, Frynas, J G and Finlay, P (2005) *Global Strategic Management*, Oxford: Oxford University Press. Chapter 12, 'Global strategic control'.

■ Mullins, L J (2005) *Management and Organisational Behaviour*, 7th edn, Harlow: Financial Times/Prentice Hall. Chapter 21, 'Organisational control and power'.

■ Pearce, J A and Robinson, R B (2007) *Strategic Management: Formulation, Implementation and Control*, 10th edn, New York: McGraw-Hill International. Chapter 11, 'Organisational structure'.

REFERENCES

1 Kaplan, R S and Norton, D P (1992) 'The balanced scorecard - measures that drive performance', *Harvard Business Review*, January–February, pp 75-85, in Hill, C W L and Jones, G R (2001) *Strategic Management*, 5th edn, Boston: Houghton Mifflin.

2 Jaeger, A M (1983) 'The transfer of organisational culture overseas: an approach to control in the multinational corporation', *Journal of International Business Studies*, Fall, pp 91-114, in Mead, R (2005) *International Management*, 3rd edn, Oxford: Blackwell.

3 Hill, C W L and Jones, G R (2001) *Strategic Management*, 5th edn, Boston: Houghton Mifflin.

CHAPTER 12

Managing failure and turnaround

Exhibit 12.1 Essential strategy model

Chapter objectives

The key purpose of this chapter is to explain what is meant by failure for businesses and to illustrate the strategies which can help a struggling business revive itself. The symptoms and causes of decline and failure are the starting point and if a company recognises these then it is in a position to tackle the causes, providing the failure is not catastrophic. A struggling company, like a successful one, needs to develop a strategy if it is to progress into the future. The first aspect of strategy for a failing business to consider is its financial position regarding, debt, assets and costs. The impact of large debts and expensive assets needs to be evaluated, and the relationship between costs, prices and profits clearly understood and managed if turnaround is to be a based on solid foundations. The second aspect of strategy for the failing business is to develop more effective competitive and marketing strategies. This includes developing effective pricing, advertising, product and market strategies.

When you have read this chapter and worked through the associated activities you should be able to achieve the objectives specified below.

1 Summarise the symptoms and causes of failure in business.

2 Comment on the feasibility of recovery for a business in a particular situation.

3 Identify and explain retrenchment strategy.

4 Identify and explain turnaround strategy.

Changes to an organisation's management and leadership can often signal the start of change or turn-around and this entry case study illustrates the changes occurring in leadership at Ford as it faces decline and the need for successful turnaround.

ENTRY CASE STUDY 12.1

Ford pares management as part of turnaround

FT

by Bernard Simon

Ford Motor has further pared its top management ranks with the early retirement of Greg Smith, vice-chairman in charge of long-term strategy. Mr Smith's departure will help Ford meet the goal under its Way Forward recovery plan of trimming its 54-strong senior management group by 12 per cent by the end of March.

Under the turnaround plan announced last month, Ford said it would cut its North American workforce by 25,000–30,000 people and close 14 assembly plants and parts factories. Ford's executive ranks were marked by high turnover even before the Way Forward plan was announce. Its North American division has gone through four chiefs, including Mr Smith, in the past five years.

Mr Smith was replaced last October by Mark Fields, who has quickly emerged as the chief architect of the turnaround plan and a possible successor to Jim Padilla, Ford's president and chief operating officer. Over the past six months, the carmaker has lost its chief of North American product development, the head of North American vehicle operations and the head of its hybrid vehicle programme. More recent departures include the group vice-president for North American marketing and sales. Mr Smith, 54, has worked for Ford for 32 years.

Source: FT.com site, 12 February 2006.

INTRODUCTION

The business pages of any newspaper talk about both the success and failure of companies, although failure and how it affects businesses and their management are often not tackled in business textbooks such as this one. This chapter introduces the types of failure situations businesses may face and then goes on to focus on the feasibility of recovery and how this could be undertaken.

The pages of any business newspaper show that actions by companies, their managers and accountants do sometimes lead to potential failure or actual decline. The spectacular failure and decline of companies like Enron, Worldcom, Arthur Anderson and Parmalat are well documented and are usually due to fraudulent business practices. In this type of situation there is no feasibility of recovery.

However, the focus of this chapter is to look at how companies which have performed poorly and are deemed to be failing or struggling can improve their position. In the UK the number of companies which failed to recognise the extent of their struggle and were unsuccessful in resolving their problems increased, as corporate insolvencies increased by 11 per cent in 2005. Well-known UK companies which became insolvent and closed in 2005 include the car manufacturer Rover, the department store chain, Allders and the off-licence chain, Unwins.[1] Hence there is a need for businesses and their managers to recognise potential failure and be able to take appropriate action.

SYMPTOMS OF DECLINE AND FAILURE

Symptoms of decline and failure are not causes of failure but are indicators that all is not well and that a company, if not already failing, is heading for failure (see Business illustration on Morrisons). Some of the symptoms of decline and failure such as falling sales and decreasing liquidity (see Exhibit 12.2) can be measured in a tangible way, and compared to previous performance and the performance of other companies in the same line of business. The presence of decline and failure symptoms indicates that the causes of decline and failure are likely to be present in the company, namely poor management and leadership, inadequate financial management, and a lack of competitiveness. If any of these symptoms of decline are initially identified in a company it is necessary to also identify the underlying causes of decline and undertake remedial action before a culture of failure becomes established.

Exhibit 12.2 Symptoms of decline and failure

- Falling sales
- Falling profitability
- Reduced dividend
- Decreasing liquidity
- Increasing debt
- Falling ROCE
- Declining market share
- High turnover of managers
- Delay in publishing financial results
- Senior management fear
- Lacking of strategic thinking
- Falling EPS

Source: based on Argenti, J (1976) *Corporate collapse: the causes and symptoms*, McGraw-Hill, in Slatter, S (1984), *Corporate Recovery*, London: The Penguin Business Library. See Chapter 4 for further discussion on ratios, ROCE - return on capital employed, and EPS - earnings per share.

Business illustration of potential failure – Morrisons

At the end of 2005, beginning of 2006, the UK supermarket Morrisons was exhibiting a number of these symptoms of failure. Morrisons had a consistent record of sales and profit growth. However, following the successful £3 billion takeover in 2003 of the supermarket chain Safeway, Morrisons have struggled to integrate the two businesses. Additionally Morrisons had not realised the extent to which Safeway was losing sales and cash. In October 2005, this led to Morrisons issuing their fifth profits warning in a year. Additionally the city had been keen for sometime to see a succession plan, as Sir Ken Morrison is over seventy years old and relationships between Sir Ken, his deputy chairman David Jones and chief executive Bob Stott continued to be strained.

Source: 'City wants to see a safe way forward from Sir Ken', Julia Finch, *Guardian*, 17 October 2005.

CAUSES OF FAILURE

There are many causes of failure and it will often be a combination of factors which will cause a company to fail (see Exhibit 12.3). Inside a company poor management and leadership can occur at all levels, with inefficiencies occurring in all areas of the business (see Business illustration on Marks & Spencer). Equally a failure to focus on the core business and poor day-to-day financial control can lead the company to slip into long-term decline, while the mismanagement of large projects such as an acquisition or capital investment means significant resources are wasted and the onset of decline can be swift.

Business illustration of causes of failure – Marks & Spencer

In mid 2004 Stuart Rose became chief executive of Marks & Spencer, and was the second chief executive to be appointed to turnaround Marks & Spencer's performance since 2000. In 1998 Marks & Spencer made pre-tax profits of £1.2 billion and by 2004 they were £763 million when Luc Van de Velde left. On taking up his new job Stuart Rose identified the following causes of failure: high costs; lack of leadership; a complicated business; neglect of the core area of clothing; cluttered stores; and a failure to compete effectively, particularly in women's wear.

Source: 'Changes in store to counter catalogue of weaknesses', *Daily Telegraph*, 13 July 2004.

Equally a company's marketing and how it positions itself in the external environment and competitive arena are also key to success; hence failure to get it right in this area will obviously lead directly to company failure. A company will go into decline if it fails to develop new competitive strategies such that previous levels of performance and success are maintained, as when previously successful products go into decline, there will be nothing to replace them.

Exhibit 12.3 Causes of failure

- **Poor management and leadership**
  - ⇨ Due to poor or dominant strategic leadership.

- **Neglecting the core business**
  - ⇨ Due to management focusing too much on exciting non-core ventures.

- **Inefficient operations**
  - ⇨ Arises from poor management of resources, resulting in higher costs.

- **Poor financial management**
  - ⇨ Financial or managerial resources are over-stretched on big projects, meaning healthier parts of the business suffer.

- **Inadequate financial control**
  - ⇨ Poor cash-flow forecasts, costing systems and budgetary control, meaning no key information on costs, sales and profits.

- **Failure to compete effectively**
  - ⇨ No understanding of the competitive arena and hence an unsuitable competitive strategy.

Poor management and leadership

An organisation heading towards decline may be doing so because the company's management is failing in any number of ways, namely poor strategic leadership, dominance of the leader or one type of employee (for example engineers), or a high turnover of strategic leaders. Entry case study 12.1 illustrates the high turnover of strategic leaders at Ford, which had four chiefs in the five years to 2006. This is in addition to losing three other senior managers in its North American division in the second half of 2005 and the likelihood of further senior management losses to come. All this change in strategic leadership has occurred as Ford have struggled to maintain market share, which dipped to 17.9 per cent in January 2006 – a whole percentage point down on January 2005.

Poor strategic leadership can lead to decline and is defined in broad terms as the failing of the strategic leader to pay attention to key factors. The external environment and marketplace will be poorly understood by the board, meaning effective competitive strategies are not developed and implemented. Poor implementation of strategy will result in a lack of clarity throughout the organisation concerning objectives and how they are to be achieved. It is also likely that a weak culture will predominate (see Chapter 5). An organisation in this position, with weak senior management and a strategic leader who have lost their way, will fare worse than one with a lost strategic leader who is well supported by strong senior management and non-executive directors.

An **autocratic** managing director runs the business in a strict and inflexible way.

A dominant and **autocratic** managing director is often found in failing companies (see Business illustration on Bank of Italy). The managing director will make all the major decisions and does not tolerate discord. The dominance of one leader is not necessarily bad, as long as the company is profitable and successful. However, as soon as trouble occurs the dominant and autocratic managing director is blamed, as the causes of early success are often the causes of later failure. Early success causing later decline is avoided if the autocrat recognises the limitations of his or her management style and is willing to adapt to a changing organisation and external environment. This means being receptive to new ideas from subordinates and customers. The unsuccessful autocrat refuses to recognise the need for change and loses the support of others, meaning business growth is jeopardised. Ultimately, this may lead to his or her downfall (see Business illustration on Bank of Italy).

Business illustration of dominant leader – Bank of Italy

The governor of the Bank of Italy, Antonio Fazio, resigned just before Christmas 2005 after more than a decade spent running the bank dictatorially under rules which date to the Mussolini era (right wing, 1930s). The resignation followed a loss of support from the bank's council, which was the only body with the power to sack the governor of the Bank of Italy. This decision by the bank's council followed Mr Fazio being put under investigation for insider trading and abuse of power contrary to EU single market rules. The Milan stock market and investors both welcomed the resignation of Mr Fazio.

Source: 'Scandal finally forces out Italy's top banker', Ambrose Evans-Pritchard, *Daily Telegraph*, 20 December 2005.

Alternatively dominance may arise from one type of employee – for example, accountants – resulting in failure to understand the nature of competition and customer needs and wants. This dominance may also be reflected in the make up of senior management, with other key areas such as human resources being ignored and not represented at board level.

Neglecting the core business

Neglecting the core business can occur when the company's management pursues exciting and challenging growth and diversification. The management focus their effort and resources on diversification outside of core products and markets at the expense of fully exploiting and maintaining the core business. The consequence can be serious decline, as the core business is that section of the business which is likely to become or be mature, and it is the mature business and cash cow products that generate the cash flow and income to fund growth and diversification. Hence, neglecting the core business to focus on growth and diversification is a short-sighted approach to developing the company.

Inefficient operations

Inefficiency is the poor use of resources, resulting in unnecessary wastage.

Inefficient operations may be found in all areas of the business and tend to arise from poor management of resources and activities, with the result being corporate decline. **Inefficiency** – directly or indirectly – causes higher costs, but can be identified by examining key measures such as **utilisation**, **productivity** and **capacity** (see Business illustration on General Motors and Chapter 11).

Capacity is a basic measure of performance; full capacity is a system producing maximum output in a specified time.

Capacity is a basic measure of performance. If a system is operating to capacity then it is producing the maximum amount of a product in a specified time. For example, a car manufacturer with the capacity to produce 1,000 cars per month is operating to capacity when 1,000 cars roll off the production line every month. Utilisation measures the percentage of available capacity that is actually used; so, for example, if our car manufacturer produces only 800 cars a month, then capacity is 80 per cent ($800/1000 \times 100$). This type of drop in utilisation can mean a mismatch between capacity and demand, resulting in unsatisfied customers or under-utilised resources. If there are unsatisfied customers, then the opportunity to make sales and profit is being missed. Alternatively if resources are being under-utilised, then the unit cost will rise as the resources are not being used to their greatest **efficiency** and the company will cut costs (see Business illustration on General Motors).

Utilisation is a measure of the percentage of available capacity that is actually used.

Business illustration of cost cutting – General Motors

In November 2005 General Motors announced plans to radically cut costs in its North American operations to allow the company to compete effectively with its global competitors. General Motors' plans were to cut 30,000 jobs and reduce its high costs in the areas of labour and materials, capacity is only 85 per cent of the capacity of Asian car manufacturers operating in the US. The company is also to change its health care programme with the aim of saving $7 billion per annum. The company's market share has been eroded by Asian auto companies and this has lead to losses in excess of $4 billion in 2005, although the chief executive Rick Wagoner retains the support of the board, but not of all major investors.

Source: 'GM races to cut 30,000 jobs', David Litterick and Josephine Moulds, *Daily Telegraph*, 22 November 2005.

Productivity is the quantity manufactured in relation to one or more of the resources used.

Productivity is the quantity manufactured in relation to one or more of the resources used. If there are a hundred employees working on the production line for cars, making 1,000 cars a month, then productivity is 10 cars per employee (1000/100). If only 800 cars are produced in a month then productivity drops to 8 cars per employee (800/100). This also drives the unit cost up, as employees are still being paid but are producing less for the business to sell, which in turn translates into reduced profits.

Additionally poor production planning, inadequate maintenance and poor plant layout can all make the production process inefficient, as can inappropriate expenditure of marketing. Advertising in the wrong place and not reaching the target market is inefficient and will mean sales decline.

Efficiency should not be confused with **effectiveness** (see Chapter 11). Effectiveness is how well an organisation sets and achieves its goals. In considering capacity, utilisation, productivity, efficiency and effectiveness, thought should be given to how these measures combine. For example, high productivity is of no use if the quality of products produced is poor or if the finished products remain in a warehouse because there is no demand for them.

Poor financial management

Declining organisations usually have some financial problems, resulting from either failure of large projects or from poor financial control. Large projects for companies include a range of ventures, such as product development, entering new overseas markets, and acquisitions. Companies heading for failure may be in that situation as a result of underestimating the capital requirements for large projects. Expenditure may escalate due to poor organisation and planning, and an inaccurate estimation of the length of time required to complete the project – and all these can be exacerbated by design changes to a building or product once the project has started. There may also be other costs associated with overcoming unexpected difficulties, such as customer hesitation or hostility.

Acquisitions are costly projects and decline can result from the expected revenues, profits and synergy failing to materialise. This can be linked to another cause of failure, which is discussed earlier in this section, namely that of poor strategic leadership. Hence acquisitions should evaluated with the same care as any other capital investment project.

Avoiding failure requires that companies do not stretch financial or managerial resources with big projects as this can easily cause other healthier parts of the business to suffer. Therefore it is essential to control expenditure and costs and to forecast potential revenues without being unrealistically optimistic.

Inadequate financial control

A lack of financial control means all or some of the following are inadequate: cash flow forecasts, costing systems and budgetary control. This lack of key information concerning products, their costs, sales and profits is due to either a lack of financial control or poor financial control. In small companies it may be an absence of financial control systems which is causing decline. In contrast, in larger companies financial control systems will exist, but will be inadequate or poorly used by management.

The inadequate nature of management accounting systems can be due to systems and how they are used. Poorly designed management accounting systems which fail to deliver information to allow the business to be run effectively will cause a business to struggle, particularly if times are tough. Equally, poor use of the correct management accounting systems and the information they generate by a management who are 'accounting illiterate' will inevitably lead to poor decisions being made, which will in turn cause decline. Also, organisational structure can hinder effective control, for example over-centralisation and placing control at too high a level in the organisation makes control difficult. **Decentralisation** (see Chapter 10) of some control and allowing budget responsibility to be held lower down the organisation may improve control and productivity.

A company may slip into decline as its failure to budget successfully starts to impact on the business. A failure to budget means short-term financial plans and forecasts will not successfully indicate potential demand and sales revenue. This in turn means the cost of meeting demand is not predicted, and neither are the flows of cash in and out of the business. Therefore, without proper budgeting companies cannot estimate profits and cash needs adequately and will experience financial difficulties, including a lack of liquidity.

Failing companies often do not know which products are profitable and which are loss making. Inadequate costing systems can result in a company not being aware of the costs of their products and services, and hence if the mix and volume of products manufactured and sold changes, the company can move from profit to loss without realising it. Equally if the company invests in new and expensive equipment and facilities to lower costs or add value, then there needs to be realisation that **fixed costs** or overheads have increased and this cannot be ignored.

Failure to identify and understand the costs incurred in making a product means it is likely that the company will have a significantly higher cost structure than that of its major competitors, putting the company at a competitive disadvantage. Hence companies in turnaround situations find themselves unable to compete on price because cost structures are too high. However, high cost structures also mean lower profit margins and less additional borrowing power than competitors, resulting in less money to invest in product development and marketing. Hence the company is more likely to end up following strategy number 6, 7 or 8 on the strategy clock (see Chapter 7 and Exhibit 7.7). Competitive strategy 6 is one of high price and standard value, strategy 7 is one of reduced value and increased price, strategy 8 is standard price and low value – all of which are strategies destined for failure. This means the company will be unable to build market share, hold on to customers and achieve competitive advantage.

Failure to compete effectively

A lack of competitiveness can result from poor cost structures as discussed previously. However, a failure to understand the nature of the competitive arena the company operates in and competitive strategy clearly also adds significantly to a lack of competitiveness. Companies unable to build market share, hold on to customers and achieve competitive advantage will clearly face fierce competitive rivalry from companies able to achieve good market share, plenty of customers and competitive advantage. Successful competitors will have launched exciting new products, improved existing products or cut costs to strengthening competitive advantage, inevitably causing demand for other products in the marketplace to fall.

Equally successful new entrants and substitute products can undermine a company's position in the competitive arena. New entrants persuading customers to switch products or brands will cause a decline in the company's sales. In the 1990s UK carpet manufacturers were badly affected by laminate floor companies supplying a fashionable alternative, which was often cheaper than carpet.

Along with a poor understanding of the competitive arena, a poor marketing effort will contribute to a lack of competitiveness. There is often complacency among management and employees at all levels in the declining company; however, it is with the marketing effort that complacency is most visible to outside stakeholders. A poor marketing effort has many features (see Exhibit 12.4).

Exhibit 12.4 Poor marketing effort

- No product development
- Unbalanced portfolio of products
- Core products ignored
- Lack of market research and knowledge of consumer behaviour
- Markets wrongly segmented
- Poorly motivated salesforce with a complacent sales manager
- Key customers not targeted effectively
- Outdated advertising and sales promotion material
- Ineffective advertising locations
- Poor after-sales service

✔ Check your understanding

- Do you understand the difference between symptoms and causes of decline?
- Check your understanding by stating if each of the following is a symptom or cause of decline.

   1 Profits warning is announced.

   2 Charging a standard price for a low value product.

   3 Three marketing managers have left this year.

   4 This year's dividend is half the dividend paid last year.

   5 Expensive suppliers are under contract.

   6 The managing director is a domineering autocrat.

Causes of decline

1 Explain the difference between symptoms and causes of decline.
2 Explain how poor management and leadership might lead a company to fail.
3 Which key measures can indicate operations are inefficient?
4 How do inadequate financial controls lead to corporate failure?
5 Summarise the competitive strategies which will lead to failure.

FEASIBILITY OF RECOVERY

The feasibility of recovery for a company depends on both causes and severity of decline and failure. A company showing many of the symptoms of decline and failure (see Exhibit 12.2) is more likely to be experiencing many of the causes of failure (see Exhibit 12.3). A company in such a situation is likely to be enduring a severe crisis. Alternatively if the industry or competitive arena faced by the company is unattractive with no opportunity for improvement or growth, then insolvency will be inevitable (see point 1 on Exhibit 12.5). A severe and long-term deep-rooted crisis, possibly linked to fraud, will also lead to this outcome (see introduction to this chapter).

Exhibit 12.5   The feasibility of recovery

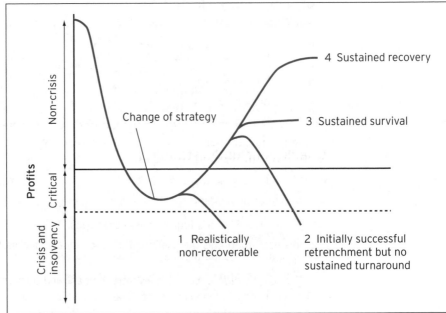

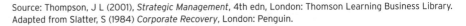
Source: Thompson, J L (2001), *Strategic Management*, 4th edn, London: Thomson Learning Business Library. Adapted from Slatter, S (1984) *Corporate Recovery*, London: Penguin.

Successful recovery for a limited period of time is possible if costs can be controlled, market share recovered and profits improved to a non-crisis level (see point 2 on Exhibit 12.5). However, unless the industry remains attractive and profitable and the company retains its competitive advantage, the recovery will eventually fail. The next possible recovery scenario is one of sustained recovery, with no likelihood of growth and expansion. This is achievable and sustainable in the longer term if costs are well controlled, prices competitive and a narrow profit margin acceptable (see point 3 on Exhibit 12.5). A sustained recovery is a genuine and successful turnaround, which includes successful long-term growth and expansion of the business (see point 4 on Exhibit 12.5).

The likelihood of sustained recovery and successful turnaround increases if poor management is the cause of decline, rather than the company operating in an unattractive industry which makes success difficult to achieve. It is possible to alter the poor management of a declining company and, while this may be difficult, it is made easier if there is support from key stakeholders for making the necessary changes. Improved management should be able to spot and take advantage of the opportunities to reduce costs, and to differentiate and refocus on core products and markets.

Slatter[2] identifies two stages in recovery: retrenchment and turnaround.

Retrenchment strategies are operational and aim to make a company more productive and profitable.

Retrenchment strategies (see Exhibit 12.6) are operational rather than competitive or corporate strategies. Therefore retrenchment strategies are aimed at making a company more productive and profitable with its current products and markets, although unprofitable products may be withdrawn from the market. The aim is for fairly swift improvements in the relationship between costs, prices and profits, with the objective of steering the company away from an immediate and more severe crisis, hopefully leading to an improvement in company performance. Unsurprisingly this requires a focus on financial matters, which are normally part of the reason for decline and failure.

Turnaround strategies aim to make the company's marketing effort more effective and improve its position in the competitive environment.

Turnaround strategies tackle those areas which need to be developed if recovery is to be sustained. Turnaround strategies are about making the company's marketing effort more effective and improving the company's position in its competitive arena. Turnaround strategies need to be successfully implemented if there is to be a sustained recovery (see Exhibit 12.8 in the section on turnaround strategies).

Review questions | Feasibility of recovery

1 Summarise Slatter's four recovery scenarios.
2 In what situation is the likelihood of recovery and successful turnaround most likely?
3 Explain the difference between retrenchment and turnaround strategies.

RETRENCHMENT STRATEGIES

Thompson[3] and Slatter[4] suggest retrenchment is about tackling a number of areas in the declining company, with many concerns being financial (see Exhibit 12.6).

Exhibit 12.6 Retrenchment strategies

■ Organisational changes	Consider changes in management, reorganisation and redefining job roles and responsibilities.
■ Financial changes	Consider cash flow, cost of production, and expenses.
■ Debt restructuring	Consider extending loan repayment periods, interest-only loans and converting loans to share capital.
■ Cost reduction in the value chain	Consider how costs can be reduced in all value chain activities.
■ Asset reduction and divestment	Consider selling assets or divesting some parts of the business.

Organisational changes

Organisational changes include changes in leadership and management and will need to occur if failure is due in to poor management rather than to an unattractive industry. New management and leadership will seek to change and improve things in the company (see Business illustration on Marks & Spencer below). This can include some reorganisation and redefinition of jobs and roles to match the needs of the company if is to attain strategic fit with its external environment. This in turn means changes to day-to-day routine behaviour and control systems (see cultural web in Chapter 5) to enable managers to achieve success in their new roles.

Business illustration of leadership change –
Marks & Spencer

Stuart Rose, the new chief executive, sought to tackle the lack of leadership at Marks & Spencer by challenging the culture of meetings, reports and poor accountability which he believed led to distraction and a lack of focus on efforts to deliver better products to customers.

Source: 'Changes in store to counter catalogue of weaknesses', *Daily Telegraph*, 13 July 2004.

Financial changes

The financial matters which are covered in developing a retrenchment strategy examine all aspects of a company's situation, from day-to-day expenses through to changes in debt and asset reduction (see Exhibit 12.6).

Financial changes covering cash flow, overheads and costs should be examined. Good cash flow is vital in a business and poor cash flow is often a feature of a failing organisation, with **debtors** taking too long to pay for goods that have been supplied and **creditors** waiting too long to be paid for goods they have supplied to the company. A tightening up of creditors and debtors, such that money owed is received from debtors before it is needed to pay creditors, will improve a company's cash flow situation. Examining costs and improving the situation with regard to costs will also improve the cash flow situation, such that enough money is available to meet bills from creditors.

The declining company should consider if it knows the actual cost of producing its various products and if it can account for all expenditure. Failing to know the answers to these key questions means the company does not understand the relationship between costs, price and profits, which is crucial if the appropriate competitive strategies are to be pursued in the best market segments. In examining costs the company should also examine overheads and expenses, as if these are high in relation to production costs then there is an opportunity to reduce costs. Establishment of effective cost systems and greater control over the cash flow can improve profitability and generate revenues.

Debt restructuring

The aim of restructuring debt is to reduce the immediate financial burden on the company by reducing the size of the regular debt repayments the company makes. Options include extending repayment dates on loans and repaying the same amount of capital over a longer period of time or converting to an interest-only loan for a period of time and deferring repayment of capital. Another option is to convert loan capital into share capital, which means that the lender foregoes repayment of the money lent, but becomes a shareholder in the company. This allows the lender to recoup the money from any **dividend payments** and the improved value of the shares at some point in the future.

Cost reduction in the value chain

Another approach to retrenchment is to consider the company's value chain and look for cost reductions and improvements in efficiency that can be achieved by altering the value chain activities (see Business illustration on Marks & Spencer on page 388).

Business illustration of reducing costs –
Marks & Spencer

Stuart Rose sought to tackle the high costs at Marks & Spencer by renegotiating contracts with suppliers; reducing stocks; examining the volume of business from 'mark-downs' or sale items; and decreasing the cost of waste food which had risen by nearly 50 per cent since 1996. Redundancies were also to take place and 650 jobs lost.

Source: 'Changes in store to counter catalogue of weaknesses', *Daily Telegraph*, 13 July 2004.

Possibilities include examining procurement and inbound logistics. Is the company getting the best deal from suppliers in terms of price or can a better deal be negotiated with an alternative supplier if the procurement function shops around? Examine what actually happens when goods are delivered to the company: do the inbound logistics run smoothly? Do goods arrive when scheduled to arrive and in the correct amount? Are there any breakages or returns of goods which are unfit for use? Is it the company or the supplier who bears this cost? Does the delivery of supplies impact detrimentally on stock control systems? Are there occasions when stock levels are high, tying up cash and costing resources to store? Can improvements be made to ensure the stock moves more quickly through the business?

Alternatively the cost of staffing could be examined. Examine working patterns and seek to manage shift patterns, overtime and redundancies to reduce costs and bring capacity into line with demand. This is necessary as it is easy for companies to slip into situations where overtime and weekend working are creating costs which cannot be recovered by charging competitive prices. If redundancy is necessary then seek to implement a redundancy programme, which will both reduce labour costs and ensure that non-essential staff and those who make the least effective contribution leave.

Finally it is always possible to cut non-essential activities in the short term, and this usually includes cutting expenditure on training, advertising, and research and development. However, if the company is to survive in the long term beyond the immediate crisis, these activities will need to be reinstated when sales revenues and profits improve.

Asset reduction and divestment

Divestment is selling off all or part of the business.

Asset reduction and **divestment** can take a number of forms and includes closing plants down or divesting, which is selling off, all or part of the business to another company or investor (see Business illustration on Marks & Spencer opposite).

Business illustration of divestment – Marks & Spencer

In 2004 Stuart Rose sought to help Marks & Spencer focus on its core business of clothing by divesting the company of its financial services business to HSBC. Additionally the company was to close its Lifestore homewares business and stop opening more Simply Food stores.

Source: 'Changes in store to counter catalogue of weaknesses', *Daily Telegraph*, 13 July 2004.

Asset reduction means plants are closed down and production concentrated in fewer places or activities are moved to cheaper facilities. BA sold its corporate headquarters in London and moved its head office into facilities at Heathrow which were cheaper than central London, resulting in reduced overheads and costs. This move not only released the capital from the London headquarters but also placed head office close to the company's major centre of operations. The other option for a company that sells a large fixed asset is to undertake a 'sale and leaseback'. The company sells the asset and then leases it back from the new owner. This allows the company access to the capital and removes overheads, which can be an attractive option if the company decides its concern is with using and not owning assets.

If a company cannot recover and turnaround from its failings, then divesting failing parts of the business may be the way forward (see Business illustration on Marks & Spencer). The decision to divest a subsidiary, division or part of the business should be supported by thorough analysis. Key questions to be asked of any potential divestment candidate (division, subsidiary, or section of the business) are shown in Exhibit 12.7.

Exhibit 12.7 Divestment candidate?

- What does the financial and strategic analysis of the divestment candidate indicate?

- Consider the current market position and opportunities for competitive advantage of both the divestment candidate and the business a whole. Do these opportunities exist? Will they be improved if the divestment goes ahead?

- How will the company's portfolio of products be altered if the divestment goes ahead? Will current and potentially profitable products be lost if the divestment goes ahead?

- How will the freed up money and resources be used? Could they be put to better and more profitable use?

- Is there a buyer willing to pay an acceptable price?

Once the decision has been taken to divest part of the business, the next decisions are who to sell the business to and for how much. It is easy to sell a business cheaply, therefore the search should be for a buyer prepared to pay a fair price. The parent company should consider if the search for a buyer is to be 'secret'. Public knowledge that a subsidiary or division is up for sale will create uncertainty among staff, indeed the good staff may leave, and the company's relationship with key stakeholders may be affected. Alternatively the view may be taken that honesty is the best policy and indeed if a **management buyout** is a possibility then the decision to divest needs to be out in the open.

However, if a management buyout is not an option then other types of potential buyer, including sphere of influence buyers, associated industry companies and unconnected companies need to be considered. Sphere of influence buyers include competitors, customers and suppliers. These types of buyers will be undertaking horizontal integration or vertical integration and will be seeking control of another section of the supply chain.

Other possible buyers include companies in associated industries with complementary and related skills, which are seeking growth via related diversification. Finally unconnected companies seeking growth by unrelated diversification are also possible buyers

> A **management buyout** occurs when the current management buy the company, usually with the aim of running it as a going concern.

✔ Check your understanding

- Do you understand how cost reductions in the value chain can be achieved?
- Check your understanding by referring to Entry case study 12.1, and explain in which areas of the value chain, in addition to HRM, Ford can achieve cost reductions in order to remain competitive.

Review questions

Retrenchment strategies

1   Explain what actions a failing company may undertake as a retrenchment strategy.
2   Specify the aspects of cost a failing company should address.
3   Summarise the options for a company seeking to restructure its debt.
4   How can use of the value chain help a company undertaking retrenchment?
5   How should a business evaluate the option of divestment for a failing subsidiary or division?

TURNAROUND STRATEGIES

Turnaround strategies are about developing the company's competitive position and market performance by improving the effectiveness of the company's marketing. This is in contrast to retrenchment strategies, which are concerned with reducing and controlling costs and getting off the bottom of Slatter's curve, and which do not directly affect customers. Turnaround strategies need to be successfully implemented if there is to be a sustained recovery (see Exhibit 12.8). The turnaround strategies outlined in Exhibit 12.8 may be used in conjunction with the retrenchment strategies and each other at any one time. This mixing of strategies will need to occur particularly if a severe and deep-rooted crisis is to be successfully managed.

Exhibit 12.8 Turnaround strategies

■ Changing prices	How will sales revenues be affected?
■ Emphasise advertising and selling	Check expenditure on advertising and selling, and whether enough sales revenue is being generated.
■ Re-focusing	Review opportunities for competitive advantage and how well products meet customers' needs.
■ Rationalising the product portfolio	Will rationalising the product portfolio help the company concentrate on the strongest market segments?
■ New product development	How will new products and product improvements help in the achievement of competitive advantage?

Changing prices

If price changes are to be considered the key question is: 'How will sales revenues be affected?' Price increases or decreases can both result in increased sales revenue. There is little point in increasing price if sales revenues are going to fall lower than ever. Increased sales revenue from price decreases are fine as long as acceptable profit margins are maintained and products do not move from being profit making to loss making. When considering price changes always review the impact of the price changes on the relationship between costs, price and profits, as this is the key relationship underpinning competitive strategy. Price changes should be supported by advertising and sales promotion, and possibly minor product changes and improvements. This allows the price changes to be justified from the customer's perspective. If the price changes are increases, then there should be a very clear link to improved added value and the creation of new competitive advantage.

Failure to carefully evaluate the relationship between costs, price and profits and the link to competitive advantage could result in the company pursuing one of strategies for failure from Faulkner and Bowman's strategy clock (see Chapter 7). Competitive strategy 6 is one of high price and standard value, which will result in customers deserting the company for competitors' more appropriately priced products. Competitive strategy 7 is increased prices and reduced value, which will also drive customers to switch to competitors. In the case of competitive strategy 8 where the company charges a standard price for low value goods, customers will realise they are getting poor value for money and switch to another supplier. The outcome of pursuing any of these strategies is a lack of strategic fit between the company's offering to the marketplace and the expectations of customers.

Emphasise selling and advertising

The first step is to examine all current marketing expenditure and try to determine where the best potential returns might be gained. Once additional advertising and sales effort are in place, the key question to ask and regularly review is: 'Do advertising and sales promotion both cover their costs and generate an acceptable improvement in sales revenue?' If necessary ask new customers how they heard about the company and its products. If advertising and sales promotion are not generating an improvement in sales revenue, then the money and effort are being wasted. In this situation it could make sense to consider the opportunity cost of the expenditure. Namely, ask the question, 'Could the same money be spent to better effect elsewhere?'.

Re-focusing

The idea behind re-focusing is to concentrate effort on identifying opportunities for competitive advantage and how products meet customers' needs. Hence the re-focusing strategy requires a thorough evaluation of why customers buy and the opportunities for improved competitive advantage and market segmentation.

Identification of opportunities for competitive advantage may mean re-segmentation of the market is needed to improve market position and tackle the competition. The possibility of profitable niche markets, which are not well served by the competition, should be considered. Re-segmentation and an improvement in market position should ideally result in specific customers and products being closely matched, which in turn should provide growth in sales revenue and profits margins. Changes should be closely monitored so that any negative responses from the marketplace can be picked up and dealt with promptly, before they push the company back towards decline.

Rationalising the product portfolio

Rationalising the product portfolio may be undertaken alongside a strategy of re-focusing, which includes re-segmentation of the market (which is discussed above). The sales revenue products make, along with their profit margin and contribution to overheads and costs, should all be examined before removing a product from the portfolio. If a product makes a small contribution to profit it could be tempting to remove it from the portfolio of products the company offers; however, before doing so the decision should be evaluated as there may be a valid argument for retaining the product (see Exhibit 12.9). In 2004 Stuart Rose cut 500 products from Marks & Spencer's food ranges, as the stores were seen as being too cluttered and the aim was to streamline the shops.[5]

Exhibit 12.9 Remove products making a small contribution to profit?

- How long has the product been made for?
- Do competitors also offer the same product?
- Has the level of performance over the last three years been upwards, level or downwards?
- Can costs be reduced or the price increased?
- Do important customers of other highly profitable products also buy products making a small contribution to profits?
- Does the product make a significant contribution to fixed costs?

New product development

New product development is a useful turnaround strategy if the company is falling behind competitors in an attractive industry. New products and product improvements can help boost competitiveness in the marketplace, which is worthwhile if improved profit margins are possible. For example, as part of their turnaround Marks & Spencer introduced the Autograph and Per Una ranges of women's clothing to improve their competitiveness in relation to other high street shops such as Next and River Island.

Alternatively product improvements can be used to extend the product life cycle (plc) of products which are in the maturity section of the plc, and this is a valid option if a profit can be made from the new version of the product. However, if the industry is an attractive fast-growing industry, a strategy of developing new products may be preferable to avoid falling behind competitors in terms of innovation and product development.

 Check your understanding

- Do you understand how to develop a turnaround strategy?
- Check your understanding by explaining the issues a struggling low-cost airline should consider if it is to achieve sustained turnaround, remain in business and grow in size.

Review questions | Turnaround strategies

1 Explain why emphasising advertising and selling is a key aspect of turnaround strategy.

2 Why should price increases and decreases be carefully evaluated?

3 Identify the actions of a company undertaking re-focusing.

4 Criticise the following statement: 'Products making a small contribution to profit should be removed from the product portfolio.'

5 Summarise the two aspects of a product development strategy.

CONCLUSION

Companies use both retrenchment and turnaround strategies to revive a failing business. Companies that are successful at turnaround will undoubtedly follow some or all of the retrenchment strategies to improve costs, budgets and cash flow. Additionally turnaround strategies are often also employed to improve the company's competitive position in the marketplace. Companies may employ retrenchment strategies followed by turnaround strategies, or indeed retrenchment and turnaround may run together in parallel.

In conclusion, do the retrenchment and turnaround strategies work? The answer is yes they can be made to work and a struggling business can revamp itself. In 2002 Mothercare, which sells baby and children's clothes, toys, prams and cots, issued three profit warnings, had high supply and distribution costs, and a pre-tax loss of £10 million.

However, by 2005 Mothercare was experiencing the success of its three-year turnaround. The overall result at the end of 2005 was profit rather than loss, with pre-tax profits for the first half of 2005 rising to £11.4 million – an increase of 4 per cent on 2004. This was done by tightly controlling costs, updating product ranges, improving customer service and increasing international sales. The turnaround was also viewed as successful by the stock market, as dividends rose from 2.7 pence to 2.85 pence, an increase of 5.5 per cent, and shares rose from 335 pence to 344.5 pence on 17 November 2005 when these figures were released.

LEARNING OUTCOMES AND SUMMARY

The learning outcomes for this chapter are specified and a brief summary of the material relating to the learning outcomes is provided.

→ **Learning outcome 1**
Summarise the symptoms and causes of failure in business

- Symptoms of decline, such as falling sales and decreasing liquidity, indicate the likely presence of causes of decline in the company.
- There are many causes of failure and it will often be a combination of factors which will cause a company to fail. Causes of failure include poor leadership, inefficient operations, poor financial management and the impact of the external environment.

→ **Learning outcome 2**
Comment on the feasibility of recovery for a business in a particular situation.

- A company may never succeed in turning itself around if it is facing a severe crisis. Alternatively a limited turnaround is possible if some of the causes of failure can be overcome. Sustained and successful turnaround requires all causes of decline to be dealt with and further growth of the business achieved.

→ **Learning outcome 3**
Identify and explain retrenchment strategy.

- Retrenchment strategies are operational strategies which are aimed at making a company more productive and profitable with its current products and markets. Retrenchment includes organisational changes, financial changes, debt restructuring, cost reduction in the value chain, and asset reduction and divestment.

→ **Learning outcome 4**
Identify and explain turnaround strategy.

- Turnaround strategies are concerned with developing competitive and market positions. Turnaround strategy includes: changing prices, emphasising advertising and selling, re-focusing, rationalising the product portfolio, and new product development.

This exit case study looks at Hewlett Packard and the plans of the new chief executive Mark Hurd to transform the business and can be used to assess the learning outcomes below.

Learning outcomes	Check you have achieved this by	
1 Identifying causes of failure in a struggling company.	Listing actions and events which result in poor performance.	Answering Exit case study question 1.
2 Explain retrenchment and turnaround strategies.	Describing the operational and competitive changes a company makes to improve its position.	Answering Exit case study questions 2 and 3.
3 Developing retrenchment and turnaround strategies.	Recommending operational and competitive changes a company could use to improve its position.	Answering Exit case study question 4.

New HP boss plans 14,500 job cuts: 10% of workforce will go to create 'nimbler, quicker' firm

by David Teather

Hewlett-Packard yesterday announced plans to cut 14,500 jobs over the next 18 months, representing 10% of the struggling company's worldwide workforce. The plans were the first significant move by Mark Hurd, who was hired after Carly Fiorina was ousted as chief executive in February following a turbulent six years in office. He had flagged a likely restructuring of the personal computer and printer maker in May, shortly after he joined the company. 'I think this will make us simpler, nimbler and

quicker,' Mr Hurd said. 'We will always be working to grow our company and to get more efficient. The two go hand in hand.'

The company said 'more than half' of the jobs would be cut in support functions such as information technology, human resources and finance. But the firm declined to say where exactly the axe would fall. Details, Mr Hurd said, would be released as they become available. HP employs 42,000 people in Europe, the Middle East and

→

Africa but does not break the figure down to country level. It has offices in Britain in London, Birmingham, Reading, Bristol, Bracknell, Warrington and Erskine.

HP aims to save an annual $1.9bn (£1bn) through the overhaul. The company said half that amount would fall through to operating profit while the remainder would be reinvested in the business. The company said the impact on the sales force and research and development would be minimal. The company is also cutting back retirement benefits for its American employees, realising savings of about $300m a year.

Mr Hurd said the board had been working on the changes before his arrival. There are no plans to reshape the business further, he added – perennial speculation suggests that the personal computer division could be spun off. 'We've been focused on optimising the current HP to make it the best HP we can.' Mr Hurd's comment echoed that of the board at the time of Ms Fiorina's exit. The company said then that the problem had been execution and not strategy.

Ms Fiorina had arguably been the most powerful woman in corporate America before she was forced from the company. She engineered the $19bn takeover of Compaq in 2002, railroading descendants of HP's founders who vehemently opposed the deal. Shortly after the merger she cut 15,000 jobs from the combined operation but failed to deliver on profitability.

HP has been struggling to compete with IBM in high-end services such as servers and consulting for corporate clients and with Dell Computer at the opposite end of the spectrum, in the largely commoditised market for personal computers. Dell began selling printers in 2003,

eating further into HP's core business. To regain market share, HP has been forced to lower prices on printers this year by 33%.

Mr Hurd, 48, joined the company in March from the technology firm NCR.

The cuts were not as big as some Wall Street analysts had been anticipating. Some had forecast up to 25,000 job losses and the lower number caused some selling. HP shares were down 7 cents at $24.85 in early trading.

HP is taking a $1.1bn charge over the next six quarters to pay for the restructuring. Outside the United States, HP said it would offer terms in accordance with local laws and regulations.

Mr Hurd had already made some changes, including the separation of the personal computing and printing business in June, five months after Ms Fiorina had combined them. The HP announcement comes a day after IBM increased its planned job cuts from 13,000 to 14,500, most of which will be in Europe.

Source: *Guardian*, 20 July 2005, copyright Guardian News & Media 2005.

Exit case study questions

1 Identify causes of failure at Hewlett Packard.

2 Summarise the strategy Hewlett Packard is undertaking to revive the company.

3 Is the strategy retrenchment, turnaround or a combination of both? Explain your answer.

4 Identify any additions to the strategy you would advise Hewlett Packard to consider.

DISCUSSION TOPIC

1 Read the paper 'Cost dynamics: scale and experience effects' by Derek F Abell and John S Hammond, Chapter 14, in *The Strategy Process*, Mintzberg, Lampel, Quinn and Ghosal, Harlow: Prentice Hall, 2003.

2 Critically evaluate the relevance of 'scale and experience' effects for the failing business.

WIDEN YOUR HORIZONS

1 Widen your horizons by identifying the turnaround strategy Stuart Rose employed at Marks & Spencer. Summarise the approach Marks & Spencer should take to maintain the improvements made by Stuart Rose.

WEBLINKS

The Ford website provides some further information on the entry case study for this chapter. The other two websites provide some useful information for further reading around the subject of turnaround strategies.

- This is the corporate website for the Ford Motor Company.
  www.ford.com
- The website of the Turnaround Management Association (UK) contains some useful definitions and articles from sponsors, which are free to non-members at the time of writing, March 2007.
  www.tma-uk.org
- Click on 'Resources of interest on turnaround management' on the left-hand side of the screen, this takes you to some useful 'papers' on turnaround management.
  www.grantthornton.ca/turnaround/index.asp

FURTHER READING

- Thompson, J L (2001) *Strategic Management*, London: Thomson Learning. Chapter 17, 'Business failure'.
- Thompson, J L (2001) *Strategic Management*, London: Thomson Learning. Chapter 18, 'Strategies for consolidation and recovery'.
- Slatter, S (1984) *Corporate Recovery: Successful Turnaround Strategies and Their Implementation*, London: Penguin.

REFERENCES

1 Press Association (2006), 'Number of insolvencies reaches three-year high', *Guardian* 6 January.
2 Slatter, S (1984) *Corporate Recovery: Successful Turnaround Strategies and Their Implementation*, London: Penguin.
3 Thompson, J L (2001) *Strategic Management*, London: Thomson Learning.
4 Slatter, op. cit.
5 *Daily Telegraph* (2004) 'Changes in store to counter catalogue of weakness', 13 July.

Glossary

7-S framework covers strategy, skills, staff, style, systems, structure and shared values.

Accessibility is the ease with which a company can communicate with a market segment.

Acid test ratio measures the company's ability to cover its short-term debts, but stock as an asset is not counted.

Acquisition is when one company buys another or a shareholding in another company.

Action is about allocating resources and making the chosen strategic options happen.

Ad-hoc pool alliances occur when parent companies contribute limited resources on a short-term basis and expect to reap the profits.

Alliances and agreements occur between two or more countries for mutual benefit.

Assessing is concerned with evaluating the impact and potential impact of both current and future external environmental factors on the organisation.

Autocracy is where government is unelected and one person or few people retain all power.

Autocratic is to be strict and inflexible.

Autocratic leadership has centralised power, which rests with a dictatorial leader.

Backward vertical integration occurs when a company establishes or acquires its own sources of inputs.

Balance of resources refers to resource excess, efficiency and excess efficiency.

Bank of England has two core purposes: monetary and financial stability.

Bargaining power of buyers depends on the opportunities to shop around for the same or substitute goods.

Bargaining power of suppliers depends on the alternative sources of supply available to the buyer.

Behavioural characteristics define the customers' behaviour and attitude to the product, including, customer loyalty, occasion and frequency of purchase.

Brokers advise on the issue price for the new shares and market the shares to potential investors.

Bureaucratic control occurs via rules and regulations.

Capability is the ability to deliver required outputs.

Capability gaps arise from specific differences in physical resources and operating systems which are routine and measurable.

Capacity is a measure of performance and if a system is operating to capacity then it is producing the maximum amount of product over a specified time period.

Category A stakeholders have low power and low interest, but should not be ignored.

Category B stakeholders have low power and high interest and should be kept informed.

Category C stakeholders have high power and low interest and should be kept satisfied.

Causal textures are interdependencies outside the organisation in the external environment.

Centralisation is the retaining of power and decision-making responsibility in one place in the organisation's structure.

Centralised structures have top management taking all the important and long-term decisions.

Champions are leaders who will push a business through the early stages of development and into significant growth.

Charismatic leadership involves judging the moods of individuals and larger audiences, and adjusting words and actions to suit the situation.

Choice is about strategic options, including competitive strategy, corporate strategy, international strategy, market options and growth strategy.

Clarity requires ease and transparency with regard to communication and co-ordination.

Coercive power is based on the subordinate's perception that the leader can and will punish staff who do not comply with instructions.

Command groups are determined by an organisation's structure and depend on hierarchical relationships.

Commitment is the ability to contribute resources or effort.

Compatibility is the ability to collaborate effectively.

Competition Commission carries out monopoly and merger inquiries and hears appeals against decisions of the OFT and Regulators.

Competitive advantage is the way in which a company makes its products or services better or cheaper than those offered by its competitors.

Competitive rivalry is the nature of competition between companies in the same industry.

Consistency is continuing success with regard to achieving objectives.

Consortia alliances occur when parent companies contribute resources on a long-term basis and expect to reap the profits.

Continuity is the company remaining committed to the same objectives and values to create a coherent and cohesive organisational culture.

Control is the ability to hold on to and co-ordinate resources and staff.

Control systems are the mechanisms for control, measurement and reward within the organisation and they monitor what is important to it.

Core competencies are the skills and abilities developed within an organisation with which competitive advantage can be created and maintained.

Core permanent employees have highly skilled jobs, with relatively good job security and career prospects with the organisation.

Cost focus is serving a narrow target market, where customers are very price sensitive and the company will deliver low-cost and thus low-priced products and services to the market.

Cost leadership is seeking to be the lowest-cost producer in its industry or sector to supply a mass market.

Cost reductions arise from the marketplace demanding lower prices, which in turn can only be met via a reduction in cost.

Creditors are individuals or other companies to which a firm owes money.

Creditors ratio measures how long it takes the business to pay its suppliers.

Cultural control is negotiated and based on trust, loyalty and mutual respect.

Cultural webs identify and draw together a number of possible determinants of organisational culture.

Current ratio indicates how easy it is for the company to cover its short-term debts immediately.

Customer characteristics are variables which can be broken down into sub-groups: demographics; socio-economics; lifestyle; geographic location.

Customer needs and wants: the needs are those things customers must have, wants are those things which customers would like to have.

Customised marketing is the development of a unique marketing mix for each customer.

Dangerous stakeholders have urgency and power, but do not have a legitimate claim and are often coercive and violent.

Debenture and loan stocks are written acknowledgements of indebtedness.

Debtors are individuals or other companies which owe money to an organisation.

Debtors ratio shows how long it takes the company to collect money it is owed.

Decentralisation is the dispersal of decision-making responsibility to operational managers.

Definitive stakeholders have all three attributes of power, legitimacy and urgency, which gives them high salience.

Demanding stakeholders possess the attribute of urgency, and without a second attribute they are for organisations annoying stakeholders.

Democracy is government via fairly elected representatives.

Democratic leadership occurs when power is split between the leader and his/her staff.

Demographic changes are changes in the age and structure of a population.

Dependent stakeholders possess legitimacy and urgency, but lack power and require others to act for them.

Differentiated market coverage strategy targets a number of market segments, all with an individually tailored marketing mix.

Differentiation is serving a broad target market, but by providing a product or service that is different and better due to its added value.

Differentiation focus is serving a narrow target

market where consumers are prepared to spend a great deal of money in order to acquire luxury, top-of-the-range goods or services (same as focused differentiation).

Disbanding occurs when a group has completed its tasks and staffs move onto different projects.

Discretionary stakeholders possess the attribute of legitimacy, but have no power or urgency in any claim they have on the organisation.

Diseconomies of scale are the loss of efficiency due to poor control and management of a business.

Distinct differences are those features of a product or service which distinguish it from a competitor's offering

Divestment is selling off all or part of the business.

Dividend cover ratio shows the number of times that current earnings cover ordinary dividend payments.

Dividend payments are the share of profits which are paid out to the shareholders of a business.

Dividend yield ratio relates the dividend to the market price of an ordinary share, giving a potential investor an indication of expected return.

Divisional structures contain separate divisions based around individual product lines or based on the geographic areas of the markets served. The divisional structure is found in diversified organisations.

Dominant stakeholders are those with both power and legitimacy, which gives them authority.

Dormant stakeholders have power, but it is unused as the stakeholder has no legitimate relationship with the organisation.

Earnings per share ratio is a measure of the earning power of each share and is closely linked to the share's market value.

Economic environment comprises bodies which make economic decisions that affect businesses and may also be shaped by political decisions.

Economies of scale are the improved efficiency gained from undertaking an activity on a large scale.

Effective managers 'do the right things' to achieve outputs and meet objectives.

Effectiveness is how well an organisation sets and achieves its goals.

Efficiency is the ratio of actual output to possible output, usually expressed as a percentage.

Efficient managers seek to use resources to achieve objectives, while minimising waste.

Embargo is a total ban on some imports.

Emergent strategy is an ongoing process which often has unclear objectives, but which develop and become clearer over time.

Enduring is being sustainable or continuing for a long time.

Equity finance is money raised via the sale of ordinary shares in a company to investors.

Ethno-centric HR strategy occurs when all management roles are occupied by home country nationals.

Eurozone is the geographic area made up of the countries which have adopted the euro as their currency.

Expectant stakeholders possess two attributes and have a medium level of salience.

Expert power is based on the subordinate's perception of the leader as someone who has specialist knowledge in a certain area.

Exporting is selling goods to overseas customers from a domestic base.

External drivers of change usually arise from another organisation over which the company has no or limited influence.

External environment is where the opportunities and threats arise from to confront the organisation.

External staff are people who can be brought in quickly to meet increased demand and include consultants, subcontractors and temporary agency staff.

Financial status ratios evaluate liquidity and solvency.

First peripheral group employees are those with full-time jobs, often with vocational skills.

Fit is used as an expression of how cohesive parts of an organisation, its resources and environment, are in relation to one another.

Fixed asset turnover ratio provides a measure of asset utilisation, measuring how many times the fixed assets are covered by sales revenue.

Fixed costs do not change directly in relation to the level of productivity, but have to be paid on a regular basis, for example rent and insurance.

Flexibility of resources is the effectiveness with

which resources can be redeployed to take account of a developing strategy and a changing environment.

Focus is often used to describe strategies serving niche markets.

Focused differentiation strategy targets a niche market where customers pay a lot of money for luxury goods (same as differentiation focus).

Focused marketing strategy targets only one market segment, despite the choice of several market segments.

Force field analysis is used to describe the impact of driving forces upon restraining forces for change in an organisation.

Forecasting is concerned with anticipating how current environmental influences may change in future.

Foreign direct investment (FDI) is investment overseas to produce goods or services in a foreign country.

Forming occurs when group members are making an impression on each other and seeking direction from a leader.

Forwards vertical integration occurs when a company establishes or acquires its own distribution channels or outlets.

Franchises are contractual agreements where the franchiser provides the franchisee with the right to sell the franchiser's products or services.

Free market economies experience little or no regulation of commercial activity.

Friendship groupings are formed by people who have a social allegiance.

From outside in and inside out linkages are **transactional dependencies**, which are links between the inside of the organisation and its external environment and vice versa.

From within to within linkages are internal dependencies or internal linkages inside the organisation.

Full-blown joint ventures occur when parent companies contribute significant resources and allow the alliance to retain the profits.

Functional structures are based around departments, and are rigid and centralised.

Gearing measures the proportion of capital which comes from long-term debt.

Geo-centric HR strategy seeks the best people for the job.

Global area structure allows a company to both sell and manufacture locally in various international markets and is based around geographic divisions.

Global functional structure allows tight centralised control by a small group of directors over a worldwide organisation and is based around functional departments such as production, HR, finance and marketing.

Global organisations plan, develop and implement a range of activities on a worldwide scale.

Global product structure accommodates manufacturing in a limited number of favourable low-cost locations and is based around product divisions.

Global strategy is used where pressures for cost reductions are high and low for local responsiveness.

Good leadership has strategic vision and is persuasive at implementing strategy to achieve tangible results.

Gross profit margin indicates the profit made in relation to the sales the business has made.

Heroes are high achievers in the organisation and personify the organisation's cultural values and hence provide an explicit role model for employees.

Holding company structures are usually found in large industrial conglomerates with a parent company acting mainly as an investment company acquiring and divesting smaller subsidiary companies.

Horizontal integration occurs when a company starts to sell the same or similar goods to those sold by competitors.

Housekeepers are leaders who can ensure the company holds its own against other competitors who may also be mature and established.

HRM is concerned with recruiting, managing, training, developing and rewarding staff to help the organisation achieve competitive advantage.

Human capital is the capabilities, knowledge, skills and experience of the individual employees.

Hybrid strategy is a combination of differentiation and lower price strategies, to achieve differentiation at a lower price than competitors.

Implementers are leaders who can achieve results via efficient and effective use of staff and resources.

Inbound logistics are concerned with managing incoming materials and components.

Industrial economies trade goods with each other and with raw material economies and industrialising economies.

Industrial structure determines a country's employment levels, income levels and products required.

Industrialising economies are those countries which are experiencing rapid growth in manufacturing and exporting.

Inefficiency is the poor use of resources, resulting in unnecessary wastage.

Infrastructure includes structure, culture and systems which are likely to reflect what it is important for the organisation to control and manage.

Initial public offerings occur when shares in a company are offered to investors for the first time.

Innovators are bold leaders who are able to search for new ideas in a complex and dynamic external environment.

Intangible resources are goodwill, image and reputation and arise from brand names, good contracts, company image and innovative capability.

Integrating mechanisms are systems and relationships which link different parts of the organisation.

Intended strategy is the planned strategy of an organisation.

Interest cover is an income-based measure of gearing and shows how well a company can cover its interest payments.

Interest groups contain people who seek to achieve a common goal.

Intermediaries' offers occur when stock exchange members apply for shares in an offer and are selling or passing the shares to their clients.

Internal dependencies are the linkages between different parts of an organisation's value chain.

International division structure centralises all the international operations and lessens the managing director's burden of dealing directly with overseas operations.

International environments are worldwide and include political, economic and cultural factors.

International licensing is an arrangement where a foreign licensee buys the rights to produce a company's products in the licensee's country.

International strategy is used where pressures for cost reduction and local responsiveness are both low.

Introductions are when a listing is granted to existing shares in company, as it already has a wide ownership base.

Key players are stakeholders with high power and high interest in the organisations.

Key success factors are those things a company has to do to successfully meet the expectations of customers and other stakeholders.

Latent stakeholders possess one attribute and have low salience.

Laissez faire leadership occurs where all power is passed to on to the staff.

Leadership is the ability to direct staff towards achieving goals.

Legitimacy is used to describe stakeholder behaviour which is right and proper.

Legitimate power is based on the employee's perception that the leader can exercise power due to their role in the organisation.

Lemon squeezers are leaders who can extract the maximum benefit from a business if is to survive and/or achieve turnaround.

Levels of strategy are corporate, competitive, and functional.

Linkages represent the interrelationships and interdependencies between value chain activities and are sources of competitive advantage.

Local responsiveness arises from variation in consumer tastes, different infrastructures and regulation requirements.

Low price strategy is charging reduced prices for products identical to competitors' products, which could result in a price war.

Management is relating to people in defined roles and working within a structured organisation.

Management philosophy is a system of principles for conduct of life as a manager.

Market development is the creation of new markets or market segments.

Market enlargement is the expansion of a company's existing markets by selling more of its existing products and services to existing customers.

Market segmentation is dividing up a diverse market into small groups of customers with similar needs.

Marketing and sales is about promotion and advertising of goods and services to customers.

Matrix structures merge decentralisation with co-ordination across all areas of the business, where there are two distinct areas which need to be managed.

Measurability is quantifying the potential size and buying power of the segment.

Mixed economies offer a choice of employment and trade, with some regulation.

Monitoring is identifying current influences on the company.

Moving to a new level is the search for answers to the difficulties faced by the organisation and implementing solutions.

Multi-domestic strategy is used where pressures for cost reductions are low and high for local responsiveness.

National culture is the way society in a country acts and behaves.

Net profit margin indicates the profit made after the deduction of expenses.

No frills strategy targets very price sensitive customers.

Norming occurs when consensus is achieved between group members and tasks are allocated.

OFCOM regulates the communications sector, covering television, radio and telecommunications.

Offer for sale occurs when shares offered direct to the public with the help of the sponsor and the broker.

Offer for sale by tender occurs when the public is invited to bid for the available shares at a price above the minimum that is set by the issuing company.

Office of Fair Trading (OFT) is a government-funded body which seeks to promote and protect consumer interests.

OFGEM seeks to promote effective competition in the energy market for present and future customers.

OFWAT regulates water supply and pricing to domestic and industrial customers.

Operations are concerned with delivering products or services of a quality appropriate for the competitive strategy being pursued.

Ordinary shareholders have their claims settled last in the event of bankruptcy.

Organic growth involves a company using its resources to establish new operations.

Outbound logistics is about rapid and accurate delivery of the product or service to the customer.

Outside linkages are called causal textures and are interdependencies outside the organisation in its external environment.

Pacifiers are friendly and sociable leaders, who have the ability to decentralise decision making to key individuals.

Paradigm is a pattern or example of behaviour or things to be taken into account in a situation.

Participative leadership seeks to involve staff and others in the decision-making process.

Perfectly emergent strategy arises when there is no intent, but there is consistency in what the organisation does.

Performance ratios evaluate profitability and efficiency.

Performing occurs as the consensus of 'norming' is built upon and the tasks are successfully completed by the group.

Person culture is found in organisations where a set of professionals agrees to collaborate to perform a specific service. These people could be self-employed, or at least would have little notion of being employees of an organisation in the traditional sense.

Personal power arises from the support and trust of subordinates and colleagues.

PEST analysis is analysis of the external environment by considering political, economic, socio-cultural and technological factors influencing an organisation.

Placings occur when a broker approaches potential institutional investors to enable shares to be issued at a fixed price to the investors.

Planned economies organise and regulate jobs, housing, production, services and food production via the state.

Political environment comprises bodies which have a political viewpoint regarding how business operates.

Poly-centric HR strategy sees key roles occupied by home country nationals and subsidiaries managed by host country nationals.

Position defines how customers perceive products and companies in comparison to competitor companies or products.

Power culture is found in small, entrepreneurial organisations where the owner works with few employees, with the centre of power and all crucial decision making resting with the owner/manager.

Power structures evolve in organisations and consist of individuals with power, sharing a common set of values that underpin the way they work together.

Preference shareholders have their claims settled third in the event of bankruptcy.

Prescriptive strategy is the sequential, logical view of strategy.

Price earnings ratio measures the relationship between a company's ability to generate profits and market price of its ordinary shares.

Primary activities are concerned with the manufacture of a product or creation of a service and their delivery to customers.

Procurement is the process for acquiring and purchasing goods and materials of appropriate quality for all areas of the business.

Product development occurs when updated or new products and services are produced and sold to existing customers.

Product life cycle is a marketing tool. The product life cycle can be used to examine the sales and profits a product or service is making, relative to the length of time on the marketplace.

Productivity is the quantity manufactured in relation to one or more of the resources used.

Project-based joint ventures occur when parent companies contribute limited strategic resources to the alliance.

Quotas are limits on the amount of goods a country will allow to be imported. **Embargo** is a total ban on some imports.

Raw material exporting economies are rich in natural resources, but have a poor manufacturing economy.

Realised strategy is the planned and emergent strategies which actually occur.

Referent power is based on the subordinate's identification with the leader who is able to exercise power because of their perceived reputation.

Refreezing is the positive reinforcement and support for the implemented changes.

Regulatory bodies for privatised utilities and industries encourage competition and see that customers are not unfairly exploited.

Resource audit is the examination of resources and how their use could be improved.

Restrictive Practices Court controls practices that are presumed to be against the public interest, including the price and supply of goods.

Retrenchment strategies are operational and aim to make a company more productive and profitable.

Return on capital employed (ROCE) ratio gives an overall indication of productivity of the capital invested.

Return on shareholders' funds is a measure of the return on the investment which shareholders have made after the company has paid its expenses.

Reward management is concerned with implementing an effective reward system linked to the attainment of goals.

Reward power is based on the subordinate's perception that the leader can reward staff who comply with instructions.

Rights issues occur when a company raises capital by issuing new shares to existing shareholders.

Rituals in organisational life can be formal or informal and are used to reinforce the routines.

Role culture is found in mature and large organisations with departments, in which everyone will have a specific job title and job description. Staff will be expected to use their skills and contribute their knowledge towards achievement of the organisational mission.

Routines are the scheduled and deliberate practices carried out as a matter of course in the day-to-day life of an organisation.

Sales promotion is the activities firms undertake to persuade customers to buy their product or services. Examples include free samples and money off vouchers.

Salience is the extent to which managers in an organisation give priority to stakeholder claims.

Scanning is concerned with identifying future influences on the company.

Second peripheral group employees provide workforce flexibility and include part-time employees, job-sharing employees and subsidised trainees.

Secured creditors such as debenture holders have their claims settled first in the event of bankruptcy.

Services in the value chain are concerned with

additional services which support the goods and services sold to customers.

Shamans, in organisational terms, are outside consultants brought in to cure the organisation's problems.

Simple structures are adopted by small businesses in the private sector, which may be established businesses or in the very early stages of growth and development. The organisation is structured around the owner/manager who manages a small number of employees.

Social mobility is the extent to which a person can move out of the social stratum into which they were born.

Social stratification is based on hierarchical social categories such as family background, occupation and income.

Socio-cultural environment includes changes in ages and structures of populations and cross-cultural issues.

Sole trader businesses are owned and administered by one person who is personally liable for all the debts of the business.

Sponsors assemble the prospectus outlining the company when new shares being offered for sale and liaise with the stock exchange.

Stakeholder attributes are power, legitimacy and urgency.

Stakeholders are any individual or a collection of individuals with an interest in an organisation.

Stakeholder's power is often based on their position in the organisation and their access to resources.

Stock market ratios evaluate the success on the stock market of ordinary shares.

Stock turnover shows how fast or slowly stock is moving through the business.

Stories represent the organisation's history and typically highlight significant events and characters in its past.

Storming is the stage of conflict with individuals in the group jockeying for position.

Strategic alliances occur when two or more businesses agree a contract to operate a joint project.

Strategic control is via efficiency, quality, innovation and responsiveness to customers.

Strategies for failure include strategy 6 – high price and standard value, strategy 7 – reduced value and increased price, and strategy 8 – standard price and low value.

Strategy as a pattern is a stream of actions with consistency.

Strategy as a perspective is a view or concept which is shared by members of the organisation.

Strategy as a plan is deliberate and developed in advance of action.

Strategy as a ploy is the threat to act in response to a competitor's actions.

Strategy as position is the company's point in its external environment which allows it to compete effectively with other companies.

Strong culture organisations are highly cohesive and have a system of informal rules, indicating to staff exactly what is expected of them.

Subsistence economies are based on simple and small scale agriculture.

Succession planning is ensuring the organisation's management provision for the future.

Symbols present in an organisation can be many and varied and indicate how much someone is valued by the organisation.

Tangible resources are physical assets such as buildings, offices, factories, warehouses, IT systems, machinery and motor vehicles.

Tank commanders are leaders who can support a team to exploit and gain maximum benefit from all possible market segments.

Tariffs are taxes levied by a foreign government on certain imported products.

Task culture is flexible and often found in organisations that frequently undertake work for a variety of customers, which will involve a team with the required skills and knowledge undertaking very specific problem-solving or troubleshooting tasks as projects.

Task groups are determined by the organisation, but do not depend on the obvious hierarchical relationships.

Technology development is the use of technology to improve products, services and their delivery to customers.

Theory X assumes that people dislike work and seek to avoid it at all costs.

Theory Y assumes people regard work as normal

activity and are self-motivated towards the achievement of organisational objectives.

Threat of new entrants arises from companies likely to enter an industry to compete with existing operators.

Three strategic Cs are customers, corporation and competitors.

Trading blocs are groups of countries that act collectively in regard to trade and commerce.

Transactional leadership works via a clear chain of command so that it is clear what is required of staff.

Transactional linkages are the links/relationships between an organisation and another organisation, such as a supplier, distributor or customer.

Transformational leadership recognises that success results from their belief in both themselves and their staff.

Transnational strategy is used where pressures for cost reduction and local responsiveness are both high.

Turnaround strategies aim to make the company's marketing effort more effective and improve its position in the competitive environment.

Undifferentiated market coverage strategy targets the whole market with one product or service.

Unfreezing is the acceptance that old behaviour must come to be regarded as unsuitable and must stop.

Unrealised strategy is the planned or intended actions which do not actually happen.

Unrelated diversification is a move into completely different goods and services to those currently sold.

Unsecured creditors such as suppliers have their claims settled second in the event of bankruptcy.

Urgency is the requirement for immediate attention and defines the relationship between the organisation and the stakeholder as dynamic.

Utilisation measures the percentage of available capacity that is actually used.

Value added tax (VAT) is a sales tax and is payable on many goods and services in the UK

Value chain is a framework for examining how an organisation configures its resources for competitive advantage.

Value system is a set of interorganisational links between the value chains of organisations and their suppliers, distributors and customers.

Values are the beliefs of the organisations that in turn determine the expected behaviours from managers and employees.

Viability of a market segment is determined by assessing if a segment is profitable enough to be treated separately.

Weak culture organisations lack cohesiveness and staff will waste time working out what to do and how to do it.

Index